BOOZE, BABE, & THE LITTLE BLACK DRESS

BOOZE, BABE, & THE LITTLE BLACK DRESS

HOW INNOVATORS OF THE ROARING 20S CREATED THE CONSUMER REVOLUTION

BY JASON VOIOVICH

Copyright © 2023 by Jaywalker Publishing LLC. All Rights Reserved.

No part of this book may be reproduced in any form by electronic or mechanical means, including information storage and retrieval systems, without permission in writing from the publisher, except by a reviewer who may quote brief passages in a review.

First Edition April 2023, BBLBD-D

ISBN 978-1-7370013-4-8 (paperback)
ISBN 978-1-7370013-3-1 (eBook)
ISBN 978-1-7370013-5-5 (audiobook)

Library of Congress Control Number: 2023903836

Published by Jaywalker Publishing LLC
Minneapolis, Minnesota USA
www.jasontvoiovich.com

For the choice-makers.

TABLE OF CONTENTS

Introduction: "Coffee for Every Purse and Purpose." 8

PART 1: BOOZE

Manufacturing Desire 17
The Manipulation Messiah 31
Flash Food 49
Cars on Time 64
Consumer Rebellion 79
Opening the Big Box 101
Housing Feminism 117

PART 2: BABE

When Advertising Grew a Pair 134
America's First Equal Opportunity Employer 151
Subscribing to Culture 168
The First District Court of Public Opinion 184
Happy Feet 201
Swampland 216
Changing the Game 236
Marketer in Chief 254
Five-Cent Trip To Hell 269
Mad Women 283
The Sensemakers 300

PART 3: THE LITTLE BLACK DRESS

Family for Sale..318
How You Got Your Kicks 334
All-Natural Ingredients. Artificial People. 349
Democratizing Fashion...362
Buying a Better You..378
Capitalism without the Capitalists....................................394
"Please, can I…" 408
Five-Star Wonderland...424

Conclusion: "The Customer Is Always Right."..................440

Key People 450
Further Reading 462
Acknowledgments 471
About the Author 472
Also by the Author 473

Introduction
"COFFEE FOR EVERY PURSE AND PURPOSE."

There was no saving her coffee maker. It had given up the ghost.

Perhaps it was leaving it running 18 hours a day, every day, since the day she unpacked it. Perhaps it was occasionally using old coffee, instead of fresh water, to *rebrew* a new pot. Perhaps it was years of brewing coffee the strength of industrial solvents. We may never know.

For my Cuban mother, now in her 70s, this was a crisis of biblical proportions. Coffee is like a parallel religion for the Havana set, and better than a half-century away from the island hadn't tempered her caffeine addiction. It required immediate attention. She wanted a new coffee maker now. Not tomorrow. Not after breakfast. *Now*.[1]

The good news: As a relief to drivers, pedestrians, and urban critters within a five-mile radius, my mother no longer drove. The bad news: Saving a hapless bunny from an untimely demise beneath my mother's Corolla meant that *her* coffee maker problem was now *my* coffee maker problem.

Luckily, there's a Target store along the way, and I didn't waste any time scooping her up and getting there. And even more luckily, the "Super" version of the store carried a full aisle's worth of choices in the kitchen section. We couldn't miss it. As we approached, the end cap display featured an interactive instructional demo for a new espresso maker. If she couldn't quite afford her best choice? *No worries*, reassured nearby pop-up signage. Target had her covered with several immediate financing options available at the check lanes.

She could choose a basic drip coffee maker. It came in one color (black), featured one capacity (10 cups), and precisely one feature (an on/off switch). Next to the base model on the shelf, Mr. Coffee offered three additional (vaguely patriotic) color choices – maroon, cream, or periwinkle – all featuring a delay timer, so she could set up her morning joe to brew the night before. That version cost about 50 percent more. Next to those, the manufacturer sold a version she could program to deliver different coffee intensities. (Though, sadly, "industrial strength" wasn't an option.) And finally, for nearly $120, she could splurge on the 4-in-1 deluxe model that brewed coffee, made hot chocolate for the grandkids,

---

1   If you know where this literary adaptation comes from, ask Raquel Welch. Or Bob Gunton. Or Stephen King. Whichever is easiest.

and crafted a variety of espresso drinks.

That scene repeated, with variations, among a handful of brands – from old-fashioned drip-style carafes, pod-using coffee machines, newer espresso models, and even a couple of French press options.[2] Only five brands dominated the shelves, each appealing to different needs, customer preferences, and price points.

With an entire career in consumer product development under my belt, I knew what I was seeing. In fact, I knew it wasn't Target's idea. This strategy was the brainchild of Alfred Sloan at General Motors, who created the original product ladder with makes and models of cars – affordable Chevrolets to luxury Cadillacs – in the 1920s. He called it a "car for every purse and purpose," using the appeal of consumer choice to unseat Ford and its iconic Model T as the best-selling car make in the world for the next 60 years.

The instructional end cap wasn't a new idea, either. Advertising agency J. Walter Thompson's Helen Lansdowne pioneered the "instructional story" approach at about the same time Sloan was dethroning Ford. It made sense. If consumers didn't understand how to use new-fangled coffee filters (invented by Melitta Bentz in Germany before World War I and just making their way to the United States in the 1920s), why would they buy a pour-over coffee maker? The 1920s saw hundreds of entirely new products hit the shelves – from radios to automobiles to washing machines to electric razors. If Lansdowne wanted to help her clients sell more widgets, she had better show consumers how to use them first.

What about in-store retail credit? You guessed it. Consumer financing came into its own during the same decade. Nearly every retail store offered some form of payment plan. But more than that, the 1920s were the first time the average person could make a major purchase – like a car or a home – without paying cash. To help teach people how to handle the deluge of credit offers, credit unions emerged as a consumer-centric alternative to traditional banks, focusing on financial education.

Even the store shopping experience itself was nearly a century old. In 1925, Robert Wood transformed the iconic Sears catalog business into the first "big box" store in the Chicago suburbs. But it wasn't just a larger

---

2   Unfortunately, Target didn't carry a stovetop brewing model – the true European and Caribbean classic – that my mother would have recognized from her childhood.

copy of the high-service boutiques downtown. This store had ample parking, thousands of square feet of showroom space, products on display you could feel and touch, and salespeople available *only when you wanted them*.

What was a radically new shopping experience in the 1920s is the norm today. But that isn't what most people think of when they envision the Roaring 20s.

When asked, what images come to mind? It might be Prohibition, speakeasies, gangsters, rum-runners, and shootouts with Tommy Guns. Maybe it's the loose morals and excesses of the *Great Gatsby* – all snappy dressing and easy sex. Or what about the one-of-a-kind architectural style of the decade? Art deco might be fun and stylish in small doses, but if it weren't for the Chrysler Building and Miami Beach, we might forget the look of the times ever existed.

But those of us who understand *consumer culture* see something more. Consumers appreciate the right amount and the right variety of choices. Consumers like to be taught how they can enjoy a new product. Consumers need flexible payment terms. And consumers love shopping when, where, and how they please. Before the 1920s, none of that would have been possible.

My mother and I spent more than an hour looking at coffee makers that morning. She loved it. It took her a few minutes to orient to what she was seeing; she hadn't bought a new machine in nearly two decades. Where I saw a symphony of choices, she saw a cacophony. But it didn't take her long to start trying out the demonstration models, comparing features, and scrutinizing prices. She was in her element, reminding me of the ruthlessly efficient shopper I remembered as a child.

She ended up with an upgraded version of her prior drip model in maroon (she loves the color red) that came with one important addition over her prior model: an automatic safety feature that would prevent her from burning down her assisted living community. (The center's director pulled me aside and thanked me when we brought it home.) To her, shopping was pure joy, and she seemed 10 years younger.

This book tells the story of the modern shopping experience and the innovators who created it, but it dives deeper than that. It shows how the consumer experience revolutionized American culture.

...

Despite my mom's "joyful" experience, consumer culture also has a dark side.

You don't need to look far to see it. If you believe the pundits and academics, buying my mom's coffee maker amounts to "a social and economic order that encourages the acquisition of goods and services in ever-increasing amounts," where Mr. Coffee designed her equipment to fail on purpose to "manipulate consumer spending," so that she could show her "conspicuous and vicarious consumption and waste" as a "display of status and not functionality or usefulness." And lest we miss the coffee shrub for the bean, our economic system would collapse without this vicious cycle of overproduction and overconsumption.[3]

The 1920s, by extension, was an era of unrestrained excess and debauchery. Predictably, the stock market collapse ended the consumptive orgy with the decade-long hangover of the Great Depression. Of the Gatsby Era's most irredeemable features was the birth of the modern shopping experience – a drug that's addicted the American public for the past century. We're all trapped in a destructive cycle robbing us of our humanity and dooming our planet.

Is there some truth to those characterizations? Yes, certainly. We've all been horrified by videos of Black Friday shoppers trampling their way to (a purposefully limited number of) $99 big-screen televisions. We've all driven by mountains of obsolete electronics and dumpsters full of discarded food while many people go hungry. Like any culture, consumerism is prone to excesses. But it's hardly fair to judge its whole by the worst of its parts.

Is the 1920s worthy of study *only* as a cautionary tale? No, certainly

---

3 These quotes come directly from Wikipedia's entry on "Consumerism." Although academics write deeper explanations, most pundits use only these summaries in their writing. If you'd like to dive deeper, Wikipedia offers plenty of ways to do that. And as of 2023, you can choose to learn more about *this book's* perspective on "choice culture" as a balance to the decidedly negative slant of the overall entry.

not. This decade gave us more than art deco and flappers; it gave the average person more freedom of choice – in more places than just the store – than they ever had before. *Ever.* In human history. That fact alone is worthy of a closer look.

To better understand both consumer culture and the Roaring 20s that created it, I'm proposing that we shift our language. Instead of taking the word "consumer" literally – the consumption of goods and services – let's redefine consumer figuratively – as a *choice-maker.* With that definition in mind, consumer culture is better understood as *choice culture* and the 1920s as the creation of *mass choice* in the American economy.

The Roaring 20s gave consumers *true* power over many aspects of their lives for the first time. The choices we enjoy today often are taken for granted. However, it's only been the past 100 years since Americans could choose where they wanted to live, travel when and where they wanted to travel, have the number of children they wanted to have, eat any type of food they liked, entertain themselves how they saw fit, dress themselves in a way they wished, and in fact, truly choose who they wanted to be. Yes, the privileged in society often had those freedoms and choices. And yes, we've had waves of migration – from the rest of the world and into the vast continental interior. But to most of the population, choice was an abstract concept. Until the 1920s, only the truly wealthy had any significant level of decision-making ability.

This book will present a new way to look at the 1920s – not as the art deco era, but as the *choice* era. It's a perspective I can promise you've never seen before. I know. I've checked. You can read *Only Yesterday* or *New World Coming* to get the shorthand version of the decade, but they skim the surface, never going deep enough to show how deep the water really is. And yes, you can find authors and filmmakers who narrow their focus so they can dive deeper. Ken Burns' 2011 documentary series *Prohibition* is an excellent example, as is the book, *Last Call: The Rise and Fall of Prohibition* by Daniel Okrent, on which the documentary draws much of its material. You can find excellent biographies of Al Capone, Coco Chanel, and Calvin Coolidge. And while each provides a greater depth of perspective into its subject – and, by extension, the era in which they lived – they're like the parable of the blindfolded men touching the elephant. To the man touching the trunk, the elephant is a snake. To the man touching the ear, the elephant is a fan. The belly is a wall. The tail is a rope. The tusk is a spear. But no one sees the elephant in the room.

Perhaps the only author who begins to see the elephant for what it is might be Thaddeus Russell. He invests a chapter in his 2010 counter-culture book, *A Renegade History of the United States*, reminding readers that it was *consumers* who delivered most of the freedoms we enjoy in our daily lives – the kind that matter in the day-to-day lives of most people. "Self-evident truths" don't mean as much to the average family as a new home, a car in the driveway, and a gas range. Russell goes so far as to christen the 1920s the *Second* American Revolution. Albeit a brief chapter in his book, it marks the beginning of a more apt description of the age.

Ultimately, consumer culture is so difficult to understand paradoxically because it's so familiar – millions of people making individual (and mostly inconsequential) decisions.[4] That doesn't mean the decisions are always correct or we aren't fooled on occasion. And yes, sometimes consumers willingly trade some of their freedom of choice because the consequences of failure are too great. But on the whole, that's rare. American consumers resist having their choices made for them by technocrats – to the tune of 70 percent of *all* economic output. Consumers aren't the tail that wags the economic dog. They are the dog. Or, more appropriately, they are the *elephant*. Because you can tell the dog where to sit. The elephant sits wherever it wants to.

...

When you take the perspective of a nation learning how to make an unprecedented number of choices for the first time, it gives us a new way to look at choice culture in general and the decade that birthed it. We'll see that choice is so much more than consumption and that the skills Americans learned during the 1920s transformed more than our market economy.

This book features 26 origin stories of our day-to-day lives: what you buy, how you buy it, what price you pay, and why you decide to buy it.

---

[4] The academic foundation of "choice culture" is rooted in behavioral economics, and especially *Austrian* economics. If you're interested in learning more about the technical side of these transactions, start with excellent books from Daniel Kahneman, Steven Levitt, Richard Thaler, or Per Bylund.

And it's so much more than buying products. Americans in the 1920s became savvier consumers of entertainment, information, politicians, advertising, and even their own identities. You'll learn about the incredible power you've been gifted to change the world – or at least, your little part of it. It's empowering, delightful, and deeply satisfying.

We'll dance the night away at the Savoy Ballroom in Harlem, sign up for the first subscription media service, get caught up in the Trial of the Century, pack our bags for the first all-American road trip, have a little fun in the sun, leave a review for that roadside motel, afford it all with five easy payments, learn how babies are made (and not) in the back seat of our car, get the resulting kink in our back worked out, shop for a new crib in the first big box store, watch our children learn to be savvier consumers than their parents, and pick up a new type of magazine to help us make sense of it all. And, of course, we'll learn about the gangsters of Prohibition ("Booze"), how sports became more product than athletics ("Babe" as in Babe Ruth), and the democratization of fashion by the indomitable Coco Chanel (the "Little Black Dress").

We'll use stories of outstanding innovators to help bring the Roaring 20s to life in a new light, but never forget that this is a personal story. *It's our story*. When innovators failed to meet our needs, they failed. When they humbled themselves, they succeeded. It's that simple. We chose its characters, its storyline, and its ending.

It's challenging to think of an area of our lives that consumer culture does *not* influence: the home we live in, the car we drive, the family we choose to create (or not), the food we eat, the places we entertain ourselves, the person we try to become, how we create social change, and even who we vote for. That's why it's vital to better understand how we got here and where we might go *from here*.

As consumers, the choice is ours. For the past 100 years, it always has been.

PART 1
BOOZE

HOW CONSUMERS LEARNED TO CHOOSE PRODUCTS AND SERVICES.

1
MANUFACTURING DESIRE

Let's begin with a thought experiment, shall we? Try to imagine your life without the following products:

> Washing Machine, Radio, Television, Vacuum Cleaner, Automobile, Electric Toaster, Electric Blanket, Refrigerator, Electric Dishwasher, Adhesive Bandages, Sunglasses, Automatic Wristwatch, Instant Camera, Speakers, Bread Slicer, Garbage Disposal, Electric Razor, Frozen Food

What you just read isn't a *complete* list of mass-market innovations of the 1920s. It's an *abbreviated* list of those products and services the average consumer might find at a department store, grocer, or car dealer. We're ignoring several behind-the-scenes innovations. A short list of those must include the assembly line, heavy construction equipment (like bulldozers), and first-generation antibiotics[1] – innovations that made other consumer products both possible *and* affordable.

Obviously, some commercial innovations are more impactful than others. Sunglasses might look sexy, but few would put them on the same level of impact as the refrigerator.[2] If you live in Miami, you're probably not jonesing for an electric blanket. You get the idea. More to the point, most products on that list feature viable alternatives – you can wash dishes by hand, and plenty of people do.[3]

This thought experiment quickly boils down to a distinction between *wants* and *needs*. Do you *need* sunglasses? Probably not. If it's too sunny, you can wear a hat. Do you *need* a radio? That's debatable. There are other places to get your news and entertainment, but you'll probably miss out (at least a little). Do you *need* a refrigerator? Not necessarily. However,

---

1 This era also saw the discovery of both General Relativity (1915) and Quantum Theory (1925), though neither spawned immediate commercial innovations. Most people think of the atomic bomb as the first "product" derived from these theories, which isn't necessarily wrong, but it's incomplete. Global Positioning Systems (GPS) could not function accurately without correcting for the influence of gravity on differing measurements of time predicted by Albert Einstein.

2 Actor Tom Cruise might beg to differ. He rocked those aviators in both *Top Gun* movies.

3 Though, counterintuitively, dishwashers tend to use water more efficiently than hand washing. The same goes for car washes.

you can't rent an apartment today in the United States without one. That seems much more like a *need*, doesn't it?

Because most of us own (or have owned) all these products, we can only *try* to imagine life without them. Consumers in the 1920s didn't have to imagine their lives without these things. These products were offered *at an affordable price* for the first time. Were the advertised benefits of an electric razor worth the costs? What else might you need to purchase if you wanted to try frozen foods? (A refrigerator or freezer, perhaps.) How might your life change when your family huddled around a radio instead of spending time talking with each other? No one in the 1920s had the benefit of 100 years of hindsight to answer those questions.

Of course, moralists at the time wasted little time tut-tutting their disapproval of supposed "luxuries" like washing machines and vacuum cleaners. (Though, not surprisingly, it was almost always those people who already had those conveniences who would look down on "less-deserving" people for wanting them too.) Moralists might have gotten ink and air time, but purchase data reveal that few people listened. When Americans could save hours of manual labor each day with a washing machine, they wouldn't listen to someone extolling the virtues of scrubbing your clothes in the river. And when Americans saw how cool they looked in sunglasses…well, that was that. Americans wanted these products. They wanted them *now*. Manufacturers, retailers, and banks lined up to deliver these innovations to a buying public seeing them for the first time.

Let's take this thought experiment to its logical conclusion. Once you had your first washing machine, why would you ever need another one?

Yes, all products have a usable life. And yes, that usable life correlates (roughly) with mechanical complexity. With a bit of simple maintenance, sunglasses might last a lifetime unless you lose them or break them. Washing machines are much more complex, with parts that will wear out over time. You may be forced to purchase a new washing machine at some point unless you can repair it, provided it's cost-effective to do so.

Why might consumers buy a new product if it's not lost, broken, or worn out? Sunglasses are easy; they're a fashion item, and tastes change. You can see why people might buy new ones, even if you might consider that a trivial reason. But would you ever buy a new washing machine simply because it was a better model? Perhaps it used less water or cleaned clothes better. That's a "good" reason for a new purchase, right? What if the latest model was smaller than its predecessor? Hmm. That reason doesn't sound quite as good of a reason as the first. What if the new washing machine comes painted a different color? Is that a "good enough" reason to upgrade? That depends on who you ask.

If moralists had heart palpations over the rise of first-wave consumer goods, *replacing* those luxuries gave them full-on cardiac arrest. We'll circle back to the moral and ethical questions later, but in the 1920s, those questions were moot. No one knew how to release new versions of products, on a predictable schedule, and not go broke doing it.

For the business community, this was an existential question. At some point, you'd run out of new customers. Sure, the population might grow, eventually creating new buyers. And yes, products legitimately wear out. However, that growth was capped unless they could figure out a way to design and manufacture new and improved versions of their products. Without revenue growth, businesses lack the resources to invest in research and development to create those new products. It's a classic catch-22.

The demand was there. That much was certain. When presented with "new and improved," Americans snapped up better products as quickly as they were available. They might have paid lip service to moral dilemmas but quickly learned to rationalize a want into a need.

That meant the faster you could develop a new product to replace the old one, the better. The cheaper you could do it, the better. The more improvements you could pack in, the better. The more appealing you could make it, the better. Henry Ford might have figured out a way to park an affordable car in the driveways of millions of Americans, but even he didn't have a good answer to those questions. His fiercest rival, Alfred Sloan of General Motors, would figure out how to get people excited about their *next* new car.

This is the story of the model year change.

. . .

The automobile market of the 1920s was far more complex than it is today. Between 1900 and 1925, over *400 new manufacturers* entered the market. Yes, you'd see nameplates like Ford (1903), Chevrolet (1911), and Chrysler (1925), but you'd also see bizarre badges like Red Bug, Wolverine, and

Davis Totem.[4] New brands were sprouting almost as quickly as others flashed in the pan.

All it takes is a visit to a classic car show or museum – one of the few that still features cars from this era – and you can't help but notice the intense experimentation and variety of consumer options. Not only were there many more manufacturers and brands, but there were also many ways to design and build cars. Safety standards didn't (meaningfully) exist. Neither did consistent traffic laws. Suppliers delivered one-of-a-kind parts for largely hand-made cars. Those cars might have been fun to look at, but they weren't a pleasure to drive, they were almost impossible to repair, and they were prohibitively expensive.

Given those market conditions, it's not surprising that Ford's approach quickly rose to the top. Modular designs, standardized parts, and assembly line construction meant lower input costs, and, therefore, lower consumer prices. By the middle of the decade, Ford's Model T accounted for about half of *all cars* sold. As a manufacturer, if you didn't adopt Ford's methods, your days were numbered.[5]

Given that success, Henry Ford saw little reason to evolve the design of his vehicle, and his rationale seemed to make sense.[6] First, Ford designed the Model T like a car "kit," allowing buyers to customize their version to specific needs. For example, a farmer might add a plow to the front of his Model T or a delivery driver might add a box container on the rear end. Second, designing new vehicles was expensive, and Ford had an evangelical-like focus on wringing every last penny from the production process to keep prices as low as possible. In the most well-known example, most were painted black because that was the cheapest color and it cured the fastest. Third, perhaps most importantly, why mess with success? Ford's strategy worked. Other companies were driving into the ditch almost as

---

4 The Wikipedia page, "List of defunct automobile manufacturers of the United States," is a fun read for gearheads. You'll notice quickly that the average lifespan of any one nameplate is less than the time it would take to pay off a typical car loan.

5 Only a few handmade vehicles (such as Rolls Royce) survived past this era. Those were only viable options for the very wealthy, and despite the mystique, they weren't high-quality machines.

6 Yes, the mid-1920s Model T adopted inflatable tires and a handful of cosmetic changes. Still, many of important improvements (like shock absorbers) were only available as aftermarket accessories.

quickly as they got on the road. A bet on Ford would have been wise in a winner-take-all race to market dominance.

However, careful observers noticed the fatal flaw in Ford's strategy. As Ford kept selling Model Ts, the company was running out of customers. It was the same problem we highlighted earlier. Henry Ford was becoming a victim of his own success.

As a moralist in his own right, Ford simply couldn't understand the consumer desire for novelty. (Or if he saw it, he thought it immoral and wasteful. Ford was an interesting character.) Ford knew how to manufacture cars at a price people could afford; in his mind, that was enough. It would be MIT-trained engineer Alfred Sloan who would figure out how to manufacture desire for your *second* new car.

. . .

Sloan's business biography, *My Years with General Motors*, calls this innovation the "Annual Model Change." He introduces the underlying rationale to begin Chapter 13:

> Each year we must produce a line of cars which embodies advanced engineering and styling features, and which will be competitive in price and meet the demands of the retail customer. The cars in this line must have some common styling features, giving them all a "General Motors look," but at the same time they must be clearly distinct from one another. They must also complement one another in price, which means that their own cost elements as well as the trend of competitive prices must be estimated well in advance of production.

As you read Sloan's account, you never get the hint he is deceiving customers or convincing them to purchase something they don't truly need. Quite the contrary. Sloan makes it clear that consumers are demanding and that competition is fierce. If General Motors couldn't figure out how to give customers what they wanted to buy, another competitor would.

Ever the engineer, Sloan decided that GM needed to create a *system* to deliver desirable upgrades on a predictable basis. An ad hoc schedule of improvements would be challenging to manage internally and difficult to communicate to consumers. By contrast, when consumers could anticipate changes, they were more likely to get excited about them. That excitement would become a positive feedback loop, driving *earned* media (reporters covering the new model releases) that would supercharge *paid* media expenditures (print and radio advertising).

Sloan identified five considerations the team must address in this systematic approach to product development: Engineering changes – those included new functions such as safety features, engine performance, and input improvements, many of which the customer would never see; styling changes – the visual look of the vehicle, distinct enough to distinguish the latest model year from the last; pricing appropriateness – ensuring all those improvements didn't make the new vehicle too expensive for its target buyer (more on this in Chapter 4); competitive differentiation – positioning each new GM vehicle favorably against rivals; and brand extensions – what Sloan referred to as the "General Motors look" among all its nameplates.

That last one made Sloan's process infinitely more difficult. Henry Ford made one type of vehicle under one nameplate: the Ford Model T. General Motors, by contrast, was a conglomeration of brands. GM manufactured cars under several nameplates: Chevrolet, Oakland, Pontiac, Oldsmobile, Scripps-Booth, Sheridan, Buick, and Cadillac.[7] In other words, Sloan didn't have to coordinate new models for one make. He needed to coordinate new models for up to *eight* unique makes. And that doesn't count models *within* each make.

Up to that point, GM had been an unprofitable mess of makes, each with independent leadership teams, engineering staff, supply chains, and sales goals. If Sloan's company was going to meet consumer demand and

---

7   When designed this way (from lowest to highest price), this range of options is called a "product ladder." Ideally, the lowest-priced Cadillac would be more expensive than the highest-priced Buick…and so on, up and down the ladder. That strategy creates a clear distinction in the buyer's mind. In practice, the options overlapped a bit in terms of features and prices, as they often do today. You can see product ladders in all manner of consumer products – automobiles, of course, but also televisions, mobile phones, clothing, restaurants, food, and hotels. In fact, it's difficult to find a product line that does *not* feature a ladder strategy. They all trace their roots to General Motors of the 1920s.

not drive the company bankrupt doing so, he would need to make changes.

...

The first (and the most important) innovation was GM's *human* organizational structure.

Sloan called this cross-functional team the Engineering Policy Group. Although it uses the word *engineering*, that word choice was a misnomer. The EPG included engineering, of course, but also design (interior and exterior), manufacturing, supply chain, advertising, marketing, sales, and finance. Because Sloan needed to coordinate decisions between GM makes, division heads had a direct say in platform-wide decisions that would impact unique customer preferences and price points for their specific brands. GM's team might have been better named the *Customer* Policy Group. That was it's *raison d'etre*.

With the team in place, the technical work could begin. Bodywork and mechanical engineering changes took the most time, so the team tackled those first. If possible, major changes would follow a two-year cycle, with more cosmetic changes filling the one-year gaps. In practical terms, if GM wanted to introduce a new body style (e.g., a longer wheelbase for more passenger room), the team would plan for a change like that every two years. It was simply too much work to design, test, and implement those changes on a manufacturing floor any quicker.[8] That balance between major and minor changes was critical – annual product introductions can take advantage of natural seasonality and rhythms that ad hoc (or every two-year) cycles cannot. You don't celebrate your birthday every *two years*, do you?

During that first six-month phase of each two-year cycle, the team would focus on how styling demands would drive engineering decisions. For example, if consumers wanted more leg room, what impact would that have on body design, total weight, engine power, or suspension? How might that decision impact different variants of the vehicle – sedan, coupe, or hardtop? Designers crafted dozens of clay and wood mockups to demonstrate each model's functional and stylistic aspects. Seeing is

---

8   Machine tooling is still a challenge, by the way. That's part of the appeal of additive manufacturing (aka 3D printing).

believing, and there's nothing like a full-scale model to focus the team's attention early in the process. Sloan wanted to know if a bigger vehicle wouldn't fit on the current assembly line *now*, not *18 months* from now.

Sloan also insisted that the team decide on key styling differences between the lines so that each vehicle would seem unique enough and provide the consumer with clear choices. Although much of the underlying engineering might be common between a Chevrolet and a Buick, each make should offer customers substantive choices. For example, a more powerful engine only available on the Buick version allows customers to decide if that's enough reason to pay the extra money to upgrade from one make to another.

The six-month mark is the first major milestone. At that point, GM's executive team would review a full proposal from the EPG, including options and price points for the entire lineup, styling models, common supply chain parts, sales estimates, and financial models. Once the EPG received its approval (often with some modifications), they moved on to the next half-year phase.

Over the following six months, the engineering and design teams needed the time to convert *concept* designs into *production-ready* designs. That meant converting clay and wood models into sheet metal, and sheet metal required machine tooling. A machine "tool" is a part used to make other parts. For example: If you're making a hubcap out of stamped steel, the tool would contain an inverted shape, like a heavy-duty crimping iron. Machine tools were (and are) difficult, time-consuming, and costly to make. Once you've made one, you need to test the resulting parts to ensure they fit with other parts made with other tools. When you consider the tens of thousands of parts in any automobile assembly, six months seems…a short amount of time to get that right. That's why shared components were so important.

The second task during this phase was less obvious but no less important: initial consumer feedback. This was an early opportunity to gauge the desirability of the new models from people most likely to purchase them. However, although this was a critical early test, Sloan realized he could never precisely predict what would happen in the dealer showroom next year. Getting feedback on a design (from advertisers, dealers, or customer focus groups) asked their *opinion* about the design or options in question. It was good for catching major mistakes but didn't necessarily translate to sales. That's because asking for an opinion differs from asking for a *sale*. On the showroom floor, if people say they liked a car but didn't buy it, their *opinion* doesn't matter. Because of that critical distinction, Sloan was always careful to avoid locking in the final decisions about a model year lineup until it was absolutely necessary. Pushing as many decisions as possible to the last moment gave GM maximum flexibility if (and when) market conditions and consumer preferences changed.

But at the 12-month mark, that's as long as they could wait. It was time to put new models into production, begin the advertising push, and train dealers.

Year two was all about the details. On a part-by-part basis, the supply chain team would decide to "buy" or "make" a particular part. If they made it, they needed tooling and production. If they bought it, they needed to write specifications, qualify vendors, check prototypes, and ensure quality delivery on schedule. Unlike Ford's production line, which stayed virtually unchanged year after year, GM needed to reconfigure major portions of its production line for each new model year and for each brand in the lineup. That meant early prototypes (used for demos and advertising), necessary refinements (although they hoped not to make *too many* costly changes), and then full production. And remember, all this happened when the factories were still producing *last year's* models.

With such a tight timeline, full production often didn't begin until six weeks before delivery. *Six weeks!* That strict schedule had benefits. The team could delay cosmetic decisions such as paint, upholstery, and minor trim features until just *days* before new cars arrived in showrooms. These could help GM respond to last-minute fashion trends more quickly than competitors, giving their salespeople an edge in dealer showrooms.

However, the most important feature might have been this: At each step, the GM team reserved the right to proceed as scheduled, make changes, or even cancel an entire line, all based on the latest consumer feedback. Sloan couldn't run GM like Henry Ford ran his namesake company. Ford's dictatorial, command-style approach wouldn't work in a system that required creativity, communication, and responsiveness. *Sloan needed to trust his leaders.* There were simply too many decisions to do it otherwise. Coordination was difficult. Decisions took guts. But consumers demanded no less.

. . .

That's not quite the image most people have of 1920s-era "scientific" managers, is it?

We're primed to think of pre-war managers as unyielding automatons who bullied hapless workers with unreasonable demands. Although Sloan was clearly driven, it's also clear GM could not have accomplished the complex logistics of the model year change without a collaborative, respectful, team-based approach.[9] For business leaders who know his story, there's ample reason Sloan's name graces his alma mater's business school 100 years later.

Sloan's approach wasn't just thoroughly modern; it worked. By the end of the 1920s, Ford's dominance of the automobile market was over. Model T sales peaked in 1924. By 1927, under pressure from consumers who wanted the variety GM offered, Ford shut down his production line to completely retool it for the new Model A. It would take Ford years to catch up to GM's ability to design new cars *and* build existing models at the same time, and by that time, it would be too late. Although Ford could boast individual vehicles with strong sales numbers (such as today's F-150 pickup truck), GM's collective portfolio of brands outsold Ford two-to-one for nearly 50 years. Only as imports from Japan and Germany began to break into the U.S. market did GM's 50 to 60 percent market share begin to decline.

GM's rigorous model year change cycle made all other automakers seem *behind* by comparison. Their strategy also proved counterintuitive. Instead of encouraging customers to wait (and buy next year's better model), GM's strategy convinced people that their *current* cars were better than their competitor's stale models. To GM's marketing team, that wasn't surprising. Buying a car is a major investment for most consumers, and a company that was always innovating and producing something new

---

[9] Labor groups in later years might disagree with that assessment, but when you strip back the arguments of those with an ax to grind, it's more a matter of union leaders demonizing Sloan (a little) to gain a negotiating advantage. To be fair, Sloan famously didn't like unions.

seemed like a safer bet.

Almost a century later, automobiles continue Sloan's model year change legacy. Even electric car upstarts – which have tended to focus on software rather than hardware – now update their cars' operating systems almost continually. However, whether it's bent sheet metal or downloaded code, all carmakers deploy some version of the complex, interrelated model Sloan pioneered to conceive, design, test, and deploy improvements.

The philosophy underpinning the model year change extends far beyond cars and trucks. Consumer electronics were the obvious inheritors of Sloan's philosophy – computers, smartphones, televisions, fitness trackers, and hundreds of other major and minor products face constant pressure to innovate and release improvements. Kitchen gadgets – like stand mixers, for example – release new attachments, motors, and color choices. Fashion brands learned Sloan's lessons to more quickly (and profitably) release clothing based on seasonal trends. It's difficult to think of *any* modern product that doesn't follow the pattern Sloan established over 100 years ago. As consumers, we expect new and improved, and we're suspicious when we don't.

Is that a good thing, a bad thing, or something in the middle?

Ah, now that's a good question.

...

That doesn't mean the moralists have gone away. In fact, they never went away. Their arguments have simply evolved.

The first modern moral argument concerns sustainability. Put simply, a desire for the new and improved encourages a throw-away culture where people give up on a product well in advance of its useful life. This leads to an increased role for extractive, finite natural resources as well as labor-intensive (and often toxic) processing of those materials. Up against glamorous new products, the "reduce, reuse, recycle" mantra can't compete. Moralists now point to mountains of bulbous, yellowed CRT monitors whose plastics will take tens of thousands of years to degrade, all the while leeching their toxic heavy metals into surrounding groundwater.

Simply offering new and improved products isn't enough, they say. Too often, product manufacturers purposely design products to fail – what they call "planned obsolescence." Worse, the product need not completely fail to encourage its owner to replace it. A computer may begin to run more slowly because new software requires processing power not available when the machine was designed…or the manufacturer may not allow the software upgrade at all. Or replacement parts for a 10-year-old washing machine might be so expensive that's it cheaper to purchase a new one. Or consumers risk voiding the warranty if they try to repair their coffeemaker. In short, it's a *conspiracy* to make bad products.

Giles Slade, environmentalist and author of the book *Made to Break: Technology and Obsolescence in America*, makes this case with repeated (and often damning) evidence.

Damning…until you scratch beneath the surface.

Slade claims the average consumer expects only two years from their computer. But be careful. That's *opinion* data, not *buyer behavior*. How often do consumers actually replace their PC? Purchase data from 2020 pegs the number at more than three times the "expected" value: 6.55 years. And that number continues to increase.

Slade claims the Model T was "the most reliable car ever built," and that cars today barely last beyond their five-year payment period. Let's verify those claims. Was the Model T the most reliable car ever built? The thriving market for aftermarket parts and the strong primary evidence of ubiquitous roadside repairs in the 1920s would say otherwise. (Every story of early road trips features at least one breakdown.) What about a car barely lasting five years? That's not true either. The average car now lasts over *12 years*.

Slade claims Boeing created the 747 jumbo jets as a way to land all the DC-3s into the scrap heap…and make airlines buy all new planes. Slade neglects to point out that the 747 is over 90 percent more efficient than the DC-3, saving billions of tons of fossil fuels and carbon emissions, while commercial air traffic has more than quadrupled in that time.

Why is there such a difference between the moralists and the evidence? Simple: Businesses have a *disincentive* to be wasteful. Moralists who make that claim have never been part of the negotiations to pay less, buy less, use less, and do more – all in the name of increasing profitability, reducing liability, and remaining competitive. Can we find examples of short-term wastefulness? Of course, but competitors tend to take care of those companies by driving them out of business.

Often, the true underlying issue is *regulatory capture*. That's when organizations lobby the government to protect their wastefulness and shield themselves from the competition. To counter those efforts, regulations such as Extended Producer Responsibility are forcing those businesses that have been able to externalize wastefulness to pass the full costs of doing business along to consumers, where they can make the choice with more complete information. Is the system perfect? No. Can we find poorly-designed products? Yes. But on the whole, today's consumer goods are high-quality, safe, and cheaper than ever. And they're getting better.

When objective arguments fail, moralists blame the perennial boogeyman: advertising. Mass marketing makes the old product seem undesirable, fooling people into a never-ending quest for new products. And worse, when they can't afford it, businesses will find a way to offer consumers credit to buy it anyway. The resulting debt traps consumers in a never-ending cycle of poverty and want.

If that were true, advertisers could dictate every fad and prop up every company. The facts point elsewhere. *Consumers* control every company's fate, and all businesses know it. GM is no longer the company it was because it lost that edge. And while some people speak to the power of Walmart, Apple, Google, Facebook, or Amazon – the average lifespan of a Fortune 500 company today is actually shorter than it's ever been. In 1958, a company could expect to be around 61 years. In 2020, that number shrunk to 18 years.

Sloan wasn't successful because he fooled customers into buying a product they didn't need. His own biography makes that point clear dozens of times. Every manager at GM lived in constant fear of shifting consumer demand. If GM couldn't deliver what they wanted, they'd simply buy a different car. Sloan simply found a way to meet that demand better than his rivals…at least for a while.

Perhaps that's the toughest thing for moralists to understand. It's not greedy corporations that create the demand for new products and services. *We created consumer culture.* Sloan simply helped to make it possible.

2
THE MANIPULATION MESSIAH

> There is only ONE Palmer School - Davenport, Iowa.
> There CAN BE BUT ONE "Palmer School" - Davenport, Iowa.
> Because there is only ONE "B.J. Palmer" - Davenport, Iowa.

B.J. Palmer seemed to enjoy screaming in print.

This angry attempt at poetry was the capstone of a 500-word screed that included the words "mislead," "innuendo," and more than 88 words written in ALL CAPS.

What got under Palmer's skin was the explosive growth of new schools of chiropractic popping up all over the midwest in the early 1920s. But instead of seeing this growth as evangelizing chiropractic into previously heathen lands, Palmer saw sprouting mushrooms – hiding in the dark and eating crap. Their clinical methods weren't his clinical methods. Their training program didn't quite follow his training guidelines. Their sales pitch for new students didn't rely on the Diva of Davenport.

That last one was the true mental sliver he couldn't tweeze out. After reading his ramblings at length (and often, they come off as only barely coherent), one comes away with the feeling that it's more about insufficient genuflecting at the Palmer altar than any actual difference in the theory or practice of chiropractic.

As the only begotten son of Daniel David (D.D.) Palmer, chiropractic's founder, Joshua Bartlett[1] saw himself on a mission to protect the soul of the profession from those who would pollute it with heresy from other natural healing methods or – *gasp!* – scientific medicine. Palmer was on a mission to save people from false prophets who denied their God-given right to wellness through the true practice of chiropractic.

If the language so far all sounds a bit, well…*biblical*, that's not a literary flourish.

As often happens in the early years of a new religion, early apostles strike out on their own to evangelize far and wide. Inevitably, they find themselves in new lands with different cultures than the birthplace of the

---

1   You read that correctly: Joshua Bartlett, not Bartlett Joshua, a pair of names that would more naturally shorten to "B.J." Palmer. Somewhat more sensibly, young Joshua often went by "Bart" as a child, which probably had something to do with the "B." coming first in "B.J." as he matured. Most histories of chiropractic omit this tidbit.

faith. To convert the masses, they must adjust[2] their message and practice to meet those realities.

Palmer would have none of it.

In the holy war between rival schools, much ink would be spilled in anger, and all cloaked in apocalyptic language – Palmer's was the one true school, B.J. Palmer was the only son of the father, and his bible and bully pulpit would be called "The Fountain Head." Suffice it to say, even considering the strangeness of the 1920s, this was odd stuff.[3]

But if we strip away all the messiah complexes and personal insecurities, Palmer was more than just a culty eccentric from a third-tier city in Iowa who fancied himself the back-cracking savior. He forced all healthcare (whether scientific or holistic) to confront some basic questions:

> Is healthcare a science or a business?
> Do doctors provide care or sell products and services?
> Are people receiving healthcare patients or consumers?

Along our journey to answer those questions, we'll have to sift through some uncomfortable facts about the state of medical practice in the 1920s, understand how different branches of healthcare competed ruthlessly with each other, and how Palmer responded to that pressure to launch the first modern commercial medical device.

As we'll see, the science of the Neurocalometer (such as it was) paled in comparison to the creativity of its sales and marketing approach. This device is important because we still live with Palmer's answers to our three basic questions.

Healthcare is a business. The doctor is a brand. And patients are

---

2   That's a chiropractic joke. "Adjust." Get it?

3   In several amateurish, but recognizable illustrations, B.J is depicted as a vaguely Christian "Jesus" or "God" figure. More artistically attractive, but even more oddly, he was pictured as a shirtless and svelte version of the Greek god Atlas. It seems that B.J. couldn't quite settle on which deity best suited him. But of all the bizarre costumes B.J. sported, his Indian Chief outfits took the cake. If you're asking yourself if "Big-Chief-BJ" was culturally offensive, yes. Yes, it was.

consumers.⁴

Let's start our journey to redemption with the state of healthcare in Palmer's day. You didn't want to get sick.

. . .

No one alive today has any concept of what healthcare was like before the 1920s.

Even a casual reading of history's primary sources (diaries, private letters, and the like) will reveal that most people lived in mortal dread of what we, today, would consider minor inconveniences – a stubborn cough, a nasty cut, or a funny feeling in the belly.

That says nothing about high-risk activities.

Childbirth is the obvious one for women. For every 1,000 births at the turn of the 20th century, six to nine women would die of complications from pregnancy, and nearly *100* babies would not reach their first birthday.⁵ Heading off to war was the other risky business, and this time it was the men who suffered. For example, in the 1898 Spanish-American

---

4   B.J. Palmer was pretty clear about this. He stated that chiropractic was founded on "…a business, not a professional basis. We manufacture chiropractors. We teach them the idea and then we show them how to sell it." His priorities don't get much clearer than that.

5   This data comes courtesy of the Centers for Disease Control and Prevention, originally published in 1999. The good news is truly astounding. From 1915 to 1997, infant mortality dropped from nearly 100 per 1000 live births to 7.2 per 1000 – more than a 10-fold decrease. However, due to a number of factors, *maternal* mortality remained stubbornly high in the 1920s, only sharply declining beginning in the late 1930s.

War, you were *ten times* more likely to die from disease than a rifle shot.[6]

The "sick and dying" part often gets sanitized when we read history books or watch documentaries. That might be because we wouldn't know how to process what we saw emotionally. Or it might be that we like to focus on the (relatively few) big wins of the 50 years before 1920 – inoculations for smallpox, Pasteurization, quinine to treat malaria, aspirin, and the stethoscope. Or we would rather laugh at the folly of blood-letting, blistering, and patent medicines.[7]

The 1918 flu pandemic was still killing people in waves as late as 1919 (probably longer), and that trauma was very much ever-present in the early 1920s. Everyone knew someone who died, and doctors could do little (if anything) to stop it.

This isn't to psychoanalyze historians, criticize doctors, or comment on the squeamishness of modern audiences, but rather to emphasize the point: It wasn't evident in 1920 that scientific medicine had the right idea.

. . .

Chiropractic preached a very different gospel.

The basic idea is that everyone deserves to be *well*, not simply free from disease. It's a vision of holistic health that physicians are only now, more than 100 years later, rediscovering. Chiropractic doesn't accept

---

6 Of the roughly 22,000 men who landed in Cuba, 332 died from battle related injuries and 2,957 died from various diseases. National Archives data claims a slightly small number of casualties (roughly 2,000 from all causes), which is sort of a quibble. Data about casualties varies depending on how you measure it. Up until modern medical treatment (mostly after World War II), this imbalance of deaths from battle and death from disease was common. I wish more histories would focus less on a general's skill commanding troops in battle and more on their ability to keep enough men alive to fight when they arrived on the battlefield. That certainly changes our popular perception of rugged Teddy Roosevelt storming San Juan Hill, doesn't it? A more accurate painting would have been thousands of men sweating it out in a field hospital waiting to die.

7 The term "patent" medicine referred to advertising a medicine under a certain trade name or (more rarely) registering a patent for the ingredient list. In that era, whether it actually contained the ingredients on its label was hit or miss at best. Before the Pure Food and Drug Act in 1907 and further prescription laws, the term "patent" referred only to the legal protection of the brand or ingredients in the formulation, not that it actually did what it claimed to do.

drugs (prescriptions or otherwise) as proper treatments. In D.D. Palmer's *original* version of chiropractic, all diseases can be traced back to misalignments of the spine.[8] The purpose of a chiropractic adjustment is to relieve the resulting pressure. At optimal levels, so the logic goes, the body's immune system and processes can address disease symptoms without additional intervention.

It's sort of like the Iowan version of Chi.

However, chiropractic faced new competition in the 1920s on two fronts.

First, medical practice was finally casting off its mystical and philosophical origins and becoming a science. Pioneers like Charles Darwin followed in the footsteps of Isaac Newton and applied the scientific method to biology and medicine. German scientist Heinrich Hermann Robert Koch worked out the broad outlines of the germ theory of disease by the turn of the century. The aforementioned Spanish-American War taught doctors that mosquitoes were a significant source of infection in tropical climates (even if they didn't know precisely why), which would allow the Americans to succeed where the French had failed to build the Panama Canal through the jungle.

The problem wasn't medical *science* any longer; it was medical *practice*.

Medical training was largely unregulated and, as to be expected, of vastly divergent quality. Even the "best" programs featured professors on staff who weren't entirely on board with germ theory in the early 1900s. That says nothing of mail-order colleges issuing mail-order degrees.[9] If you wanted to call yourself a doctor in the early 1900s, well...you just did.

Founded in 1847, the American Medical Association (AMA) finally began to address physician training in the first decades of the new century. They set educational standards, certified physicians, established standards

---

8   If you research the origins of chiropractic, it gets a little weird. D.D. Palmer claimed to receive the tenants of chiropractic from a doctor who had been dead for 50 years communicating to him from "the other world." There's plenty more about the concepts of "subluxation" and "innate intelligence" that don't bear a full discussion here. If you want to learn about chiropractic, go visit a chiropractor. There are two major types – "straights" (the pure Palmer version) and "mixers" (the majority, who will incorporate other alternative medicine techniques.)

9   The final exam surely included the questions, "Pay to the order of" and "Amount." We'll meet other mail order doctors in this book.

of evidence, and began to test (and sanction) pharmaceuticals for actually doing what they claimed to do.

But it was more than simply improving medicine by improving the quality of physicians. It also meant actively ridding the field of quackery and pseudo-scientific approaches – faith healers, magnetics, and most importantly, chiropractic. It used a multi-pronged strategy to lobby federal and state governments to restrict or ban non-scientific medicine.[10]

However, taking on scientific medicine was a fight Palmer relished.

Palmer took every opportunity to lambaste the inconsistency and hypocrisy he saw in medical practice (for example, doctors routinely prescribed whiskey, especially during prohibition, because it was a big moneymaker) and to tout the miracle cures offered by chiropractic. Palmer's biographer Joseph C. Keating, Jr. called him the "P.T. Barnum of Science" – an apt description of his promotional style.[11] It didn't matter if the attention was positive or negative; the *attention* was the critical part. In one example, when the *Illinois Medical Journal* called him the most dangerous man in Iowa *not* in a prison cell, Palmer had posters made up that pictured him behind bars. Palmer understood that the more people heard of chiropractic, the more it would be perceived as an "option" alongside "standard" medical practice. Instead of hurting chiropractic, criticism

---

10 It took an antitrust lawsuit in 1976 to finally overturn "basic science" laws in 24 states, including Iowa. In fact, the American Medical Association (AMA) was so successful in its more than 100-year campaign to rid medicine of what it called "quackery" that most other non-sanctioned professions disappeared or were folded into standard practice. Chiropractic was one of the few that survived. You can learn more in the AMA's own ethics journal. Since the late 1970s, other alternative healing methods (including the anti-vax movement) have resurfaced – with a vengeance. They don't trust medical science, pointing to this campaign (and other misdeeds) as evidence for their position. It says something about the nature of Americans that suppressing information (even when it's "wrong") often backfires.

11 Keating's biography, *B.J. of Davenport: The Early Years of Chiropractic*, is the definitive guide to its subject. Deeply researched and packed full of (hysterical) screeds and cartoons, it shows the messy evolution of chiropractic as it worked to free itself from Palmer's grip. If you're wondering if I'm being fair with my characterization of Palmer as a megalomaniac and shameless self-promoter, you can read the ample direct evidence yourself. Keating spares nothing. I needed to find the book in a chiropractic library in Minneapolis, and there don't seem to be too many copies left in print. That's too bad. Like many primary sources covering this era, they're fading away. I'm hoping Google gets around to digitizing this one soon. We need to keep these sources around.

elevated chiropractic, making people curious and sparking natural conspiratorial instincts.

Palmer may have enjoyed fights with doctors, but the battle *inside* the profession threatened everything he had worked so hard to build.

Chiropractic training was becoming deeply inconsistent. The practice snowballed after World War I, mainly on the back of Federal funding for vocational programs for returning soldiers. Ever the business opportunist, Palmer's school raked in those dollars and pumped out new chiropractors by the thousands.

It didn't take long for other aspiring chiropreneurs to see the same opportunity and begin opening competing schools, not necessarily following the "pure" Palmer methods. Many new schools saw the AMA's standards and training as opportunities and guidelines, not as a heresy to fight. They incorporated additional training on nutrition and other natural healing methods, lengthening their training programs in the process.

Palmer called it exactly as he saw it. Medical science might be full of overeducated, ivory tower pontificators, but so-called "mixers[12]" were worse. They were *heretics*. They diluted the "correct" practice of chiropractic.

The trouble was that mixers adopted the core principle of the scientific method: evidence. Where Palmer saw chiropractic more like an article of faith – above questioning – mixers did not. They were more comfortable asking core questions: Does chiropractic work? If so, how? What are the key measurements that would prove it? After a chiropractic treatment (the adjustment), what changed? How would you measure it? More specifically, if pressure on spinal nerves was the problem, how could you measure that pressure? Patients reporting they felt better wasn't good enough – even in the 1920s, the placebo effect was (roughly) understood. If people believed something worked, they often would report feeling better. Standards of evidence required objective measurements and controlled experiments.

The answer that came next – from Palmer, no less – remains with us today. It transformed the fight over medical evidence into an argument over

---

12 Palmer loved his nicknames for his enemies. That's one of the reasons I use so many to describe him. Turnabout is fair play.

business models, and in the process, transformed patients into consumers. We're finally ready to learn about the Neurocalometer.

...

"THE MOST VALUABLE INVENTION OF THE AGE BECAUSE IT PICKS, PROVES, AND LOCATES THE CAUSE OF ALL DIS-EASES OF THE HUMAN RACE."[13]

Palmer's initial success made sense. He heavily advertised the chiropractic training program for its effectiveness on patient health *and* its impact on the chiropractor's bank account. In 1918, a 12-month program cost $250 for a single person and $312 for a married couple.[14] (This "married partner" innovation should not go unstated. It was not only rare for the time, but absolutely genius. It created families of chiropractors, not simply individual practitioners.) The 18-month program cost a bit more – $300 for singles and $375 for married couples – but at the end of your training, you got to call yourself a "Doctor of Chiropractic" and not simply a "Chiropractor."

A recession in 1920 and 1921, coupled with Federal vocational training reimbursements for veterans, heavy advertising, and a lack of competition, made for some heady years in Davenport.

But by 1924, the Palmer school was in financial trouble. It's not hard to understand why. Once you trained a chiropractor, you had no new sources of revenue. You can't earn more income from practicing professionals if (as you claim) they have nothing more to learn. What's worse, Palmer's insistence that chiropractors required only about 18 months of

---

13   This description comes from a 1924 issue of the *Fountain Head News*. I have so many questions about this description. What's the difference between "picks" and "locates"? And *all* diseases? Really? If I get into a patch of poison ivy, how does a spinal adjustment help? And why, precisely, could you not use this on…say…your dog? Isn't your furbaby worth it? (Is there such a thing as a chiropractor for pets?) And more ALL CAPS. Sheesh.

14   About $5,000 to $6,000 in 2020 dollars. Not bad, huh? I checked around. In 2020, the Palmer School charged just over $9,000 for its program. Other chiropractic schools charged a bit more – $12,000 to $19,000. That's still a bargain compared to most 4-year college programs, and you're done in a fraction of the time.

training in a universal set of methods backed him into a corner.

Even worse, some of those chiropractors decided to open their own schools, increasing competition for students. In the immediate years after World War I, Palmer's school could (rightly) claim to be, if not the largest vocational training program in the country, certainly in the top 10. Attendance mushroomed from a few dozen before the war to more than 1,200 in 1919, 1,500 in 1920, and nearly 3,000 in 1921. That would be fine if the number of students continued to grow, but that wasn't the case.

By 1923, the school was shrinking, and Palmer almost said "no" to the invention he hoped would save it.

The device that would become the Neurocalometer was the brainchild of a fresh graduate of the electrical engineering program at the University of Arkansas and a veteran of the new field of radio communications working for the U.S. Secret Service in Mexico.[15]

The basic idea is pretty simple. Dossa Dixon Evins sought chiropractic help for a bout of tuberculosis in 1916. He was fascinated by that doctor's attempt to detect "hot boxes" in the spine – a possible indication of a pinched nerve – that would tell him where to perform the chiropractic adjustment. Where chiropractors used their hands to detect the difference in heat or pressure, Evins took the obvious next step: He would use a thermocouple. This simple device would measure the difference in heat (a proxy for "pressure") between two points on the left and right sides of the spine. If it worked, it would revolutionize chiropractic by adding objective, quantitative data of a measurement that before required a trained craftsperson. Evins was so intrigued by the idea that he enrolled in the Palmer School in 1920, graduating in 1922.

At first, the Davenport Deity showed little interest in the device. He turned Evins down flat without a second thought. Keating hints (but doesn't come out and say) that part of Palmer's reluctance was an aversion to anything that smacked of scientific origins polluting the pure practice. That seems reasonable. He also could have been distracted by falling enrollment and his insistence that new schools were churning out

---

15   Mexico was a big deal in World War I. Germany tried to convince Mexico to attack the United States if the U.S. entered the war on the side of the Allies. It was a solid gambit, but when it was discovered, it helped convince the Americans to enter the war. You can read more about it by searching for the Zimmerman Telegram.

substandard practitioners.

Whatever the reason, Palmer regretted his initial brush-off as soon as Evins received his patent. Luckily for Palmer, Evins was a true disciple. He returned to Palmer, who graciously received him back as soon as Evins said he would hand over the patents to the school for only a tiny share of the profits.

It seems most likely that Palmer, the *businessperson* saw what Palmer, the *chiropractor* failed to grasp during the first meeting: The Neurocalometer was a golden goose.

Finally, there was an opportunity to earn additional revenue for every new graduate. More importantly, given falling admissions numbers, was the potential to sell a device to every chiropractor with an already-established private practice. What's better, he could refute the claim from the medical profession that chiropractic failed to deliver evidence. The device took a measurement. The chiropractor made an adjustment. The device took a second measurement. The change was evident and quantitative, or it was not. It not only showed the impact of a treatment,[16] but also the impact and quality of the *practitioner*. (Make a mental note of that last part. It'll be important later.)

Palmer's turnabout on the Neurocalometer was part of his bipolar persona – he could be prickly, egotistical, and demanding regarding chiropractic dogma. But when it came to business opportunities, he could admit he was wrong and change tactics.

As we'll see, it was only when his chiropractor persona resurfaced that everything fell apart. What happened next might have been a trainwreck, but it's essential to bear witness. Medical science watched the wreckage

---

16 Trained researchers would jump out of their chairs at this point: Where is the control group? How are you calibrating the devices? What about preconditions? Are the changes in heat before/after statistically significant? Are the causal of relief in symptoms? Or simply correlated? But all those questions mattered to scientists more than to chiropractors in practice and their discussions with patients. The Neurocalometer looked sophisticated and generated simple numerical measurements anyone could understand.

unfold, and it would not make the same mistake.

First, however, here's what went right.

. . .

Palmer was familiar with the "Ford" strategy – make a lot of something and make them cheap. That way, most people could afford one. It's an excellent idea for a mass market but a terrible idea to create an aura of exclusivity. The Neurocalometer, by contrast, would be priced high *on purpose*.

When Palmer announced the device was ready for pre-orders (another savvy strategy to generate excitement and help the factory know how many to produce), he set the price at $1,500 – about $30,000 in today's dollars, or what you might pay for a decent car. Palmer also made it clear that if you didn't commit right away, the price would go *up* – to $2,200 (almost $45,000 in today's money) – now the price of a *very* nice car.

Palmer justified the high price on several grounds, none of which were related to what the device cost to manufacture (although the packaging, design, and construction *were* top-notch). He made it clear that the national advertising and support for the device, including traveling staff to help train chiropractors in its proper use, required a hefty initial profit to cover those expenses over time. That's not an unreasonable line of logic.

Additionally, he set an MSRP – otherwise known as a Manufacturer's Suggested Retail Price – for each measurement performed by an authorized chiropractor using the device. At $10 per measurement session, the buyer would earn back the $1,500 investment in 150 visits. At five patients per day, you could see a full recoup of your cost in about a month.

When he found other entrepreneurs trying to cash in – and there were a few, including such fun variants as the NUEROpryoMETER – he sent his lawyers after them. Aggressively and *successfully*. He would jealously guard his intellectual property like any business magnate of the age.

That was a solid exercise in Marketing 101, but here's where Palmer took it to the next level.

After considering multiple options, including selling the device outright, Palmer settled on a "lease" model, which isn't exactly what that word commonly means today. It wasn't like renting or leasing a car. You didn't *purchase* a Neurocalometer; you *licensed* it for ten years. During that time, your fees covered training and repair services.

The specifics aren't important to the story other than to say that it was an odd layaway/lease combination. You needed to pay $100 up-front and commit to $50 monthly at 6 percent interest to secure your spot in line. Once you reached $1,500, you could take delivery while making the rest of the payments. Oh, and one more thing. If you paid the full $1,500 up-front or accelerated your payments, you'd move to the front of the line.[17]

Another key feature of the licensing model was that it was restrictive. Because the device required a trained chiropractor (Palmer made it clear that use by an untrained person could be dangerous, but for what reason remained unclear), only chiropractors would be allowed to purchase one. Even more to the point, Palmer strongly implied that only *his graduates* were eligible. That meant graduates of knock-off schools and mixologists[18] were out of luck. Palmer wanted to create exclusivity and uniqueness among *his* followers.

Palmer's strategy here was about as sound as it could be. It had all the elements: exclusivity, premium price, the money-making potential for its buyers, strong advertising support, aggressive legal action to counter the counterfeits, flexible payments, incentives for buyers to pay faster, and

---

17 Presumably, after you passed 30 months (or 44 months at the higher price), your payments would end and Palmer would remain on the hook for training and repair service during the remaining time on the 10 year license. That's a classic maintenance sustainability problem that still plagues businesses today. There's an argument that it would have been smarter to move to a rental pricing model – say, $25 per month for the length of the license term – but that would have generated less up-front cash flow. The evidence of incentives for faster payment tells me Palmer needed the money right away and was willing to cross that repair bridge when he came to it.

18 To my knowledge and reading, Palmer didn't use this turn of phrase, but he should have. I think had I been able to tell him, he totally would have. He had an eye for a good insult.

immediate cash flow for the Palmer School.

Or, at least, it *had* the potential.

Had B.J. Palmer not been B.J. Palmer.

. . .

Now, here's what went wrong.

From the moment Palmer introduced the Neurocalometer, chiropractors complained about the high price, the restrictive license, and the suggested patient procedure pricing. Those deals would become common in the years to come with all manner of "capital equipment" (as we'll see shortly), but they were new in 1924.

It would take a skilled communicator to patiently explain the virtues of the arrangement – how it would help convince more patients to see a chiropractor and how it would help them demonstrate their clinical skill with quantitative evidence.

Unfortunately, Palmer had all the tact of a drunk uncle during a wedding toast. Here's a taste:

> About 50 percent of the chiropractors haven't any ability to be chiropractors and ought not to be; about 25 percent haven't the ability to run an office commercially…[19]

Not only did he use his in-person meetings and bully pulpit in the *Fountain Head News* to lambaste chiropractors who were unworthy or unqualified, but he went a step further. He insulted their ability to run a business as well. He called them narrow thinkers and unable to see the big picture. When he estimated how many Neurocalometers he thought they could sell (a "market sizing" exercise every competent businessperson does – although usually not publicly), he put it this way in a *live* speech:

> Out of 20,000 gross, we can discount 10,000 as being unworthy; then, out of the remaining 10,000, 5,000 can save themselves yet by studying Chiropractic at some competent and qualified school. Out of the

---

[19] From a longer Palmer speech (republished later) called, "The Hour Has Struck." Palmer certainly had a flair for the dramatic with his titles.

remaining 5,000, probably 3,000 can now afford to buy at reasonable terms, beginning tomorrow, at eight o'clock in Room 12. This will cull about 5,000 good out of 20,000, and leave a substantial number of competent and qualified chiropractors to construct a professional house that would be worth living in, where we think and talk the same language and feel acquainted on the same subject.[20]

Did you catch that?

Only 25 percent of chiropractors were "good," and only 60 percent of *those* could afford it – 3,000 out of a total market of 20,000. In later remarks and editorial cartoons, Palmer again justified the high price by claiming chiropractic as his "birthright" and that he should profit from the cumulative effort he had put into the profession over the years.[21] When chiropractors (obviously) saw the light? Palmer would be gracious, forgive them, and welcome them back to the flock. Like any good savior.

Let's just say this strategy didn't go over well.

It's not a bad strategy to be exclusive. Luxury brands use high prices to create exclusivity all the time, but they usually don't do that in a speech in front of mixed company, and they don't come out and say how they're explicitly doing this to recoup the expenses of supporting you schmucks all these years. Palmer's influence in the chiropractic community would never recover.

Palmer had a golden goose. But before it could lay its first egg, he slit its throat to cook it for dinner.

. . .

Nearly a century later, Eric Donnenfeld wanted eggs more than he enjoyed poultry. He and others like him in the medical profession took Palmer's ideas and ran with them. We'll meet Donnenfeld in a minute. But before we meet the good doctor, let's turn our attention back to the medical profession's reaction to the trainwreck that was the Neurocalometer.

Medical doctors didn't take Palmer's threat lightly. According to a

---

20 From that same "The Hour Has Struck" speech. Read in its entirety, this speech is a case study in how *not* to introduce a new product.

21 There was cartoon asking who gets to milk the chiropractic cow. Seriously.

sneakily, sly AMA spy, the Davenport school was off 90 percent from its peak at the beginning of the decade, now reporting only 316 enrollees.[22] They knew the launch of the Neurocalometer wasn't going well, but that didn't lull them into believing Palmer was beaten. The newly christened WOC radio tower in Davenport – aka "World of Chiropractic," as Palmer coined it – was among the most powerful broadcasting platforms in the country. When most radio stations stayed on the air only a couple of hours per day, and even those schedules proved inconsistent, WOC was one of the first stations to feature reliable, full programming days. That predictability and audience reach brought in the advertisers.[23]

Ever since, medical doctors have paid attention to Palmer's successes and have carefully avoided his mistakes.

As diagnostic medical devices became more complex and expensive over the following decades, innovators would use Palmer's business methods to become some of the largest companies in the world. They wouldn't steal the idea behind the Neurocalometer, of course. They thought it was hooey. However, the animosity of the medical profession towards chiropractors in general, and Palmer in particular, would not extend to his innovation in business practices.

Let's fast-forward 100 years to see how the story turned out.

Just a few of the devices common in clinical and hospital settings today, in the medical imaging subcategory alone, include Magnetic Resonance Imaging (MRI), Computerized Tomography (CT) Scanners, and breast imaging equipment (both 2D and 3D). That last one, used for mammograms, typically costs between $20,000 and $30,000, oddly similar to a Neurocalometer in today's dollars, isn't it? Because we're focusing

---

22 This wasn't so uncommon then, or now. The technical term is "industrial espionage" and it's *sort of* legal. As long as a Journal of the American Medical Association representative didn't misrepresent himself – like counting cars in a parking lot today – there's nothing explicitly unethical about gathering that data. That said, this is another tangible example of the perceived threat chiropractic posed to scientific medicine. You don't gather competitive intelligence on someone you don't consider a competitor.

23 Ronald Reagan (yes, *that* Ronald Reagan) got his broadcasting start in Davenport at WOC in 1932. Palmer fired him for flubbing an insurance ad. Reagan got a job down the street at a competing station that Palmer bought a few years later. It's unclear if Palmer fired him twice. I have to wonder if Palmer saw the young broadcaster's potential.

on big-ticket diagnostic medical devices used by clinicians, we won't dip our toes into the fetid swamp that is prescription drug marketing, but many of the same economic factors are at play.[24]

It's not just imaging and diagnostic equipment or prescription drugs. For example, robotic surgery equipment is commonplace in larger clinics and hospitals. This equipment can often lead to more reliable surgery outcomes, but it also can *increase* the cost of care. Why? A doctor, even a specialist, can do many things – see patients, perform multiple surgeries, do research, and consult with other doctors. A piece of capital equipment can (usually) do just one thing – a mammogram, for example. The larger hospital systems can afford to purchase the equipment outright, but many smaller clinics use some version of the same licensing model pioneered by Palmer in the mid-1920s. Every moment that machine isn't squeezing a breast and taking a picture, it's losing money. They must keep the device operating, or the owner will have trouble making the payments.

Ever wonder why you see robotic surgery equipment advertised on billboards? Or why you seem to be getting more screenings than you used to? Economics isn't the only reason, but it's a big one. Doctors and insurers who push back on the evidence that we might be over-diagnosing (and, therefore, over-treating) face an uphill battle against basic assembly line economics.

You can be forgiven for thinking that you don't have a "consumer" choice in the matter and that clinicians, hospital administrators, and insurance providers will figure this out…eventually. You're a patient. The doctor has an ethical responsibility to do right by you. You can always rely on that.

True. (Or at least, true-ish.)

But we see the same thing happening with so-called "cosmetic" procedures, each featuring expensive devices doctors need to purchase to offer the service. Consider how many advertisements you see for eye correction surgery, skin-tightening injections, face-lifts, chemical peels, hearing aids, tooth whitening, "invisible" braces, liposuction, and cryotherapy. And

---

24 The Government Accounting Office (GAO) found that drug manufacturers spent $17.8 billion on direct-to-consumer advertising (DTCA) for 553 drugs from 2016 through 2018, or about $6 billion each year. Most of that spending focused on only 39 drugs.

there, because healthcare insurance often won't cover the costs, the business practices are much more Palmer-esque.

Let's take the first one as a mini-case study. About 700,000 people get LASIK surgery in the United States *each year*. Remember Dr. Eric Donnenfeld? He's a former president of the American Society of Cataract and Refractive Surgery. He has performed over 85,000 procedures *himself* during a 28-year career.[25] That works out to over 3,000 procedures per year, or about 10 per working day. For just one doctor. When you consider the bigger picture, the overall "market size" of LASIK in the United States is about $3 to $4 *billion* each year, depending on who you ask. Since 1999, over 10 *million* Americans have gone under the knife (and laser).

To make the big numbers a bit easier to visualize, one patient (consumer) comes off the eye correction assembly line every 45 minutes during every 8-hour shift. When caring for people features the same economic incentives as building a car, it shouldn't be surprising that your clinic feels like a factory.

To be fair, Donnenfeld is not alone. He simply responded to the pressures of expensive equipment, capital financing, training requirements, marketing support, and suggested pricing. To maintain a pipeline of patients (consumers), he needed to become successful at knowing which psychological buttons to push to move people from "considering surgery" to "scheduling the appointment" in the shortest possible time. Equipment needed to appear "high tech" to inspire the patient's (consumer's) confidence. The overall patient (consumer) experience was just as important as the medical outcome. Advertisements featuring celebrity doctors fill mailboxes, flood web browsers, and illuminate billboards.

Highlighting his business skill doesn't mean Donnenfeld isn't a good doctor. He clearly is. It also isn't to say that he and Palmer wouldn't have had deep philosophical disagreements on the nature of medicine and healthcare. That's true too.

But B.J. Palmer would have been proud of him nonetheless.

---

25 Donnenfeld's example comes from a longer story on LASIK risks published in 2018, nearly 20 years after the FDA authorized the procedure in 1999. Doesn't a two-decade lag to talk about the risks seem a bit much to you? Can you see where a bit of the mistrust from chiropractors and other skeptics comes from?

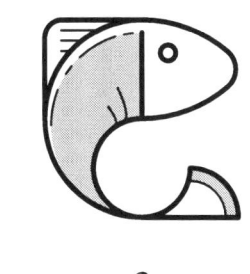

3
FLASH FOOD

Clarence Frank Birdseye would eat anything. Once.

That's a good thing, too. His career choices – cataloging ticks in the Montana backcountry or completing survey work in the Arizona and New Mexico deserts made him something of a connoisseur of odd meal choices. No animal in the vast American wilderness was safe from his fork. He wrote prodigiously about what he ate, though thankfully, his penchant for amateur photography focused more on landscapes than scorpion skewers.

Here are a few examples:

Birdseye is famous (infamous?) for his field mice stew, but he'd prefer the bigger rodents should they unwisely wander his way. His recipe adapted well to chipmunks, gophers, woodchucks, and beavers. He loved rattlesnakes fried in pork fat – he claimed it tasted like frog's legs, which given his culinary adventurousness, is utterly believable. Skunk meat was a "treat." (Not for the skunk, of course, and probably not for Birdseye. One imagines Birdseye getting his fair share of sprays in his attempts to wrangle the smelliest members of the weasel family.[1]) Gulls made great gravy, though birds of all shapes and sizes would do. He even ate lynx, which he loved, especially soaked in sherry wine.

Given the stunning variety of wild cuisine, one wonders whether he was the first person in recorded history to eat a particular animal. Certainly, he was the first to write about it.[2]

For most other people, being flat broke would be the only thing that could convince them to move with their spouse to the icebox that was (and is) Labrador, Canada, to learn about the commercial fishing business. But this is Clarence Birdseye we're talking about. He hadn't tried seal

---

1   There's some debate on Skunk classification under the *Mephitidae* family. Recent genetic analysis suggests these little stinkers should be in their own "stink weasel" family.

2   In his book, *Birdseye: The Adventures of a Curious Man*, journalist and author Mark Kurlansky doesn't rely on the mythology of the man; he went to the sources – Birdseye's diaries, published firsthand accounts, and living friends and family. It's an impressive work, and utterly invaluable to books (like the one you're reading) that must rely on a mix of primary and secondary sources when one topic (such as the birth of consumer culture) spans multiple subjects.

blubber or polar bear steaks, and a job is a job.

(Did we mention that his wife Eleanor went along with all this? Not only that, she *married him* during their time in Labrador. One struggles to find a better example of true love.)

Biographer Mark Kurlansky called Birdseye a promiscuously "curious" man. That's an apt description. Because what he noticed during the 24-hour winter nights when temperatures routinely dipped to 40 degrees below zero changed our (eating) lives forever.

...

Before we begin, we need to step back and understand what makes water unique, especially as it gets "Labrador" cold. (Don't worry, the science lesson will be brief, and you probably already know it – if not from tenth-grade chemistry, certainly from personal experience.) H_2O is a weird and wonderful molecule. Because of a quirk in the geometry of how water molecules fit together when they freeze, they do something almost no other molecule does: they *increase* in volume. *Water expands when it freezes.* If you've ever forgotten a bottle of water outside during a cold Minnesota winter night, you already know this. It's the same reason you don't fill up an ice cube tray to the very top with water. And there's one more thing. The increase in volume depends on how long it takes for the water to freeze – faster freezing; less volume. Cool water down slowly enough, and the resulting ice will take up about nine percent more space than the original water.

That's pretty much exactly what happens in your kitchen freezer. When most of us freeze food at home, we give the water inside the muscle cells in meat or cell walls in plants lots of time to expand. The resulting pressure bursts their cell walls. When we reheat that food, those cell walls don't magically reform. That's why most reheated, home-frozen food tastes like mush.[3]

But when Birdseye and his wife munched on cooked fish originally

---

3   It's also why cryogenic freezing doesn't work. If you were to freeze yourself in the hopes of waking up in a utopian future, you're more likely to be the human equivalent of reheated pot roast.

frozen in Labrador, it was still flaky and tender. *Why was that?*

During his time on the tundra, Birdseye watched the Inuit people ice fishing in negative 40 degree temperatures.[4] As they pulled fish through their augered ice holes, they would immediately flop them onto a fresh patch of ice. At that temperature, the water molecules didn't have much time to arrange themselves into neat little lattice structures and go on a cell wall-bursting rampage. Yes, the water did increase in volume as it froze, but not nearly as much as a slower freezing process. This *flash-freezing* process meant Inuit anglers could cook tasty fish stew whenever they wanted it.

Birdseye wondered: If he could flash-freeze fish and maintain its flavor, could he mass-produce other frozen foods? Could he get them to market? Would people want to buy them?

The short answers: Lots of things. With difficulty. Eventually.

Here's how he did it.

. . .

Birdseye was lucky to come of age in the Roaring 20s. He was able to ride the wave of several other critical technological innovations just coming into commercial use at that time – most notably, chemical refrigeration and the assembly line.

Before chemical refrigeration, the only (practical) way to get ice was to find it occurring naturally. The process involved finding a frozen lake or pond, sawing blocks of ice from it (with difficulty), packing it in straw as an insulator (to prevent too much melting along the way), and lugging it (again, with difficulty) to where it was needed.

Chemical refrigeration works differently. It involves taking advantage of an *endothermic* chemical reaction – one that absorbs heat from the environment, making the immediate area surrounding the reaction colder. Human sweating is a classic endothermic reaction. As water evaporates from our skin, we cool down. It's an extraordinary adaptation. Most other

---

4   You're probably wondering, did Birdseye steal this idea and claim it for his own? Nope. He credited the Inuit for their ingenuity every chance he got.

animals need to resort to panting.[5] In the 1920s, scientists and engineers commercialized Freon, the first in a long line of chemical refrigerants. That allowed product designers at Frigidaire to create the first self-contained refrigeration and air conditioning units. These were a far cry from the household freezers that would come later (many homes still used "ice boxes" well into the 20th century), but they were within reach of commercial buyers…albeit with some help with the cost. Remember that last point; it'll become important later.

The other major innovation was the assembly line. Although many manufacturers pioneered this technique, Henry Ford was its undisputed master, and its influence is hard to overstate. The idea that the item to be manufactured *moved* and the people or assembly machinery *stayed in one place* allowed workers to specialize and increase their efficiency and freed planners to reconsider the entire idea of throughput as a function of the speed of the assembly line.

Birdseye would combine these two inventions – commercial freezing and the assembly line – to solve one of the most practical problems of all: thawed, slow-frozen food tastes terrible.[6]

. . .

Why was solving the freezing problem so important? Americans wanted options.

Modern readers have a difficult time understanding just how limited the diet of the average American was in the early 1920s. Supermarkets, with rows and rows of convenient, processed foods, didn't exist. Food was fresh not because it was trendy but because there was no alternative. And although that may seem like a crunchy hippie paradise, it was not. Food

---

5   Kangaroos in Australia mimic human sweating by licking themselves. Obviously, you can only cool where you can reach with your tongue, so kangaroos have evolved reachable areas with lots of blood vessels to maximize the effect. The more you know…

6   In some circles, the fact Birdseye invented neither commercial freezing nor the assembly line meant that he wasn't a "true" innovator. That's not only examining his career too narrowly (his name appears on over 200 patents) but also confuses *invention* with *innovation*. Inventors create new things. Innovators introduce them into the marketplace. Sometimes those are the same person, but often (most often, actually) they are not.

was fussy and expensive.

People are resourceful when facing limited food supplies and learned early in our history to take advantage of surplus seasonal foods. The core techniques of food preservation – dehydrating, salting, and canning – hadn't changed much in hundreds (if not thousands) of years. Today, only country grandmothers, game hunters, and thrifty hipsters retain the skills that any average homemaker in the 1920s could do blindfolded. If you wanted to preserve meat, you dried and salted it – the origin of jerkies and bacon. Pickled vegetables, including the ubiquitous cucumber pickle, came in all shapes and sizes. Sugars do the work preserving fruits into jams, jellies, marmalades, and curds.[7] The need for bread that would keep longer than a couple of days was the origin of hard tack, biscuits, pasta, and even beer. Dairy converts tastily to cheese.

That sounds like a lot of options. It also sounds like we might all be healthier without modern food preservation technology. However, the reality was that food preservation took significant time and resources. You risked foodborne illness when you got any part of the process wrong, and it often led to malnutrition for families less well off (aka *most* families). But let's put it in straightforward terms: Imagine a grocery store, or your home, without a refrigerator.

Because keeping different foods fresh was a finicky business, production and distribution companies tended to specialize tightly. Butchers slaughtered animals (largely) on demand, right when a buyer handed over the cash. Bakers baked what they could sell that day. If you didn't catch your milkman fast enough, your milk got warm waiting for you outside. Today, all that is nostalgic and quaint. In the 1920s, it was normal.

Perhaps a lynx stew with gull gravy doesn't sound so weird, does it? (Okay, maybe it still does.) For the everyday person not willing to grill up an overgrown kitty, food choices were limited and highly dependent on your local environment and cultural background. Those in more concentrated urban areas enjoyed a bit more variety, but only if they could afford it. Malnutrition, especially among children and the elderly, was a constant worry. How do we know that? Not only do we have diaries and other primary sources from ordinary people at the time, but we also have

---

7   Ask your grandmother about the difference between these.

the advertising messages used to sell them foodstuffs. Look for yourself. Pudgy was ideal because many children were malnourished.

That's the world Birdseye knew and the problem he set off to solve.

. . .

The first question Birdseye needed to answer was the most obvious: How did flash-freezing work? He noticed that Inuit anglers would allow the fish to freeze on the brutally cold Labrador winter ice, where the temperature routinely dropped below negative 40 degrees Fahrenheit.[8] Simply flopping the fish on the ice at that temperature would freeze it in seconds, but how would that work in the summer? Or, more to the point, how would that work in cold, but not *brutally cold* climates, like the fishing port cities of Maine or Massachusetts? Labrador's weather was the inspiration, but it couldn't be the solution.

Birdseye needed to rely on chemical freezing, not climatic freezing. That part was obvious. But what wasn't obvious was *which* chemicals would be best on a mass-production line. He experimented with multiple options, including liquid oxygen and hydrogen. Although effective at creating an endothermic reaction, they are notoriously difficult to work with.[9] Birdseye abandoned what would become rocket fuel to focus his attention on various types of salts. To be clear, these aren't the table salts you're thinking of. A chemist would tell you that a "salt" is any ionically-balanced combination of an acid and a base.[10] The details aren't important here other than that different salts can produce varying degrees of endothermic reactions at different rates. One wonders how much Clothel Refrigeration Company appreciated thawing fish in its factory while he was experimenting, but Birdseye was nothing if not persuasive. The specific winner (Calcium Chloride) could mimic a Labrador winter. Still, that answer didn't solve the bigger problem: Freezing

---

8   Fun fact: That's the same temperature on both the Fahrenheit and Celsius scales.

9   Even in the 1920s, manufacturers could produce ultra-cooled elemental gases that would liquefy at shockingly low temperatures. They're dangerous, though. Liquid hydrogen and oxygen combine to make water…and rocket fuel.

10 Salt is an ionic compound that contains a cation (base) and an anion (acid).

one fish at a time wasn't commercially viable. That's where the assembly line came in.

...

Why did Birdseye need the Clothel Refrigeration Company, you ask? Simple. Cracking the code on the correct chemistry to flash-freeze *one* fish is (relatively) easy. Flash-freezing thousands of fish per hour is…more challenging. He quickly realized he could not use the one-at-a-time process, akin to bringing fresh fish into a dedicated "flash-freezing" room. Moving fish crates into and out of a closed room is highly inefficient. (For a familiar demonstration, watch the temperature of your home freezer quickly rise when you open the door, even for a moment.) Instead of the batch approach described above, Birdseye adapted Henry Ford's assembly line concept with one important alteration: Everything needed to *stay* cold throughout the process. Why? If your assembly line stops, car axles won't quickly thaw and rot on your shop floor.

Here's how the first flash-freezing assembly line worked. Workers would add fresh fish in a box to a moving conveyor line. (We'll talk about the box shortly.) Along that line, the fish would move through an area of the line between two chemically super-cooled metal plates, never coming into contact with the metal plates or chemical refrigerant. That was a big deal. Warm fish could stick to the metal plates in the cold – a la the flag pole scene in the 1983 film *A Christmas Story* – or take on odd tastes and smells from the chemical salt itself. Both were bad. Flash-frozen fish came out the other end of the line, ready for sale.

Birdseye called this an "indirect" flash-freezing method, as he described in Patent 1,773,079, issued on June 18, 1927. It was the symbolic beginning of the frozen foods industry. It wasn't long before Birdseye set up his own company – Birdseye Seafoods Inc. – to perfect the flash-freezing process and market his product.

What could possibly go wrong?

. . .

No one wanted them.

Birdseye stumbled onto the classic innovator's dilemma.[11] Simply stated, just because you built a better mousetrap doesn't mean people are kicking their cats out of the house. Somewhat predictably, his company promptly went bankrupt. But like any curious person, he paid attention to the key reason he failed. Launching a new consumer product into the market, especially something as central to everyday life as food, requires more than working out the production process – regardless of how impressive an accomplishment that was. His next company, General Seafood Corporation, would focus on the "downstream" activities – packaging, distribution, and marketing.

Let's start in the obvious place: packaging. Remember when we mentioned the "box" the fish came in would be important? Here's where we need to revisit a surprisingly relevant detail. No one wants to chisel a frozen fish from a cardboard box or wooden crate. That might sound obvious, but packaging materials as they exist today weren't quite what they were in the 1920s. One of the big differences between Birdseye's first and second ventures was developing a package for frozen fish that made sense for distributors and retail outlets.

Although wholesalers might purchase frozen fish by the crate or the pound, retailers often sell *by the fish*. Birdseye needed to package his product so that sellers could work with it. Again, this is one of those things that Birdseye didn't invent, but rather adapted to the need. He used existing (but still reasonably new) materials – parchment, cellophane, and wax papers – to help line the box and separate individual fish.

Once Birdseye figured out a better way to package fish before the flash-freezing process, he needed to convince the transportation networks

---

11 For more explanation, read Everett Rogers' *The Diffusion of Innovations*. In this 1960s classic, he coined the terms "innovator" and "early adopters" to describe people who were more willing to try new things than the average person. It's unclear where Birdseye's lynx stew would fit on that scale. He was one-of-a-kind.

to carry them. Refrigerated railway cars weren't new, but they were still *new enough* to be somewhat less than 100 percent reliable. Refrigerated *trucks* were even newer and riskier. Remember, frozen fish didn't just need to stay cold; they needed to stay cold enough to remain *frozen*. Railway operators worried about the potential liability of thousands of pounds of frozen fish thawing during a maintenance stop.

In what would become Birdseye's trademark business strategy, he engaged in hand-to-hand diplomacy. He was a tireless promoter of flash-freezing and its benefits, which extended to every part of the process from factory to dinner table. He worked with railway operators on the specific procedures they would need to ensure quality delivery even during "worst case" scenarios. The effort paid off. Skeptical railway and distribution executives often become his biggest supporters.

However, the challenge didn't end at the rail stop. Birdseye took that same frenetic energy door-to-door – quite literally – to mom-and-pop neighborhood grocers. Very few owned a commercial freezer, and even fewer had the financial means to purchase and maintain one. Birdseye faced not one, but two, distinct challenges. First, he needed to convince them of the quality of the end product itself (by this point, not only fish, but flash-frozen vegetables as well), and second, how they could afford the equipment necessary to offer those new products to their customers.

The quality demonstration was easy. That involved a sample. Answering the second question was more consequential. In an innovation that would be repeated in dozens of industries (and that would become standard practice over the coming decades), Birdseye helped arrange affordable financing for the equipment necessary for grocers to offer a new product to their customers. (Though, in the beginning, he did need to give away some freezers.)

Business types call this path from factory to sales floor the "value chain." That's fancy language for examining where meaningful improvements are made at each step in the process. In our example, the first value step was the factory itself, the second was wholesaler packaging, the third was transportation procedures, and the fourth was retail equipment. Examining the value chain is the key difference between creating an innovative *product* and pioneering an entire *industry*. However, the careful observer will notice we forget two important steps – one at the beginning and one at the end. The factory isn't actually the first step, and the retailer isn't the final one.

. . .

Fish don't come from a factory, a railway car, or a grocery store (or, for those of you on the coasts, a fishmonger.) They come from a body of water because, well, that's where they live. And it should also be clear they don't simply jump into the boat hoping hairless monkeys want to eat them. Anglers need to *catch* those fish. To extend that reasoning, chickens don't roll their wings in hot sauce and jump into the deep fryer on their own accord. Dairy cows don't squeeze their milk into convenient storage bottles. Vegetables don't leap out of the ground.

This may seem ridiculous, but consumers often forget that *producers* control the food supply, and they serve at the pleasure of Mother Nature. If the fish aren't spawning or the ground is frozen, no "market forces" can magically produce food through sheer will.[12]

We need to make this point because those people – anglers, farmers, and ranchers – needed to agree to provide their product to the flash-freezing production process. But wait, you say. Why would anglers care where they sold their fish? A buck is a buck. *Not so fast.* Remember, people knew what frozen food tasted like once thawed and prepared. If they sold their catch to Birdseye, and he sold it to grocers, who then sold it to consumers, who *hated it*, what would it do to the future demand for their product?

Additionally, what would that mean for seasonal production schedules if consumers could safely store fish (or other meats and vegetables, for that matter)? Would that lead to surpluses that needed to be dumped on the market at lower prices one month and then shortages and a scramble the next? It's not simply a matter of people resisting change. Entire agricultural production and labor schedules rely on a certain rhythm and predictability.

In the same way Birdseye convinced the railroads to carry frozen foods, he went belly-to-belly with producers. He demonstrated the techniques and the finished product, but more than that, he helped them see

---

12 Hydroponics and fish farming, for example, hope to address some of these issues, but they still require inputs. None of which are necessarily more efficient or sustainable just yet. In the 1920s, they simply did not exist.

the *positive* opportunities rather than just the downside risks. Flash-freezing could extend the buying season and geographic reach for their bounty. More availability in more markets meant more sales. That's a pretty compelling argument.

...

If you've ever frozen your leftovers and reheated them the next day, you know precisely why consumers of the 1920s were hesitant. On the whole, reheats taste terrible.

It's worse than that. We can look back on the 1920s with personal experience of freezing and thawing last night's chicken pot pie. They could not. If people *did know* what reheated food tasted like (and many didn't), they knew it wasn't good. If they had experience eating frozen foods (like ice cream), they knew it was an expensive treat only available on special occasions. In any case, homemakers wondered if frozen foods were as nutritious for their families as fresh foods. That reheated food tasted bad didn't help convince them.[13]

Beyond the flavor and nutritional value questions, not everything lent itself well to flash-freezing. Birdseye experimented with hundreds of foods. Some, like fish, flash-froze quite well. Once blanched (quickly boiled), peas, carrots, and other root vegetables tasted great reheated. Fruits? Less so. Birdseye knew that if he tried to sell something that wasn't a good candidate for flash-freezing, he might not just fail to sell that single poor example; he might ruin the entire market.

Birdseye couldn't do what a P.T. Barnum might have done a generation before – lie, exaggerate, or both. That's because, unlike a circus that rolls into town once a year, people need to eat every day. You might fool people with a slick sales pitch on mushy fish once. You won't fool them twice.

Advertisements and commentary of the time reveal the strategies used to convince skeptical buyers about this new, flash-frozen food option. The first was the use of the word "frosted" instead of the word "frozen" – or even "flash-frozen." Birdseye felt that it was important to distinguish this

---

13 This persists today in the "raw" and "uncooked" movements.

new process from any hint of the negative connotations of "slow frozen" foods and their poor taste, even though the gentle word "frost" almost conveys the opposite of rock-solid, flash-freezing. Although that descriptive word choice wouldn't persist past the middle of the century, it did provide an important distinction in the early days.

Other advertising messages described Birds Eye Frosted Foods[14] as "little short of magic," and the fish "as fresh flavored as the day [it] was drawn from the cold blue waters of the North Atlantic." To drive home the benefit regarding out-of-season produce, other ads featured "June peas, as gloriously green as any you will see next summer. Red raspberries, plump and tender and deliciously flavored. Big, smiling pie cherries – and loganberries. Imagine having them all summer-fresh in March!"

Birdseye was a savvy cultivator of popular media as well to help bolster his claims. Publications as diverse as the *New York Times* and *Popular Science Monthly* sang the praises of Birdseye's new frozen foods – often overstating the quality and similarity to their fresh counterparts. Today, that sounds a bit silly, but imagine never eating fish out of season, or if you do, only eating canned tuna, and you can see the appeal.

The era of frozen foods began not when Birdseye filed his patent, but when the first homeowners bought flash-frozen foods to prepare at home.

...

We're skipping over quite a bit of detail about the business side of Birdseye's ventures. Suffice it to say, it wasn't all savory lynx stew and gull gravy. On multiple occasions, financing dried up as investors lost patience. That said, if you were a betting person, you could have done worse than place your money in Birdseye's hands. He was more than simply observant. He was an inventor who could transform that observation into a repeatable production process. He was also more than an inventor. He was an expert negotiator who could convince reluctant suppliers, transporters, and retailers to invest in his vision. He was also more than a negotiator. He was a crafty marketer who could convince a skeptical homemaker to

---

14 Yes, he split his last name. He even went by "Bob" instead of Clarence to make it easier for people to say. He was willing to change his name if it would help. That's commitment.

use frozen peas in her stew that night.

One hundred years later, our industries (including food) are so mature that specialization is key to success. But when industries don't yet exist, it is the *integration* that's important. It's so rare to find people so multi-talented today that we hardly recognize how different each of those skills truly is. There were plenty of people who knew more about each specific step in the process than he did, but only Birdseye knew how they all fit together.

Perhaps in a stroke of what might be called the best business decision of all time ever in the history of the universe, Birdseye decided to accept an offer from Goldman Sachs and Postum Foods for $22 million, or about $325 million in 2020 money, in early 1929.

In October 1929, the stock market crashed.

Not a bad result for a guy who, only ten years before, was freezing his nuts off watching Inuit anglers.

. . .

Despite the trials of the Great Depression, frozen foods took quite a while to become a staple in the American diet. After the sale, Birdseye continued to work for his company's new owner for a while, mainly focusing on improved freezer designs and more cost-effective transportation schemes. By the mid-1930s, without any worries about money holding him back, Birdseye moved on to improve light bulb designs and invent food dehydration techniques.

Most people trace the beginning of the frozen revolution to the wide adoption of freezers in homes in the 1930s and 1940s, or the cultural phenomenon of the "TV Dinner" in the 1950s. But none of that would have been possible without Birdseye's trailblazing work creating the industry.

From the high ground of 100 years of hindsight, it's easy to critique the entire frozen foods industry as a net negative for American public health. Those (usually privileged) critics focus on the health benefits of fresh, in-season foods without noting the costs and availability of those foods – and the unique challenges not only in bringing them to market but also keeping them fresh while they wait to be eaten. In 2020, the U.S. Food and Drug Administration estimated that Americans *waste*, on average, about 40 percent of all foods produced.[15] Freezing is a critical weapon in the arsenal to fight food waste.

Another way to look at it is that Birdseye's innovation meant that many healthy foods were available to people at a price they could afford at any time of year. One could argue that he was *so successful* that the most significant public health challenge would utterly reverse itself – from "fattening up" to avoid malnutrition to "slimming down" to prevent the negative health consequences of widespread obesity.

Today, the annual market for frozen foods is about $300 billion, or about a third of all food sold. Ready-made meals cook up about a third of that total, with meats, vegetables, potatoes (primarily fries), and soup each accounting for meaningful percentages. Perhaps most oddly, frozen seafood is one of the *smallest* categories of frozen foods.

Given the eventual success of frozen foods, one wonders what Birdseye would have thought of the "local" and "fresh" food trends of the 21st century. At first glance, you might think he would think *we* were the crazy ones – that he brought us a literal and figurative bounty of affordable and healthy food and that we're all a little too bougie and snooty to appreciate it.

But that's not a good reading of the kind of person he was. If Birdseye were alive today, what would he do? He probably would have done precisely the opposite of what he did in the 1920s and figure out how to bring *fresh* food to the masses more efficiently.

> I do not consider myself a remarkable person. I am just a guy with a very large bump of curiosity and a gambling instinct.
> – Clarence Birdseye

Who knows? Maybe there's another Birdseye grilling up some crickets in Montana who can help.

---

15 For foods like strawberries, the number is closer to 90 percent. Really.

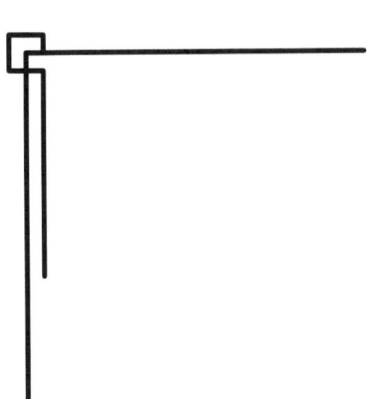

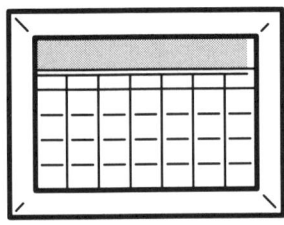

4
CARS ON TIME

Before the Civil War, producing just one shirt took about 14 hours of labor. To be clear, we're talking about a *woman's* labor hours. When you add in the number of other household and agricultural chores women needed to complete in an average day, you can start to understand how exciting the invention of the sewing machine was.

Like all innovations, early sewing machines were clunky, unreliable, and expensive. Only small factories and wealthy customers could afford one. Still, the promise was there. Even early models shaved stitching time by half; by the 1880s, that time could be measured in minutes. Think about it: 14 hours versus 14 minutes. That's compelling.

As the decades passed, sewing machines *did* become cheaper, but not *that* cheap. They were almost within reach of the average household's budget, but not quite.

In 1880, a new sewing machine cost about $40. That might not seem like much until you do the inflation conversion. $40 in 1880 is about $1,000 in 2020 dollars, and the first credit cards were decades in the future. If you wanted one, you needed to pay cash upfront. When you think about the price of a sewing machine as equivalent to about two weeks' income, it was *nearly* affordable for the average family.

The Singer Corporation, the biggest maker of sewing machines at the time, devised an ingenious plan. Instead of forcing strapped households to front the entire cost, they would let you take delivery of your machine on an installment payment plan. They called it, cleverly, "a dollar down, and a dollar per week."[1]

As you might guess, demand *exploded*.

It wasn't just sewing machines. Other manufacturers didn't take long to copy Singer's strategy and offer their installment payment plans. For the first time, jewelry, pianos, tools, and farm equipment (among many other products) came within reach of the average family.[2]

As you might also guess, overextensions of credit, defaults, and

---

[1] Alex Askoroff has written several books on Singer and the sewing machine industry. Check out his books if you're interested in learning more. His more recent is, *A Brief History of the Sewing Machine*, published in 2019.

[2] Including, not surprisingly, clothing. Why buy the machine when you can buy the clothes?

financial problems *also* exploded.

To observers of the time, overextending your credit was either (a) a profound moral failing on the part of the borrower stemming from a lack of discipline, (b) a lower-class person attempting to live beyond their means and put on airs, and/or (c) duplicitous advertisers and salespeople fooling good people, tempting them like the devil tempted Jesus in the Bible.[3] To them, the smattering of reports of financial distress (often more juicy anecdote than reality) was proof positive that installment plans were a one-way ticket on the road to damnation.

No one seems to have bothered to ask the housewife who could finish a shirt in a fraction of the time what *she* thought about all this. Moralist observers of culture rarely do – then or now. She might have nodded her head at the preachers, held her tongue with the Victorians, and then went ahead and bought a new sewing machine on a payment plan.

So, what happened?

Not what the moralists would have expected. In fact, it was precisely the *opposite* of what they thought would happen. Instead of Americans financing debauchery, installment plans *encouraged* the discipline and careful budgeting they desired in the unwashed masses. It *kept* people at their jobs. It *anchored* communities. The reason is so apparent that any first-year psychology student could explain it: A family that now owned a sewing machine, piano, and wedding ring couldn't imagine life before (or without) them. They'd do just about anything to keep them, including making better financial decisions to ensure no one could take their precious possessions back.[4]

In short, it's a myth to claim that people in the 1920s had no experience with installment loans. They'd been around for decades, but only for certain items and only from a handful of sources. On the whole, they were

---

3   Many of these observers couldn't decide if they were Victorians and classists, deeply religious, or both. All of this language was common. If you want to look at the original source notes, you'll see plenty of Biblical language along with the word "uppity." (Remember, this was a different time. The word did not have the racial overtones it does now.)

4   If you're interested in learning more, search for "loss aversion" or "prospect theory" in the psychological literature. The impacts are quite well documented. Every advertising person learns how to use these techniques. You should too…so that you know how to recognize them.

available only on goods that generally followed the "two-weeks income" rule. Options were limited, as was the potential financial risk on both sides. But that was all before the newest, shiniest, biggest ticket consumer product of the 1920s: the automobile. The desire to buy a new car, more than any other single purchase, raised the stakes. By the end of the 1920s, auto financing had permanently changed a thrift culture into a finance culture.

. . .

When most people think about automobiles in the 1920s, they can't help but think of Henry Ford and the iconic Model T, and for good reason. By 1927, when the last Model T rolled off the production line, Ford had sold nearly 15 million of them. To get a sense of the scale of Ford's success, that accounted for more than half of *all* cars sold during the Model T's production run.[5] But as we learned in Chapter 1, it was General Motors' strategy of offering multiple lines that changed *each year* that won out in the end. Although no single GM model outsold the Model T during the same period, by the end of the decade, GM outsold Ford *overall* and would continue to do so for the next six decades.

That naturally leads to speculation that it was operational mastermind Alfred Sloan, the architect of the GM product strategy, who was also behind the innovation in auto financing. That's only partially true. Although the General Motors Acceptance Corporation (GMAC) gets ample time in Sloan's business autobiography, *My Years with General Motors*, auto financing wasn't his idea. We need to back up a step and introduce a new character most people don't know.

Everyone knows Henry Ford. Businesspeople know Alfred Sloan. Far fewer people know the mercurial founder of General Motors: William Crapo "Billy" Durant.

Confused? If you had been around in the first couple of decades of the 20th century, you wouldn't be. Not knowing who Billy Durant was in 1920 would be like forgetting Steve Jobs today. Durant was just as

---

5   Because of the way Ford set up its production line, the company needed to completely shut down production to retool for the Model T's replacement. During that time, GM overtook Ford in market share and never looked back.

well-known as Ford, if not more so, and much more recognized than Sloan, who was in charge of a parts supplier before 1920.

Like Jobs nearly a century later, Durant was more than just an auto enthusiast. He was the consummate salesperson. Durant had an instinct for people, honed from a talent for active listening. Not surprisingly, like Jobs (but unlike Sloan), Durant was an "instinctive" manager – he went with his gut. That was great for the early days of the automobile industry when no one knew what to do, but it proved disastrous as the industry consolidated in the mid-to-late 1920s. That said, he was a smart enough businessperson to understand that not every car brand would survive. Those that did would need to understand their customers.

What did he know about people from careful listening? Something completely unintuitive. Early cars were unlike the (generally reliable) machines we drive today. Stories of road trips routinely include breakdowns, washed-out roads, and getting lost. Every car owner carried a complete set of tools, spare parts, extra food, and camping gear. Seriously. It was part of the adventure. Here's the funny part: *People loved them*. In those days, a car wasn't just a means of transportation. The haps and mishaps along the way wove their way into the emotional attachment to the vehicle in a way a "reliable" vehicle could not.

Durant is most famous for buying up the family of car brands that would eventually become General Motors – Cadillac, Oldsmobile, Buick, Chevrolet, and a handful of others. But Durant wasn't buying car designs, manufacturing plants, and dealer networks. Durant collected the strongest *brands* – the names that meant the most to people. The cars would improve with time, but the emotional attachment was irreplaceable.

You can read plenty more about Durant, but we'll set that aside for now.[6] It's enough to know that Durant had a knack for knowing what customers wanted. His instincts (and listening) told him that automobiles meant so much more to people than simply getting from point A

---

6 The best book to describe the relationship and contrast between Durant and Sloan is *Billy, Alfred, and General Motors: The Story of Two Unique Men, a Legendary Company, and a Remarkable Time in American History*, by William Pelfrey.

to point B. The problem wasn't desire; the problem was money.

Consumers couldn't afford the car they wanted.

...

Finding the money to buy an automobile was never a problem for the wealthy, and for the most part, that was good. Before the 1920s, cars were unreliable science projects, driving on very few roads, with no traffic rules, that were not only spectacularly expensive to purchase initially, but also difficult and expensive to maintain. The average consumer didn't have the means to hire a mechanic, a carpenter, and a medic to follow them around town…even if they could afford the car.

Henry Ford's answer to that problem was to build a car cheap enough that most people *could* afford it. In fact, unlike cars today, the Model T price *dropped* nearly every year as production efficiency improved. Despite a lower price, a new car was a tremendous investment – much bigger than a sewing machine or piano. If the automobile was to reach the mass market, it would take a *combination* of lower prices *and* more flexible financing. We're going to focus on the financing here.

Here's why financing a car was so difficult in the early 1920s. You only had a few options.

First, you could pay upfront. As we've already discussed, that's difficult for expensive 1900-1920 vintage cars, but even the $260 Model T was too expensive for many people (that's just over $4,000 in 2020 money). Could people "save up" for the purchase? Sure, and some people certainly did. That's actually what Henry Ford *wanted* people to do. More on that later.

The second option was going to a bank and doing something called "pay debt call" – in other words, the bank will give you the money, but they get to say when they want it back. Not familiar with that option? Most people aren't. It's more common in investment circles, where people with money will provide entrepreneurs with the capital they need to get started. Sometimes, they'll accept ownership in the company, sometimes a loan with an undetermined payback date, or a combination of both. Pay debt calls might be an option for delivery drivers who use their trucks to make a living (keyword, *might*), but they don't make sense for the average buyer.

The third option was nearly the opposite of a pay debt call: dealer credit. It's as if you went into a car dealer and said, "put it on my tab," and you paid your tab as you saw fit. You can see where the average grocery store might trust you to pay for those eggs and butter next week, but the dealer would be…leery…of relying on you to pay back a car when you felt like it. No, that wasn't going to work, either.

You might be wondering about a fourth option. The obvious one. The one that the sewing machine folks figured out 50 years before. You're on the right track, but hold that thought. There were two critical *financial* differences between a sewing machine and an automobile.

The first difference was the price. A new car cost ten times as much as a new sewing machine. That fact meant that banks were the only choice with enough capital to finance the transaction. For lower-ticket items, it was feasible for the manufacturer to assume the role of the bank. Singer made the machines. It understood them. It knew how reliable they were. And they deeply understood their customer and how they used the machines in the home. That level of knowledge made the company confident that it could make sound credit decisions. Worst case, a $40 possible loss was a reasonable risk if a customer defaulted. A $400 loss (a typical price for many automobiles at that time) was not. Only a bank could take on that risk.

However, by and large, banks didn't want to. That's the second difference between a sewing machine and an automobile. Not unfairly, cars were seen as "rich guy toys." Only the wealthy could afford them, and they tended to "play around" with them – racing was the ultimate trust fund baby pastime for the auto enthusiast of that era. What was the average person supposed to do with a car, even assuming they could afford one? That was unclear. Banks *hate* to lend money when there's no apparent use for the product. Remember, cars were famously unreliable. It wasn't just the purchase price; the customer also needed money to *maintain* the car. If they couldn't (or wouldn't), the risk of default skyrocketed. If one customer defaulted, the bank could handle the loss. Hundreds of defaults could ruin the bank.

Of course, cars *were* getting better. Roads were improving. Suburbs were growing. (We'll talk more about that in Chapter 6.) Additionally, waves of immigration that crashed on America's shores over the prior 20 years meant a *lot* of new potential customers. For example, from 1901 to

1914, nearly one million people arrived in the United States *each year*.[7] The opportunity was right in front of the banks, waiting to be seized.

But the banks wouldn't bite. Instead, General Motors would copy Singer and dominate auto financing (and the auto market) for half a century.

...

The most straightforward answer to the auto financing problem was the *installment loan*. The technical definition gets wonky, but it's not complicated in practice. An installment loan involves paying for a large purchase over time in "installments" – usually a small proportion of the total amount each month plus interest. The interest provides the incentive for the lender to allow you to use the money to buy what you want. It also protects against the risk that some people might fail to make their payments. (Yes, a lender could repossess the property in that case, but reselling a used car rarely makes the lender whole.)

Let's keep the math easy in a simple example. Let's say a new car costs $1,000. An installment loan with 5 percent interest and ten monthly payments would mean the buyer pays $105 monthly for ten months. In other words, to own the car outright, the buyer must pay back the purchase price of $1,000 plus interest of $50 for a grand total of $1,050.

Obviously, this example is oversimplified.[8] The 5 percent interest is *annualized* (not compounded monthly, daily, or continuously). The purchase price could be more or less. The buyer could make a down payment (pay a portion of the total upfront to lower the remaining balance). The lender might lower the payments by stretching out the payback period. Additionally, many installment loans feature a clause that says if the buyer fails to make payments, they forfeit any prior payments in a repossession. In other words, if you make eight of the ten payments and then stop, the lender repossesses the car and gives you nothing. The buyer may have used

---

7 According to U.S. Census data, between 1845 and 1900, 322,000 people arrived in the United States each year. Between 1901 and 1914, that annual number nearly tripled to 923,000 before dropping again between 1915 and 1965 to 270,000 each year.

8 We'll ignore balloon payments, variable interest, and other tricks of the trade.

the vehicle during that time, but they earn no equity (partial ownership) in it.

As we've discussed, the mechanics of the installment loan was not the issue. Bankers clearly understood it. Calculating interest rates and terms was simply a math problem. It wasn't the *terms* of the loan; it was the *amount*. The average person didn't have the savings necessary to purchase a car outright, even as cars dropped in price during the 1920s. Because most bankers thought cars were toys, they weren't inclined to accept the risk.

Perhaps a more significant issue than the amount of the loan or the car's perception as a toy was the sticky creditworthiness issue. Remember, these are the days before easy-to-access credit scores. Wealthy people can get into financial trouble, but they usually have the money to make their payments. The *average* person is trickier.[9] Making a loan was a judgment call. It was personal. And squishy decisions make bankers nervous.

One of the simple things that made bankers nervous was the obvious question: When does the buyer take possession of the car? Do they drive it off the lot with only a signed commitment? Do they need to make a down payment or post collateral? Do they need to make a certain number of payments? (Or, ideally, *all* the payments?) Those were all unanswered questions in the 1920s.

Finally, as if all that wasn't enough, car buying was seasonal. That meant a much greater demand for financing during certain times of the year. Seasonality creates crunches and gluts – much like electricity demand can fluctuate between day and night. The bank (or utility) needs to maintain capital (or power grid capacity) to handle spikes in demand. That's difficult and costly.

In other words, auto financing involved multiple unpredictable variables and stubborn unanswered questions. Smaller manufacturers who self-financed smaller equipment purchases were one thing. Singer understood sewing machines, and the price was low enough to make the risk manageable. But cars? They were too expensive, and banks *didn't* understand them. The net effect was a messy market where some people could get financing some of the time, but most people couldn't get financing most of the time. This unmet demand starved the auto market of the fuel

---

[9] Today, we look at credit scores and wonder if they're biased. Sure. But what about judging credit risk without any data? Is that less so?

it needed to grow.[10]

However, much like Singer, General Motors understood cars. They also had a strong incentive to sell more of them, especially as Ford's Model T seemed to be taking over the market. If GM could find a way to finance automobiles, it could take advantage of the unmet demand in the marketplace and halt Ford's advance. If they couldn't, there was a genuine chance Ford would drive everyone else into the proverbial ditch.

. . .

Billy Durant wasn't the type to document his strategy. Luckily, his successor, Alfred Sloan, was. He captured Durant's March 15, 1919 announcement in a formal letter:

> The magnitude of the business has presented new problems in financing which the present banking facilities seem not to be elastic enough to overcome.
>
> The constantly increasing demands for our products, particularly the passenger cars and commercial vehicles, has correspondingly increased the difficulty of our dealers in commanding at the seasons of the year when most needed the banking accommodation necessary properly to handle the volume of business which their ability as salesmen and the merit of our product as merchandise has developed.
>
> This fact leads us to the conclusion that the General Motors Corporation should lend its help to solve these problems. Hence the creation of the General Motors Acceptance Corporation; and the function of that Company will be to supplement the local sources of accommodation to such extent as may be necessary to permit the fullest development of our dealers' business.

In other words, if the banks wouldn't finance cars, GM should set up a new division to do it.

By today's standards, GMAC started conservatively. Customers would

---

10   When you look at a growth chart, you might question that claim. However, most graphs don't show the aftermarket for used cars, which are even riskier prospects. With no financing, there were limited opportunities to sell a used car and trade up to a new one, constricting the overall auto market.

be required to provide a significant down payment – often as much as 35 percent – to ensure customers had skin in the game. Additionally, GMAC wouldn't let customers extend their payments that long. Advertisements and other sales records of the time often tout 10-month payment schedules. Still, compared to the uneven bank financing options available to car buyers up until 1919, and frankly, throughout the 1920s, GMAC was a godsend.

To be clear, customers weren't *required* to use GMAC financing. Dealers weren't required to offer it. That's part of the plan's brilliance. GM didn't *need* to force anyone to use it, but with the lack of good options available, it became the *fait accompli*. Durant understood that customers *loved* making a choice – even when GMAC was up against only a few other poor options – and *hate* being forced – even when GMAC would have been the best choice.[11]

It gets better for GM. To understand how, let's use a simple example.

In 1925, the cheapest production car you could buy was the Ford Model T "runabout" model for $260.[12] GM's answer to the Model T was a bargain model Chevrolet, which might cost $300 for comparable features. Yes, the Ford is cheaper, but what if you only have $50 in savings right now? Neither option works unless you can convince someone to loan you the money.

GMAC would be that "someone."

The Chevrolet dealership's financing option is straightforward: Your $50 down payment leaves $250 remaining to finance. Over each of the next ten months, you'll need to pay $25 against that balance and another $5 in interest. Within a year, the car will be yours. Yes, you'll (eventually) pay $350 for a $300 car, and it would be more expensive than the Ford in either case, but you can drive it off the lot *that day*.

How did that discussion go at the Ford dealership? Not so well. Come

---

11 As it turned out, banks responded to competition from GMAC throughout the 1920s. Once GM showed car financing was possible and profitable, conservative bankers got on board.

12 According to Model T enthusiasts (you can find multiple sites dedicated to the iconic car) this was the cheapest price. Model T's could range as high as $1,590, but most averaged $400 by the end of its run in 1927. That's a steep 50 percent *reduction* in price from the first model year in 1909. The first year's model cost roughly $800.

back when you have the money. Ford didn't need to worry about anyone defaulting on a loan, but he also didn't need to worry about making that sale. That buyer bought a Chevy.

The situation gets worse for Ford and even better for Chevy.

Our buyer might have bought a *more expensive* Chevrolet model. Or perhaps even an Oldsmobile (the next rung up on the product ladder). Here's why. Let's say our buyer spies that upgraded model on the showroom floor. It costs more (say, $400), but if the *monthly payments* remain affordable, the car's sticker price doesn't matter as much. Not only did GM now have a tremendous competitive advantage when comparing similar models, but it could also shift the perception of affordability from the *total* price to the *monthly* price – a much smaller number.

By 1928, this micro example played out at the macro level so often that although Ford's Model T was the best-selling car through most of its production run, General Motors grabbed the steering wheel and took the driver's seat.[13]

This is what Durant understood so well from his sales training. Most people think about sales as manipulation or control, but Durant (and, to be fair, the best salespeople) see it differently: They are problem-solvers. The problem was affordability. The solution was flexibility.

Henry Ford was not a salesperson. At least, not a salesperson at Durant's level. Despite that, Ford *was* a tough competitor. He soon realized what GMAC could offer and worked to build a duplicate system. However, Ford had…let's just say…problems with "finance" people. In his mind, they ruined his first venture and nearly scuttled his (ultimately successful) second. He understood they were necessary, but he didn't trust them. He certainly didn't like them. And he didn't like the idea of finance people conniving to convince good, God-fearing people that they didn't need to save up to make a large purchase.

Here was Ford's idea:[14]

While many Ford dealers offered their own payment schemes, the

---

13 Do you like the car metaphors? Come on. They're fun. Just roll with it.

14 For more, read Lendol Calder's *Financing the American Dream – A Cultural History of Consumer Credit.*

Ford Motor Company stuck to an old-fashioned layaway plan. It was called the "Weekly Payment Plan." Customers could select the style of car they wanted and make a down payment. Ford asked people to bring in $5 to $10 a week and deposit it in an account run by their local dealer. And then when they had enough money in the account - only then could they take delivery.

How well did that go over? Just about as well as you'd think.

By 1928, Ford set up its own financing arm, but it was too late to recover the lost ground. Ford was one of the lucky ones. Financing drove many smaller carmakers out of business by the decade's end. Only the dozen or so largest remained independent, but it was mostly a three-car show: General Motors, Ford, and Chrysler. In that order. For the next 60 years.

. . .

Alfred Sloan gets a lot of credit for formalizing and building GMAC during his time as president and chairman. He's often misquoted in (even otherwise reputable) history books as *creating* GMAC. Not true. Did you notice the date on Durant's letter? 1919. Sloan's previous company was absorbed into GM in 1918, but Sloan didn't have a meaningful role until 1920 and didn't take over as president until 1923. Yes, he grew GMAC. No, it wasn't his idea.

Only a trained *listener* and observer of human nature, like Durant, would understand how powerful an impulse it is to get what you want when you wanted it. That said, Ford's Model T was such a uniquely strong competitor that it would take a better part of the 1920s for auto financing to finally turn the tide in GM's favor for good.

Did Durant realize what he had done? Did he know that he added the final leg in the stool to support the consumer economy? Perhaps he did. The first was mass production, brought to the world by the Industrial Revolution a generation before. The second was mass marketing, with its practitioners trained by the government for World War I propaganda. The third ingredient was mass finance. If consumers couldn't afford what they wanted, no amount of supply or advertising would help.

The consumer economy exploded.

By the decade's end, financing had expanded to enable nearly every major purchase. Aside from home mortgages (such as they were, see Chapter 7) and automobiles, the most popular items were: Household Furniture, Pianos, Sewing Machines, Phonographs, Washing Machines, Radio Sets, Jewelry, Clothing, Tractors, Gas Stoves, Electric Refrigerators, Vacuum Cleaners, Farm Equipment, and Improvements to Buildings.

A growing mass finance consumer culture caused no end of hand-wringing and opining. Those lamentations came in a few distinct varieties.

First, they claimed people didn't understand the finance options, couldn't do the math, and therefore, didn't know what they were signing. Hmm. There likely was some truth to that. However, data from GMAC showed that even in the worst years of the Great Depression, losses amounted to no more than one percent of all loans. Perhaps GMAC was simply good at judging credit risks? It seems just as likely that opinionated commentators didn't like the choices, but that doesn't make consumers dumb.

If people knew what they were doing, they were doing it for the "wrong" reasons. Without discipline and patience, consumption was simply a way to satisfy immediate desires – not the least of which was to "keep up with their neighbors." As personal finance author Steve Rhodes lamented:

> People are gauged, not by their worth, but rather by what they seem to be worth. For these are times of show, more than of substance. It is one of the foolish and unwarrantable expedients for maintaining credit, to keep up an expensive domestic establishment; and you know not from any outward symbols, whether such an establishment is an evidence of wealth, or simply a device to preserve the appearance of wealth.[15]

Hmm. The data shows that installment plans created disciplined behavior, not the other way around. When consumers knew that if they failed to make their monthly payment, someone would repossess their wedding ring or washing machine, they find a way to make the payments. That doesn't mean consumers didn't (occasionally) regret those choices, but they made them willingly. It seems just as likely that opinionated commentators didn't

---

15 Personal finance author Steve Rhode (aka the "Get Out of Debt Guy") quotes this gem from the 1853 book, *The Bible in the Counting-house: A Course of Lectures to Merchants*, by Henry Augustus Boardman. It gets requoted often in 1920s-era publications.

like the reasons, but that doesn't make consumers hedonists.

Ah, but wait! If people knew what they were getting into, they didn't understand its implications. Consumers have become wage slaves, trapped by their possessions and ready for exploitation. When the thought of losing possessions weighs on the mind, it's challenging to advocate for higher wages and better working conditions. Again, is there some truth to that? Absolutely. Loss aversion is real, but the logic here is strained. It's not as if debt was a new concept only born in the 1920s. If anything, a greater number of creditors forced *lower* interest rates and *better* payment terms as the American standard of living increased dramatically.

Finally, when all arguments failed, consumers didn't *need* that car, sewing machine, or wedding ring. They *wanted* it. True, of course. But those same arguments had been leveled against chimneys in the 1400s. No one *needed* heat in their home when they could wear more clothes. The same argument was leveled against indoor plumbing in the 1800s. No one *needed* to use an indoor toilet when they could go outside…or simply empty the chamber pot. Yes, our idea of wants and needs has evolved, but consumers find it funny that it always seems to be the people with a lot telling people without that they should be happy with less. Consumers have finely tuned hypocrisy detection systems. "You first," they say.

On March 5, 1927, after struggling through the pros and cons, the *Literary Digest* seemed to come to the inevitable conclusion:

> We believe that the installment system performs a useful function in our economic structure and that it is here to stay. There are abuses which must be eliminated, such as extending credit without regard for any principles of sound credit. This kind of installment credit brings disaster to both borrower and lender as does the unwise extension of every other kind of credit. Then, too, there are dangers lurking in the use of the system which must be guarded against. But we believe that the system is an important contribution to modern economic organization, and that in time to come it will be recognized as such, even by those conservative people who, at the present time, see little good in it.

Whether you'd consider the preceding argument a strawman or not, the reality was that consumer financing was here to stay, that some people like complaining about it, and that consumers don't care.

5
CONSUMER REBELLION

On January 17, 1920, the most extensive blockade in naval history began to form off the East Coast of the United States. It was far larger than the British blockade of its rebellious colonies or the similar blockade of the Confederacy.

It spanned the northeast port cities, from Boston to New York. It continued off the coast of Maryland, where the Potomac River empties into the Chesapeake Bay, just a handful of miles downstream from Washington D.C. It didn't stop there. Ships lined the coast, near every major port city (and plenty of minor ones), all the way to Miami. The flotilla numbered hundreds – and sometimes thousands – of individual vessels, each lined up exactly three miles from shore.[1] To the untrained eye, it looked like a military invasion force – something the United States, due to its blessed geography, has never had to worry about.[2] Yet, there it was.

But this was no invasion force or naval blockade. What's the opposite of those words? "Devasion?" "Allowcade?" It's worth flipping through the thesaurus for a better word because the *opposite* of a blockade was precisely what this was. Hundreds of unarmed ships anchored offshore aren't exactly a threat to national security, and from a military perspective, they were sitting ducks. The biggest ships in the fleet were massive tankers carrying highly flammable cargo. It was the *smaller* ships that did the dirty work. They'd run the three-mile gauntlet back and forth, ferrying smaller loads to shore – usually under cover of night. The trips weren't exactly easy. The nondescript rendezvous points were nestled in out-of-the-way inlets and bays. Unmarked trucks would take it from there to the big markets and buying public.

Why all the cloak and dagger?

Because to the "drys" on the mainland (those who supported Prohibition as the law of the land), this *was* an invasion.

Those ships were filled with booze. Lots of booze. *Thousands of cargo*

---

[1] In the later years of Prohibition, this would be extended to 12 miles. Predictably, it did *not* slow the flow of illegal booze into the United States.

[2] The two greatest generals in American military history are General Atlantic and General Pacific.

ships of booze.

It was all legal so long as it stayed three miles from the American shoreline. (Or for the zillions of other exceptions and caveats, which we'll discuss shortly.) But when the so-called "rum-runners" crossed that imaginary boundary…

. . .

Watercraft design is as good a place as any to begin our story about the consumer innovations born of the Prohibition era.

As we've mentioned, the giant container ships *anchored* three miles offshore. They were huge and slow. There's no way they could make their way into Boston Harbor (and out again) without anyone noticing.[3] In other words, they couldn't use the ports for what the ports were good at – efficiently disgorging vast amounts of cargo.

The smaller craft would sail out to the container ships, load up as much as they could carry, and scurry back to a secluded port where trucks waited to whisk the illegal hooch into the vast thirsty underbelly of American speakeasies and private buyers. It was the swift boats and sweet spirits of the Caribbean that gave this practice its name: *rum-running*. (To be fair, it should have been called rum-*boating*, but that doesn't sound as snappy. Phonetics matter.) These rum-runners were the first high-speed motorboats, the precursor to everything we see at the marina today.

To be clear, what these rum-runners were doing was illegal.

To be even more clear, it was *totally* worth it.

Successful rum-runners could earn several *hundred thousand dollars* each year. (Even lazy ones could make tens of thousands of dollars.) By comparison, the Commandant of the Coast Guard earned $6,000 each year, and a seaman earned just over $1,500. If you're starting to sense a… disparity…between legal and illegal income potential, that's what we'll call a "running theme" in this chapter. (Pun intended.)

Entire port cities got into the act as well. That was especially true along the coast of Newfoundland in Canada, where local anglers largely *quit* fishing. Warehouses in town stored alcohol shipped in from the

---

3   As we'll see, enforcement was both lax and doomed to fail from the start, but c'mon. Docking a cargo ship was too much.

Caribbean or Europe, waiting for captains to load it up and head for Maine, Massachusetts, or New York.[4] (To be fair, scotch does smell better than cod. That's a fact. Look it up.) What's an underpaid Coast Guard Commandant to do?

Well, first things first. You need to *create* a modern Coast Guard. That meant trained, professional crews, better radio communication technology, and aircraft surveillance. One more thing: You also needed faster ships. There's no way to catch a 10-foot craft with an outboard motor with a 40-foot clipper in tight inlets. The smaller craft is simply too fast and too maneuverable. To solve the problem, the Coast Guard did what any law-abiding government agency needed to do: It put out a bid to boat manufacturers for *their own* speedboats.

Can you guess what happened next? Sure, you can.

Rum-running was far too profitable to let the cat catch the mouse. (Is there an nautical equivalent of this metaphor?) In a move so bold as to defy belief, they got their hands on the Coast Guard specifications and approached *the same bidders* to build *them* a faster model. If you're wondering, that's why you can buy an *average* speedboat today that clocks in at over 60 miles per hour on the water, with some performance versions skimming the waves well over 100.

There are plenty of ways to tell the story of Prohibition. Daniel Okrent's *Last Call: The Rise and Fall of Prohibition* is perhaps one of the best history books *ever written*. It's certainly one of the most entertaining. Ken Burns' documentary mini-series *Prohibition* is a powerful companion. However, often missed in these histories is the impact on consumer culture. It's one of the best ways to tell just how powerful consumerism would become and how little the government truly controlled.

This is the classic story of how cat-and-mouse competition sped up innovation in sectors as wildly different as speedboat design to women's

---

4   Search for "Main Duck Island" on Lake Ontario's inland shore for a typical example.

restrooms. (Really! You'll see.)

And gangsters. Don't forget gangsters. We'll talk about them too.

. . .

Before we ponder why Walgreens was *so* popular during the 1920s, how taking a leak changed for the better (at least for women), and why Al Capone was a hero to so many people, we need to step back for a brief diversion into the world before Prohibition to understand why banning liquor seemed to make so much sense.

Alcohol consumption goes *way back* in human history. The origins of most beers, wines, and spirits are clouded in a historical stupor, but the records we *do have* mix a great cocktail. For example, Egyptian laborers were often paid in beer. (At least, an early version of it.[5]) Beer is basically fermented, shelf-stable *bread*. In other words, it was a dense, calorie-rich, portable food that would stay edible (drinkable) in Egypt's climate much longer than a flatbread loaf. Oh, and it was *much safer* to drink than water. The brewing process (and the distilling process for spirits and fermenting process for grapes) kills microorganisms responsible for some of the nasty epidemics of that era. The Egyptians didn't know *why* fewer people got sick drinking beer than drinking Nile river water, but they put two and two together. Ask yourself: What would you rather drink? A warm jug of beer or a scoop of water with floating crocodile dung? Easy decision, really. When you look at the pyramids, don't think aliens; think beer temple.

Fast forward a few centuries, and the Roman Republic figured out the same thing. Heck, they probably learned it from trading with the Egyptians. Most people think of the Romans as excellent conquerors (and they *were* that), but they were *even better* at food preservation and transportation. That's the only way to feed nearly one million urban residents in the pre-modern era in the city of Rome alone, much less other major cities across the Mediterranean. Aqueducts brought in water, but they didn't purify it. Making wine was not only a tasty way to preserve grapes; it was also safer to drink. Besides, the Romans' party habits were legendary. (They even shared a god with the Greeks for boozing it up.) Wine's

---

5   Check out *A History of the World in 6 Glasses*, by Tom Standage.

popularity was probably a combination of "hey, we're not getting sick as often," "this tastes better than Po river water," "that person looks way sexier when I drink this," and "let's party!" Since then, alcohol consumption has become part of the social and religious rituals in nearly all cultures around the globe.[6]

Unfortunately, alcohol *abuse* goes way back too.

Alexander the Great was probably the world's greatest party bro. Sure, historians know him as one of history's great military commanders, but we *also know* that he threw epic parties that lasted *days*. It was so intense that even modern frat guys would say, *hey man, take it easy. You've had enough.* We don't know why exactly he died at age 32, but the likely culprit is alcohol-related – blood poisoning from a bender, acute liver failure, choking on his own vomit, take your pick. That said, alcohol wasn't quite strong enough to do much damage unless you could afford to drink a *lot*, and most people couldn't. At an estimated average of 2 to 3 percent alcohol by volume, beer was weaker than it is now. Wine was routinely watered down, even by partygoers, and the resulting drink contained about 6 to 8 percent alcohol. Yes, plenty of people got drunk, but no, it wasn't quite as common as you might think.

Spirits – distilled beverages that convert the sugars in food into sugar alcohol – changed *everything*.

Blame the so-called *Age of Discovery* in the 15th century, at least partly. As more agricultural cargo needed to be preserved over ocean-going distances (trips that took weeks, or even months), inventive entrepreneurs needed to find ways to preserve staple crops into something that still had value (more than rat food) once they arrived at their next port of call. All the major grains were distilled – wheat, barley, corn (maize), sorghum, and rice – but also sugar cane, agave, and many others. The higher the sugar content, the better, and the New World featured many of these crops in abundance. This era birthed whiskey, vodka, brandy, gin, tequila, and rum – just to name a few. Seriously, if people could figure out how to

---

6   It's not just a human thing. Even elephants are into it. They get hammered on fermenting fruit. This should go without saying, but if you ever encounter a drunk elephant, don't taunt it.

distill cabbage, they would.[7]

What truly made spirits different, however, was their alcohol content. They were strong. *Very strong.* Distilled spirits routinely clock in between 40 to 60 percent alcohol by volume. And they were cheap. *Very cheap.* Spirits were available at a fraction of the cost per unit of sloshiness. And that meant lots of people could get drunk. *Very drunk.*

By the time you get to the 18th century in the United States, you have an entrenched history of locally-made rum and moonshine with a drinking culture to match. Drinking wine was still a rich person's hobby, and beer was seen as a German drink. (The latter was mixed up with the issue of immigration; that'll be important in the story later.) No matter. The average working Joe (not Jane, we'll get to that too) had plenty of cheap hard liquor to choose from. The best data we have at the time that compares beer, wine, and spirits consumption shows spirits were *by far* the most popular, making up 70 to 80 percent of all intoxicating drinks.

Where would Joe drink that liquor? Not at home, usually. He drank at the *saloon*. These were different than the bars we know today. In those days, the saloon was part drinking establishment, part payday lender, and part local political headquarters. The saloon became a cultural institution, and not necessarily a positive one. In addition to alcohol abuse, the saloon's drinking buddies included gambling, prostitution, family neglect, spousal abuse, and financial ruin. People quite literally drank away their earnings while their families starved. Diaries and newspaper reports are rife with stories recounting these grave social ills. In short, drunkenness had become a public health crisis.

---

[7] They did. At least, they tried. Cabbage has very low sugar. In 2006, someone on the "Home Distiller Forum" posted his experience. He stunk up his house for a month distilling 200 lbs of cabbage into one pint of rancid-smelling cabbage hootch. *Not. Worth. It.* One hopes he was not married. One thinks if he was, he no longer is.

If that's hard to grasp, imagine a Friday night wild party in a college town. Now imagine that party is happening everywhere. With men of all ages.

Not good.

...

The idea of "temperance" predates the founding of the United States. However, for our purposes, the first coordinated movement to eliminate alcohol consumption coincides with the rise of first-wave feminism and political organizing. The saloon didn't offer much to women except a place to find their husbands passed out in the corner or betting away the family's food budget. (Remember that point. Speakeasies in the 1920s would not make that same mistake.) When you wonder why women's suffrage and Prohibition were linked at the tail end of the 19th century, now you know.

The most colorful organizer straddling the 19th and 20th centuries was Caroline Amelia Nation – better known as the "Hatchet Granny" – who would use an ax to physically demolish saloons when prayers and preaching failed to convince them to close their doors and repent. She was…well…precisely the kind of person you think she would be. She described herself as "a bulldog running along at the feet of Jesus, barking at what He doesn't like." However, if you harbored any lingering thoughts that Nation had a redeeming streak of Christian charity, lower your expectations. When President William McKinley was assassinated in 1901, Nation quipped that drinkers "got what they deserved." The name of her biweekly newsletter? *The Hatchet*. That said, she did have a way of bringing people together in those racially-segregated times. Many saloons began hanging a sign that read: All Nations Welcome But Carrie.

Nation might have represented the extreme fringe of the Women's Christian Temperance Union (WCTU), but the women *did* have a point. As we've learned, most saloons were sleazier than even the sleaziest dive bars today. They were also sources of political power – a power generally opposed not only to temperance but also to women's suffrage. It was the nature of that political power that gave both the prohibitionists and the suffragists their opening.

. . .

Before the Civil War, most of the eight *liters* of liquor consumed per capita per year in the United States were spirits of some kind. Beer and wine each accounted for just a sliver of that total – less than ten percent each. By 1900, the amount of wine consumed stayed low (only wealthy people could afford to drink wine), but the proportion of beer *skyrocketed* to nearly half of all alcoholic beverages consumed by volume.[8] It was new European immigrants who brought their brewing expertise. They had names like Yuengling, Pabst, Anheuser, Busch, and Miller. Do you notice something similar about each of those names? You guessed it. They're *German*. And they weren't simply brewmasters; they took to American capitalism like sauer on kraut. To encourage saloons to serve more beer (and offer it at affordable prices), they helped subsidize the saloon's expenses. The breweries would supply signage, tables, chairs, taps, glasses, counters, rails, and (when needed) direct financial support in the form of deferred payments, loans, or money under the table.[9]

Being German might not raise eyebrows in the United States in the 2020s, but before the 1920s, being German *was* a big deal. *A bad deal.* Like a story repeated many times in American life, new immigrant groups were not trusted. Think about it: The saloons were hubs of local political organizing. The German immigrants were subsidizing saloons. How long would it be before they began to *exercise* that political power?

That increase in beer consumption and the German connection to the political power scared the crinolines off of the organizers of the WCTU. (The German brewers were far better businesspeople than they

---

[8] This data was compiled by the National Institute on Alcohol Abuse and Alcoholism based on census data and sales estimates. There is a notable gap during Prohibition showing "zero" consumption, which is certainly not true. After Prohibition, consumption remained lower during the 1930s. In overall terms, total consumption has varied a bit, but the proportion of wine, beer, and spirits has changed markedly. The big winner since the 1940s has been wine.

[9] Does that seem familiar to what you see in bars today? Yep. It's the same story. The liquor industry subsidizes most bars.

were politicians, but the WCTU couldn't know that.) The real trouble was the first letter in the WCTU. Women couldn't vote. They needed help to achieve their objectives.

They would get it.

It's time to meet the Anti-Saloon League.

...

The ASL was founded in the tiny hamlet of Oberlin, Ohio, in 1893 to promote temperance with a decidedly evangelistic bent. In contrast to matrons with machetes, the ASL would not rely on theatrics. Although its publishing arm became a force of nature – pumping out nearly 40 pamphlets each month – its true objective was *legislation*. The ASL meant to change laws.

In its early days, the ASL focused on local laws and ordinances. If you're wondering why some cities (even today) have restrictions on where a bar may be located, its hours, and what it can serve, that law may be a holdover from more than 100 years ago. The ASL took advantage of a core feature of American governance to build its momentum: *distributed control*. According to the U.S. Constitution, powers not explicitly identified as the federal government's purview are reserved for the states. (For example, the Feds reserve the right to declare war, regulate interstate commerce, etc.) In a mirror of the federal system, many states leave local decisions in the hands of counties, cities, and towns. Ideally, at the most fundamental level, those powers not identified anywhere else are in the hands of individuals to decide as they see fit. The idea is that decisions are best made by the people closest to their consequences.

Reread that paragraph from the perspective of the ASL. Logically, they had two basic strategic choices. First, they could go for the gold medal – a constitutional amendment. In one fell swoop, Prohibition would become the law of the land and supersede any other *state* law. Or, second, they could work to change laws at the local and state level. The result would be a confusing patchwork quilt of legislation, but they wouldn't need to meet the (purposefully) high hurdle that passing an amendment required. National Prohibition might have been the goal all along, but the ASL knew it didn't have the support it needed in the 1890s. It needed to build support by getting laws passed and, more importantly, electing friendly legislators at all levels of government. How they accomplished those goals would change American politics forever.

In practical terms, the ASL strategy amounted to supporting "dry" candidates – put simply, those who opposed alcohol – or at least, would vote that way. That was the ASL's main innovation. In sharp contrast to Nation's approach, the ASL didn't care what you did in private or what you thought; they cared that you *voted* the way they wanted you to. They were one of the first "single issue" political organizations and certainly the most successful to date. The power of that approach cannot be understated. For candidates who would vote dry, the ASL would not simply *support them* passively; they would throw their entire organizational weight behind that candidate's campaign. But for those that wouldn't…well, you can guess how aggressive they'd be in opposition. And the ASL was smart, too. They knew they would have limited success in the industrial and financial capitals of the northeast. Instead, the ASL built a power base in the religiously-conservative south and midwest – mainly in smaller communities where they could exert a powerful influence over local zoning laws.

Most troublesome in *both* regions was sharing common cause with the Klu Klux Klan. In that, the ASL was agnostic. They knew these partnerships were critical to their ultimate objective. That's why they supported the WCTU's push for suffrage along with Prohibition, but they also tacitly supported the KKK's race-baiting and violence. (One of those two associations would come back to bite them later. Can you guess which one? Sure, you can.) However, in the lead-up to national Prohibition, the ASL's strategy worked like a charm. It racked up victory after victory changing laws and electing friendly legislators.

For those who know this part of the story, you might find it odd that we haven't mentioned the architect of this single-minded, seemingly amoral strategy: Wayne Wheeler. More than any other person, he sharpened the ASL's ultimate focus on a constitutional amendment. For any legislator who owed their seat to Wheeler, his influence was all-powerful. He had what amounted to an office on Capital Hill, and journalists of the time routinely noted the comings and goings of anyone who was anyone in Congress. That's how influential Wheeler – and, by extension, the ASL – had become.

The political story of the eventual passage of the Eighteenth

Amendment to the United States Constitution is fascinating. Okrent details the *surprisingly* easy path the amendment took through the required two-thirds majority in Congress and a three-fourths majority of state legislatures. You can read more about the arm-twisting and bargaining in his book, but suffice it to say, what happened shocked almost everyone… except for Wheeler. He was playing chess with everyone else's checkers. It wasn't even close.

Anti-German sentiment following World War I helped. All the big brewers were German. Rampant anti-Catholic sentiment helped as well. Wine was (and is) part of the Catholic tradition. Anti-Black sentiment helped. The KKK (with the backing of the ASL) worked to spread stories of drunken Black men terrorizing helpless White women. It was, in retrospect, pretty sick stuff, but Wheeler didn't care. He did whatever it took.

On January 16, 1919, the amendment was ratified as a part of the Constitution after receiving the okay from the 36th of 48 states.[10] One year later, on January 17, 1920, national Prohibition went into effect.

After decades of tireless work, Wheeler and the ASL had won.

. . .

There's an old saying in revolutionary politics: It's easier to blow up the trains than to make them run on time. The underlying wisdom of that saying is simple: The strategies and tactics you use to overthrow the status quo are not the same strategies and tactics that will work to build a new one. Wheeler's single-minded, heavy-handed approach to securing an amendment would implode when it came to rule-making and enforcement. The forces of wet might have been caught dry-mouthed in the middle of January 1919, but they had an entire year to begin their counterattack.

What follows is the text of the Eighteenth Amendment *in its entirety*, and you can ignore Section 3. That's boilerplate language. The meat of the amendment is a scant 62 words.

Section 1. After one year from the ratification of this article the

---

10 It would eventually be ratified by 46 of 48 states; Connecticut and Rhode Island rejected it.

manufacture, sale, or transportation of intoxicating liquors within, the importation thereof into, or the exportation thereof from the United States and all the territory subject to the jurisdiction thereof for beverage purposes is hereby prohibited.

Section 2. The Congress and the several States shall have concurrent power to enforce this article by appropriate legislation.

Section 3. This article shall be inoperative unless it shall have been ratified as an amendment to the Constitution by the legislatures of the several States, as provided in the Constitution, within seven years from the date of the submission hereof to the States by the Congress.

Any new law, including something as important as an amendment, requires regulatory detail. They don't work simply as written. You must define your terms to enforce the law, and that's where it gets sticky. Even a non-lawyer can see the problems. What, precisely, is an "intoxicating liquor?" How does that translate into a percentage of alcohol by volume? Was 1 percent alcohol by volume too high? What about half a percent? Did the number need to be zero? How would you measure and validate that? Some beverages (especially medicines) had a negligible amount of alcohol. What about those? Furthermore, there are plenty of industrial uses for alcohol. Were those okay, even if they could be converted (quite easily) into something drinkable? That's another thing – *drinkable* – what was the difference between a "food" and a "beverage?" Additionally, the amendment mentioned the "manufacture, sale, or transportation" of intoxicating liquors but not the *consumption* of said beverages. How would that work?

And that's just Section 1.

In Section 2, note the phrase "joint enforcement." Have you ever heard the saying, *when you have to ask who is in charge, it's not you?* Joint federal-state authority meant inevitable confusion (at best) to willfully ignoring laws states didn't like (most common) and active sabotage (at worst).

We'll step through just *some* of the issues with the forthcoming Volstead Act, which operationalized the enforcement of Prohibition, but as you might have guessed from the preceding discussion, it was problematic from the start.[11] Sure, there were plenty of poorly-conceived details, but Wheeler himself was the most troublesome part of the whole debacle. Single-issue politics work great when you're trying to get a new law passed, but they work much *less well* when it comes to the appropriate enforcement environment necessary to make Prohibition last. However, in Wheeler's mind, *to the victor, go the spoils.* He owned so many politicians that he believed he had nearly king-like powers to craft the new laws in his image, and he was not inclined to be a benevolent monarch.

We already talked about the birth of the modern Coast Guard and how it created a perverse incentive to build ever-faster speedboats.

Buckle up. It's about to get weird.

. . .

The first issue with the Volstead Act is something you could already guess from the booze flotilla anchored three miles offshore in *international* waters. A constitutional amendment is a big deal…to people in the United States. To everyone else? Not so much.[12] Islands in the Caribbean didn't count. Embassies didn't count.[13] Mexico didn't count. Canada didn't count. Those last two? You don't need a boat in most places. You simply walk across. There is no practical way to secure every mile of the land border to the north and south of the United States; that's especially true on the Canadian side. In fact, the very first arrest under the new Volstead Act was a rum-runner making an over-*lake* crossing from Ontario to Detroit. It wouldn't be the last. The best guess on how many were caught versus how many succeeded? Perhaps one in one hundred, but that's a

---

11 Specifically, this was H.R. 6810, named after Judiciary Chairman Andrew Volstead of Minnesota. By all accounts, he was a reasonable person, like most midwesterners. However, he wasn't really in charge. It would have been more accurate to call it the Wheeler Act.

12 The United States wasn't the only country to try national Prohibition about that same time. Many Scandinavian counties did. In a bizarre turn of events that only a tone-deaf communist revolution could envision working, so did Russia.

13 The Belgians loved Secretary of Commerce, Herbert Hoover. He helped save their country from starvation during World War I. They thanked him each day after work with a (legal) cocktail.

guess. We *could* try to estimate based on annual liquor consumption rates, but the government stopped tracking that because…well…booze was illegal. The number should be *zero*, right? Wheeler didn't want to keep track of something people shouldn't be doing. That would admit defeat.

But let's leave the illegal activity aside for now. Nothing in the amendment said an American citizen couldn't enjoy a tipple *overseas* or in some other country where drinking was permitted. How do you think the Caribbean cruise industry got started? You guessed it. For a small fee, passengers would board a big, fancy ship headed out into the beautiful blue waters off the coast of Florida. The champagne corks would begin to pop as soon as the vessel reached international waters. However, those boats didn't simply slosh around and head back to port. They'd stop off in Cuba, Puerto Rico, the Bahamas, or (what would become) today's island destination vacations. If you wanted an even faster trip to the drunken isles, you could hop on one of the new passenger *aircraft* that started daily flights by the mid-1920s.

More than that, booze wasn't as *illegal* as it seemed.

Remember that part about the *consumption* of intoxicating liquors? (As in, there was nothing written in the amendment about that?) If you had liquor in your possession before the law went into effect, there was nothing to say that you couldn't drink it or share it with friends. You simply couldn't move it around, buy it, or sell it. What followed was precisely what you think happened. Anyone who could afford it spent 1919 hoarding vast quantities of liquor and wine in storage cellars. Did you note that part about *affording* it? As the 1920s dragged on and newspapers continued to tell increasingly salacious stories about drunken benders at rich people's homes, the drumbeat of hypocrisy began almost immediately: *Prohibition for thee, but not for me.* That went over with the average working stiff just about as well as you think it would. Wheeler's influence, strong as it was, didn't reach that far. The Volstead Act would not confiscate private property, especially when it was legally obtained. What's more, remember that part about how the ASL didn't care what you did or thought so long as you voted the right way? Lots of politicians hoarded hundreds of bottles. This was when those hypocritical hens came home to roost.

The next carve-out in the law came from the farm and ranch communities. Remember how we talked about how one of the original uses for alcoholic beverages was preservation? That hadn't changed. Orchard operators routinely made apples (and other fruits) into ciders. The Volstead Act rewarded some of the ASL's most prominent supporters with the right to distill enough cider for "personal and family use." Despite the trend to smaller families over the past five decades, some "families" miraculously expanded to include dozens – sometimes hundreds – of members.

(Just wait. We haven't even gotten to the outright criminal element yet. We're not even close. That's how poorly executed Prohibition was.)

What happens when two amendments come into conflict? Namely, the First Amendment, which prevents the establishment of a state religion, and the newly-minted Eighteenth, which prohibits alcoholic beverages. Remember the anti-Catholic sentiment that fueled the adoption of Prohibition? Catholics weren't pleased that the government could curtail a vital aspect of the celebration of mass, wherein the wine served transubstantiates into the blood of Jesus. You couldn't have that, now could you? That became another carve-out in the Volstead Act: wine for religious services of all types, and not just Catholic masses.

Caught flat-footed by Prohibition, many vineyards plowed under vintage vines until the Catholic Church started ordering in bulk. The Jewish synagogues followed suit. With the combined demand, many of the California region's most famous vineyards started supplying sacramental wine during Prohibition. Moreover, because all you needed was a "congregation" to call yourself a "religious minister," mail-order priesthoods proliferated – hundreds of new priests, pastors, and rabbis managed their flocks through hastily-constructed storefronts where they'd hand out wine after a cursory prayer or blessing. One hazards to guess that not all these transactions were…spiritual. (Or, in a different reading of the word "spiritual," perhaps they were.)

Speaking of mail-order degrees, physicians also found a way to earn a little extra cash on the side. Although it may seem odd today, doctors of that era routinely prescribed a shot of whiskey as a medical treatment. Getting a script from your doctor for your slug of Johnnie Walker wasn't a big deal *before* Prohibition, but after? Records indicate that in the *first six months* after Prohibition went into effect, over 15,000 doctors and 57,000 pharmacists got their licenses to prescribe "medicinal" alcohol. The best estimates record more than 11 *million* prescriptions written during the 1920s, but that number is almost certainly *too low*. One doctor, cited by the hapless Prohibition Commissioner John F. Kramer, wrote 475 prescriptions in a *single day*. (One suspects he needed to write himself a shot of Glenfiddich to treat wrist cramps.) Finally, in a head-scratcher-only-if-you-don't-consider-the-obvious, historians suspect Charles Walgreen's stunning expansion from 20 to 525 stores during the 1920s might have had something to do with medicinal alcohol. (*Might*. Snicker.)

And this was the *legal* stuff – or at least, the drinking of alcohol under some sort of legal guise, no matter how flimsy that white Roman collar might be.

Charged with enforcing these carve-outs to the Volstead Act and all the illegal activities that would follow were 1,500 federal agents and an inconsistent smattering of state law enforcement…when the states decided to help…which was not often.

1,500.[14]

You read that correctly.

That's the number of people who typically show up for a high school sporting event. Those 1,500 poor souls were charged with monitoring about 6,000 miles of coastline, 5,500 miles of the Canadian overland border, 2,000 miles on the Mexico side, and any illegal activity *within* the United States. *But wait, you say.* You've heard about people like Elliot Ness, his "Untouchables," and the famous Texas Ranger, Frank Hamer. Sure, they were real people. And yes, they did their jobs admirably. But they are famous precisely because it was so rare that anything enforcement agents did could stem the flow of liquor *at all*.

. . .

> For those willing to risk the perils of unlawful activity, selling liquor without having to pay state or federal taxes was a business model of considerable appeal. Vastly enhanced profit margins could underwrite a lot of the overhead associated with lawbreaking – for instance, the cost of corrupting police, judges, politicians, or anyone else remotely involved in enforcement. William Howard Taft, serving as a professor of law at Yale during the interval between his presidency

---

14 The U.S. Census Bureau tracked that as a job category in the 1920s. You can find the original job notice in the *New York Tribune's* archives.

and his eventual appointment as Chief Justice of the Supreme Court said, "The business of manufacturing alcohol, liquor, and beer will go out of the hands of law-abiding members of the community, and will be transferred to the quasi criminal class." The only ill-chosen word in that sentence was "quasi."

That last sentence, from Chapter 7 of Okrent's remarkable history of Prohibition, might be one of the most concise summaries of a situation since *Veni, Vidi, Vici* two millennia before.

The booze business has always been ridiculously profitable; Prohibition made it even *more so*. That's not just because alcoholic beverages are relatively easy to make, and consumer demand has always been high. No, the underlying reason is quite simple: taxes.

Ever since President (and General) George Washington crushed the so-called "Whiskey Rebellion" in 1794, the United States government had successfully taxed the production, distribution, and sale of alcoholic beverages. That taxation happened, in varying degrees and amounts, at the federal, state, and even local levels.

When Prohibition took hold, the only ones who could make money on liquor – aside from the exceptions we've already mentioned – were criminals. And do you know what criminals *don't* do? They don't pay taxes. As we've discussed, there were plenty of exceptions in the Volstead Act, but all those barely made a dent in overall demand. The remaining "business opportunity" went primarily to organized crime. Overnight, mobsters earned another five to ten percent premium on their activities. Why is that? Let's say a case of beer cost $5.00 before Prohibition, and that $0.50 of that price was some type of tax. To the consumer, the case of beer cost $5.00, not $4.50. After Prohibition, that case of beer cost… you guessed it…*$5.00.* The price didn't go down because the government wasn't taking its cut. The mob was collecting that extra revenue without changing the consumer's perception of its price. In short, Uncle Sam gave the mob a ten percent bonus out of its own coffers.

Organized crime was well-established in the United States before Prohibition, running all sorts of illegal enterprises: gambling, extortion, bid-rigging, and prostitution. However, nothing was as profitable as bootlegging – simply defined as doing what the Volstead Act said you couldn't do. Reasonable estimates put the value of bootlegging at $3.6 *billion* annually in 1925, or $55 billion in 2020 money. Income from other illegal activities didn't even come close. More than any other single factor, bootlegging gave mobsters the financial muscle they needed to build powerful criminal organizations. Legitimate businesses required some sort of legal cover. Boozy doctors, mail-order pastors, whatever Charles Walgreen thought he was getting away with – they did have a metaphorical fig leaf, teeny though it might be. The mob? They were content to run around buck-naked.

There was no one more comfortable running around in a metaphorical birthday suit than criminal mastermind Al Capone. Capone certainly wasn't alone. He wasn't even alone in Chicago, though he did (famously, bloodily, and ruthlessly) eliminate his competition. Although his in-the-open strategy ultimately led to his downfall, it does provide a rare window into the usually-hidden world of illegal activity.

First, however, we must understand that many stories we've heard about Capone were (at least in part) fabrications. In her book, *Al Capone: His Life, Legacy, and Legend*, biographer Deirdre Bair examines the evidence (such as it is) that he brutally rose to power after he arrived in Chicago in 1919 and had full control by the time he turned 26 in 1925 (true), that he used a baseball bat to bash in the brains of two rivals after a nice dinner (likely false), and that he hated being called "scarface" (maybe, maybe not).

Some of Capone's most famous quips? Of that, there is no doubt. There are plenty of versions recorded. When asked about the southerly flow of booze across the border, Capone claimed he "didn't know what side of the street Canada was on." He was keen to call out the hypocrisy of the prissy elites who condemned him: "When I sell liquor, they call it bootlegging. When my patrons serve it on silver trays on Lake Shore Drive, they call it hospitality." Perhaps best of all was his self-description, more perfect for our continued discussion than any other: "I am just a businessman, giving the people what they want."

Bair makes the case that Capone understood – and actively *cultivated* – this image in part to stoke his ego, in part to scare off rivals, but mostly because he understood that it was good business. Then, as now, interesting people attract customers. And Capone attracted a *lot* of customers. Seeing consumer innovation through Capone's eyes might seem distasteful, but it's useful. Most criminal activity happens in the shadows, but in Chicago, it started spilling onto the streets.

Inspired by the killing machines of World War I, gun manufacturers started innovating with new models of handheld automatic weapons. When gangsters began using them on the streets of Chicago, law enforcement knew they needed to change as well. They realized that simply attempting to stop Capone with increased police presence and matching firepower wouldn't be enough. Trying to rope him in on a bootlegging charge wouldn't be enough. They needed to attack the *true* source of his power – his image.

They worked to cultivate the image of "bad" liquor you might get in a speakeasy lounge. Yes, a handful of people died drinking (essentially) flavored wood alcohol from home-distillers. However, Capone's organization – and organized crime in general – wanted nothing to do with buying liquor from a home still. Not only *could they* easily secure supplies of the real stuff, but they also had every incentive to do so. Remember, if people got sick, they'd stop coming.

Speaking of speakeasies, law enforcement cultivated the image of the "seedy" dive bar, where you were likely to be assaulted...or worse.[15] The air of mob ownership may have added a bit of a dangerous veneer to the experience, but it was not the main reason people went. Capone's organization ran some of the safest clubs, all featuring the best musicians and dancing. Why? Every club needed a legitimate "front," which encouraged a dramatic increase in the quality of the club-going experience. (See Chapter 12 for more about the clubs in New York.) Again, there were so many speakeasies, consumers had choices. They needed to *choose* Capone's clubs.

Who would go to those clubs? Not just men, as was the case in the saloon days. Young women, many just arrived in the city, wanted a speakeasy experience just as much as the men did. (The music and dancing helped attract a broader audience.) When nature called, a room out back with a hole in the floor to urinate wasn't...appealing to women. Capone and his contemporaries remodeled their establishments to feature elegant "powder rooms" and restrooms for women.

In all this, doesn't Capone seem like many of the other successful

---

15 Are you wondering if people were worried they'd get arrested and have to go to court? Sure, but they weren't really *that* worried. It was hard to get a jury to convict their peers. Why? They drank too.

business people you'll read about in this book? Dale Carnegie, the author of the (still) best-selling *How To Win Friends and Influence People* thought so. He observed that Capone was a "modern" business tycoon. Yes, business success was key, but just as important was that person's public image and active management of the media.

. . .

Unfortunately (fortunately?), Capone's flamboyant nature caught up with him. Growing increasingly disgusted with the crime in Chicago, President Herbert Hoover finally authorized a massive federal intervention and a novel law enforcement approach: convict mobsters on tax evasion, not bootlegging. Juries – usually drinkers themselves – didn't like to convict violators of the Volstead Act, but tax evasion was a different story. The best estimates were that Capone's criminal organization was worth something like $100 million – a vast sum in the 1920s – that wasn't paying a dime in taxes. The details aren't important here, but Capone was eventually convicted and sent to prison.

By the time law enforcement was bringing down Capone, the amendment and law that made him powerful was collapsing as well – and that included its chief architect. Wayne Wheeler's power began to ebb in the mid-1920s as Prohibition became increasingly unpopular. Like the parable of the turtle and the scorpion, many of his Congressional lackeys turned on him, questioning the ASL's operations, tactics, and campaign contributions. In 1926, Wheeler's wife died in a horrible kitchen accident, and his father died of a heart attack trying to help. Wheeler was personally crushed, and he never recovered. Wheeler died in 1927 a broken man, with his crowning achievement, Prohibition, also near death.

The onset of the Great Depression would be the final straw. In 1933, President Franklin Roosevelt signed the Cullen-Harrison Act, which authorized the sale of 3.2 percent beer and wine for non-religious purposes. Later that year, the states ratified the Twenty-first Amendment, repealing the Eighteenth and ending Prohibition.

All this begs the question, did the "Grand Experiment" work?

Maybe.

A little.

Although the government wasn't tracking alcohol consumption, per se, it *was tracking* health outcomes. Some evidence points to lower rates of liver cirrhosis, alcoholic psychosis, and infant mortality, though those are correlations, not causations. In other words, it's impossible to know if Prohibition *caused* those outcomes.

Speaking of politics and government, Prohibition distorted the process and led to the "innovation" of single-issue lobbying groups. It showed politicians (and, more importantly, interest groups) just how effective that focus could be in passing legislation – though few (if any) have figured out how to *implement* effective legislation once that has been achieved.

The fact that Prohibition decreased tax revenues for the government is indisputable. That those revenues flowed into the pockets of criminal elements is also indisputable. Did that increase crime? That's a silly question. Of course, it did. And not just the shady doctors, mail-order priests, and violent mobsters. *Everyone who bought illegal liquor during Prohibition was breaking the law.* They risked their freedom to resist a law they disagreed with. Not everyone, of course, but vast numbers of people.

However, we need to stop right here and make the obvious point. Without consumer demand, there would have been *very little incentive* to innovate anything we've discussed in this chapter. In each case – from speedboats to powder rooms – innovators (both legal and illegal) responded to consumers' wants. It's tempting to think of Prohibition as a well-meaning but misguided idea, poorly executed and leading to numerous unintended consequences. But it's much more than that. In an era that taught consumers how to vote with their wallets, Prohibition was their most prolific instructor. By the time it was repealed, consumer culture would never be the same.

America was thirsty. They would choose their drink by any means necessary.

6
OPENING THE BIG BOX

Robert Elkington Wood was the type of guy who read U.S. Census data for fun.[1]

Surprisingly, he was not a jerk. Nor was he going crazy from a mosquito-borne illness he caught sweating it out in the Panama Canal construction zone. No, despite being obsessively detail-oriented, he was a worker's manager. Wood was the kind of leader who never asked anything of his staff that he would not gladly do himself.

Wood was an army officer at the turn of the century, but his true crucible wasn't West Point; it was the aforementioned sweltering jungle that was the Panama Canal railway line. In the mid-1800s, the attempt to upgrade the railway crossing the tiny strip of land between the two oceans into an ocean-going canal nearly bankrupted the French government and claimed the lives of thousands of workers – primarily due to mosquito-borne diseases, devilish engineering challenges, and a poor understanding of both.[2]

The Americans would do better a couple of decades later. In warfare, there's an old saying: Generals win battles, but quartermasters win wars. If you chose to think of the Panama Canal as a war (and that made sense given the death toll), the bean counters would be the true heroes. Wood doesn't get much play in David McCullough's epic love letter to the Panama Canal, *The Path Between the Seas*, but his role was central. His expertise in the army wasn't shooting people or flying planes; it was logistics.

Once you solved the mosquito problem (which is a story all its own), the next challenge wasn't as much engineering as it was *supplies*. Reliable shipments needed to arrive in the canal zone at the right *time*, in the correct *order*, and at the negotiated *price*. Any hiccup in the delivery of any single item could lead to months of delays and mounting costs. Workers still need to be clothed, fed, housed, and paid during that delay. As a simple example,

---

1   As one of its many quirks, *Time* magazine insisted on publishing the middle names of every public figure. We'll read more about what made that publication special in Chapter 18.

2   Historian David McCullough's biography of the canal and its builders, *The Path Between the Seas*, is a story of the effort in two parts: first, French, and second, American. But it's so much more than that. It's also a story about the birth of modern engineering, logistics, and infection control. There's just something about "big projects" that catalyze advancement.

imagine the impact of a missed shipment of spare parts for one of the massive dredgers along the canal line. If you can't dig, work stops.

Suppliers, of course, knew this. Many would take advantage of the situation to purposefully delay shipments to inflate prices or ship inferior products to increase profit margins. Wood understood *this* enemy quite well.

He pioneered what we would call today "zero-based budgeting," also known at the time as "bottoms-up" costing. That's just fancy business-speak for deeply knowing the input costs of what you're buying, adding what you consider a fair profit margin, and only then setting the price you're willing to pay.[3] Suppliers may not have liked it, but they respected Wood. He was a fair dealer, and he knew his stuff. You don't easily fool a guy who enjoys reading statistical tables. Within a few months, delivery schedules stabilized, prices came down, and progress on the canal sped up.

Fast forward a few years, and our intrepid lieutenant colonel (and soon-to-be brigadier general) would find himself as head quartermaster for the U.S. military forces in Europe during World War I. When he left the military, the business community couldn't wait to get their hands on him – especially the mail-order companies. They faced some of the most complex logistical challenges in the business world.[4] They needed skilled logistical talent who could help them succeed, and Wood ended up taking a job with the biggest mail-order success story in the early 1920s: Montgomery Ward.

You thought it was *Sears*, huh?

You're not alone. Richard Warren Sears and Alvah Curtis Roebuck created the Sears mail-order engine in the final decade of the 1800s by essentially *inventing* the winning combination of efficient mail-order delivery and a lavish catalog to show people what they could buy. It was the first time rural customers had access to these products, and they couldn't get enough of them.

But by the early 1920s, Monkey Wards was throwing their poop in

---

[3] Contrary to popular belief, this doesn't mean "beating up" suppliers. A good buyer knows that an unprofitable relationship is unsustainable and will lead to quality and delivery problems.

[4] Even modern e-commerce giants can't come close to the level of challenge of running a mail-order business at the turn of the 20th century. Imagine running an e-commerce business without roads, without trucks, or without even standardized mailing addresses.

Sears' face (figuratively, of course).[5] From 1920 to 1924, Ward's business was *up* 47.5 percent. During that same period, Sears *declined* 15.9 percent. Sears remained king in terms of overall market share but had fallen from 71 to 58 percent of all U.S. mail-order business. Montgomery Ward simply did what any smart business leader would do when facing a lumbering competitor – it pressed its advantage. Hiring Wood was the equivalent of kicking Sears when it was down.

Had Montgomery Ward simply let Wood do some kicking, he might have finished off Sears.

Remember that pesky habit of reading census data? When other men of a certain age were busy getting wood flipping through their deck of naughty playing cards before bed, the real Wood stayed busy scrutinizing page after page of demographic trends. In the wee hours, he noticed that more city residents were moving away from traditional city centers. In those days, retail had a split personality – rural folks ordered by mail, and city folks took the train downtown. But automobiles were changing that. Wood saw that as people bought cars, they moved farther away from the city for cheaper land, bigger homes, quieter neighborhoods, and better schools. In these new "suburbs," growing families had no place to shop.

Wood's idea was to bring the store to them, creating a hybrid of the two approaches – the selection and "buy on your own without a salesperson" mail order, but the physical touch and feel of the downtown store. These stores required plenty of display space for merchandise and even more room for parking lots. Luckily, in the suburbs, the land was cheap. The data were sound. The logic held. The idea would work.

He presented his idea to the monkeys at Monkey Ward. They through their poo in *his* face.

So, Wood cleaned himself off and took a job offer from Julius Rosenwald at Sears.

. . .

It bears just a moment to linger on Rosenwald.

In 1924, when he hired Wood to take the company in a new direction,

---

[5] Yep, that's what our parents called it. Ask a Boomer.

Sears' elder statesman was nearing the end of his career. (He would die in 1932 at the age of 69.) His focus had changed. Part of a reform Jewish congregation, Rosenwald met activist Booker T. Washington. It was Washington who eventually convinced Rosenwald to serve on the board of the Tuskegee Institute and advocate for African American education.[6] Rosenwald was one of those rare business types who put his money, time, connections, and resources where his mouth was.

He had more than earned the right to step back and focus on his passions.

Rewind the clock 25 years, and Sears was in trouble. During the Panic of 1893, the company drowned in supplier inventory as demand dried up. Rosenwald was one of those suppliers – of menswear, specifically – and he faced one of two options. He *could* try to play hardball and demand payment. But then, as now, that strategy rarely works. The problem wasn't that Sears didn't *want* to pay; the problem was that they *couldn't* pay. Simply demanding they do so doesn't help. It's like speaking louder when trying to communicate with someone who doesn't speak your language. You're just being noisy.

Luckily for Sears, Rosenwald accepted option two: He'd get an ownership stake in the company in lieu of payment. By 1895, Rosenwald began to take the reigns, eventually establishing complete control of the company by 1903. After a tense few years, Sears diversified its offering dramatically. Clothing and gifts would remain mainstays of the catalog, but Sears began to include electronic gadgets, hardware, tools, furniture, drugs, medical supplies, and dry goods of every description. Sears would sell *anything* the American farmer could want and deliver it through the mail.

And when Sears said anything, they meant *anything*.

The rules were different back then. You could buy just about anything you wanted through the mail.[7] Want medical equipment to perform surgery at home? Here's your scalpel set! Want some cocaine? Score! Fancy

---

6 There is so much more to say here. If you're interested, read Peter Acosti's book, *Julius Rosenwald: The Man Who Built Sears, Roebuck and Advanced the Cause of Black Education in the American South*.

7 Check out classic versions of the catalog online. Some parts are weird and archaic, but it looks strangely modern in many ways.

a new vibrator? Yes, ma'am! Remember that the Sears team managed all that inventory – literally, thousands of different items – with pen, paper, and telegrams. Also, remember that Sears didn't make that stuff. It was a *reseller*. It needed to buy items (usually) before receiving an order from a customer. Guess wrong, as Sears did in 1893, and the new volume and variety of inventory could bankrupt the company.

Add to that the challenge of simply getting things to rural communities in the first years of the 1900s. (Zone Improvement (ZIP) Codes weren't introduced until 1963.) There were no trucks before the 1920s. All that inventory needed to move with a combination of trains, horses, carriages, and human muscle. It was worth it, though. In 1900, over 40 percent of Americans lived directly on farms, and another 20 percent lived in rural areas. Mass markets were, originally, farmers' markets.

Impressive as managing those challenges was, what made Rosenwald special wasn't the product expansion or logistical brilliance; it was his attitude. Instead of "*seller to* the American farmer," Sears became the "*buyer for* the American farmer." Think about that for a second. Instead of placing Sears and all its suppliers on one side and the customer on the other, Sears put itself and the farmer on the same side and the *suppliers* on the other. That change in perspective provided clear guidance for decision-making. Should Sears offer a money-back guarantee? Yes. Should Sears include an item in the catalog that only a small number of customers in a specific region might want? Yes. Should you play fair with suppliers so that Sears would get the best prices? Yes. Should you play fair with employees so that Sears could recruit the best talent? Yes.

Rosenwald saw his company's power as a means to a positive end for everyone involved. However, even the best intentions couldn't prepare Sears for what would happen next.

. . .

In 1917, the United States entered World War I. In 1918, the flu came home with them.[8] As the world recovered, the American economy collapsed in the worst Depression before the "Great" one. The triple whammy nearly crushed Sears, though Rosenwald was able to lead the company through it.

That said, the effort exhausted Rosenwald. Biographer Peter Acosti says that Rosenwald began searching for his successor as soon as the crisis eased. That's probably why competition (most notably from Montgomery Ward) was starting to overtake Sears. To be fair, Rosenwald's company had more to lose in an economic downturn simply because it was so large, and upstarts like Montgomery Ward had a lot to gain simply because it was so much smaller. However, those charitable explanations hid two larger shifts in the market.

The first change was demography. The shift from a rural to an urban way of life was well underway. Sears might be the "buyer for the American farmer," but there were fewer of them every year. As people moved to urban areas, distance mattered much less. Local neighborhood stores offered same-day convenience that multi-week mail-order catalogs could not.

The second change was a bit more subtle, but it's a recurring theme in this book. Until the 1920s, simply aggregating the explosion of new consumer products was good enough. In this, Sears was the only "buyer" option. But as the 1920s progressed, Sears faced competition – not only from Montgomery Ward, but from a new type of retailer: the chain store.

. . .

Asking a modern consumer to define a chain store is like asking a fish to describe water. Chains are so pervasive that they almost blend into the cultural scenery. It wasn't always that way.

To begin, let's start with a simple definition: A chain store is a single business (usually focusing on retail or dining) with several locations operating under a single brand. Typically, they also share centralized

---

8   Though there's some doubt about the actual origin of the 1918 flu pandemic. It probably wasn't Spain, it could have actually been Kansas, but it was certainly made worse by the cramped conditions, poor nutrition, and major mobilization and displacement of people from the war.

management teams, standardized operations, and common supply chains.[9]

When pressed for their opinions, many people attribute chain stores' success to conspiratorial practices wherein large organizations, fat cat founders, and in-the-pocket government officials deliberately make it difficult for "mom-and-pop" stores to succeed.

That criticism is as old as chain stores themselves. Chain stores often lobby federal, state, and local governments to set standards and rules that, while noble sounding on the surface (safety requirements, training standards, etc.), often have the net effect of protecting certain companies and industries.[10] However, it didn't take long for communities to learn to fight back – slowing or stopping the spread of new chain businesses in their communities. They do this often by delays in licensing, outright rejection, or other punitive requirements.[11]

However, competing with one is spectacularly difficult even when chain stores have no "unfair" advantages.

The first advantage is not what comes readily to mind when you think about the 1920s: *data*. As we will see in Chapter 17, the ability to compile large data sets confers massive advantages. Imagine you're Sears, and you notice consumers beginning to purchase a new style of clothing. The purchase might go unnoticed at any individual store or in any single catalog order, but across a vast number of stores, the trend becomes apparent. Chain store managers enjoy the same advantage with employee staffing patterns, prevailing wages, supplier negotiations, advertising effectiveness, and much more. Their buyers can be the first to secure the best deals – and even exclusive products – with critical suppliers. An independent store simply cannot access data as quickly as its large, multi-site competitors.

The next advantage is simpler: *volume*. All else equal, the larger a chain store is, the more it buys. The more it buys, the stronger its negotiating position. Better negotiation results in lower prices. A chain store could

---

9   There is a precise legal distinction between a "chain store" and "formula retail." It's not important here, but if you're considering starting a chain store, check with a lawyer.

10 The process is called "regulatory capture," and the preeminent scholar on the matter is University of Minnesota professor Morris Kleiner.

11 Some practices stand up to legal challenge. Others do not. However, when faced with a hostile city council, many chain stores will simply move on to the next community.

offer the same product – a radio, let's say – for $10 to the customer, pay its supplier $6, and still make $4 profit on the transaction. A smaller store, buying in far smaller quantities, might not get the radio for less than $9. To match the chain store, they'd need to sell for only $1 profit – about a quarter of what the chain store makes for the same product. And that's if they could negotiate a deal directly with that supplier *at all*. Often, smaller stores need to buy through a broker or wholesaler, with a corresponding middleman markup, resulting in even lower profit margins.

To counter that impact, independent retail stores justify their higher prices with intangibles – "better service," "support for local communities," or "personal relationships." These sound like compelling reasons, but given a choice, people demonstrate that they would rather have the same thing for less money. That's not to say that small stores can't compete, but over the long term, they struggle.

By contrast, all that data and undeniable buying power allow *chain stores* to hyper-focus on customer desires. That means a lot more than simply having the products people want at the lowest price possible. It means having the profit margins (see the $4 versus $1 example) to invest in extras that customers actually value. Macy's started a holiday parade in downtown New York. Sears could invest in money-back guarantees. Other chain stores offered free delivery, setup help, and training classes.

Rosenwald knew all this as he considered choices for his successor. He had been a careful observer of retail chain stores of that era. He knew he needed a leader who could bring Sears into that world. That's why Wood wasn't his first choice – Wood worked at a mail-order competitor, not Macy's. But as other candidates fell by the wayside, Rosenwald took a closer look at Wood's (admittedly, a bit crazy) plan and decided to give him a shot.

What happened next would transform retail forever.

. . .

As we've mentioned, retail chain stores were not new.

They featured multiple "departments" for housewares, clothing, and gifts – which is why we call this particular type of chain store a *department* store. Modern readers may struggle to remember the appeal of such places, but ask a Baby Boomer what it was like to walk into a downtown

Macy's store in a major city. They spanned multiple floors and anchored the best corner real estate. They sold all the hottest fashions and gifts. But for all their purported variety, most department stores focused on a limited array of products for the urban elite. It's why companies like Sears still had an advantage by focusing on the farmer who lived in "mail-order" country (today's "fly-over" country). Farmers rarely drove into the city.

However, that urban/rural split was changing. As more people moved into the cities, it became more challenging to get around. Cities were the centers of energy, commerce, finance, and fashion, but the larger they grew, the less appealing they were for people who wanted to raise a family. Frustrated with both the disconnection of rural life and overcrowding in the cities, a new type of real estate zone emerged: *the suburbs*. They are, quite literally, near cities. They were (and are) dependent on city cores as a center of gravity, but they're far enough away to offer a unique balance of room to grow and connection to culture. However, suburbs had drawbacks. With all retail options concentrated in core downtowns, suburban residents still needed to venture into the city to shop. As cities became more crowded, making that pilgrimage became an unwanted tax on suburban life.

If only someone would build a store near where people lived, right?

What seems so obvious in retrospect was not obvious at the time. Even Wood had trouble convincing Sears management to take up the idea. To make the decision a little easier to swallow, the first Sears retail store was at North Lawndale in the Chicago area – physically adjacent to its largest mail-order distribution center.

The move made sense for several reasons.

Like other major metro areas, Chicago was growing fast. The city was large enough to be a good test site but not *so large* or geographically constricted as to skew the results. It also helped that Sears was headquartered in Chicago. If you're going to run an experiment, you might as well do it close to home. There are advantages to walking across the street and checking on things. Experiments need constant fiddling, and Wood understood this intuitively. And finally, locating your test store next to a mail-order center reduced the logistical burden (shipping amounted to wheeling merchandise from down the hall) and the perceived risk of making mistakes. These geographic features meant that it would be the *midwest* that would incubate a new era in retail.

But geography and convenience aren't quite what made the first Sears store special.

Wood understood that people in these "middle zones" wanted a mix of merchandise – fashion and gifts that you could find in the city, along with home improvement and gardening tools that you could find in the country. For their part, shoppers didn't expect (or need) the same level of fashion they'd wear in the city, and they also weren't growing acres of soybeans. A modest home with a yard in the suburbs needed the *right* balance of products and services – sort of a Goldilocks zone.

Wood also noticed the increase in the number of cars, especially as Ford's Model T became the de facto mode of transportation. While popular in the cities, cars were *essential* in spread-out suburbs. Those areas didn't have the density to justify effective public transportation options, and walking a few miles home carrying groceries and hand tools in a Chicago winter is not appealing.

The new Sears store would need the physical space for a new type of real estate: the parking lot. As Wood started opening stores away from crowded mail-order locations, he could get away with leaving most of the land of the retail site "empty" so that shoppers would have a place to park.

Wood also understood how consumer expectations were changing.

The 1920s saw a flurry of new fashions, gadgets, tools, and appliances – many running on electricity – unlike anything seen before. A catalog simply couldn't do them justice. People needed to see, touch, and feel them. However, what most people don't realize about the 1920s is that most retail stores were *salesperson-directed* shopping experiences. One simply didn't walk into Macy's and pick out a bedspread.[12] You asked a salesperson to show you bedspreads. When you decided what you wanted, the salesperson would "go to the back" and get it for you.[13] In other words, most retail operations of the day solved the problem of overwhelm and confusion with a curated, personal shopping experience.

Wood suspected consumers might be ready for a different type of shopping journey. From his experience at Montgomery Ward and Sears, he

---

12 If you understood that reference, Speak Friend and Enter.

13 Doesn't that drive you berserk about some shoe retailers today?

knew that people *would purchase* products sight unseen through a mail-order catalog. They didn't necessarily *need* a salesperson to assist them. If his hunch was correct, the store simply needed to display all the items on the sales floor. Shoppers would browse and choose for themselves. An open sales floor takes up more physical space than a downtown display rack, but these new stores had the room.

That's not to say Wood had it easy. He had to learn (mostly the hard way), what this new type of suburban retail would require.

Location was key. If you got that wrong, and there weren't enough people in an area, that store's sales might not justify the expense. Some store locations were obvious; the homes were already there. However, because suburbs were still new in the early 1920s, Wood needed to get good at projecting population growth. Luckily, that's the sort of thing he loved doing. (One struggles to imagine his children enjoying *those* bedtime stories.)

Once sited, the store must have easy access from local roads, clear (and big) signage, and adequate parking for peak hours. That meant working with city planners to ensure the infrastructure was in place to handle the traffic. Sears began the decades-long love/hate relationship with city councils. They loved the tax revenue. They hated the demands.

Once people got to the parking lot, the building needed to be clean, well-lit, and spacious. At first, Wood's team simply stacked merchandise in a way that was easiest for warehouse staff to manage. Warehouse organization schemes are designed to economize space, not maximize sales. Pan-head screws, paper clips, and chewing gum are all about the same size, but putting them together in the same display doesn't make sense. At least if you want people to buy them. Screws should sell with hardware. Paper clips, with office supplies. Gum, with snacks. You get the idea. Wood hired architects to create beautiful product displays. Everything you see today in modern retail stores – racks, shelves, islands, etc. – was designed by Wood's team.[14]

To meet these new expectations, Wood needed to train employees to offer just the right amount of assistance to shoppers. Answer questions, but don't hover. Customers did not always need a salesperson's help, but

---

14 When you see pictures of Sears stores on the 1920s, it's uncanny how modern they look.

Wood wanted to ensure staff was available when they did. Wood leaned on his experience leading workers in the Panama Canal zone to pull off that tricky balance. He realized that top-down management must work to support bottom-up decision-making at the store level – not the other way around. Employees "on the floor" understood what customers wanted and how they behaved. Wood would use aggregate data from all stores to validate those findings and cultivate the best customer services approaches. That meant that when it came to training staff, Wood quickly discovered that transplants from "traditional" retail also brought their bad habits and assumptions. He found it faster and easier to train them from scratch, leading to a culture of internal advancement and loyalty that outside competition couldn't quite match. He also wouldn't let his leaders sit behind their desks. He required they spend time in stores, on the sales floor, listening and watching. Yes, customers loved Sears, but employees *also* loved Sears.

Behind the scenes, it was easy to assume that a Sears retail location would simply be a "catalog in a building," meaning that anything you could buy in the catalog would be displayed in the store. That wasn't the case. That might seem obvious, but it wasn't. Sears needed to learn what would sell, at which stores, and at what time of the year.

The classic example is winter wear. Warm clothing only sells in the fall and winter, and only in stores in northern climate zones. Try to sell mittens in Houston, and people look at you funny; but try to sell mittens in Minneapolis in July, and people will get mad. They don't want to think about winter just then. That's the easy example, but there were so many others. Suburban stores attracted both women and *men* – something downtown department stores struggled to do. That meant understanding what products each gender wanted, how they wanted to be displayed, and what prices drove sales.

This new form of shopping led to a massive increase in the sophistication of accounting and merchandise planning systems to ensure the right item was in the right store at the right time and in the right quantity. It remains the most vexing issue in retail nearly 100 years later.

Management guru Peter Drucker might have said it best when he analyzed what made Sears so successful:

> True marketing starts with the customer, demographics, realities,

needs, and values. It does not ask 'what do we want to sell?' It asks 'what does the customer want to buy?'

Robert Wood would also include "where they want to buy it."

. . .

In retrospect, Wood may have seemed like a genius, but in reality, Sears' path to retail success was slow, deliberate, and careful. The first experimental store opened in 1925. Wood opened seven more in the first year because, as he reminded Rosenwald, you can't experiment with only one location. However, he opened only *one* more store in 1926. Within three years, there were only 22 Sears retail locations, and all were sited in cities with over 100,000 people.[15]

To its credit, Wood's former employer wasn't sitting on its hands.

Managers at Montgomery Ward noticed their former employee's success, and by 1926, crafted its own retail strategy. In a move that would hearken forward to Walmart's business idea more than a generation later, Montgomery Ward had more locations in smaller cities, whereas Sears focused on fewer stores in bigger cities. The strategy made sense: Rural was still king, and having stores near rural centers meant those customers wouldn't need to travel as far. Moreover, because the rural market was so well-served by its mail-order catalog, Montgomery Ward stores would be "display only." In other words, you couldn't buy anything in their first iterations. You could just look.

This is a classic example of skating to where the puck *is* rather than skating to where the puck *will be*.[16] The difference between the two approaches couldn't be more evident. A Sears store averaged $558,000 in annual revenue per store to Montgomery Ward's $197,000 – almost three times as much. Worse for Montgomery Ward, as Sears expanded, Wood found that he could go down-market to smaller cities easier than his competitor could go upmarket to larger ones. He created the "A-B-C"

---

15 Except, inexplicably, Green Bay, Wisconsin.

16 Midwesterners will understand this analogy. Because we're talking about Sears, based out of Chicago, it seems appropriate.

store ranking scheme to operationalize this strategy. "A" locations were the full-line, large metro stores – the no-brainers. "B" stores were located in smaller, growing cities with the potential for rapid growth in the coming decades. Most of those cities were found in the South, Southwest, and West. Their reduced offering was conditional. The idea was to grow the store's offering only as its sales numbers justified it. "C" stores were either in smaller communities or niche stores in larger cities. Montgomery Ward never got the formula quite right, and it never again mounted a serious challenge to Sears.

For the first time, customers could buy (nearly) everything they needed in one place: clothes, home repairs, car tires, electronics, tools, gifts, appliances…*everything*. Because a family could supply their entire home from one store, shopping became an anticipated experience for the whole family.

The era of the "big box store" had arrived.

. . .

The numbers speak for themselves.

By the end of the 1920s, retail stores accounted for a full *third* of Sears sales. Ten years later, at the height of the Great Depression, retail sales doubled to two-thirds of all sales, relegating the iconic catalog to second-tier status. Wood took advantage of the retail chaos of the 1930s to refine Sears' product mix, improve store design, and strengthen its supply chain. He also supported President Roosevelt during those years when many other business owners would not. Wood was no socialist or communist, but he saw employee and customer success as linked to the company's success. And just like Rosenwald, he took concrete actions – raising wages and lowering prices. After the war, Sears would dominate the American retail landscape for decades, giving us not only the template for other department stores, but also giant physical retailers Walmart, Target, and Best Buy, e-commerce giant Amazon, and even the modern shopping mall – often anchored by a Sears store.[17] None of those businesses could have existed without the trail blazed for them by Rosenwald's catalog and

---

17 The very first modern, enclosed shopping mall was another midwestern invention: Southdale Shopping Center in a suburb of Minneapolis, Minnesota, in 1956.

Wood's big box store.

Has that change been entirely positive? No.

Commentators as early as the 1920s lamented the impact chain stores had on small, independent retailers. Chain store magnates of the time, with names like Filene and Penny, actively tried to counter their attacks. Since then, chain store operators have become much more adept at redirecting negative public attention from depleted and boarded-up small-town main streets. That's why you see large brands sponsor community contribution campaigns, run feel-good advertising, and even provide "help" for small businesses. Even that help, however, proves self-serving. It can be challenging to innovate as a large business; small businesses are more agile and responsive. By bankrolling them, large corporate padrones often get the first crack at what they come up with.

Despite the noisy partisan outcry, the average consumer continues to vote with their wallet.

In 2019, the average revenue of the top ten U.S. retailers accounted for $1.41 trillion of the $4.85 trillion in total retail sales, or nearly one in three dollars spent.[18] Although by definition, that means that 71% falls into the long tail of smaller retailers, one could argue their impact goes beyond that. The major retailers are so large that they define the terms of supplier relationships and set wage rates. On the flip side, big box stores counter that they negotiate with suppliers in a way that the average person could not, meaning better prices and availability for everyone.

When we step back from those arguments, we can appreciate what Sears accomplished. Wood gave shoppers a new option – one that fit their location, their lifestyle, and their growing families. He created the modern retailer as a place where consumers could see, touch, and feel a lot of merchandise all under one roof.

With its catalog, Sears invented shopping. With its stores, Sears invented the shopping experience.

---

18 According to public filings, the annual revenue of the Top 10 U.S. retailers in 2019 was: Walmart ($524 billion), Amazon ($158 billion), Costco ($153 billion), Kroger ($122 billion), Home Depot ($110 billion), CVS ($87 billion), Target ($77 billion), Lowes ($72 billion), Albertsons ($62 billion), and Best Buy ($43 billion).

7
HOUSING FEMINISM

Herbert Hoover would like to give you some home ownership advice. Yes, *Hoover*, and you should listen to him.

Most people remember (and misremember) Hoover as the president who presided over the economic collapse of the Great Depression. But in 1923, in a surprise to most, Hoover was one of the most popular public figures in the world. He nearly singlehandedly prevented German-occupied Belgium from succumbing to starvation in World War I. He was an engineer by training, a progressive by temperament, and the ultimate bring-people-together-to-solve-problems kind of guy.

Hoover's tireless advocacy for home ownership remains one of the best examples of his can-do spirit. Let's hear what he has to say.

If you're renting right now, you probably feel some insecurity. At any point, the landlord could decide to raise your rent, making it unaffordable and throwing your living situation into chaos. Owning a home means no one can change the terms of the mortgage.

When looking for a home, you need to take an inventory of what you *want*, what you *need*, and what you can *afford* – ideally, before you even start looking. That way, you'll know how to evaluate the specifics of the home: square footage, number of bedrooms and bathrooms, neighborhood, schools, transportation options, and the neighbors. But it's more than just location, location, location. You also must dispassionately evaluate the home itself: its current condition, what repairs it might need, and what potential it holds for future needs. That might include raising children or caring for elderly parents.

Once you've done that, you can balance those considerations with what you can afford. That means more than simply adding your savings and income, but also involves accounting for the impact of interest rates and mortgage terms. Payments that seem affordable at eight percent interest may seem oppressive at ten percent. And don't forget to add in any state and local taxes.[1] Hoover used a $7,500 home for his monthly payment example. For reference, that's about $105,000 in 2020 money, so

---

1   These are the days before the familiar 30-year, fixed-rate mortgage that became the standard. Homebuyers navigated a much more complicated lending landscape – if they could find a bank (or credit union, see Chapter 24) to lend to them at all.

he's not talking about that era's equivalent of a McMansion.

And finally, you need to consider building or buying and what it will take to furnish and maintain the house. You can also get creative – buy what you can afford now, but with the space to add a deck or porch later – to stretch your budget.

If you were considering a "speculative" purchase, Hoover warns against it. Some people were tempted to buy more home than they could afford or purchased with the hope that their property would quickly appreciate (and they could turn a quick profit). That's not what home ownership and community building are all about. Buying your home is a long-term investment in your family and your community.

Pretty good advice, wouldn't you think?

His advice appears in the forward to the government publication: "How to Own Your Home: A Handbook for Prospective Home Owners." It's a well-written, clear, and practical guide to the mechanics and finance of home ownership.[2] Sure, when you read Hoover's introduction, there is plenty of language we today would consider archaic – male pronouns for the buyer and female pronouns for the decorator – but on the whole, with a couple of tweaks, this would be sound advice *today*, 100 years later.

But to look at home ownership as a purely rational decision misses the point.

Homes mean more to people than simply a place to live. They build generational wealth for families, stabilize communities, and strengthen nation-states by giving people something tangible to protect. We'll explore those reasons in more depth shortly. However, a more significant, yet underreported, aspect of home ownership is *feminism*. Owning a home gave women of that era a tangible place to exercise power within the family. Homeownership was linked with suffrage, reproductive rights,

---

2   If you're curious, yes, redlining occurred during this era. That's the practice of excluding certain ethnic, racial, or religious groups from certain neighborhoods. However, there was nothing about that in Hoover's pamphlet, even obliquely. Despite a mixed record (at best) regarding civil rights, his views on race were strongly influenced by his Quaker upbringing, which believed in the fundamental equality of all people. He desegregated the Commerce Department in 1928, lived in China for a time and learned Mandarin, and served with an Indigenous American (Charles Curtis) as his vice-president. Hoover believed in all citizens assimilating into American culture; housing was a critical step on that path.

and financial independence. It didn't happen all at once. It wasn't perfect. Nevertheless, the impact was undeniable.

Hoover understood this. Although he could provide significant material support and leverage the government's bully pulpit as the first Secretary of Commerce, the Department of Construction and Housing couldn't do what was truly needed. What follows is the story of two tireless women who made the idea of home ownership a tangible, living thing in the United States. Largely, Hoover stepped aside and let them take the lead.

Marie Mattingly Meloney and Dr. Caroline Bartlett Crane created the American Dream.

. . .

Before we can talk about Meloney and Crane, we must step back into their world. Specifically, the world as it related to finding homes for everyone who needed them. It was not going well.

In the decade before the 1920s, nearly one million immigrants arrived in the United States each year. Although immigration slowed as 1920 approached, population growth did not. Between 1920 and 1930, the U.S. population would jump from 106 million to 123 million – an increase of more than 16 percent. So, what's the problem? America is a big place, right? The issue was that people didn't spread themselves out evenly over the vast continental interior. New people tend to congregate where existing people already are. That's somewhat obvious when it comes to newborns, but it's also the case with new immigrants. It's nice to live somewhere they speak your language…at least, until you can learn the new one.

We'll sidestep many of the cultural conflicts and tensions that arose during this time to focus on the most immediate problem: housing. That meant certain cities – large, mostly port cities on the east coast (New York, Boston, Philadelphia, and others) – bore the brunt of the rapid population expansion. All those newly-arrived people needed a place to stay, enough food, clean water, functioning sewers, and other necessities. Even large cities strained to meet the demand. It turns out, they met that demand in the worst possible way: the slum.

Today, people might bristle at the use of the word "slum" to describe barely-standing, rat-infested tenement buildings, but that's what they were. As you might guess, these buildings were not built "to code" – if such a thing existed, which it essentially did not. Substandard plumbing meant sewage routinely backed up into rental units, causing rampant disease. Substandard electrical wiring (if such a thing existed, which it sometimes did) meant frequent fires, causing rampant terror and occasional death.

In that environment, doesn't it seem reasonable that these communities became breeding grounds for crime? Organizations such as the Italian mafia secured a foothold because they could offer what the government could not: jobs, stability, dignity, and a sense of belonging in a frightening new place. If the Black Hand didn't recruit you, the local communist party might. "A chicken in every pot" sounds pretty good when you're struggling to find work and feed your family.

It was the sort of classic *systems engineering* problem that Hoover understood well. A simple cause – waves of poorly-managed immigration – caused complex ripple effects. To be sure, some of those impacts were positive, including energetic entrepreneurship, new cuisine, and dynamic politics. But many impacts, as we've seen, were quite negative – from poor public health to violent crime to political instability.

If the root cause of the problem was the lack of adequate housing, the root solution was a house. And to be clear, when Hoover, Meloney, and Crane (among many others) said "house," they meant a *single-family* home. Why were they so insistent on that solution? Wouldn't better *multi-family* rental housing solve the underlying problem more quickly and efficiently? Not necessarily.

Single family homes give their owners a stake in their communities that no rental property could match. Homeowners invest in their physical property and the neighborhood surrounding it. They get to know their neighbors. They're less likely to tolerate crime in their communities and more apt to work with law enforcement to root it out. Owning property also stabilizes local politics and blunts the persuasive communist/socialist appeal of collective ownership. In short, owning a home encourages families to put down roots. Like a mature tree, those roots anchor the soil of their communities and provide shade for newcomers and habitat for businesses, schools, churches, entertainment, and fraternal organizations.

As one Realtor put it in an address to the Interstate Realty Convention:

> The most sacred institution in the world is not the Church…nor the State…it is the Home, and the man, who, in these times of high costs and hard conditions, buys a home… secures for it a happy wife, and raises therein patriotic well-educated American children, and sends them out to high moral ideals, to be a blessing to the community, has done the most patriotic and religious thing possible and incidentally the more opportune thing for the betterment of human conditions. Upon the home rests our moral character; our civic and political liberties are grounded there; virtue, manhood, and citizenship, grow there. American citizenship in the long run will be, must be, what the American home is…

This was the homeownership ideal Hoover, Meloney, and Crane were working to create: your own single-family home somewhere in the suburbs. That's the why. Now, we need to work on the how.

. . .

The first thing we tend to think about when we consider the "how" of homeownership is *how* people will pay for it. For the most part, that means thinking about mortgages, because that's how most of *us* finance a home. However, the 20 or 30-year home mortgage we know today didn't exist until 1934 with the creation of the Federal Housing Administration (FHA). Before the 1920s, prospective homebuyers needed to come up with at least 50 percent of the purchase price and were *lucky* to be able to finance the balance over the next five to seven years (paying interest only during that time) and finishing up with a balloon payment at the end. Suffice it to say, only the well-off could afford to buy a home at all.

The 1920s saw a new type of loan. As housing values rapidly increased (see Chapter 13 for more), banks allowed buyers to buy a home with *interest-only* payments and a smaller (or nonexistent) down payment. The logic was simple: By the time the loan came due, the property had appreciated so much that buyers could refinance using home equity to pay back the original loan or, at worst, sell the home and pay back the loan with the profits.

Can you guess what happened when the financial markets collapsed in 1929? Sure, you can. But that's ten years in the future. For now, it's enough to know that *many* more people could afford a home. Furthermore, the payments were reasonable enough that they could *also afford* to fill that new home with all the stuff they saw (and heard) advertised.

With financing out of the way, the real issue became how to make a house a *home*. Hoover was smart enough to realize he wasn't the person to answer that question.

. . .

In 1920, at the age of 42, Marie Mattingly Meloney was described as "small, very frail, almost an invalid; a childhood accident had made her slightly lame. She had gray hair and immense, poetic black eyes set in a lovely pale face."

Perhaps tiny, but fierce.[3]

In her description of the Better Homes in America (BHA) movement, you can read a more inclusive statement than we saw before, but with an even crisper sense of purpose.

> The American home is the foundation of our national and individual well-being. Its steady improvement is, at the same time, a test of our civilization and of our ideal. The Better Homes in America movement provides a channel through which men and women in each community can encourage the building, ornamenting, and owning of private homes by the people at large. We need attractive, worthy, permanent homes that lighten the burden of housekeeping. We need homes in which home life can reach its finest levels, and in which can be reared happy children and upright citizens.
>
> The Better Homes movement stands on the belief that our people, by well-planned measures, can obtain for themselves a finer type of home and family life...The work of Better Homes committees has promoted character training in the home, and reading, music, and other forms of wholesome home recreation. It has encouraged saving and wise expenditure for the building and equipping of homes, and thereby helped to raise living standards, reduce drudgery, and make

---

3   Giving credit where credit is due for this description of the fictional Karrin Murphy in *The Dresden Files*, by Jim Butcher. It's an apt turn of phrase to describe Meloney.

the conditions of life more attractive.

This is the real vision of home ownership in America. It was a place where families would build, decorate, and maintain nurturing environments to raise children, and in so doing, elevate the standard of living for the entire country. It's bold. It's positive. And it was going to take a lot of work to pull off.

That's why Meloney approached Hoover to get involved. She started the BHA in 1922, right about the same time Hoover founded the Department of Construction and Housing within the Commerce Department. They knew and respected one another. In 1923 and 1924, as the BHA movement was going national, Hoover signed on as President of the organization, with Mattingly serving as Vice President.[4]

Hoover added the voice of the government's bully pulpit to Meloney's BHA to publish pamphlets and secure audiences with key financiers, but that wasn't what most people remember. Based out of New York, Meloney's *The Delineator* magazine served as the true mouthpiece for home ownership – less the mechanics of mortgages and more the transition from house to home. Because it was the latter that was the most important, it would fall to the women of America to take the lead.

Have a look at just a *sampling* of the table of contents from the January 1926 edition:

6   "Runaway" is a story by Albert Payson Terhune, "whose stories of champion dogs begin appearing in this issue."
15 "Christmas in Delineator Homes" by The *Delineator's* Department of House Decoration and Home Building.
20 "What Price Beauty?" shows how to furnish a house, room by room, at three different income levels. Costs are included.
21 "The Home Gymnasium" discusses the requirements and benefits of regular exercise, especially as a way to lower the death rate

---

[4] To those who feel this was a bit sexist, you're right. But this was 1924, and having Hoover's name on your initiative was a big deal. To his credit, Hoover was a figurehead and saw his role that way. He knew Meloney was the force, and most importantly, treated her as such. He supported her with the pamphlet we excerpted and many other efforts, giving her efforts the full weight and power of the U.S. government. Note: That's what we mean by "allyship" a century before anyone used the term.

among young women.
22 "Has it Beauty?" advocates the search for beauty in material things as well as in life experiences.
23 Paris fashion sketches and Butterick patterns imitate the French designer look.
35 Advertisement for Campbell's Soup.
39 Advertisement for Fleischmann's Yeast includes a testimonial about its ability to relieve constipation.
40 Whole wheat flour recipes accompany a discussion of whole wheat's nutritional benefits and improved storage qualities.
41 Advertisement for Listerine promotes it as a means of controlling bad breath.
49 Advertisement for Kotex stresses that women who use these sanitary napkins will have a more active and sociable lifestyle.

Up to this point, you would have thought homeownership was all about mortgages, financing schemes, and construction. Sure, we read about the bigger vision, but no one had translated those aspirations into something tangible that women could do *today* in their homes. If you think about what you read in the table of contents, you'll start to get an idea of the specifics Meloney had in mind.

Consider the story about pets in the home. Until then, pets didn't exist in the public consciousness. That's not to say that many people didn't care for animals or that they didn't have experience with livestock (or even that they had an emotional connection), but this was the first time Americans learned how to make pets a part of the "home" experience.

Consider the story about how to decorate your home for Christmas. Yes, churches decorated for the Holidays. And yes, families celebrated shared meals and exchanged gifts. However, *home decoration* was a new concept – not simply inside the home (what your Christmas tree "should" look like), but also how you might decorate your yard, the outside of your home, or your neighborhood.

Consider the story of the home gymnasium. Written by Dr. Lillian Shaw, the article featured common sense advice for women to stay fit and healthy.⁵ Again, this was not something people worried much about in a rural lifestyle. (Ask someone who works a farm. They don't "need" a gym membership.) City life changes things. Dr. Shaw recommends using the empty space in a two-car garage and filling it with modest, practical equipment. "This is not half as difficult or expensive as it sounds," she advises, and it doubles as a place for children (boys and girls) to burn off excess energy.

Was fashion neglected? Not at all. *The Delineator* featured guides on how to copy French styles they might see from the likes of Coco Chanel (see Chapter 23) on an *American* middle-class budget.⁶ Recipes featured prominently, as did advertisements for key ingredients. Creating healthy meals was an essential expectation of the mistress of the house, and Meloney's magazine made it a point to highlight things she might try. The magazine opens with an article from Angelo Patri on child-rearing (see Chapter 25), how to grow plants indoors, and how to prevent the common cold.

Those are all excellent examples, but let's call our attention to one article in particular: "Has it Beauty?" Here's how it begins:

> Every inch of you must be lovely to have real beauty. You can't have a peaches-and-cream complexion with a dumpy body and still be beautiful. You can't be lithe and well-groomed with a dark-brown personality and still be beautiful. Celia Caroline Cole will gladly help you correct your faults if you write her at *The Delineator*.

At first read, Cole's article seems like the rasping of a sharp-tongued advice columnist who's holding women to an unattainably high standard. No "dark-brown" personalities or "dumpy bodies," please. (Does "dark-brown" mean what you think it means? No, likely not. This wasn't an oblique reference to race. Does "dumpy" mean what you think it means? Sadly and impolitely, yes.)

But no, that's not it. Beauty was a broader concept; you knew it when

---

5   You can find downloadable copies of *The Delineator*, and many other publications, by searching the Library of Congress for the "Prosperity and Thrift: The Coolidge Era and the Consumer Economy, 1921-1929."

6   This issue contains at least 12 pages of illustrated women modeling the latest fashions. It could have come right out of a Coco Chanel catalog.

you saw it. You could try to find beauty in harmoniousness, coordination, or rhythm, but ultimately, beauty is about *both* outer appearance *and* inner joy. Yes, that implied a woman must care for her appearance – no "sagginess of body" – but also must care for her mindset – no "sagginess of mind." Reading a little deeper, Cole focuses the reader's attention on the whole meaning of beauty and genuine aspiration: *Does it bring you joy?* Beauty was more than skin deep. True beauty meant joyfulness. Maintaining that joyfulness was the responsibility of the home's leader.

Meloney's signature publication, *The Delineator*, was crucial, but the BHA movement was much more than that. Reading about creating the good life was one thing. Experiencing it for themselves was quite another.

The "Better Homes Week" was a neighborhood-organized event featuring model homes, lectures, slide shows, window-dressing contests, and block parties. The local focus allowed more women to participate (either as hosts or attendees), encouraged camaraderie, built personal relationships, and ensured sensitivity and alignment with distinct neighborhood styles, cultures, and values. In short, every event followed the same script but allowed for improvisation.

You'll often see prominent *men's* names in newspapers and advertising when you read reports from the time. Like Hoover, they were figureheads. It was essential to get the head of the local chamber of commerce to support the effort (it encouraged business in the community, after all). Still, it was the women who did the actual legwork and made all the important decisions.

In her book, *American Queenmaker: How Missy Meloney Brought Women Into Politics*, historian Julie Des Jardins details Meloney's organizational genius:

> Turning local women into publicity agents, [Meloney] gave them nut-and-bolt directions for erecting miniature playhouses in the public square, holding school essay contests on home ownership, showing BHA films in local movie houses, and collaborating with local newspapers, Rotary and Kiwanis Clubs, real estate boards, business and trade associations, home-building and-furnishing industries, chambers of commerce, women's clubs, and local departments of education, ignoring no grassroots angle of the campaign. Missy was a big-ideas thinker, but she also visualized the follow-through on the granular level.

In an innovation familiar to any prospective homebuyer 100 years later, Meloney took experiential up a notch. Along with *New York Tribune* marketing executive Helen Rogers Reid, Meloney created the first walk-through concept home. It featured indoor plumbing, a sewing machine, a washing machine, kitchen appliances, an electric vacuum, and washable wallpaper.

In an era starved for guidance on what to do after you signed your mortgage documents, Des Jardins makes the case that Meloney did more to promote the middle-class homeownership ideal than anyone else. Millions of people would tour model homes, and many more would read her magazines or hear her advertisements on the radio. She would leverage that success and her political connections to lift other women into higher positions in their communities and government – sometimes behind the scenes, but just as often, into elected office.

In every meaningful way, Better Homes of America was a woman-led organization. The only critique, if there is one, is that Meloney offered an authoritative but decidedly *east coast* approach. Not that there's anything wrong with that, but New York elites have a habit of (intentionally and unintentionally) ruffling the feathers of non-New Yorkers. People outside the five boroughs listen, and even (sometimes) follow along. However, if homeownership (and homemaking) was going to catch on outside the cultural centers, the effort needed a champion who was a little…let's just say, midwestern.

Here's where we finally get to meet Dr. Crane.

. . .

Never heard of her? You wouldn't be alone. Des Jardins doesn't mention her, which isn't surprising, given her focus on Meloney, but neither do many of the books on first-wave feminism in the United States. If it wasn't for Loren Stack Moulds' University of Virginia dissertation in 2014, we might not know Dr. Crane at all. That's a shame. Because without Dr. Crane, we might not have the "down home" vision or "grandma's house" idea we see portrayed in literature, movies, and popular imagination. Let's correct that oversight and get to know her a bit better.

The woman who would become known as "America's Housekeeper" was born in Hudson, Wisconsin, in 1858. Unusual for women of her era, she attended college and married another doctor (Augustus Warren Crane, an early researcher of X-rays in medicine). She was a frequent traveler, and while in England, she worked on public sanitation. To put it mildly, she was *horrified* by what she saw in the tenements and slums. Given her training, she was acutely aware of the health implications of poor personal hygiene and inadequate public sewers.

When she returned to the United States (this time, taking up residence in Kalamazoo, Michigan), she dedicated her talent to addressing the sanitation problem in American cities. The queen of clean was born.

Her work drew national attention – not from Meloney, but from Hoover. As President of the Better Homes of America movement, he asked her to lead the event in Kalamazoo in 1924. His trust was not misplaced.[7] Dr. Crane created the winning model home, drawing 20,000 visitors.

Where Meloney focused on style, beauty, and experience, Dr. Crane focused on the practical aspects of home management. She also added more focus on churchgoing and faith – something the New York types tended not to bring up as often. (Dr. Crane knew her audience.) Her designs were workable, practical, and science-focused. As Moulds put it:

> Crane's focus on improving the physical conditions of the home placed her within a larger intellectual conversation concerned with sanitary science, home economics, and environmentalism. Writing about Crane's housing reform work in Kalamazoo, one contemporary believed that her work "was the result of the recognition of the profound influence which the physical home has upon the family."

In short: happy home, happy life. She crystallized her ideas of home economics and the impact a well-planned home could have on family under the broader concept of "*Euthenics*." Careful observers will note this word sounds quite a bit like *Eugenics* – the belief that traits received through heredity were deterministic. In other words, you were born that way, and there wasn't much you could do about it. Many of that day's scientists expanded that concept, layering it with racial ideas. Euthenics wasn't like that. If Eugenics was "nature," then Euthenics was "nurture." Through her observations, Dr. Crane saw that careful control of *environmental* factors

---

[7] That's not to say Meloney wouldn't have approved, but there's no evidence Hoover asked her. As a scientist, Dr. Crane had more in common with the engineering-trained Hoover.

was more important than heredity and background.[8] So the logic continued: improve the home, and you improve its inhabitants. Improving the inhabitants would improve the entire *nation's* health.

Also, unlike eugenicists (who tended to value theorizing over actions), Dr. Crane's euthenics movement put its effort where its mouth was. In her model home, she focused on the functionality and practicality of each room. She called it the "Everyman's House," which is a bit of clever marketing but also a misnomer. The home had much less to do with the every *man*, and focused instead on the every *woman* and her baby.

> [The home] was not a hobby, it was not an art project, it was not a trophy to show off to friends and enemies: it was a house meant to surround and protect and assist the average American mother in her twofold high calling of taking care of her baby and making a good and happy place for all the family.

Unfortunately, most homes weren't designed with that ideal in mind. (Dr. Crane didn't come out and say, "they were designed by *men*," but she implied it.) Those homes were poorly designed, and because of that, they encouraged inefficiencies and created clutter. The more time a mother spent taking unnecessary steps and cleaning up messes, was less time she could spend guiding and nurturing her children. Her model home corrected these errors, especially in the kitchen, where women spent much of their time in the 1920s.[9]

Contrast this approach with the "Has It beauty?" question asked in *The Delineator*. It's not that Dr. Crane didn't believe in an attractive home, but in her mind, *form* followed *function*.

One hundred years later, we might cringe at the portrayal of traditional gender roles, but that's not how people of the time saw it. More to the point, that's not how most *first-wave feminists* thought about it.

---

8   You can read more in *Euthenics: the Science of the Controllable Environment*, by Ellen Richards.

9   For example, consider the so-called kitchen triangle – sink, stove, and prep area. By arranging those three as a triangle, you simply need to pivot your body from one zone to another. It's not as efficient for mass production (as in a restaurant), but it's perfect for the home.

By carving out a defined role and unquestioned sphere of influence, Dr. Crane helped to create a power base for women in society. From that power base, other rights and privileges would be possible.[10]

According to Dr. Crane, one of the immediate areas of that expanded influence was a much more vital role for women in manufacturing, designing, and marketing products made for the home. If those products wanted a place in the home, and women were in charge of the home, then women should make the decisions. She encouraged women to speak up and speak out. As more women did, manufacturers of products for the home listened…or they found themselves out of business.

In many ways, Dr. Crane had just as much influence on what we see as "homemaking" today as Meloney. One focused on function; the other, form. So, why don't we know more about her? Was it because she was "midwestern" and didn't have connections in the literary arena? That's tough to say. She knew Hoover, after all. Was it too much practicality and not enough style? Maybe. Many "middle America" publications, even today, have huge audiences yet garner little recognition from the coastal presses.[11] But it was something more about her midwestern style and ethos. She wasn't loud. She was simply determined, no-nonsense, and got results. That approach doesn't often win awards.

...

Meloney and Dr. Crane's lasting impact on American life cannot be understated. By any stretch of the imagination, home ownership is central to American life. In 2020, over 65 percent of Americans owned their home – a number that climbs to nearly 80 percent in Maine and Minnesota. That's almost *double* what it was before the 1920s. Additionally, home products and building account for 15 to 17 percent of *all* annual American economic output. In 2008, the impact was so pronounced (in a bad way) that U.S. housing nearly brought down the entire *global* financial system. And yes, the legacy of redlining retains deep racial disparities,

---

10 She even worked on a screenplay of the homemaking experience. Although people loved it, the screenplay never made it to screen.

11 *Taste of Home* and *Good Housekeeping* are too excellent examples.

even decades later.

However, all of those overall statistics ignore the fundamental question: What was the impact of home ownership on the *individual* family?

For his part, Hoover's advice is good 100 years later. Most of the consumer choices we discuss in this book are small, but not this one. Americans of the 1920s needed to learn to make financially meaningful choices as well. It probably also stabilized communities. Owning a home probably did blunt the popularity of communism in the United States. That said, although homeownership rates *did* increase during the 1920s, they declined sharply in the 1930s, only recovering with the broad introduction of 30-year, fixed-rate, government-backed mortgages.

Meloney's focus on true happiness and beauty remains the guiding light of a strong family. We can argue with the details of her approach all we like, but a stable home life is one of the most significant predictors of long-term health, happiness, and success. We may not associate that legacy with feminism today, but it was one of its most enduring contributions to American life.

Dr. Crane had an important point as well. It's not all about style. A home needs to *work* for those who live there. Today, we're seeing more evidence that our home environment *does indeed* impact our physical and emotional health – the materials we choose (or don't, like lead paint), adequate airflow and ventilation, clean water, and effective sewage removal. If your home is sick, your family is sick. Our homes are as safe and healthy as they are because of Dr. Crane's legacy.

In the end, however, the true judge is…all of us. Did *we* make the right choice as consumers? Are our homes just places to put all our stuff? Sure, that's one way to look at it. But why do many elderly adults resist leaving their big house well after their families have grown up and moved away, and well past the point they can physically take care of them? The answer is obvious. That's because it's not about the house. It's about the *home*. A house is a physical place. A home is a set of emotions.

Hoover understood the house was essential for plenty of rational reasons, but it was Meloney and Crane who understood what a home meant.

PART 2
BABE

HOW CONSUMERS LEARNED TO CHOOSE INFORMATION AND ENTERTAINMENT

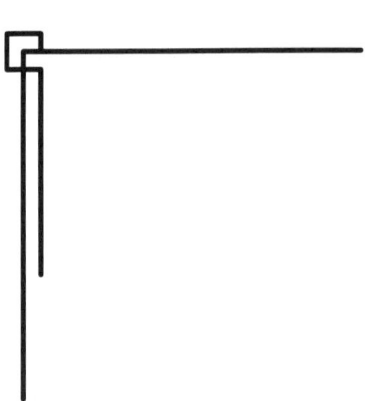

8
WHEN ADVERTISING GREW A PAIR

Wh13at makes a good testicle?

On the walk from his office in rural Milford, Kansas, to the outdoor pen where Dr. John Romulus Brinkley kept his bulbously-endowed herd of goats, the conversation surely drifted to gonad greatness. Did you want the largest testicles? Or paradoxically, were the smallest ones the most potent? Were aggressive goats more virile than their friendly cousins? Or was it more about a billy's impregnation rate? Or perhaps it's all about the average number of kids his nannies produced? So many questions. The good doctor seemed to have all the answers.

One imagines a process similar to selecting the victim for dinner from the lobster tank near the front of a seafood restaurant. But oh no, you wouldn't be munching on these salty balls. After selecting your prize (prizes?), both you and the unlucky billy would go under the knife. The billy's kid-siring days would be over, sacrificing his vitality to allow Dr. Brinkley to implant gonad tissue *into you*. And we won't discuss precisely where.[1]

Why on earth would anyone trust him to do that?

If you are a man of a certain age, you might have a sense of why you'd trek to Nowheresville, U.S.A., to ponder goat scrota. If not, let's just say that 1990s late-night advertisements didn't invent erectile dysfunction. Almost a century before the little blue pill hit the market, coy advertisers (like our new friend, Dr. Brinkley) used the newly-popular automobile to coin euphemisms to make it easier for embarrassed men to discuss their…"flat tire."

Dr. Brinkley was to medical doctors what Olive Garden is to Italian food. Still, just like chocolate lasagna, he did have a knack for understanding the desires of his target market. In the early 1920s, your mail-order

---

[1] I know what you're thinking. Dr. Brinkley would transplant goat reproductive tissue into a human testicle. Not exactly. The evidence we have (and it's limited, thankfully) indicates the implantation was performed somewhere north of home base. You can read all about it in *Hello, Everybody!: The Dawn of American Radio*, by Anthony Rudel. It's not the only place to find this story, but it's one of the best.

medical degree didn't matter.[2] Only results counted. And surprise! It worked! At least, people *believed* it worked.[3] Brinkley used testimonials from thrilled, erect customers (and their wives) to generate word-of-mouth advertising to build a thriving practice.

There was a problem. (No, not the obvious one.)

What happens when you've "cured" all the limp men within earshot of tiny Milford? It's simple. More people need to hear about it. Sure, you could advertise in newspapers, catalogs, and magazines, but those were expensive and impersonal. Finding the right words to convey the urgency and emotion of a customer's flaccid predicament was difficult. In the 1920s, there was a brand new answer to the problem of getting the word out: the radio. And what happens if there's no radio station in your area? You do what any enterprising testicle farmer does: You build one.

It might seem odd today, but in the 1920s, no one knew how anyone could make money on the radio. The brightest executives in the country (and even a future United States president) had no idea what to do. But a quack doctor in the middle of Kansas with an obsession with goat nuts sure did.

What follows is the story of the early days of radio – not the radio's invention or how its technology works, but how advertising came to dominate the new mass medium. It's *that* story that created the expectation that all media should be free, paid for by your local sponsor.

(Thankfully, this is also the end of our story about goat testicles. For now.)

. . .

---

2 The specific diploma mill in question was something called the Kansas City Eclectic Medical University. Only two of the five words in that name are accurate. Can you guess which two?

3 Before you sneak a scalpel into your local petting zoo, please read up on the "Placebo Effect" and buy the 25-cent goat feed pellets instead. The billys will thank you for it.

> The wireless music box has no imaginable value. Who would pay for a message sent to nobody in particular?
> – *Unnamed RCA executive, 1921*

Shilling quack medical procedures over the air wasn't the first idea on how to pay for radio. You'll be happy to know that. Plenty of intelligent people had other ideas, but as is often the case with *truly* new ideas, being smart isn't that helpful. What we think of as intelligence often masquerades as simply knowing how the world *currently* works. Often, the smarter you are, the less able you are to see new possibilities. When it comes to a new thing like radio, all of those smarts weren't worth more than a mail-order medical degree.

Let's begin this exploration of alternatives to goat nuts by picking on the very smart people at the Radio Corporation of America.[4] It didn't take long for the snappy engineers at RCA to shamelessly copy Henry Ford's efficient assembly line and ruthless supply chain management techniques. In a few short years, their factories began to disgorge radios by the tens of thousands, and then by the millions. And just like the Model T, the prices for shiny new RCA radios finally fell to the point your average household could afford one.

That was not an insignificant point. Radio certainly showed its value in World War I. Instead of guessing where your ships or troops were when they wandered out of sight, you could simply ask them. (Ask any military historian. Poor communication was a *literal* killer.) As is often the case with new technologies, hobbyists cobbled together Rube Goldberg-style contraptions in their garages to operate little "ham" radio stations of their

---

4   I'm leaving out plenty of detail about the history of the creation of radio and its technology because its not central to the story. If you want more, I'd recommend *The Early History of Radio: From Faraday to Marconi*, by Gerald Reginald Mansel Garratt, and published by the Institution of Engineering and Technology in the United Kingdom. The Brits not only know how to write a stellar technology book, they're also spectacularly obsequious with their names.

own.[5] In both cases – military and porky – radio equipment was expensive, hard to use, or both.

By contrast, RCA concentrated on making radio equipment for the home market, where the technical knowledge required amounted to (a) plugging it in and (b) tuning it to an existing broadcast station. In the 1920s, when both electricity and radio were new-fangled, vaguely scary things, that strategy made a lot of sense.

The trouble was, making a radio wasn't the hard part.

The problem is obvious if you think about it. Who wants to buy a radio if you'd hear nothing but static? Or worse, some weirdo rambling about his pet conspiracy theories. (If you think weirdos are a product of the modern internet era, they most assuredly are not.)

Faced with the prospect of selling what would amount to expensive footrests, RCA did the obvious thing. They got into the radio broadcasting business. By 1923, RCA operated three stations in the New York market and one in Washington, D.C. Most importantly, they began to produce their own programming so buyers would have something to listen to.[6]

There were problems from the start.

First, because of a licensing agreement from AT&T (who held essential patents), RCA couldn't operate a *commercial* radio station – aka *one that made money* – because AT&T wanted to keep that business to itself. It was AT&T that was actively experimenting with sponsored messages and syndicated programming, although those efforts were clumsy compared to what would come next. AT&T was on the right track, though, and it figured one-to-many voice communication (radio) seemed like a natural extension of its

---

5   The word "ham" was used in the 1800s to refer to railroad telegraph operators so incompetent or drunk (or both) that they caused train wrecks. Needless to say, being called "ham handed" with a telegraph machine wasn't a complement. Nonetheless, amateur radio operators owned the insult and adopted the term as their own. Pride in their bumbling heritage did not endear them to military types, who promptly shut down all non-military radio stations during the war to avoid a similar "train wreck" on the airwaves. It's hard to blame them.

6   If that business model sounds bizarre, it shouldn't. In the 1980s, Nintendo used the same strategy packaging the games *Super Mario Brothers* and *Duck Hunt* into their new Nintendo Entertainment System console. Otherwise, the NES was an expensive, ugly, gray paperweight.

existing one-to-one voice communication service (telephone and telegraph).

Second, building a radio station was expensive. (It *still is* expensive.) That's fine when lots of people are buying new radios because they don't have one, but it didn't take long for the competition to increase and the rate of new product acquisition to slow down. Fewer sales meant less money you could allocate for big construction projects.

However, the biggest problem was the *ongoing* cost. No, not upgrading equipment. That's easy. *Producing programming is hard.* Check that. Producing *good* programming that people want to listen to is hard. Check even that. Producing good content that people want to listen to *consistently* is hard. Manufacturers of radio equipment (namely, RCA) don't tend to be very good at producing the programming that aired on those radios. One task involves product design, electronics manufacturing, retailing, logistics, and supply chain. The other requires creativity, talent management, and scheduling. Could the same group of people do both? Sure. Will they be good at both of those things? Unlikely.

Let's use an example to make the problem a bit more concrete. Imagine you're a manager at RCA. You plan to sell 500,000 new radios next year at $50 each. You were willing to allocate five percent of your revenue to programming to give buyers something to listen to on your new radio. Your annual income is a cool $25 million. Multiply that by five percent, and you'll have $1.25 million to invest in programming for the year, or a little more than $100,000 each month.

That might sound like a lot, but it's not.

You're not simply paying for broadcast programming – which is expensive and challenging all by itself. You *also* need to build and maintain a radio station. Those expenses include facility construction and rent, high-dollar broadcasting equipment, even-more expensive equipment upgrades, maintenance of said finicky equipment, and technical staff to do the fiddling.

More to the point, investing five percent of revenue for a manufactured technology product was *not* sustainable over the long term. Profit margins tend to erode as new competitors enter the market. Most radio stations (including those owned by RCA) couldn't afford to be on the air for more than a few hours a day. Would people want to buy an expensive footrest that played scratchy programming for only two hours a day?

Bottom line: selling radios to pay for broadcast programming wasn't going to work. AT&T might have the right idea about sponsorships, but it's easier to charge money for one-to-one communication services (like the telephone or telegraph) because you know who the "one" and "one" are. On the radio, you only know the "one" (the radio broadcaster), not the "many" (the listeners).

If the underlying problem of broadcast revenue is finding enough to talk about, there's one group that shouldn't have a problem with that: the newspapers.

You'd think so, but you'd be wrong.

Newspaper magnates of that day liked *newspapers*. They enjoyed the written word. They produced articles through deep research and a deliberate editorial process. Radio, by contrast, was more akin to giving a 24-hour extemporaneous speech that you couldn't practice. Writers tend to *hate* that, and by and large, newspaper reporters and editors made terrible broadcasters. (It turns out that writing and speaking are very different skills. Who knew?) They simply couldn't see the point of broadcasting a story that you couldn't come back to and re-read later, or that they might not have time to get all the facts straight before they went on air, or that radio seemed like more performance than journalism. To be fair, they did see *some situations* where it made sense – natural disaster announcements come to mind – but they didn't like it.

Unfortunately for the ink jockeys, this was a horse race they wouldn't win.

In the 1920 presidential election that eventually elected Warren Harding, fresh-faced broadcasters at the newly-minted KDKA radio station in Pittsburgh announced state-by-state vote counts during an 18-hour marathon broadcast as the results came in.[7] A few months later, Newark-based WJZ would be the first to broadcast the 1921 World Series of Major League Baseball.

Despite these clear successes, newspapers saw radio as a threat. The newspapers saw themselves as the guardians of public opinion. They alone should decide how to interpret election results, not some pimply punk with a microphone. The results of a sporting contest might not command the attention of the "top" journalists, of course, but sports writers loved

---

7   Seriously. They had just received their broadcasting license a few days before their presidential results marathon broadcast. That's a pretty gutsy way to start.

the witticisms they could come up with during a few rounds of editing. Writers don't tend to be good on-the-spot people, and they were jealous that people would be repeating a clever expression made by a broadcaster in the moment rather than waiting for tomorrow morning's report on how they should feel.

Like it or not, given the choice of immediate or delayed gratification, most people fail the marshmallow test.[8] Newspapers would not make significant inroads into radio.

(If you're noticing a pattern about how existing types of businesses do not quite understand how to make new types of businesses successful, you're starting to catch on.)

Another idea involved charging people for subscriptions to radio services. That could work if broadcasters had some way to administer that process.[9] In the 1920s, sending bills by mail was expensive without automation equipment and software. And more to the point, who would you send them to? The person who bought the radio? What if they weren't listening? Or how about the 50 other people in earshot? Do they get to listen for free?

Yet another business model for radio involved envisioning it as not a business at all. In what could only make sense given the politics of the time, progressives like Commerce Secretary Herbert Hoover advocated for a tax on people who bought radios.[10] The government would then redistribute that money to broadcasters to be used for the public good. Although this idea would evolve into National Public Ratio (and the BBC

---

8   This was the now-famous (infamous?) test given by Stanford researcher Walter Mischel in 1972. The basic idea is that kids who could resist immediate gratification (*not* eating the marshmallow in front of them for a certain amount of time) would get a second marshmallow as a reward. The videos of the kids are hysterical. Subsequent experiments have challenged the validity of the test, but it hardly matters. Once results like this sneak into pop culture, they're like a mental tick in our collective consciousness. They're very hard to pull out.

9   Even in 2020, the biggest problem for subscription broadcaster Netflix is, you guessed it, password fraud. Or, as it's more gently known, password sharing.

10 It didn't help that President Calvin Coolidge told his progressive-minded Commerce Secretary Herbert Hoover to go suck a goat testicle if he thought he would sign a bill with a radio tax…in so many words. Given his penchant for brevity, Coolidge would have simply said, "suck it."

in the United Kingdom), it never quite captured a mainstream audience.

The solution wasn't going to involve adapting an old model to a new medium. You couldn't mass produce entertainment. That meant manufacturers didn't know what to do. You couldn't delay radio broadcasting until it followed a newspaper story. Why would you listen to something you have already read? That meant newspaper writers were flummoxed. And taxing radio was unworkable with 1920s technologies and politics. That meant the government could offer little help other than licensing stations.

No, the solution needed to address the unique qualities of radio as a new form of media. Whoever did that would win.

. . .

Radio is all about *time*.

If you want to listen to a specific program, you not only need to tune in to a specific frequency (station), you need to listen at a specific time. In the 1920s, recording and playback technology was decades in the future. Unlike a newspaper or magazine that might be read at different times by each reader over the course of the day, week, or sometimes month, radio is happening *right now* for everyone listening. If you don't tune in *now*, you miss it. Radio created a sense of urgency, immediacy, and shared experience no print media could match.

Even more importantly (and obviously), time is limited. While a newspaper or magazine can expand to fill the content available (within reason), a radio announcer can only speak so fast. The available broadcast schedule is celestially limited to 24 hours each broadcast day. In the early days of radio, when broadcasters barely filled a few hours, this wasn't a problem. But it didn't take long for content to quickly fill the available time. This forced an inevitable Darwinian evolution of broadcast strategy. To increase the variety of programming available, time slots shrunk. What began as multiple-hour programs condensed to single hours. Then half hours. Then quarter hours. Then minutes. Then *seconds*. Radio rewarded impact and brevity in a way print media did not.

Finally, time is mutually exclusive. Put very simply, if you listen to one station at a particular time, you cannot listen (easily) to another station at the same time. That difference is more obvious when you compare it to print media. There's no practical restriction on reading multiple newspapers to compare how different reporters covered the same event. You're limited only by the amount of time you'd like to devote to the task. Radio, by contrast, is a zero-sum game. Listen to the Cubs on WDAP (see Chapter 14), and you couldn't listen to "World of Chiropractic" on WOC (see Chapter 2). This forced radio producers to understand what their audience wanted to hear. Otherwise, they'd turn the dial.

Let's boil it down.

The new medium of radio required live attention, rewarded shorter and more impactful programming, and encouraged careful alignment with a specific audience. Print media of the day allowed you to read on your own time, rewarded depth of coverage, and served multiple audiences simultaneously. Is it any wonder most "smart" businesspeople of the day didn't understand what they were hearing? Does it make a little more sense now why a quack doctor with a goat fetish and a very motivated customer base understood radio better?

. . .

> This afternoon the radio audience is to be addressed by Mr. H.M. Blackwell of Queensborough Corp., who through arrangements made by the Griffen Radio Service Inc. will say a few words concerning Nathaniel Hawthorne and the desirability of fostering the helpful community spirit and the healthful, unconfined life that were Hawthorne's ideals.
> – *5 pm, August 28, 1922, on WEAF New York (the prelude to the generally agreed upon first radio advertisement)*[11]

If this doesn't sound like a modern radio advertisement, you're right. Mr. Blackwell took the mic from the announcer and went on for *ten full minutes* about the "high-grade dwellings" in Jackson park that featured "all the latest conveniences and contrivances demanded by the housewife." (Contrivances?) Blackwell might have characterized the woman of the house as petty and demanding, but he also implied the man of the house was a

---

11 This comes directly from the October 15, 1956, issue of "Broadcasting and Telecasting." Most modern recreations cut out the details because we wouldn't know what to think of a 10-minute ad. It's spectacular to have the details.

grade-A moron who "deluded himself" into thinking an outdoor life was only available by buying a home in the country.[12]

This was…not a good start for radio advertising. Hang in there. It'll get better.

But all this explanation of the basics of radio, and the academic quibble over what precisely was the first time someone paid someone else to advertise over the air, doesn't really answer the question of why it needed to be *advertising* that paid for the bulk of radio programming. To do that, let's look a little deeper at the practical implications for broadcasters. Again, it's all about time.

Here's a programming schedule from Pittsburgh radio station KDKA for Monday, January 23, 1922:[13]

10:00 to 10:10 am	Music
12:30 to 1:00 pm	Music
2:00 to 2:10 pm	Music
4:00 to 4:10 pm	Music
7:30 pm	Uncle Wiggily Bedtime Story from the Pittsburgh Sun and Music for the Kiddies, and Grown-ups who still enjoy them
7:45 pm	Special News, Government Market Reports, Summary of New York Stock Exchange, Weather Report
8:30 to 9:00 pm	Musical Program
9:00 to 9:05 pm	News (United Press Service)
9:05 to 9:30 pm	Musical Program
9:55 to 10:00 pm	Arlington Time Signals

Depending on how you add up the time noted in this schedule, the most generous estimate of total broadcast time is just over two hours. *For the entire day.* And KDKA was one of the more sophisticated radio stations in the early 1920s. They actually published a schedule. Many others

---

12 Here's an advertising tip for free: Insulting your audience usually doesn't make them want to rent your apartment. Let's just say that Brinkley never insulted his audience. His customer's flaccid penis was firmly in his mind.

13 From the January 22, 1922, issue of "Radio Broadcasting News," published by KDKA, in Pittsburgh.

did not. (It makes a bit more sense now that Mr. Blackwell could insult potential apartment buyers for ten whole minutes, doesn't it? He had time to spare.)

Do you notice something else? How compelling is it to drop the equivalent of a month's wages on a new radio for two hours of programming interrupted by odd gaps of dead air?[14] Until 7:30 at night, an ill-timed trip to the bathroom meant you'd miss most broadcast windows. Radio stations were under pressure to make that (significant) investment worth listening to. Otherwise, the naysayers would be right. Radio would fade away, like pole sitting and mahjong – other fads from the era.

Part of the answer seemed obvious. Radio was an audio medium. Musicians make sounds. And more to the point, they *make money* with those sounds. Perhaps they would pay the radio station to broadcast a short performance in the hopes that a certain number of those listeners might purchase a ticket to attend a live performance. That was the same idea behind early baseball broadcasts at Wrigley Field, as we'll see in Chapter 14.

How would you set the price for that advertisement?

You might ask how long a musical performer needs to play to convince people to attend a live performance that night. Is it 60 minutes? 30 minutes? 10 minutes? Even less? Each of you (the broadcaster and the performer) is incentivized to select the shortest possible time that results in the maximum number of people attending the live show. You might also consider shared benefits. As the broadcaster, you'd benefit from the advertising revenue and the music's inherent entertainment value. As a performer, you'd benefit from more exposure and higher live event ticket sales. As a listener, you'd get to "try before you buy." Win. Win. Win.

However, that's not a consistent source of revenue if that performer doesn't have a live performance happening right now or if baseball is out of season. It's a good idea (that's still used today), but there simply aren't

---

14 Full disclosure. When I was a in Kindergarten in the late 1970s, I *loved* airplanes. In my parent's copy of *TV Guide*, I noticed a program titled "Off the Air." In my 5-year-old mind, that was a potentially cool show my parents wouldn't tell me about… probably because it was on overnight. I couldn't stay up until midnight when it started (I tried), but maybe if I got up at 4 a.m. I could catch the last hour. I actually set an alarm to wake early for several days until I realized "off the air" was not a program. I still love planes, but not quite enough to watch television static before dawn.

enough musicians and baseball games to pay the bills.

Radio needed a bigger pool of potential advertisers. Luckily, the explosion of consumer products provided the answer. They had all the incentive in the world to use the radio to sell their products – and even better – they were not dependent on a live performance.

To explain how it works, let's return to goat testicles.

Let's say Dr. Brinkley sells a quack medical procedure.[15] He knows the radio station can reach 10,000 people in a given range of its signal. Only five percent of those people (50) are potential customers; of those, two percent (1) will come to his clinic. Savvy math people will see that's one person out of 10,000, which, if you talk with savvy marketing and advertising people, is a reasonable proportion of the target audience you can expect to purchase this.

Let's also assume that our friendly neighborhood quacker makes $500 each time a patient goes under the knife. He knows that for every $50 he spends on advertising, he makes $500 from the one patient who walks through the clinic door.[16] In marketing speak, we say his promotional budget is 10 percent of revenue.

That, in a nutshell, is how media advertising works.

Sure, there are caveats.

Our quack can't know if all 10,000 people will be listening during that 10-minute window, so he'll negotiate a package of time slots – perhaps 20-30 shorter repetitions of his message within a few days – to ensure he catches everyone in his target audience at least once.[17] If you ever wondered why so many broadcast messages seem repeated ad nauseam, now you know why.

And because time is money, and he's dividing his 10 minutes into 20, 30-second time slots, he won't have enough time to explain all the details of his procedure. He'll learn (through trial and error) which specific, punchy messages are the most memorable and, most importantly, bring

---

15 Kids, please don't try this at home.

16 There's some debate on the actual price. You'll see references to $500, $750, and other figures. It hardly matters, does it? A $500 price makes the math a little easier in the example.

17 The magic number of repetitions in advertising usually is seven times. That's a rule of thumb, not physics, but it tends to work.

in the largest number of new patients. If you ever wonder why messages compete for laughs or shock value, now you know why.

Finally, because certain programs appeal to certain audiences, our quack will carefully study which programs his audience is most likely to listen to, choosing only *those programs* to sponsor with his messages. The better he is at this, the more efficient his advertising budget becomes. For example, suppose he can tune his advertising to just the right message to just the right audience, and by doing so, he gets two people to show up at his clinic instead of one. In that case, his cost of advertising drops from 10 percent of revenue to five percent of revenue. That's a big deal. If you have ever wondered why certain products get advertised during certain programs, now you know why.

In Dr. Brinkley's case, he owned the radio station as well. In the early going, he would ramble on and on about goat balls. But it didn't take him long to realize his audience's testicle attention span was limited, and he started filling his programming day with music, news, and religious programs. Eventually, entertainment programming crowded out *infotainment* programming, even on the station that gonads built.[18]

As the 1920s progressed, the tango between radio and advertising became so intimate they might as well be copulating. In practical terms, advertising led to more money. More money led to better production values for programming. Higher quality programs led to a greater variety of programming to appeal to ever-narrower audiences. A greater variety of audiences meant extending the length of the broadcast day. Better (and more) programs made listening to the radio more exciting, and the purchase of one easier to justify. More people with radios created more reasons to advertise to them via the radio.

All major formatting types sprang to life in the 1920s as part of this positive feedback loop: call-in advice shows, debate programs, sports broadcasts, sports commentaries, cooking shows, morning talk shows, and dozens of other variants and concepts. As radio stations competed for listeners (remember, you can only listen to one radio station at a time), Darwinian competition refined and improved programming quality.

On the advertisers' side, bigger audiences and better programming

---

18 Infomercials are still a thing, but they tend to only get broadcast when few other advertisers are buying.

increased per-minute rates. As the rates went up, they faced pressure to measure actual results. Calls to action (visit this store!) became more common. Demographic surveying got so much better during this era that advertisers often knew more about who lived in an area than the government did. And advertising got more creative so people wouldn't go to the bathroom during commercial breaks.

For its part, RCA realized managing *this business* was wholly unique from running a manufacturing and technology business. In 1926, when AT&T decided to throw in the microphone and get out of the radio business, RCA bought up its assets. Alongside General Electric and Westinghouse, it created an entirely new kind of broadcasting company: the plainly-named National Broadcasting Corporation, or NBC.[19]

Blessedly, quacks like "Doctor" Brinkley found themselves crowded out by big-name advertisers with much deeper pockets. That's good, of course. But it's also bad. Those ads must have been a hoot.

...

> It is therefore primarily a question of broadcasting, and it becomes of primary public interest to say who is to do the broadcasting, under what circumstances, and with what type of material. It is inconceivable that we should allow so great a possibility for service to be drowned in advertising chatter.
> – *U.S. Secretary of Commerce Herbert Hoover, speaking at the first radio regulatory conference, 1922*

The "Great Humanitarian" and progressive lion of the 1920s didn't stand a chance. Although Hoover would use his tremendous organizational and negotiation skills to craft some of the first broadcast spectrum regulations, he was powerless to prevent consumer culture from dominating radio and its future evolution.

To be fair, the demand outstripped everyone's ability to keep track of it.

By the end of the 1920s, the number of radio stations went from single digits to over 600. Over 60 percent of all U.S. households owned at least one radio in their home – many more than one – and that didn't

---

19 ABC came later.

count radios blaring in public offices or private businesses.

The radio business model, at its core, hasn't changed much in the past century. The same dynamics are at play, albeit with a higher level of sophistication. In fact, as print media advertising in newspapers and magazines has declined, audio/visual advertising has *grown*. Radio advertising still accounts for about 14 percent of *all* advertising spending in the United States, or about $10 billion annually, despite the growth of digital advertising platforms, including search engines and social media.

Radio also formed the foundation of the television business model in the 1940s and 1950s – with precisely the same dynamic leading to the rapid adoption of television with ever-better and more sophisticated programming production quality. Digital media followed the winning formula as well. Search media (mainly Google) and social media (mainly Facebook) adopted and improved the business model with ever-better ways for advertisers to measure their impact.

However, given the popularity of cable television and the explosion of streaming media services, it would be tempting to believe that the advertising-centric media business model was falling by the wayside in favor of a return to subscriptions and pay-per-view.

It's not.

In 2020, advertisers supported mass media producers to the tune of $250 billion. By contrast, Netflix, the largest ad-free, subscription-based offer, only raked in $31 billion – a number that is shrinking as its consumers now have several choices in streaming services. Several of those services, Netflix included, offer "advertising-supported" versions to compete on price. Cable television still earns about $80 billion, but the number of subscribers has remained stagnant for years, their revenue growing only when they raise their prices. Satellite radio is growing, but it has struggled to reach the $10 billion mark – oddly enough, about what traditional radio earns.

Add it all up, and advertising pays the bills for most media by a margin of at least *two to one*.

To say that consumers prefer advertising-supported media because they "like free stuff" snobbishly misses the point. Listening to the radio, watching television, browsing the internet, or enjoying social media isn't *free*. Consumers not only understand that they need to purchase their preferred media consumption gadget, but they also know that advertisers are paying the bill. Generally, they don't mind. People may *say* they don't like advertising killing their buzz, but when asked to pay up to escape it, most won't.

The true reason the advertising-supported media idea is so powerful is that consumers are making a conscious trade: ever-better free entertainment in exchange for the low, low price of learning about a product or service you might want to buy.

Are there problems? Sure. Sometimes advertising leads to reality television, hour-long infomercials for healing bracelets, and perfume that smells like a celebrity's vagina. But it also helps produce epic television programs, communication technology straight out of a sci-fi movie, and the totality of the world's knowledge behind a simple search box.

For the past 100 years, consumers have called that a fair deal.

9
AMERICA'S FIRST EQUAL OPPORTUNITY EMPLOYER

Imagine being 25 years old.

Since the age of seven, when your parents separated, you've traveled regularly from tiny Little Falls to giant Washington, D.C., with your father – a Congressperson representing Minnesota's 6th District – in an age when most people never ventured farther than a few miles from home. You grew up idolizing him and his public lifestyle. He was a staunch isolationist in an age when speaking out against the government (and its involvement in Europe's "Great War") would certainly get you censored, and could even land you in jail.[1]

While your father railed against the war, you couldn't help being fascinated by that war's most eye-catching innovation: the airplane. It was barely a decade since the first powered flight at Kitty Hawk, and already, it was changing the face of modern warfare. What else might the airplane mean? As a young (but worldly) man, the idea of flying was an irresistible tonic.

You decided to follow that dream.

Next, you did the unthinkable. In your single-engine aircraft, you crossed the Atlantic Ocean. Non-stop. *Alone*. Your tiny single-propeller plane left New York on May 20, 1927, and landed in Paris the next day. You flew for thirty-three and a half hours and just over 3,600 miles with no stops, no breaks, and no hope of rescue should anything go wrong.

That's what it was like to be Charles Lindbergh.

The story of the flight is fascinating, even if you're not an airplane geek, but what came afterward might be even more important than crossing the ocean by yourself, one propeller away from certain death.[2]

President Calvin Coolidge awarded Lindbergh the Medal of Honor, the highest military decoration in the United States, along with the

---

[1] Charles August Lindbergh, father of the more famous son, published pamphlets and books critical of U.S. war involvement. Federal agents confiscated his manuscripts and destroyed the printing presses. They were published only after the war. Were you thinking this couldn't happen in the United States? Think again. Democratic president Woodrow Wilson vigorously enforced wartime censorship laws.

[2] The biographer A. Scott Berg wrote what many argue is the best treatment of the subject in 1998. The appropriately titled, *Lindbergh,* won the Pulitzer Prize. Did you know Lindbergh also invented a perfusion pump, was a staunch environmentalist, and remained (like his father) suspicious of American intervention in foreign wars?

Distinguished Flying Cross. The next president, Herbert Hoover, appointed Lindbergh to the National Advisory Committee for Aeronautics in 1929, which jumpstarted air mail and passenger air travel. *Time* magazine named him the very first "Man of the Year."[3] Lindbergh received too many parades and local awards to count.

Lindbergh's honors weren't limited to the United States. The French President made him a member of the *Légion d'honneur*. Even the defeated Germans loved him, and that brings up a sticky topic we need to cover before we move on…the part about Lindbergh being a Nazi. That's not hyperbole. President Franklin Roosevelt thought so (and *said* so) to his advisors.[4] Despite FDR's frustration (which probably had more to do with Lindbergh parroting his father's anti-war rhetoric), you already have all the clues to suss out the truth.

Here's the backstory. The American military command was under no illusion about Germany's intentions in the late 1930s. Although the country resisted involving itself in another European war, military planners needed to understand the strength of the German military in general, and its Air Force, specifically. But how would they get the intel they needed? Well, one idea would be to send the guy Herman Goering (yeah, *that* Herman Goering) desperately wanted to meet.

Lindbergh did as asked, gathering military intelligence from a foolish Goering too starstruck to hide anything. To be fair, Lindbergh *was impressed* with what he saw and told his American counterparts so. The gotcha was the little surprise Goering had in mind for the after-banquet. On the orders of the Führer himself (yeah, *that* Führer), Goering presented Lindbergh with the Iron Cross.

Let's pause for a moment. Remember, Lindbergh is not yet 30 years old. Adolf Hitler is handing you that country's highest honor. If you don't

---

3   Until 1999, *Time* used "Man" or "Woman" of the year. After that, they switched to "Person" of the year. Sometimes, they've also named unnamed people, inanimate objects, and even planet Earth.

4   When you read Lindbergh's speeches about how the British "race," the Jewish "race," and the Roosevelt administration were pushing America towards war, you can hardly blame FDR for questioning the aviator's loyalty. Lindbergh did, however, fly multiple Pacific missions as a sort of quasi-civilian. When you realize he's simply taking after his father, his "loyalty" is less questionable than his tact.

accept it, would they get...upset? The Nazis weren't the type you wanted to make upset. Short story: Lindbergh took the award because his American handlers hadn't expected it, he didn't know what to do, and no one wanted to create a diplomatic incident.

The problem with the whole Nazi sympathizer image is that when Lindbergh returned, he wouldn't toe FDR's interventionist line. He saw communism (the "Asiatic threat" as it was known at the time) as the bigger deal. Lindbergh thought it would be better to have Hitler's attack dog pointed toward the Soviet Union rather than the West. If the Jews were in the way, Lindbergh argued, they should get out of the way. They weren't America's concern either. He gave sold-out speeches to that effect.

With more than 100 years of hindsight, we might question Lindbergh's positions, but ask yourself a question: What decisions would *you* have made in your mid-20s being the most famous person in the world? Was Lindbergh a bit naive? Sure. Was he an anti-Semite? It sure seems so. Was he a eugenicist and race purist? You bet, but no more than Margaret Sanger (who we'll meet in Chapter 19) and a *solid majority* of Americans at the time.

Lindbergh had no idea what he was getting into, and he wasn't alone. The 1920s created the first truly modern celebrity – a list that included Louis Armstrong, Albert Einstein, Coco Chanel, Henry Ford, F. Scott Fitzgerald, Babe Ruth, Al Capone, and dozens of others. Had there been "notable" people before? Sure, but this was different. Before the 1920s, famous people were usually politicians, wealthy industrialists, or military leaders. They had experience being "notable" and the baggage that came with it. Lindbergh was utterly different. He was just an average kid from Minnesota who did something really, really, outstanding.

This is the story of the creation of the modern celebrity and how Lindbergh happened to be in just the right (wrong) place at just the right (wrong) time.

...

Definitions of celebrity prove elusive.

Celebrities draw our attention for so many reasons that it's difficult to pin down what makes a celebrity a celebrity. People are endlessly fascinating, but that hardly seems enough. On the one hand, they have a story arc to their lives that mirrors ours. They are born, grow up, lead an adult life, grow old, and eventually pass away. That's where the similarities end. Sometimes, they're born into a notable family. Other times, they're child prodigies. Sadly, those child stars often flare quickly and fade just as fast (or even more sadly, they die young). Exceptional individuals, like Charles Lindbergh, achieve the impossible. Yet other times…well, we just don't know what makes them so appealing.

We can name celebrities, and when prompted, we can even recall groups of them at a time – notable athletes, musicians, or political pundits. But that's identification and categorization, not a definition. Simply being able to recall the names of 12 movie stars doesn't tell us why we remember those names and not others.

Pressed for more specifics, we next assume those people (like the movie star names we just came up with in our minds) must be people with "positive" characteristics. They wouldn't be famous if they weren't physically attractive or artistically talented. If we're being charitable, we could extend that reasoning to count prominent scientists or civil rights activists as celebrities.

However, that logic falls apart quickly. We can probably think of just as many famous serial killers as we can Nobel laureates (sadly, probably several more). Even if reality television stars don't run around slitting throats and keeping body parts in their freezers, we all can agree that the positive-negative talent continuum doesn't seem to help us define celebrity.

What we seem left with is that celebrities are famous people. That's not only a pretty flaccid description but also circular reasoning. Synonyms are not definitions. For our efforts, all we've done is describe a group of people with shared characteristics. It's like we looked at everything with feathers and wings and said: We'll call those things 'birds.' It's helpful but doesn't tell you much about how feathers or wings work.

We can do better, but we'll need to rely on some concepts from consumer marketing to help.

. . .

Oddly enough, the trouble comes when we think of celebrities as people.

They might bear a passing resemblance to the rest of us, but they're not people. (Just to be clear, there's a person under the metaphorical mask, so don't go around stalking them.) The modern celebrity is a carefully-cultivated mirage. They are *products* made for our consumption. When we shift to that perspective, we can look to the product development process as a way to understand how one might create a celebrity from scratch ingredients.

In product development, we look to three co-equal criteria a new product must meet to succeed in the marketplace: desirability, feasibility, and profitability.

Desirability is obvious. People have to want it. Not everyone needs to like the new product or service, of course, but *enough* people need to for the effort to be worth the trouble. Feasibility simply means that you can *actually* make the product. People might want a flying car, but if the technology doesn't exist to build one, desires don't matter. And finally, profitability means more than simply making money; it's about *sustainability*. You're not truly profitable if you can't make enough money to reinvest in product improvements, run out of scarce resources (raw materials or talent), or act so recklessly that the government shuts you down.

No part of the three-part equation can be missing. If a product is desirable and feasible, but not profitable, no one will want to go through the trouble to bring it to market. (Usually, those are the products and services we must rely on governments to deliver.) If a product is feasible and profitable, but not desirable, no one will buy it. That's the classic "build it, and they will come." *They* rarely do.[5] And finally, if a product is desirable and profitable, but not feasible, you have a flying car.[6] You need to wait for technology to advance, fund basic research, or learn the aerodynamics of ground effect flight yourself.

How does this relate to celebrity as a consumer product?

Social science researcher Sharon Marcus makes the same case we did, except with different words. In her research, a celebrity is the joint combination of the person, the public, and the media – all three elements must

---

[5] The 1989 movie, *Field of Dreams*, gave voice to this cautionary business parable.

[6] Companies such as ASKA might disagree that flying cars are not feasible. As of this writing, they might be right, but they're only talking about the technology. Regulatory feasibility matters too, no matter what Uber and Lyft might say. Given average driving skills displayed on American roads, do you want those same people flying airplanes?

be present. To make her point, she asks us to consider the obvious: Many people who "should be" famous simply aren't. Think of a top physician whose surgery success rate is off the charts, an engineering team that completed a major public infrastructure project, a scientist who cracks the genetic code, or artists who fail to find an audience during their lifetime. (Or even horrible people who simply commit ordinary crimes.) In this book, we'll meet Cy Avery in Chapter 20 and we met Clarence Birdseye in Chapter 3. Within certain circles, people knew them, but they weren't household names.

Simply doing the right things isn't enough to become a celebrity. Marcus makes the point well below. She debunks the fallacy that the media can create a celebrity out of thin air:[7]

> Publicists, marketers, and entertainment industries are not omnipotent kingmakers. Stalled campaigns abound. If relentless publicity alone created celebrity, then every one of the many songs that ever benefited from payola[8] would have become a major hit, and every heavily promoted actor would be a star.

How many failed attempts do we see by the media to prop up an artist, an athlete, or even a business leader? Most of those effects flame out. To become a celebrity, the person must have the right "stuff" for their area of expertise – musical talent, athletic ability, or business acumen. The public must see value in it – not everyone, but at least a critical mass. And the media must be incentivized

---

7   *The Drama of Celebrity*, by Sharon Marcus, is probably the most readable book on the subject. Most academics take sick pleasure in making exciting things as boring as possible. If you're into that, or having trouble getting to sleep, try *A Short History of Celebrity*, by Fred Inglis.

8   Payola is the (illegal) process of paying a radio station to play a particular song more than they otherwise would. Marcus is making the point that simply exposing the public to crappy music won't make the artist famous. Despite conventional wisdom, pop artists who endure are actually quite good.

to amplify it – and those reasons must not include legal (or illegal) bribery.

Now that we know how to manufacture celebrities, let's start building them.

. . .

Let's start in the natural place: the people themselves.

It's a common trope that celebrities are mindless, vapid shells of people whose only skill (if you can call it that) is to do outrageous things to get *and keep* the public's attention. There is no shortage of past and present examples, and you've probably got a bunch on the tip of your tongue. Let's briefly ignore people like Neil deGrasse Tyson and Celine Dion. It's evident to most people that Ph.D. astrophysicists and Grammy-winning singers have some "worthiness" behind their "celebrity." No, the people we're thinking of fall into what many derisively call "Kardashian" territory.

To her detractors, big sister Kimberly Noel Kardashian is nothing but a reality television star who wasn't content with simply winning the genetic lottery, augmenting her good looks with lip injections and butt enhancements. She then "accidentally" released a sex tape, married another celebrity – Kanye Omari West, aka Ye[9] – had four kids, named them North, Saint, Psalm, and Chicago, divorced Ye, and (reportedly) had the butt implants removed in a never-ending disgorgement of publicity stunts.

Hmm. You can agree or disagree with the validity of each of those so-called publicity stunts – that reality television doesn't require acting talent (it does), that she should not have had sex on camera (why do you care?), that Kim Kardashian should not have married Kanye West (why not?), she should have named her children something "normal" (what's normal, exactly?), that she shouldn't have divorced her husband when the couple had small children (do *you* know her reasons?), or that she should not have had plastic surgery (then, who gets to?). However, it must be clear that these decisions were not random. They were a planned series of engagements with the public that created an image and persona that served (and continue to serve) Kardashian's interests.

How well served? In 2022, at age 41, Kim Kardashian was worth nearly $2 billion. In her 30s, she started a line of clothing for the now-defunct

---

9   Aka Yeezus, Saint Pablo, Yeezy, and Louis Vuitton Don.

Sears, the Kardashian Kollection, which brought in $600 million in 2013. She owns the Kardashian Beauty cosmetics line, Kardashian-branded tanning products, and the boutique-line DASH with her sisters. She earns nearly $1 million when she posts for another brand on her Instagram account.

You can call Kim Kardashian many things, but stupid is not one of them. (Crazy like a fox comes to mind.[10])

In her book, Sharon Marcus pushes back on earlier scholars who made the circular argument that "celebrities were well-known because of their well-knownness."[11] It's not true now, and it certainly was not true as celebrity culture heated up in the 1920s. We've already seen that with Charles Lindbergh. The seed of the celebrity *must* be something special about the person. It can be looks, talent, or accomplishment, but it's not "nothing." If you don't see it, you might not be the right "buyer" of that particular celebrity's value.

. . .

Who is that buyer? That brings us to the second critical part of the celebrity formula: desirability.

The public needs to want to "buy" what the celebrity is "selling." The people who criticize Kim Kardashian's success aren't typically those who read fashion magazines, watch reality television, or buy cosmetics. *Her target audience* gets it. By contrast, Kardashian's fans probably don't

---

10 Let's not go down the road of why so many people call Kim Kardashian (and others like her) stupid, vain, shallow, or promiscuous. It's too easy to say the root cause is sexism. Deploying that argument shuts down broader debate. It's like asking if you've stopped beating your spouse. That's not to say there is *not* an element of sexism; it's simply that those explanations blind us to the three-part harmony of why celebrity is so effective.

11 If you're curious, she's referring to cultural historian Daniel Boorstin, who wrote in 1961 that the "hero created himself; the media created the celebrity." Marcus' point is that Boorstin overplayed the role of the media and the driving force. Yes, the media creates a catalyst, but the other two ingredients must be there. And yes, Boorstin is trying to make a distinction between the "right" kind of notable person (the hero) and the "wrong" kind (the celebrity). If a hero wins in the forest, and no one is there to hear him, did he really win? We can debate that philosophically, but not economically. If no one saw him do it, the hero does not exist.

understand why nerdy men get a science erection when they watch Neil deGrasse Tyson on public television. Those contrasting perspectives help point out that the public can have multiple "desires" for different classes of celebrities.

The appeal could be as simple as a celebrity's opinion on relevant matters of the day. For example, both Coolidge and Hoover saw Lindbergh as an expert in the early field of air travel. But there is something less than satisfying about the "expertise" explanation. Both Lindbergh and the field of aeronautics were young, so there wasn't a deep bench of gray hairs to call on. Additionally, Lindbergh wasn't the only person with expertise in air travel a president could have called to the White House. However, can you name *any other* famous pilots of the 1920s? No? One suspects neither could a president.

The simpler explanation is that Lindbergh's accomplishment added an air of credibility to the new field of air travel that no one else could bring. Presumably, someone who understood how passengers embarked and debarked, like a train operator, would be a more critical team member. And presumably, those people were involved as well. But no one remembers them now, nor cared at the time. Lindbergh's star power made air travel seem real (and, more importantly, attainable) to the average person.

Lindbergh was the first person to show government and business leaders how to harness the public's positive associations with a celebrity and link those to their policy initiative or product offering. At first, it seemed relevant that the endorsement should be something related to the celebrity's *raison d'etre* – think of professional golfer Tiger Woods endorsing a brand of golf clubs. But it didn't take long for business leaders to discover that the celebrity's positive halo effect meant the association hardly mattered – think of Woods endorsing Buick automobiles.[12]

The relationship provided a positive feedback loop. In the past, a celebrity might have limited opportunities to cash in on their notoriety. Fifty years before, Charles Lindbergh might have landed a cushy job somewhere, but that's it. A great entertainer might have been able to sell concert tickets, but not much more. Endorsements not only helped the celebrity earn extra money, but they also helped keep the celebrity's name

---

12 For more on the social psychology of why this works, read *Influence*, by Dr. Robert Cialdini.

front and center with the public.

Celebrity appeal involves more than an expert opinion or regular exposure. As Marcus puts it, we want to have some connection with the celebrity, although we know we're not going to have a *personal* relationship. Celebrities are exciting because they're like us *and* more than us. That mix of closeness and distance is critical.

Every celebrity who wishes to remain a celebrity must master this balance. That's why you can buy a Kardashian cosmetic, buy her clothes, or follow her on social media, but she won't follow you back. That said, there's something more than just the celebrity themselves and the careful balance they need to strike with their adoring fans. Without the media as a catalyst, celebrities could never achieve mass market appeal.

...

Think of the media's role with celebrities the same way you think of the advertiser's role with a product. Their job is to amplify.

It might surprise you that most celebrities aren't as rich as a *modestly* successful Wall Street investment banker or a *reasonably* successful small business owner. When we talk about the media's role in making celebrities profitable, we're not talking about the celebrity earning money themselves – although many do, and some (like Kim Kardashian) become quite wealthy, but it's not a requirement. When we talk about profitability, we're talking about the *media's* profitability.

It's critical to understand that all media require a sustainable business model. That was just as true for newspapers or radio stations in the 1920s, as it was for television stations in the 1950s, as it was for internet sites and social media platforms in the 2000s. Even so-called "public broadcasting" outlets require significant supplements to their taxpayer-driven income, usually in the form of memberships and sponsorships.

With that perspective in mind, it's not difficult to imagine the following trade-off: The more money you invest in high-quality programming – original dramas, investigative journalism, and the like – the less money you make. In a nutshell, that's why the media *loves* sports programming, game shows, and reality television. They're cheaper to produce. *Far cheaper*. But the most inexpensive programming, by far, is celebrity coverage.

Celebrity gossip coverage requires none of the skill of creating dramatic programming. Anchors don't even need to know anything about a particular sport. In the 1920s, media outlets learned that all they needed to do was send some schmuck with a notepad and camera to follow a celebrity around and wait for them to do (or say) something.[13] Nearly anything would be "newsworthy" because the public is endlessly interested in seemingly trivial things done by famous people. Celebrities work hard to ensure they wear the right clothes, shop at the right businesses, and say quotable things. If those choices are controversial, all the better. Bad choices keep people talking.

Although it's not what Lindbergh had in mind when he toured Luftwaffe HQ in Germany, public discussion of his (purported) Nazi sympathies led to no end of press coverage in the United States. While all evidence suggests that he wanted nothing to do with that perception, a modern celebrity coach would advise him to keep that debate going in the media as much as possible. Without media coverage, public attention can wane. That's especially true as other celebrities (not to mention more serious concerns) vie for limited public attention.

For good or bad, simply being seen is a celebrity's primary job. That's why most celebrities are keen to keep themselves in the public eye – if they don't, their ticket sales drop, merchandise sales evaporate, and speaking gigs dry up. That's why many "accidental" celebrities quickly discover they don't want to live under a microscope and crack under the media's harsh light. Children are especially vulnerable, and the history of child stars is heartbreaking.

However, too much attention isn't necessarily a good thing. All celebrities risk *overexposure*. We can understand that better now. What makes a celebrity exciting and appealing to us is the balance between accessibility and distance. We want someone we can relate to, but not so much that they lose their specialness. The media, for its part, wants to expose celebrities as much as possible. Some media even specialize in celebrity coverage – tabloids are the most notable, whether they're online, in print, on air, or some combination of those. It's cheap and easy programming.

The trick for celebrities, then, is managing the *right* amount of

---

13 In 2020, it's even easier. All you need is a smartphone. Or even easier, you grab social media footage that *someone else* captured with their smartphone. Some reporters never even need to leave their desks.

distance. Those who get it right have long careers. Those who don't risk flaming out. Or worse. In Lindbergh's case, his overexposure led to the kidnapping and murder of his child. Had he been just "anyone," it's unlikely that would have happened. That's why celebrities today invest (heavily) in security services and often lock themselves behind sturdy gates unless they're putting themselves on display on purpose.[14] Many people scoff at those precautions as another example of vanity, but it's like wearing a hard hat on a construction site. An I-beam might not hit you on the head each day, but when it does, you want to be wearing that helmet.

Marcus sums up the three-part balance perfectly:

> Because publics, members of the media, and celebrities themselves all actively shape what it means to be a celebrity, their contests are too evenly matched for their outcomes to be easily predicted. That unpredictability makes celebrity culture a suspenseful, interactive, serial drama. Though the drama of celebrity has momentary winners and losers, its contests never definitively end; the resulting suspense keeps millions engaged.

. . .

Why were the 1920s so catalytic for celebrity culture?

It wasn't simply that the public had access to *more* media choices but that those new options were more engaging and exciting. Radio and movies were *richer* and *hotter* media than newspapers and magazines.

In the book, newspaper, and magazine era, printed sheets of paper could discuss the exploits of famous people to a mass audience – or, at least, an audience who could read. But think about that experience. Unless the writer included a direct quote, it was a bit "removed" from the experience of hearing the person speak those words. If this is a tough distinction to grasp, imagine only getting Kim Kardashian's words quoted in a printed newspaper along with a poorly-lit black and white photo. Not

---

14 Most celebrities have assistants that do all the "ordinary stuff" for them – groceries, coffee runs, school drop-offs, everything. It's sort of a sad life when you think about it. Most people want the kind of celebrity that you can turn on and off. On when you want a great table at an exclusive restaurant. Off when you just want to sit on the beach on vacation. Unfortunately, you can't have it both ways.

as compelling, is it?

Imagine then what a mind-blowing experience it would be to hear Charles Lindbergh's voice on the radio for the first time. Reading is one thing. Hearing him brings him that much closer. You hear the tone and tenor of his voice, the unique way he pronounces words, and how he pauses for effect. Imagine you can see Lindbergh live in a newsreel or motion picture clip. You can see how he stands, how he carries his body, and how he gestures when he speaks.

As the 1920s went on, radio ownership exploded. Movies with sound quickly displaced silent films. The media landscape became much more exciting.

In 1986, scholars Richard Daft and Robert Lengel described Media Richness Theory. The basic idea is that media that engage more senses are *richer and hotter* than media that don't.[15] Richer media carry more information, and therefore – so the theory goes – can communicate faster and better. Books, newspapers, and magazines are on the cold side – they communicate only through the written word and a limited number of photographs. Radio is a bit warmer, mainly because it's broadcast live, but there are no photos and little opportunity for audience feedback (call-in shows notwithstanding). Films are even warmer media because of the moving images, even though they're not live (adding sound to silent films was a big deal).

Celebrities learned quickly in the 1920s how to take advantage of the newer, richer media. You wanted your media hot, *but not too hot*. Strategic distance is vital, and these new media were perfectly suited to that task. Radio and movies allowed celebrities to craft a compelling image without appearing *too accessible* to the average person.

When you add a cultural environment brimming with new opportunities for extraordinary people to thrive, a consumer culture ready to buy all manner of innovative products and services, and a hotter media landscape, all the ingredients are in place for an explosion in the number

---

15 Oddly, they never "wrote the book" on their theory. Ah, the good ol' 1980s. These days, researchers routinely leverage novel research findings into a book, companion training course, live seminars, and consulting. If you saw what academics are paid these days, that shouldn't surprise you. When you read the theory, they show live, one-to-one, in-person communication at the pinnacle of the "rich and hot" scale. For our purposes, we're leaving out those media because they're not as relevant to 1920s-era celebrities.

of diverse people who became celebrities in the 1920s. If you were going to design a social science experience to create celebrities, you could hardly pick a better time.

The positive feedback loop between personal ambition, public appetite, and media access spurred demand for ever more celebrities to fill the gap. That, in turn, opened the door for people who otherwise would not have had the opportunity to become famous. Anyone could now become a celebrity – White men, yes, but also women, Black Americans, and people from diverse immigrant groups. However, as the opportunity for different types of people expanded, the "scripts" those celebrities could use on their path to stardom narrowed. By the end of the 1920s, our modern concept of celebrity had crystallized.

Let's make it more concrete with some examples, including a few we've already mentioned.

Let's start with Charles Lindbergh. He's followed the "accomplishment" path to celebrity status. His claim to fame was that he did something everyone thought was impossible. Fast forward a few decades, and Neil Armstrong and Buzz Aldrin would find fame on a much longer trip. Mary Lou Retton did it in the Los Angeles Olympic Games in 1984. What happens after that magic moment is up to them. They can fade into obscurity or leverage that achievement into something more.

F. Scott Fitzgerald and his wife, Zelda Sayre, were the original "power couple." Their script is different – the two people are a unit, and what's most interesting about them is their relationship. There have been countless examples since then. Sonny Bono and Cher come to mind, and we've already mentioned Kim and Kanye. Power couples can follow two paths. They can become a power couple after they join forces. Fitzgerald and Sayre followed that script; neither was *that* well-known before they married. In the second, two existing celebrities can merge into a more-compelling single unit. Kim and Kanye followed that path.

Although they could have become noteworthy before the 1920s, military and political leaders created their own celebrity scripts in that decade. Herbert Hoover was the first in a long line of celebrity politicians – larger-than-life people whose influence far outstrips their time in office or official capacity.[16] Charisma matters in this script, as does a desire to cultivate the limelight. For his part, Hoover's celebrity status catapulted him into the White House, and then the same forces dragged him through the mud as the Great Depression got going. Eleanor and Alice Roosevelt were good examples (although they didn't much like each other.) Douglas MacArthur also suffered from the Icarus problem, flying too close to the sun and getting fried (and fired) by President Harry Truman in 1951. Chelsea Clinton and Ivanka Trump follow the same script today.

Henry Ford created the modern business celebrity. The script here requires the (perceived) success of your namesake company.[17] People forgave Ford for all kinds of weird stuff – like controlling workers' book choices, what religion they practiced (he hated Jews), and restricting all alcohol use (even before Prohibition). Elon Musk follows the same playbook today. He can get away with crazy stuff (planning for Mars, tweeting strange things) because he's seen as a successful businessperson.

There are so many more.

Both men and women can follow the sex symbol script. That's related to, but distinct from, the "fashion icon." Celebrities of any gender can follow that script. (We'll meet Coco Chanel in Chapter 22.) Babe Ruth was the first "sports star" celebrity – a script that dozens of men and women of all races would follow for decades. Along with sports, the musician was one of the easiest (and most profitable) scripts for Black and other minority groups to adopt. It's the one place you'll recognize more Black names than White or Asian ones. We'll meet more of the musicians in Chapter 12 and talk about Black culture's influence on entertainment. Even the most complex subjects could become accessible through the power of celebrity. Albert Einstein was the original "popular scientist," a script that involves making science easy to understand for the average person. (Though it would take decades for more than a handful of people to truly understand the theory of general relativity.) Author Edith Wharton wrote *The Age of Innocence*, becoming the first woman to win the Pulitzer

---

16 One could argue Teddy Roosevelt was the template for the celebrity politician, but he didn't have radio and movies to boost his image. It's nearly certain he would have used them.

17 This helps explain why Donald Trump remains a business celebrity even though the objective financial results of his namesake brands don't quite measure up.

Prize for literature in 1921, and writing the "writer" script along with other notables such as Earnest Hemingway. Perhaps most strangely, even criminals could become celebrities. Al Capone was the first of the modern "gangsters." He was the first admitted criminal to truly understand how to court a "Robin Hood" persona in the media to his advantage. Bonnie and Clyde were a 1930s power couple/gangster combination.

This narrowing of celebrity scripts is a direct result of increased public demand. Paying attention to a new celebrity takes work; people have limited attention spans. It's easier for celebrities and the media to follow an existing trail rather than blaze a new one. In other words, in the three-part celebrity formula, it's the *public desire* that's the true driving force. Celebrities are popular because *we want them to be popular*. Celebrities are diverse because *we want them to be diverse*. Celebrities are compelling because *we want to see ourselves in them*. Celebrities and the media simply give us the tidy storylines we're asking for.

Ambitious people didn't create the modern celebrity. Hotter and richer media didn't create the modern celebrity. *We created the modern celebrity.*

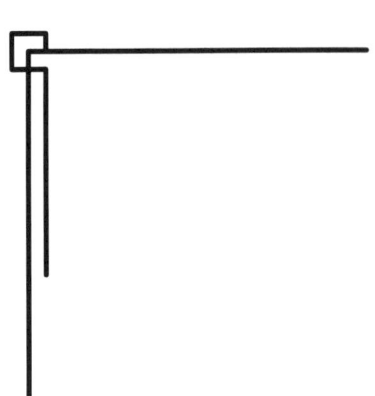

10
SUBSCRIBING TO CULTURE

D id you know that Shakespeare sold cigarettes?

It's true.

In the early decades of the century, packs of John Taylor Tobacco Company cigarettes depicted a famous character or scene from one of the Bard's plays. Not to be outdone in the promotional goodies department, the folks at Ty-Phoo Tea took it up a notch. In each box, you might find a playing card featuring Olivia from *Twelfth Night* – an artist's rendering on the front and a brief character sketch on the back. (They're quite beautiful.[1]) In the high-brow arms race, chocolatier Whitman's took culture-in-a-box to its peak. Purchase a special-edition assortment of you-never-know-what-you're-gonna-gets, and you might find a full-length, leatherbound (albeit pocket-sized) Shakespeare play. Today, all you're likely to get is diabetes.

Between the end of the Civil War and the outbreak of World War I, all kinds of people read classic literature. It was a sign that you, as a middle-class American, were cultured and sophisticated.[2] That's why tobacconists, tea-makers, and chocolatiers used Shakespeare in the 20th century like we might use Shakira in the 21st. They increase sales.

In 1919, Emanuel Haldeman-Julius and his wife, Marcet, decided to go one step further. Out of their tiny publishing house in Girard, Kansas, they published the "Little Blue Book" series. The idea, born of their socialist leanings, was to make the classics accessible to the average person.[3] They produced cheap paperbacks with stiffened blue covers because it was the most affordable way to fashion a durable booklet. (It still is.) At 3.5 x 5 inches, they were small enough to fit in a shirt pocket. They fan-

---

1   That wasn't a bad strategy in the 1920s. There were many more cigarette and tea brands than there are today. Anything that could differentiate your brand of cancer sticks or bland American tea was welcomed. You can buy originals on eBay and Etsy. And yes, baseball teams stole this idea for playing cards.

2   Before the 1900s, people read the classics regularly, attended plays based on those works, and generally enjoyed them. Then, academics came along and decided there was a "right way" to appreciate these works – coincidentally, *their way*. Literary academics are, for the most part, completely insufferable. Janice A. Radway's book, *A Feeling for Books: The Book-of-the-Month Club, Literary Taste, and Middle-Class Desire*, is deeply informative but falls into this same trap.

3   Socialism and communism were bigger deals in the 1920s.

tasized that the proletariat would read according to his abilities and buy according to his needs.

Emanuel and Marcet probably didn't like what happened next. Advertisers are the consummate capitalists, and it didn't take long for one of its best and brightest to combine two good ideas into one *even better* idea.

Harry Scherman, a middling copywriter from the J. Walter Thompson advertising agency, combined the variety of Little Blue Books with the snazziness of Whitman's leather into his "Little Leather Library." Adding in one more good idea, he decided to sell them through the mail like Sears. It would have been *four* good ideas had he come up with a better name, but c'mon. Three out of four ain't bad. That's an even better ratio than Meat Loaf.[4]

It took a collaboration with business partners Max Sackheim and brothers Charles and Albert Boni to lock in that fourth good idea. No, not a better name. Instead, they came up with one of the most effective sales pitches in history: "30 Great Books For $2.98." Or, about ten cents a book. It was so popular that the team sold *40 million* copies in their first five years. It wasn't long before Scherman and his partners founded their own marketing agency devoted *only* to selling books.

However, that level of success wrote its own tragic ending.

Many aspiring middle-class Americans wanted a handsome, leatherbound library of classics on their shelf. And yes, there were plenty of newly-arrived immigrants who would buy the books as a symbol of acculturation. (Whether they read them or not wasn't the point, as we'll see.) But although those are *mass* markets, they're not *infinite* markets. Scherman and his crew risked running out of customers.

What do you do when you sell a shelf of leatherbound classics to everybody who wants one?

. . .

Even a "middling" copywriter at J. Walter Thompson was smarter than

---

[4] Two out of three ain't bad…RIP Michael Lee Aday.

the average bear.[5]

What made Scherman special, however, wasn't his advertising writing skill.[6] He was a keen observer of culture and human behavior, and in the 1920s, he knew that it was changing. Part of that was rapid urbanization – a shift from a disconnected, rural, agrarian life, to a centralized, bustling, chaotic city life. Instead of culture determined by deep tradition and religious observance, the culture shifted to something more cosmopolitan. In practical terms, that shift created the paradox of city life: On the one hand, people surround you in a way you'd never experience on the farm. On the other hand, the sheer number of people gives each person (who's not a celebrity, see Chapter 9) a degree of anonymity they wouldn't experience otherwise.[7]

Imagine you're a rural boy from Kansas making your way to Chicago for the first time. You came from a tight-knit Catholic community where you were expected to inherit the family farm, marry the girl down the street, and produce future tithers. But through a twist of fate, you've moved to the city. No one knows who you are, and frankly, no one cares. Cultural opportunities engulf you – people living different lifestyles, wearing spectacular colors, cooking exotic meals, and practicing odd religions.

You probably read about mass production as part of the Industrial Revolution, but what surprises you most isn't simply the material possessions; it was the number of varieties of the *same* stuff. It wasn't merely that you might see an automobile for the first time, mass-produced clothing, or frozen food. It's that you would see multiple makes and models of cars, a full spectrum of clothing styles, and even competing brands of frozen peas.

After initial disorientation, you realize that you're now free to create a

---

5   He's only middling because of the place he worked. Scottie Pippen was an outstanding basketball player for the Chicago Bulls in the 1980s, but when you were on the court with Michael Jordan, even Pippen looked average. JWT produced some of the best advertising talent in history; many of its campaigns are unrivaled, even today. See Chapter 17 for examples.

6   Which happened to be better than his literary skill (he toyed with becoming a novelist). Which was even better than his knock-off Keynesian economic ideas. He wasn't quite a Renaissance Man. Scherman was more like a Renaissance Fair man. That might seem a little harsh, but you haven't read his books.

7   Those same insufferable academics refer to this concept as "modernity."

life you imagined for yourself. *Any life at all.*

Let's use our friendly farm boy to continue the example. We'll call him Westley.[8] After a few weeks in the Second City, he goes by "Wes," and he's ditched the pope. In his hometown, he would have been lucky to own two outfits of clothes – one for everyday work and one "Sunday best." In Chicago, without *il Papa* to please, Wes could visit the local haberdasher to select the styles that spoke to him.

How did he know what his clothes would say to him? Easy. He listened to what those clothes said about the multitudes *around him*. Like every big city of that era, Chicago featured role models on parade. Wes watched, learned, and created a new version of himself. Your *possessions* could define the *person* you are. For the first time, the place you were born or your family history did not define your identity.[9] Through your consumer choices, you could decide who you wanted to be. Bringing the discussion back to books, *reading* the classics wasn't the point. *Having* the classics was the point. That was Scherman's insight.

But that didn't really answer our question, did it? Once you sold a fancy set of classic books for every Westley in Chicago to keep on his mantle, what then? To answer that question, we need to take a detour to understand a little about the realities of publishing.

. . .

Being a new author is challenging in three unique ways.

The first challenge is the obvious one: writing. Not only does that require a command of the grammar rules and a broad vocabulary (doubly difficult for anyone learning a new language), writing requires a sense of style and grace. Yes, using active voice is important to be learned. You can remove, omit, and correct needless and superfluous words. You can even learn to literally use the word literally figuratively. But rules can't tell you when to break the rules – because when we break the rules, we create

---

[8] If you don't get the reference, you're not a Gen Xer. Watch *The Princess Bride*. It holds up. You'll understand why Westley's transformation in this example makes sense.

[9] Race and gender would come later, and that's still a work in progress. That's the point. Identities aren't fixed in time or space.

impact.[10] For most people, creative writing ranks near public speaking in the category of *activities to be avoided*, and very few ever attempt it.[11]

It gets tougher.

The next challenge is publishing. That process not only involves formatting the book into printed pages with a cover, table of contents, chapter headings, and page layout, but also includes production logistics: securing copyrights, setting a price, and deciding how many to print. Publishers front those costs for the author because most promising artists are not independently wealthy. Before on-demand publishing services such as Amazon's Kindle Direct Press, publishing costs were prohibitive, necessitating an elaborate gate-keeping process. This system of literary agents and acquisition editors ensured (and for the big houses today, still work to ensure) a high quality standard.

Wait a second, you say. There are *sooo* many crappy books out there, even from reputable publishing houses. Why is that? That brings us to challenge number three: promotion. In other words, how many books will an author sell? Or, more to the point, because the publishing house bought the rights to the book, how many can *they* expect to sell?

That question is easier to answer for series authors, and that's why you see so many of them. If you bought the first, second, and third *Harry Potter* books, you're likely to purchase books four, five, six, and seven. (You'll probably buy the extra goodies too.) Celebrities also are a good bet – whether they wrote the book themselves (unlikely), whether they had it written for them (more likely), or whether it's about them (very likely). That presents a chicken-or-egg problem for first-time authors who aren't yet household names. Editors work hard to sense which books will be good, but it's more like astrology than any hard science. It's full of smart-sounding guesses and intellectual voodoo. Even with today's publishing data, predicting a hit is nearly impossible. In the 1920s, it was *entirely* impossible. Mostly, publishing companies do their best to screen out the obviously-poor books, take their best guess based on how other

---

10 You may have heard of artificial intelligence software that can write by itself. The resulting writing feels "artificial" because it's following rules. Good writing follows rules. Great writing breaks them.

11 Yes, Amazon makes *publishing* a book easier. No, it doesn't make *writing* a book easier, and it certainly doesn't make them better.

books in the same genre sold, and hope for the best. If a teen vampire thriller just sold 10,000 copies, the next one probably will too.

The three-part reality of rare (good) writers, high publishing costs, and sales uncertainty leads to a risk-averse, insular culture where the offering of new books is surprisingly similar to what you've seen before. Now you know.

If Scherman was going to do better than the major publishing houses, he needed to come up with a better idea for a chicken dinner than an ugly paradox.

. . .

> [The Book of the Month Club] establishes itself as a sound selector of good books and sells by means of its own prestige. Thus, the prestige of each new title need not be built up before becoming acceptable.
> *– Harry Scherman*

The secrets to Scherman's success were hiding in plain sight…if publishers only stopped to notice them.

At first glance, it might be tempting to think that the cost of the book is the problem, but the dollar value is rarely the issue. With the growth in disposable income and lower printing costs, nearly everyone could afford books. No, the problem is a different kind of cost. The first is risking the social stigma of buying and reading a book not approved by your circle of friends and family, or that creates a social image for yourself that is embarrassing.[12]

People reliably bought books in a series or picked up books from famous (or infamous) people because they knew what they were getting. That sense of certainty lowered the perceived risk of choosing a new book and enhanced the image of the person buying it. By owning a specific book, you signaled to your social group that you shared interests with them, even if you didn't (actually) read it.

The other risk is *time*. Reading a book isn't like skimming a new article in a magazine from an author you haven't heard of. Long-form reading

---

12 It's the reason many people today won't admit to reading romance novels. That aside, bookstores would go broke without the romance genre.

takes a commitment to enjoy – especially for complex non-fiction and long fiction epics. With dozens of other entertainment options, including movies, radio, amusement parks, and new products, a new book is a risky (and, frankly, less exciting) entertainment option. We enjoy novelty, of course, but only to a point. If you haven't heard of the author, and one of your friends hasn't recommended it, or you're embarrassed to open that kind of book, you aren't likely to give the new book much attention.

Yes, publishers can purchase advertising for a new author, but that's expensive. Worse, for every dollar a publisher spends to build the name recognition of an unknown author, that's one less dollar they make on the book. Most books (then and now) don't make back the initial advance they provide their authors.[13] That's the hard truth.

Buying a book meant trusting its author.

But what if Scherman could sidestep that problem? With the Little Leather Library, readers didn't need to know *all* the classical authors. They might know most of them, but there were undoubtedly a couple on the list they didn't recognize by name, even if they were familiar with the general storyline. In this case, people weren't trusting a specific author. They trusted the Little Leather Library to curate a group of classical books. Scherman's new idea for his "Book Club" would make the same shift for newly-published books.

Did buying a book now mean trusting the curator? Not exactly.

Instead of boosting the profile of specific authors, Scherman focused on the selection committee – the "eminent experts" who would identify the best books. Although the people he chose for the committee were qualified, Scherman understood that it wasn't important precisely who they were, or even what books they chose. The most crucial qualification seemed to be a lack of condescension for people who bought "coffee table books" – people who bought books for what they said about themselves,

---

13 An "advance" is a set amount of money provided by the publisher to the author in exchange for rights to publish the book. Authors earn royalties on books, but only *after* the initial advance has been "paid back" through book sales. In a simplified example, let's say the author received a $1,000 advance and will earn $1.00 in royalties for each book sold. In order to begin seeing a royalty check, that book must sell more than 1,000 copies ($1,000 divided by $1.00). This may surprise you, but most books don't sell more than a few hundred copies.

not necessarily for their literary value.

Assuming the selection committee remained non-snobby, it was more important that the committee chose books predictably and consistently. Remember, people were buying the *idea* of experts selecting books for you, not the specific experts (that would simply mean building the reputation of the selector) or even the specific books (that would simply recreate the same problem the publishers faced).

Scherman's innovation was that buying a book meant trusting the *process*.

It was a great idea, but it begged the question: What books would they choose?

. . .

The second leap of faith would transform a good idea for a "book club" into a transformative innovation: the "Book *of the Month* Club."

It's obvious in retrospect, but in 1926, literary folks (grudgingly) accepted that while you could sell *classic literature* through the mail, you could not catch the same lightning in a binder with popular books. Classics had an established "brand" – they were already known and respected, making them as much a status symbol as something you read for pleasure.

Here's where Scherman's advertiser mind kicked in. He understood intuitively (and through experience advertising new products) what publishers of the time did not: People crave new things, but they're sometimes afraid to crack the spine of a new novel. He solved that problem by transferring the needed trust from the book's *author* to the book's *curator* to the book club's *system*. There was no longer any reason to limit the selection of books solely to "classic" titles. Any new book would do; plenty of them were available, and new ones were published all the time. The curation board would have dozens of books to choose from each month. They could afford to be choosy.

What's more, as incomes rose, people were spending more on many types of consumer products, and books were no exception. Between 1898 and 1916, the average American household spent $4.41 on books. Between 1922 and 1929, that figure more than doubled to $9.02. In other words, people not only had the money for books but also demonstrated they were willing to spend it.

If all this seems obvious, it's only because of hindsight bias.

Buying things through the mail was established, but very few had thought of buying products through the mail *each month,* the same way you might subscribe to a newspaper or magazine. That was new. That was the big idea.

Here's where it all comes together: the Book of the Month Club asked people to *subscribe* to an *ongoing fee* where they would be mailed a book selection by an expert panel each month.

Think about that from the *consumer's* point of view. Each month, you have something to look forward to. Everyone likes the pleasant surprise of receiving a gift, and part of that joy is not knowing what it might be. And it's not a *scary* not knowing; it's an *excited* not knowing (that's the critical difference) because you trust the person giving you the gift. It's like Christmas in your mailbox every month.[14] The Book of the Month Club transformed the book into a "gift-like object," adding something beyond its pure literary value.[15]

Subscribing to the Book of the Month Club meant you could purchase cultural status. You need no longer worry about carrying around some untested book. You were a member of a club that guaranteed you were reading the best there was to read. If there was a conversation about the new hot thing, you could know you were in on it. If you hadn't read the book yet, you knew that you had it on your shelf and could get to it anytime. Sometimes you read it. Sometimes you didn't. It was important just to have it.

You *could* read it, though, and many did. Subscribers wanted books that were relatable but sophisticated, and intelligent without being insulting. Curators needed to carefully balance high-brow and low-brow choices

---

14 Or probably more like Hanukkah. The Jewish festival of lights features more gift-giving days.

15 This is one of advertising expert Dr. John Eighmey's turns of phrase. He's part of the reason for this author's fascination with advertising history.

to skate a razor's edge of *middle-brow* culture.

. . .

The Book of the Month Club's subscription idea transformed its business value for Scherman and his team.

Recurring revenue (otherwise known as people paying each month) ensured a certain predictability and stability in cash flow. From a practical perspective, they knew how many books they would need to ship to subscribers each month and could easily calculate the cost to buy the books, package them, and send them through the mail. Additionally, Scherman knew how much he could pay his curation staff, and even when to get them additional pre-reading assistance as the number of books reviewed increased.

Most importantly – *and this is a critical part* – as the number of subscribers increased, the *cost per subscriber* decreased. To illustrate the point, let's use an easy-math example.

Imagine you had 5,000 subscribers who paid $10 each month. For that, each subscriber would receive five books in the mail. Assuming $1 per book, your monthly cost to deliver the books was $5, and your monthly profit was $5. So far, so good. Let's say you also needed to pay seven curators at a monthly rate of $1,000 each, for a total monthly personnel expense of $7,000. (To keep this easy, we'll ignore other overhead costs.) To summarize, with 5,000 subscribers, you'll earn $50,000 each month. Your expenses include $25,000 monthly for the books and $7,000 monthly for the curators' salaries. Do the simple math, and you'll earn $18,000 in monthly profit. Divide $18,000 in profit by 5,000 subscribers, and you get an average profit per subscriber of $3.60.[16]

Got it? Good. Now let's rerun the example with 50,000 subscribers.

If you're a savvy businessperson, you'll probably negotiate better per-unit costs for books, postage, and mailing supplies. Instead of $5 per month per user in costs, now it's $3.50. Rerun the math at the same monthly subscription price. That equals $500,000 each month in revenue against only $175,000 in costs. You probably won't need additional

---

[16] In the subscriber business today, we commonly use the acronym ARPU (Average Revenue Per User) – in this case, we're calculating APPU (Average Profit Per User).

curators because once you've selected books for the month for 5,000 people, you don't need more curators to choose books for 50,000 people.[17] Let's save you the trouble of finding your calculator and cut to the answer: $6.36 per subscriber, or nearly double the profit margin.

This is *the single reason* subscription business models are so powerful. Like mass production approaches, economies of scale reduce costs. However, unlike most other manufacturers, subscription services have predictability that other product manufacturers rarely enjoy. For other manufacturers, the sales clock started over at zero each month. The Book of the Month Club started each month knowing exactly how much money it would make.

. . .

Put very simply, the idea worked *spectacularly* well.[18]

Within its first year of operation, the Book of the Month Club exploded from 4,750 subscribers to 46,539. (Hence, the relevance of the financial illustration above.) Despite that, many experts – notably those in the snooty circles in publishing – predicted book clubs were a flash in the pan. Scherman was an advertising person, not a literary expert. His experts weren't the *real* experts. The books they chose weren't the *best* books. They were – *gasp!* – books the average person would want to read.[19]

That's not to say Scherman and crew didn't need to make some changes.

When you signed up for the Book of the Month Club in the early days, you got the books they picked for you. That was that. The entire idea was that you did *not* get to make a selection. That was the point. You abdicated that choice to the experts so that you could rely on their judgment.

---

17 Of course, that assumes you've only curated *one* group of books. As the Book of the Month Club grew, Scherman and his team added to the curation staff to review and select different sub-groups of books. But for this example, the general principle holds.

18 In her book, Radway uses the phrase "disconcertingly well" instead, which says more about her point of view. Words matter.

19 If you're continuing to get that feeling that experts struggle when it comes to periods of intense change, you're catching on.

If subscribers could make choices, it would defeat the purpose and make the logistics of running the operation much harder. Management couldn't know how many copies of each book they'd need each month, opening up the company to supply chain delays, printing problems, and higher per-unit costs.

But what if readers had a *little* choice? Could the Book of the Month Club provide options for its subscribers *and* maintain its profitability?

Max Sackheim, one of Scherman's trusted lieutenants, came up with the idea for the *negative option*. Instead of simply receiving a set of books in the mail each month, subscribers also would receive a postcard featuring *next month's* selections along with a brief review.[20] If they chose to, subscribers could return that postcard and *opt out* of a particular book selection. If they did nothing, the entire book selection would arrive as scheduled.[21]

Scherman, for his part, understood the benefits immediately.

It not only gave subscribers some say in what they would receive, but paradoxically, it gave the business even *more* predictability than it had before. If a higher proportion of people than average rejected a particular book selection, the curation team would have a way to gauge public interest not only for that specific title and author, but also for other similar books in the same genre. The ability to gauge interest *before* the sale is critical intelligence to improve the selection process. Over the intervening decades, Scherman would incorporate more people with marketing and advertising experience, in addition to those with literary backgrounds, into the curation team. Yes, "expert" literary editors would look down their noses at the Book of the Month Club process, but by now, you should be able to see that criticism for what it is: sour grapes.[22]

The Book of the Month Club built a business system that balanced

---

20 Yes, this meant that the selection committee needed to work ahead to make their choices, but only by about a month. It wasn't a big deal.

21 You see this at work all the time. It's the same reason rates for retirement account contributions are higher when structured as *opt-out* rather than *opt-in*.

22 If you wonder why experts don't get listened to, expert authority only tends to work if they don't show disdain for their audience. There's a lesson in there somewhere. One wonders if experts will learn it.

literary excellence with consumer tastes. When you're trying to create something that appeals to the broad middle, this is the balance you must strike.

...

Over its nearly 100-year history, the Book of the Month Club sent more than 570 million books to its subscribers. It was one of the largest wholesale buyers of books, making it a force to be reckoned with in the business of publishing.

More than simply an economic success, the Book of the Month Club jumpstarted the careers of some of the most notable American authors to peck at a typewriter. The Club's very first selection was Ernest Hemingway's first novel, *The Sun Also Rises*. Other notables included *Gone With the Wind* by Margaret Mitchell, *The Catcher in the Rye* by J.D. Salinger, and *By the Rivers of Babylon* by Nelson DeMille – at the time, each was largely unknown to the general public. The curation team passed on *The Grapes of Wrath* and *All the President's Men*, but even the negative publicity of a missed choice kept people talking. As an advertising person, Scherman would have understood that all attention is good attention.

For all its success, the Club's second half-century in operation hasn't been as kind as its first 50 years. After a merger with Time, Inc. that seemed to make sense in 1977 (see Chapter 18 for a better understanding of why), subsequent moves did not. After the marriage with *Time* soured, the Book of the Month Club stumbled through multiple owners and reincarnations, finally ending up as part of the portfolio of a private equity firm as of 2022. This story is unlikely to have a happy ending. Private equity firms do not have a strong track record of building strong companies.[23] They're sort of like capitalism's cockroaches.

The rise of big box bookstores in the 1990s, and their ability to offer massive discounts on hardcover books, made the core idea of the Book of the Month Club decidedly less appealing for both consumers and investors. It didn't help that later management got rid of the judges'

---

23 Thomas Levenson's *Money for Nothing: The Scientists, Fraudsters, and Corrupt Politicians Who Reinvented Money, Panicked a Nation, and Made the World Rich* retells the story of the so-called "South Sea Bubble" in the 1700s. So, yeah. Cockroaches are hard to kill.

panel concept entirely in 1994 and handed the selection process to the marketing team alone. That move shattered the delicate balance that provided credibility to selections. If there was no judge other than popularity, what's the point? You can buy popular books far cheaper at the "Walmart of Literature" down the street (aka Barnes & Noble) or the "Walmart of Literature" online (aka Amazon).[24]

However, to see the Book of the Month Club's legacy as revolutionizing book sales, creating the middlebrow genre, and jump-starting American authors misses the shelf for the book.

It's all about *subscriptions.*

No, it's not about copycat subscription services like the Columbia House Record Club that started when Scherman's company sold out to Time, Inc. Since then, the subscription business model has evolved into much more than books and music. Although, to be fair, purchasing subscriptions to books, television, movies, and games is *the way* much of that is purchased today, overtaking DVDs and even Apple's brilliant $0.99 per song iPod and iTunes combination. As you might have guessed, the true catalyst for the broad adoption of subscription services was something business people call "reducing logistical friction," and everyone else just calls "the Internet."

It didn't take long for entrepreneurs to expand the definition of media to include software of all types – the sorts of software that run desktop applications such as word processing and spreadsheets, but also (and more importantly) the kinds of big-business software that manage vast databases of financial information, medical records, and telecommunications. They take advantage of the same benefits Scherman enjoyed 100 years ago, mainly the consistent, monthly revenue stream. That predictability means the software developer can continue to update, patch, and improve the product as long as people keep buying it. And they need to. Because if people decide the software no longer meets their standard, they'll simply

---

24 Walmart, Sam's Club, Costco, and Target got into the popular book game too. They're some of the biggest buyers now, especially with Borders gone. The biggest bookseller is Amazon, of course.

cancel their subscription and choose a competitor.[25]

Running a subscription business is like running on a treadmill. You can never stop.

Despite the risk of getting thrown off the back of a piece of figurative gym equipment, the allure of the subscription muscle beach is strong. You can subscribe to fashion (clothes in a box), personal care (shaving in a box), dinner kits (food in a box), and pleasure (sex toys in a box). That's just to name a few. In 2021, the "subscription economy" (which covers everything from dishes to dildos) reached nearly $75 billion annually. It almost doubled in 2022 to $120 billion, and it shows no signs of slowing down. By the decade's end, it almost certainly will pass $1 trillion, and it will account for five percent of *all* economic activity.[26]

If you're so inclined, you can even buy an annual subscription to "Shakespeare in a Box" from an independent bookstore in Paris. The Bard must be proud. At least it's not cigarettes.

---

25 In the subscription business, that's called "churn." Watch a financial analyst report from Netflix and you'll hear the word tossed around a lot. Now you know what it means.

26 This number comes from a 2022 report from The Business Research Company and several other sources. Their predictions should be taken with a grain of salt, but the growth rate – otherwise known as CAGR – seem to support the claim.

11
THE FIRST DISTRICT COURT OF PUBLIC OPINION

In the dramatic final scene of the 1960 film, *Inherit the Wind*, famed defense attorney Henry Drummond (played by actor Spencer Tracy) picks up a copy of Charles Darwin's book *On the Origin of Species* in one hand and a copy of the Bible in the other. Wordlessly, he weighs the two books against each other, slaps them together under his arm, and walks out of the courtroom.

The symbolism was clear: Both books deserve our respect, albeit for different reasons. Darwin's book represents science and progress, whereas the Bible instructs us on morality and faith.

However, this 1960 movie adaptation of the so-called "Scopes Monkey Trial" in 1925 plays fast and loose with the facts. For starters, none of the key names are the same. Defense attorney Henry Drummond? In the actual trial, his name was Clarence Darrow – one of the most recognized lawyers of the 1920s. The movie's prosecuting attorney was Matthew Harrison Brady. In 1925, it was William Jennings Bryan – a name you might remember from American history class. And the movie's defendant, schoolteacher Bertram Cates? You might know him better as the namesake of the real-life trial: John Thomas Scopes.

In addition, the movie created new characters and motivations from whole cloth. For example, Scopes didn't have a fiancé; Cates did. Unlike the fictionalized townspeople, Dayton, Tennessee residents welcomed journalists flooding into town, and the real-life Bryan wasn't as unyieldingly fundamentalist as his "Brady" portrayal. When asked, co-writer Jerome Lawrence was unapologetic. His purpose wasn't a historical retelling of the Scopes trial of the 1920s, but only to serve as a backdrop to critique the hostile anti-communist climate of the 1950s. He altered the details for dramatic effect.

That's a shame. People who saw the film version may have come away with the impression that they understood the issues, the characters, the trial, and its impact. They would not.

The 1925 trial was more dramatic than its movie adaptation, the characters were surprisingly colorful, and its impact was further reaching. It's time we learned the true story of the real issues, the real people, and the real trial that served as the coming out party for science in American life.

. . .

The Scopes Monkey Trial wasn't really about *Scopes*, only obliquely mentioned *Monkeys*, and was more theater than a legal *Trial*.[1] Let's set the scene – the real one, this time – not the movie version.

First, why Scopes?

It didn't need to be Scopes, specifically. It could have been anyone who violated the law and was charged with the resulting crime. Passed only weeks before, the new Tennessee law didn't forbid public schools from teaching evolution *per se*. To be precise, it wouldn't allow "any theory that denies the story of the Divine Creation of man as taught in the Bible, and to teach instead that man has descended from a lower order of animals." In other words, teaching evolution was acceptable so long as humans weren't a part of it. The American Civil Liberties Union (ACLU) agreed to represent John Thomas Scopes, a 24-year-old substitute math and science teacher in Dayton, Tennessee. He would serve as the defendant in a test case to challenge the so-called "Butler Act" in court.[2] We'll talk about why Scopes was a great "made for media" choice soon, but all you need to know now is that it could have been the *Johnson* Monkey Trial, the *Adams* Monkey Trial, or the *Kowalski* Monkey Trial. It wouldn't

---

1   History geeks will recognize the paraphrase of Voltaire's more famous quip: "The Holy Roman Empire is neither Holy, nor Roman, nor an Empire."

2   Here are the critical 83 words: *Section 1. Be it enacted by the General Assembly of the State of Tennessee, That it shall be unlawful for any teacher in any of the Universities, Normals and all other public schools of the State which are supported in whole or in part by the public school funds of the State, to teach any theory that denies the story of the Divine Creation of man as taught in the Bible, and to teach instead that man has descended from a lower order of animals.* Like many cultural hot-button issues, a few motivated legislators created (essentially) a strawman argument about children coming home and telling their parents the Bible is "nonsense." For his part, Governor Austin Peay didn't think it mattered that much to the day-to-day operation of schools. However, he was happy for the support of Christian conservatives (including Bryan), who still considered Darwin's theory "unproven" and "dangerous" to the minds of students.

have made any difference who the defendant was.

Second, what's this about Monkeys?

That explanation takes us on a brief diversion into Darwin's theory of evolution by natural selection. In the crib notes version, all life forms face pressure to survive in a changing environment. Although Darwin didn't understand the genetic mechanisms at the cellular level, he observed that when individuals reproduce, random changes in their offspring mean that some individuals have a greater chance of surviving than others. Those with favorable changes tend to survive and reproduce more often than those that don't possess those advantages. Over time, beneficial traits become more common throughout the population. There's more to Darwin's theory than that, but that's the core idea.[3]

Most people accept the idea of evolution in the context of animal and plant breeding. The results are self-evident to any cattle rancher or wheat farmer. However, the sticky part comes from a misunderstanding of how *humans* evolved. To say humans evolved from monkeys (or apes) is not correct. Both apes and humans evolved from a common ancestor. That ancestor probably looked more like a modern ape than a human, but it was *neither*. However, in attempting to explain evolution to laypeople, many writers and journalists (and teachers who didn't quite understand it themselves) would show a modern ape on one end of a continuum, extinct earlier forms of humans as "intermediate forms," and finally, modern humans at the other end in a linear progression. It's easier to understand intuitively, but it's not quite correct.[4]

That misunderstanding fed directly into racial stereotypes of the time. If humans evolved from apes, and apes are native to Africa, then (it follows) the earliest forms of humans should be found in Africa. And although that is indeed true (to the best of our current knowledge, all

---

3   Any dog breeder can tell you evolution works. How do you get a Pomeranian from a wolf in recorded human history? By selective breeding. In other words, *artificial* selection. Darwin's *natural* selection refers to random environmental pressures making decisions, not human beings. That said, so far, nature has failed to create fluffy ankle-biters with poor dispositions without our "wise" intervention.

4   It's wrong for plenty of other reasons. Biologists have learned that the cladistics we learned in school – where earlier forms gave way to new ones in a sort of branching tree – is not exactly right. The so-called "tree of life" is more like an interbreeding bush where species share genetic material.

humans evolved first in Africa), that's not how people of the 1920s saw it. They misinterpreted Darwin's theory to provide evidence that Africans represent "lower" forms of humans, bolstering the case for racial hierarchies. It's not included in the main storyline here because, frankly, most people of that era accepted racial hierarchies as accurate. But for most people, the true sticky wicket was what evolution implied about a human's unique place in creation. In the Bible, God created humans in His image *after* he had created animals and plants.[5] Or, in other words, certainly *not* an ape's image.

Finally, what's so unique about the Trial?

Ask anyone who reads case law or cites Supreme Court opinions, and they'll tell you that although a few can be modestly readable, for the most part, they're just not that interesting to the average person. Legal language is, by design, persnickety. Most *written* legal opinions are dense logical arguments that only trained people can decipher. Oral arguments, however, can get saucy. The two primary attorneys were craggy firebrand Clarence Darrow for the defense and religious iconoclast William Jennings Bryan for the prosecution – both renowned for their spicy tongues. Their verbal jousting and procedural sparring would shape how people remembered the trial. Why? This was the first significant trial *broadcast* on the radio. Instead of reading a dry legal opinion months after the case was settled, or written transcripts the day after, radio listeners could hear the drama unfolding in real-time. For many Americans, this was the first time they would experience a court proceeding. They couldn't have asked for two better adversaries.

One last thing. Spoiler alert: Scopes lost. As we'll see, the result of the trial wasn't the point. The fine was only $100, and the ACLU was prepared to pay it. They had a different audience in mind. This fight would play out in front of a judge and jury in rural Tennessee, but also in a new forum: the court of public opinion.

. . .

Now that we know the backstory, let's meet the main characters in this

---

5   If you believe Michelangelo's interpretation, His image meant an aging White guy in a beard giving life to a younger, svelte, clean-shaven, naked White guy with tiny genitals.

made-for-media drama in a bit more detail.

Although it could have been anyone, John Thomas Scopes *did* make a good defendant. A high school teacher in Dayton, Tennessee, he grew up in Kentucky and Illinois, started college, dropped out for health reasons, and finally got his undergraduate degree in law with a minor in geology. It wasn't just that he'd studied the right subjects in school; Scopes was picture-perfect. Photos at the time show a wiry, earnest young man of twenty-four with a fashionably off-kilter piano-man hat and thick, round glasses. (Imagine a cross between John Lennon and Harry Potter.) If you wanted to pick the ideal schoolteacher who would participate in a test case about science, it would be tough to make a better choice.

Defending him in court was Clarence Darrow. Craggy and 67 years old when the trial opened, the contrast between the men at the defense table couldn't have been starker. Where Scopes was earnest and smart, looking like he just came from central casting, Darrow's piercing eyes, slicked gray hair, ill-fitting suits, and ruthless questioning style made him equal parts feared and admired in the courtroom. Even his smile seemed a little ominous. Darrow was a country lawyer in the classic American tradition. He believed many Wilsonian-era laws passed in the wake of World War I and the "Red Scare" in 1917-1920 were unconstitutional.[6] But Darrow wasn't content to simply complain about it; he was one of the founders of the American Civil Liberties Union (ACLU). A brilliant lawyer, Darrow was a dog with a bone when he took a case.[7] Like many brilliant jurists, however, he had a knack for ruffling feathers…even on his own side, not to mention presiding judges. However, if you needed someone to make an epic, convincing speech or tear an argument down through pointed witness questioning, this is the lawyer you wanted.

On the other side of the aisle, along with a team of prosecutors, was

---

[6] No one called it "World War I" in the 1920s. They would have called it "The Great War" or "The War to End All Wars." For modern readers, familiar that there would be another "Great War" just a handful of years later, using the names they would use at the time gets confusing.

[7] In many ways, the Scopes trial is one of Darrow's least important cases. Although just the year before, he had spared two rich kids from the electric chair for a murder they actually did commit, Darrow was considered a hero of civil rights law. For more, look up the Ossian Sweet trial, where Darrow defended a Black doctor and his family from a White mob trying to run them out of their neighborhood.

the famous William Jennings Bryan. Presidential historians will remember him as the perennial loser – to William McKinley twice and to William Taft once. Although most people may not remember him today, he was a powerful force in politics from the 1890s through the early part of the 1920s, largely because of his ability to captivate an audience. Historians routinely credit him with being the most influential politician of the Progressive Era who did *not* become president. The public's most recent memory of Bryan was his steadfast advocacy for Prohibition, though this was only one of many feathers in his public cap.[8] To be fair to his position (and unlike his movie portrayal in the *Inherit the Wind* film), Bryan wasn't so much *anti-evolution* as he was against allowing classroom teachers to step into what he believed to be the church's domain. But by 1925, the baby-faced "Boy Orator" seemed worn out when he arrived in Dayton to put a capstone on his crusade against teaching evolution in schools. He couldn't have known he was only weeks away from death, but in retrospect, this trial would be Bryan's swan song.

The fourth character in the drama was a growing force in the 1920s: the broadcast media. The so-called "fourth estate" had been a part of American politics since its British days and played a key role in the American revolution. As a thank you, the founders granted journalists a semi-divine status in politics, spelling out the media's freedom to operate in the first amendment to the U.S. Constitution. But the image of journalism in the public's mind was already changing when the trial opened. So-called "yellow" journalists were charged with goading the American public into the Spanish-American War in 1898 with sensational stories and outrageous headlines. Although investigative journalists like Ida Tarbell were repairing the "afflict the comfortable" image of the profession, one person's investigator is another person's muckraker. In other words, people had come to expect (rightly or wrongly) a certain amount of entertainment value in their news. Much more than simply the teller of news or the synthesizer of ideas, broadcast technology brought immediacy and excitement to journalism that no print newspaper could match. In the days before radio, you needed to be *in the courtroom* to witness the drama.

---

8   Bryan's support of Prohibition probably helped his public image in the minds of his core Christian audience, but as we saw in Chapter 5, many people secretly sidestepped the law while praising it publicly.

Now, radio would take you there, live and in person, with no journalist's filter. *The State of Tennessee v. John Thomas Scopes* would be the first major trial where live, audio coverage of the proceedings would be available.⁹

In the middle of July, Dayton was a broiling sweaty mess in the way Tennessee summers often are. A young, dapper schoolteacher stood accused of bringing radical scientific ideas into the classroom. The best two orators of their time squared off at the height of their respective careers. However this turned out, the trial would be a *great* show.

. . .

Edward Larson's 2006 Pulitzer Prize-winning biography of the trial, *Summer for the Gods: The Scopes Trial and America's Continuing Debate Over Science and Religion*, recounts the day-by-day drama of the trial in clarifying, rigorous detail. As we'll see, it was fundamentally different than other courtroom dramas.

In most criminal legal proceedings, the point – the entire reason for an adversarial legal system – is to determine the guilt or innocence of the defendant. In those cases, the burden of proof rests on the prosecution. For the Scopes trial, that would mean Bryan's team needed to produce evidence that Scopes had violated the Butler Act. By contrast, Darrow didn't need to prove Scopes innocent. Scopes would be *presumed* innocent until and unless a jury said otherwise.

However, as a "test case," the point wasn't to show Scopes was innocent. Quite the contrary. Scopes was guilty…but guilty of violating an unconstitutional law and, therefore, innocent of the resulting crime. The defense wanted to put the *Butler Act itself* on trial. In that role reversal, the Butler Act was presumed innocent, and Darrow needed to prove to the jury that the *law* was unconstitutional. Of course, that's not a legally correct interpretation, and the judge in the case wouldn't buy it, but it's easier to make sense of what happened in the trial when you switch perspectives

---

9   To handle the crush of reporters and coverage technology, Dayton leaders transformed the small town. Its main street would become a pedestrian mall. The courthouse lawn now featured a speaker's platform. City leaders upgraded the courtroom with wiring for telephone, telegraph, radio transmissions, and movie newsreel camera platforms. Chicago's WGN radio would claim the trial cost more than $1,000 each day in broadcast fees, or nearly $15,000 daily in 2020 dollars.

on the defendant in the case.

Darrow didn't take long to deliver the kind of speeches and fiery rhetoric everyone expected. In a particularly quotable line in his opening statement, Darrow lays down the challenge:

> We find today as brazen and as bold an attempt to destroy learning as was ever made in the Middle Ages.

At stake here wasn't just evolution; it was *learning itself* that was on trial in Tennessee.

From there, Darrow only sharpened his attack. Seeing another opening, Darrow objected to the *opening prayer* on the third day of the trial. Raulston overruled him, saying that he had instructed the preachers not to mention the issues in the case in their prayers and Bible verses. The next day, Darrow objected again, this time asking Raulston to declare the law unconstitutional because it violated the establishment clause in the United States Constitution.[10] The judge also dismissed that motion, reasoning that the Bulter Act:

> …gives no preference to any particular religion or mode of worship. Our public schools are not maintained as places of worship, but, on the contrary, were designed, instituted, and are maintained for the purpose of mental and moral development and discipline.

Only after point and counterpoint, charge and counter-charge, did the obvious happen. The defense team entered a plea of "not guilty" for Scopes near the end of the trial's third day.

This was the kind of drama the journalists craved and, by extension, the tit-for-tat jousting the American public also clearly wanted. Readers could explore full transcripts and a detailed legal analysis of both arguments the next day in the newspapers. The intellectual and elite crowd reveled in Darrow's objections and motions, demonizing Judge Raulston

---

10 The first amendment to the U.S. Constitution opens with the phrase: "Congress shall make no law respecting an establishment of religion…" In this, the framers meant "state-sponsored" religions, as in the Church of England, but it has been interpreted more broadly to mean simply favoring one religion over another.

and lampooning the simpletons in the jury box.[11] The religious faithful took the opposite side, though you don't find as much evidence from them in print. (That'll be important later.) They saw Judge Raulston as a defender of the faith – much like they saw Bryan – unfairly under attack from the "devil's influence" to reduce God's creation to "survival of the fittest." And yes, some readers simply loved the drama, like they would love a closely-fought baseball game. But it was the radio listeners who were in for the treat. The careful after-the-fact analysis made for all-caps headlines and in-depth magazine articles, but the real star of the show were radio and film producers on hand, providing live broadcast and movie newsreels. Listeners could *hear* Darrow's pacing, his energy, and his delivery. Viewers could *see* the sweat rolling down faces in the courtroom as the days dragged on. It was the first multimedia trial, captivating in an entirely new way, and amping up the emotional intensity of each legal maneuver.

The drama soon faded. Judge Raulston focused the attention back on Scopes as his defense team entered his plea. Working to keep the focus back on the core issue, the prosecution called students to the witness stand to testify if Scopes had discussed evolution in his classroom. Scopes may not have remembered, exactly, if he had done so, but they said he had. This part of the trial also featured the only actual scientist – a zoologist, Maynard Metcalf – who explained to the jury that evolution was widely accepted in the scientific community.

If you thought the trial would now begin to delve into the scientific issues, you would be wrong. The next day, July 17, Judge Raulston agreed with a motion from the prosecution that further scientific witnesses weren't necessary. They claimed, and the Judge agreed, that the trial was *really* about Scopes and his alleged violation of the law. Science was

---

11 Much of what we know now about the Scopes Monkey Trial, if not from the movie version, was written by the "winners" – those public intellectuals and journalists who saw the Tennessee law as repressive and those who supported it (at best) simpletons and (at worst) zealots. H.L. Mencken's reports created the dismissive narrative. There was no journalistic objectivity here. Dayton residents were "yokels." Bryan was a "buffoon," and his speeches were "theological bilge." Oddly, though he was broadly supportive of science in general, Mencken also called advanced mathematics (even probability theory – basically, anything he didn't understand) "nonsense." Mencken certainly was an authority on buffoonery. He simply needed to look in the mirror.

not on trial. Scopes was. They had all they needed to know from the testimony gathered the day before. At that, many of the journalists decided to pack it in. What additional drama could play out if the defense couldn't talk about evolution? The case might not be over, but the balloon deflated.

That determination was a mistake. It's like they didn't know Darrow at all. In the most dramatic moment in the trail – after many reporters had left – Darrow called *Bryan* to the stand as a "Bible expert." If the trial wasn't going to be about science, Darrow would make it about religion.

What followed can only be described as a grilling of Bryan and, by extension, the Christian faith. The entire cross-examination lasted less than an hour and clocks in at about 3,000 words.[12] Here's a taste:

> Darrow: Mr. Bryan, do you believe that the first woman was Eve?
> Bryan: Yes.
> Darrow: Do you believe she was literally made out of Adams's rib?[13]
> Bryan: I do.
> Darrow: Did you ever discover where Cain got his wife?
> Bryan: No, sir; I leave the agnostics to hunt for her.
> Darrow: You have never found out?
> Bryan: I have never tried to find out.
> Darrow: You have never tried to find out?
> Bryan: No.
> Darrow: The Bible says he got one, doesn't it? Were there other people on the earth at that time?
> Bryan: I cannot say.
> Darrow: You cannot say. Did that ever enter your consideration?
> Bryan: Never bothered me.
> Darrow: There were no others recorded, but Cain got a wife.
> Bryan: That is what the Bible says.

To some readers – especially those who read the transcript or accounts

---

12 Thanks to the University of Missouri – Kansas City School of Law for the transcription.

13 There's some debate about the translation of the word "rib." We think of it as one of the bones surrounding our chest organs, but that might not be correct. Most male mammals have a bone in their groin area to aid in mating, assisting penile erection and insertion into the female vagina. Humans don't have that bone, and the early Biblical stories about God removing the "rib" from man could have been a clever explanation for that anatomical difference.

later, it may seem that Darrow scored point after point on the "yokels" who believed these "crazy" stories. But that's not how it *sounded* in the courtroom, and certainly not how it sounded to the religious faithful who heard it. The transcripts feature more than one exchange like this one (note the emphasis):

> Darrow: Do you know anything about how many people there were in Egypt 3,500 years ago, or how many people there were in China 5,000 years ago?
> Bryan: No.
> Darrow: Have you ever tried to find out?
> Bryan: No, sir. You are the first man I ever heard of who has been interested in it. *(Laughter.)*
> Darrow: Mr. Bryan, am I the first man you ever heard of who has been interested in the age of human societies and primitive man?
> Bryan: You are the first man I ever heard speak of the number of people at those different periods.
> Darrow: Where have you lived all your life?
> Bryan: Not near you. *(Laughter and applause.)*
> Darrow: Nor near anybody of learning?
> Bryan: Oh, don't assume you know it all.
> Darrow: Do you know there are thousands of books in our libraries on all those subjects I have been asking you about?
> Bryan: I couldn't say, but I will take your word for it.

The *audience* in the courtroom certainly sided with Bryan. Throughout the exchange, you can hear a calm, faithful man resisting the urge to stand up and slap the guy questioning him. It's quite impressive. But even Bryan had his limits and exercised his verbal power over his questioner by choosing the time of its closure:

> Bryan: Your Honor, I think I can shorten this testimony. The only purpose Mr. Darrow has is to slur at the Bible, but I will answer his question. I will answer it all at once, and I have no objection in the world; I want the world to know that this man, who does not believe in a God, is trying to use a court in Tennessee…
> Darrow: I object to that.
> Bryan: …(continuing) to slur at it, and while it will require time, I am willing to take it.
> Darrow: I object to your statement. I am exempting you on your

fool ideas that no intelligent Christian on earth believes.

Judge Raulston had had enough. He adjourned the court for the next morning. When court resumed the next day, the Judge expunged the entire exchange from the record, claiming it bore no bearing on Scopes' guilt or innocence. Darrow asked the Judge for an immediate guilty verdict to bring this trial to a speedy conclusion and set the stage for a planned appeal. The jury obliged him. It took them only nine minutes of deliberation to return their verdict. Scopes was found guilty and fined $100. In his only statement of the entire trial, Scopes said he would:

> …oppose this law in any way I can. Any other action would be in violation of my ideal of academic freedom – that is, to teach the truth as guaranteed in our constitution, of personal and religious freedom.

. . .

The ending of the "Trial of the Century" was a bit…anticlimactic.

The ACLU appealed, but the Tennessee Supreme Court eventually upheld the Bulter Act, although it threw out Scopes' conviction on a technicality. For its part, Dayton's School Board wanted Scopes back in the classroom so long as he agreed to abide by the law. (An offer he declined.)

Those courtroom successes led other religiously-inclined legislatures to pass their versions of the Butler Act, mostly throughout the Deep South. Just as it seemed anti-evolution forces would take their victory in Tennessee and make a righteous march across the country, they were stopped cold in places like Minnesota, where the law failed spectacularly despite a strong lobbying campaign.[14]

William Jennings Bryan died five days later in Dayton. The timing was auspicious for the faithful; they viewed him as a martyr for their cause, exhausted and "killed" by the relentless heathen Darrow. His tombstone reads: "He Kept the Faith."

Darrow's speechifying might have made for quotable one-liners, but it wasn't well received by his broader legal team. His style created as many

---

14 That's a Minnesota joke. It's cold there.

enemies as it did friends, and it certainly didn't win the case. For his part, Darrow learned his lesson. In future cases – most notably the Ossian Sweet civil rights case – he used his formidable oratorical skill to benefit his *clients* and less to score rhetorical points.

In many ways, the media "won" the case. The Scopes trial dominated the front page of the *New York Times* for days. Reporters swarmed in from across the country (and even a couple of London). Sweaty telegraph operators pecked out over 165,000 words each day. Announcer Quin Ryan broadcast the play-by-play of the trial for Chicago's WGN. Movie crews flew film out each day from a custom-built airstrip to get their newsreels into theater showings. And in a piece of brilliant showmanship worthy of the long-dead P.T. Barnum, trained chimpanzees performed on the courthouse lawn.

One of the Scopes trial's most significant legacies might be how it changed Americans' perception of the courts in general. Interest in the inherent drama of legal proceedings spawned hugely popular fictionalizations – from Perry Mason to Columbo to multiple versions of the *Law and Order* franchise. This mix of reality and drama meant that lawyers in significant cases could never again ignore public opinion. The jury might decide the legal case, but the public chooses the true winner.

Larson makes the case that evolutionists – primarily east coast intellectuals – were satisfied that they won in the "court of public opinion" even if they failed to save the young schoolteacher from a guilty verdict. In a surprisingly short time, they moved on to other issues. But the faithful were faced with a deeper choice: Do they accept the conclusions of the intellectual elite that science had triumphed over religion? Or do they reject that characterization and side with Bryan and religious leaders?

Many Protestants and Catholics – especially in the north – chose a third way. They did what Spencer Tracy did in the final scene of *Inherit the Wind*. They chose to accept the Bible for its moral teaching and science for its practical instruction. They took the Bible seriously, not literally. They were also careful to hide outward displays of their faith in intellectuals' company lest they be lumped in with the hillbillies and yokels who took Jonah's story as literal truth.

Another group of Evangelical Christians – a large group, mainly in the south – never forgave Darrow. They cast themselves as the early Christians in the Roman Empire, ready to face not *literal* crucifixion but death in the sense of a place in elite society. They accepted it and retreated into their own world. They wrote their own textbooks. They chartered their own schools. They even built their own theme parks.[15] Even today, this isolation is why intellectuals, journalists, and even marketers still struggle to understand this segment of the American public.

The whole kerfuffle does raise an interesting point. The trial never quite answered the charge about the *lesson* itself. Today, we think about Scopes' "crime" in terms of his teaching of "evolution" and the broader concept of "freedom to teach." But what exactly was Scopes teaching children in his class? Was his textbook, *Civic Biology*, really as "dangerous" as Bryan claimed?

This is the part that gets…uncomfortable, especially for the intellectuals who consider themselves the "winners" in the court of public opinion. Let's have a read, shall we?

> The Races of Man. – At the present time, there exist upon the earth five races or varieties of man, each very different from the other in instincts, social customs, and, to an extent, in structure. These are the Ethiopian or Negro type, originating in Africa; the Malay or brown race, from the islands of the Pacific; The American Indian; the Mongolian or yellow race, including the natives of China, Japan, and the Eskimos; and finally, the highest type of all, the Caucasians, represented by the civilized white inhabitants of Europe and America.

The "highest type of all" was the "civilized White inhabitants of Europe and America." While we might bristle at that characterization, let's be careful not to slip into anachronistic thinking. Many people of that era, including prominent scientists, would have agreed with that statement. But the book went further. After discussing (positively) the role of Eugenics in improving the human species, and the impact of "parasitism" of lesser people on the rest of society, it suggests a "remedy" for that problem:

> If such people were lower animals, we would probably kill them off to prevent them from spreading. Humanity will not allow this, but we do have the remedy of separating the sexes in asylums or other

---

15   The most famous is the Ark Encounter in Williamstown, Kentucky.

places and, in various ways preventing intermarriage and the possibilities of perpetuating such a low and degenerate race. Remedies of this sort have been tried successfully in Europe and are now meeting with some success in this country.

The "remedy" sounds quite a bit like a certain "final solution" in the 1940s, doesn't it? In other words, who was on the right side of history is unclear.

...

In the final reading, there's something a bit unsatisfying about the trial and its high-minded interpretations. Was this simply the first public culture war battle, fought for the first time on the radio? Is that really what people were concerned about?

It turns out, however, that we *do indeed* have a source that more closely mirrors the concerns of the average person as it relates to science and its place in the world in the 1920s. Scopes should have given us a clue: science *teachers*. More specifically, the textbooks they used to instruct students. We may have focused on some of the nasty aspects of *Civic Biology*, but it doesn't quite represent what was happening. It was the shiny light bulb, not the marquee sign.

In 2021, scholars John L. Rudolph from the University of Wisconsin in the United States, and Tor Ole B. Odden and Alessandro Marin from the University of Oslo in Norway, completed a quantitative assessment using Natural Language Processing of the topic areas found in the academic journal *Science Education* over the past 100 years. Conveniently for us, that analysis began in 1920.

Their analysis helps us focus on a very different form of evidence than historical accounts, speeches, and magazine articles. Away from the media buzz, this journal gives us a window into the issues science educators grappled with when no one was looking. What they discovered challenges the notion that the conflict between religion and science was the *main thing*. It wasn't even a sideline. The most prominent single topic, by far, in science education of that era was "Science in Everyday Life." It outranked all other topics – 21 in all – by an order of magnitude during the 1920s. The author described this topic as:

> early attempts at science outreach through written descriptions of natural and mechanical phenomena: for example, the life cycles of trees and insects, the development of the match, and the laying of undersea cables

Scopes was *not* a typical science educator of his time. Not even close. Most science educators weren't interested in a culture war; they struggled with helping students understand the transformative impact of science and engineering on daily life. When you think about it for just a moment, that task makes sense. Put yourself in the shoes of a science teacher of the 1920s. What questions are your students likely to ask?

> How do radio waves travel through the air without a wire?
> How does electricity make a light bulb bright?
> How does an internal combustion engine power a car?

It was these and dozens of other questions that science teachers needed to explain to their students. Today, we take the innovations in this book for granted. When the Scopes Trial began in the summer of 1925, they were brand new. Student (and parent!) curiosity was only natural.

The analysis is even clearer when we consider the *second* most popular topic, at about one-fifth the frequency of the first topic: Science Teacher Preparation, Program Development, and Technology. If science teachers were going to need to train students on these questions, their teaching methods would also need to change. Put another way, science teachers were responding to consumer demand. As the fight raged in the sultry courtroom in Tennessee, the American public was hungry for information about what *precisely* evolution was, less because of its religious implications and more because they were curious about *everything*.

As a science teacher, Scopes *was* the innovator, just not in the way he thought.

12
HAPPY FEET

> One night, somebody came over and said, 'Hey man, Clark Gable just walked in the house.' Somebody else said, 'Oh, yeah, can he dance?' All they wanted to know when you came into the Savoy was, do you dance?"
>
> – Stories from the Savoy Ballroom, Harlem[1]

The Savoy Ballroom in Harlem, New York, was demolished in 1958 to make way for an apartment complex.[2] In its heyday, the raucous club nestled between 140th and 141st Streets on Lenox Avenue. Anyone who was anyone played there, including names even people without a lick of rhythm will recognize: Duke Ellington, Ella Fitzgerald, Count Basie, Dizzy Gillespie, and Louis Armstrong.

The club did not disappoint…in more ways than one. The Savoy featured two bandstands. That way, there would never be a break in the music on busy nights. It was a live, human version of the two turntables and a microphone. More than performance logistics, the Savoy featured audience innovations as well. Unlike its Harlem neighbor, the (perhaps) more famous Cotton Club, the Savoy was *integrated*. At the Cotton Club, the performers were Black, the guests were White, and the owners were mobsters. It was a place where fancypants White audiences could get a glimpse of Black music without the "fear" of actually interacting with a Black person if they didn't want to.

The Savoy was different. Both featured all the top artists, but more to the point, anyone who was anyone *danced* there. Because when you went to the Savoy, you went to dance. From the historical records, we know most nights, the audience was 85 percent Black and 15 percent White. But when the big names came in, the Savoy packed in a nearly equal split – a salt-and-pepper dance floor where the only thing that mattered was how you moved your feet. A little nervous sharing the dance floor with the spectacular "Lindy Hoppers?" They had you covered. For a quarter,

---

1   There are plenty of sources for this quote in slightly different versions. The exact words don't matter as much as the sentiment. At the Savoy Ballroom, not even celebrities received special treatment. This version comes from a 2006 *New York Times* article titled, "Where the Feet Flew and the Lindy Hopped," by Manny Hernandez.

2   Originally named the Delano Apartments, the complex has since been renamed the Savoy Park Apartments in recognition of its heritage.

the uninitiated could get a swing dance lesson on the spot. No, they might not be able to hold a candle to some of the regulars, but they could *participate* in the club's atmosphere. The Savoy wasn't a sit-on-your-hands and politely-clap-at-the-end sort of place. Black or White, you were expected to get out onto the floor.

The Savoy influenced music clubs for generations afterward. It forced innovation in dance floor design. (The Savoy's floor wore out regularly. That experience taught future architects and builders about reinforced flooring and better materials.) It paved the way for White performers Frank Sinatra, Elvis Presley, and Marshall Mathers. It planted the seeds for blues, rock and roll, rap, hip-hop, and pop music. And most importantly, it brought Black and White people together in a way almost unheard of in American culture of that era – not in some milquetoast discussion of "race" or ineffectual legislation, but in pure, unadulterated joy and dance.

But aside from pictures – and the memories of people who experienced it – nothing is left of the physical Savoy building but a boxy apartment complex.

There's a sadness to that, but all hope isn't lost.

It's important to understand the story of "America's Classical Music" and how it helped transform entertainment into consumer culture. It's important to understand how that is primarily an outgrowth of *Black* culture and the debt America owes to some of the best musicians ever to play and dancers ever to move on the dance floor.

In the end, we'll check out a way we might even have a chance to bring it back.

But for now, let's get out onto the floor.

. . .

Jazz is so common in everyday American life that it's almost become life's soundtrack. Unfortunately, you might not hear Satchmo (Armstrong) on the trumpet as you ride an elevator, but you might hear one of its genericized derivatives.[3] You'll *certainly* hear your fair share of R&B, rock, hip-hop, or pop numbers. They're all jazz at heart. However, if you *know*

---

3   Sadly, much of the jazz heard today is of the "elevator music" variety.

anything about "America's Classical Music," and you're not a musician yourself, it probably came thanks to Ken Burns' 10-episode miniseries. First airing in 2001, *Jazz* charts the story of this unique art form – its origins, its heyday, and its legacy. Being a documentary, Burns can weave in actual performances, adding depth and vitality to the subject matter that a printed (or read) page cannot. In other words, we won't do justice to the appreciation of the art form here.[4] Instead, we'll focus on the influence of jazz on consumer culture and choice-making, specifically as it relates to the entertainment industry. Consider what follows the short version of the art form's history – just enough to give us the context to understand why it was so powerful.

As we know it today, jazz was born of a mix of cultures and influences. Its roots are quite deep, tracing across the Atlantic Ocean and anchoring in three continents. Some of the ingredients in that melting pot were born from a deep legacy of African music going back hundreds of years. That tradition includes heavy beats, rhythmic chants, a focus on dance, and an overall high energy level. When enslaved people were brought to North America, South America, and the Caribbean Islands, they brought their traditions with them. In their forced homeland, their music continued to evolve as they interacted with Indigenous music and other European settlers. Jazz owes part of its heritage to spiritual music and anti-slavery anthems. It also draws influence from the mix of cultures in the New Orleans area, where raucous joy and intense emotions were on display in the clubs and brothels of the notoriously wild port city. And it even adapts influences from the lightning-fast banjos, strong beats, and drunken dance of hill country music from Appalachia.

What's important to understand about jazz and its origins is how *different* that was from *European* classical music. When most people before the 1920s thought about music, they thought of Beethoven, Bach, and Mozart. Those composers wrote the basis of Catholic and Protestant church music (which most people recognized) and inspired a legacy of symphony orchestra performances (which only the wealthy could

---

4 You'll hear plenty of great music in the documentary, but with the advent and popularity of streaming services, you have plenty of options.

regularly enjoy).⁵ Part of the reason is obvious: Not only was European classical music part of most White Americans' heritage, but in an era before recording technology, you also needed to be physically present to hear it. Classical music requires significant investment in both the musical instruments and the training to play them competently. That reality bred an elitist culture that's (fair or not) *still* hard to shake.

European classical music *is* deeply emotional, but it requires a certain level of appreciation to get the full experience. Jazz isn't like that at all. As musician and historian Ted Gioia explains in his book *Music: A Subversive History*, jazz was born of poverty and struggle, not privilege and refinement. It was dirty, raw, violent, sensual, and joyous – emotional, yes, but in a tangible way for people. You didn't need a trained ear to feel the emotion in Ella Fitzgerald's voice or the timbre in Armstrong's trumpet. Gioia argues against trying to sanitize jazz. To do that is to rob it of its heritage and make it into something "palatable" for "sophisticated" audiences to "analyze." Jazz was for *everyone*.

To be clear, just because jazz was raw and powerful didn't mean it didn't take tremendous talent *and* years of practice to master. Instead of cloistered concert halls and private music lessons, jazz musicians would develop their craft in front of live audiences – more like how comedians develop their skills than classically-trained musicians. They listened to what their audiences responded to; they weren't trying to copy a violin virtuoso who had been dead for 200 years. Jazz was *current*. It evolved in real-time in the small clubs that dotted New Orleans.

That responsiveness led to a culture of improvisation. Improvisation was a live experiment on the audience. And the audience, like Darwinian "environmental pressure," pushed jazz into higher energy, stronger talent, and most importantly, danceable *swing* music. (Pay attention to that last part; it'll be important later.)

At this point in the story, we've arrived at 1917. American troops were heading off to World War I. They'd come back to the worst flu pandemic they'd ever seen. The immediate post-war spiraled the county into a short

---

5   Before the 1920s, learning classical music and reading classical literature was a middle class aspirational activity. This helps explain the popularity of pianos in many "average" homes, paid for on installment plans. See Chapters 4 and 10 for more background on installment plans and middle class buying patterns.

(but painful) Depression in 1920 and 1921. What had been a musical curiosity in the sweltering club scene of New Orleans was ready for its national debut.

. . .

Jazz began its migration just ahead of the 1920s. There are plenty of reasons: War mobilization moves people, especially young men, many of whom were musicians. The flu pandemic killed hundreds of thousands of people (675,000 according to the best current estimates) in the United States alone, and that impact was felt disproportionately in poorer neighborhoods. Many New Orleans neighborhoods certainly qualified as poor; then as now, death encourages change. To stem the tide of sexually-transmitted diseases among soldiers (a critical public health challenge for mobilization), authorities largely succeeded in shutting down the "red light" district and curbing (though not eliminating) prostitution. But demand is demand, and many simply migrated to less vigilant cities. Many simply wanted better work opportunities. Others wanted to escape the racially-charged south.

Perhaps it was inevitable that jazz would have left New Orleans in any case, but this unique mix of factors greatly accelerated the process. By 1920, Jazz musicians had established themselves on a northward and eastward track – St. Louis, Chicago, Detroit, and most importantly for the consumer side of this story, New York.

However, jazz was *Black* music. White audiences *might* have heard it if they frequented the club scene – that was especially true in New Orleans – but that was limited to those with the right mindset for it. They were the adventurous types – "early adopters," as we might call them now. The fact is that although the move to the cities from the farms was well underway, more than half the U.S. population still lived in rural areas and small towns. The thought of going into the city was a bit exciting but vaguely scary for them. The thought of going into a club was not *vaguely* scary at all…it *terrified* them. Yes, racism played a part in that, but that's too trite an explanation and not quite correct (as we'll see). It was more lack of awareness. White audiences simply had never heard this music before and had never experienced a dance club. That was more of the root cause of the apprehension than anything else.

At the risk of making the discussion even more uncomfortable, we need to clarify what we meant by "White" audiences because it's not what we mean today. In 1920, "White" referred to people of British and Scandinavian descent (and perhaps those from France and the Low Countries). They were, by and large, Anglo-Saxon Protestants. Germans might have pale skin, but the Kaiser wasn't popular during the war years for obvious reasons. Russians and Eastern Europeans were "Slavs" – not quite at the same level as other Whites in the racial hierarchy.[6] Italians? They were Catholics and mobsters – either taking their orders from the Pope (subversives) or their "Don" (criminals). Irish? They weren't genuinely British; the vast numbers fleeing the potato famine created huge numbers in the United States whose speed of entry unnerved the political power structure. And they were also Catholic. That didn't help. Religious bigotry was a real force. Jewish people? Antisemitism was rampant. In short, when we say jazz wasn't familiar to White audiences, we mean "White," as we described it *narrowly* above. Those *other groups* quickly saw the opportunity to partner with Black performers to open new clubs.

That cultural background is essential because it helps us understand what happened in the 1920s to bring jazz mainstream and make it America's music.

. . .

Several other trends helped electrify the growth of jazz in the United States. (In the case of recording technology, quite literally.) We've already seen how the migration of Black musicians out of the south and into northern cities planted the seeds of jazz in fertile new ground. We've also seen how marginalized groups found common cause and (surprisingly) common culture. Together, these groups pooled their resources to build new clubs in urban areas. Those clubs featured free-flowing alcohol and sexual

---

6 If you weren't uncomfortable enough, yes, the ethnic term "Slav" has a etymological relationship to the English word "slave." People with "ski," "sky," "vic," and "vich" in their last names (among many other variants) were commonly enslaved well into the modern era. The circular reasoning held that if you happened to be enslaved at some point in your history, your "people" somehow "deserved" it.

tension. Remember, these weren't the formal dances and coming-out parties of WASP Americana, where women wore flowing dresses, men wore tails, and everyone watched for the chaperone. These clubs featured unattended young adults wearing the latest fashions. In practical terms, these clothes allowed for much more freedom of movement (see Chapter 22 for more details). In sexy terms, there was a lot less…fabric, and they showed a lot more skin. All the better to dance with, isn't it? You can't do Swing, the Charleston, or the Lindy Hop without a bit of touching, now could you? And if a little *extra* skin-to-skin contact happened, well, how unfortunate. (See dictionary definition of "facetious.")

As Prohibition took hold in January of 1920, the clubs took on a decidedly anti-establishment vibe. That suited the Germans, Irish, Italian, Jewish, and Black proprietors and performers just fine. They simply hid the bar behind a special door behind the dance floor. (We learned more about that in Chapter 5.) Predictably, it didn't take long for the tut-tutters to cluck their disapproval for the "respectable" young people patronizing these dens of iniquity, they might as well have put up a blazing sign that read: GO! HAVE FUN! (They would have been better off simply ignoring the club scene, but then, as now, they simply *can't* resist.)

In other words, if illegal alcohol, energetic music, close dancing, comfortable anonymity in the big city, and unchaperoned meetings with the opposite sex weren't enough reasons for young people to visit one of the new clubs, an authority figure telling them they shouldn't sealed the deal.

Who doesn't want to go? Don't you want to go now? Like, right now? Sure, you do.

Who might you see?

All of the best clubs featured spectacular ensemble bands – the foundation of any good club scene in that era. Augmenting their appeal were some of the biggest names of the era. We've already mentioned Duke Ellington, Ella Fitzgerald, Count Basie, Dizzy Gillespie, and Louis Armstrong. You might also hear Chick Webb, Fats Waller, Willie Bryant, Adelaide Hall, Ethel Waters, or Bessie Smith. We won't be able to give these artists the recognition they're due because this isn't a chapter about the music as much as it is a chapter about how music impacted consumer culture. More importantly, listening to them play is the only way to truly appreciate their talent.

That said, there is one critical difference between the evolution of jazz in the 1920s and much of what followed. As we've mentioned, jazz clubs weren't "politely listen and applaud when finished" sorts of places. They were *alive*, and the performers were connected to their audience in a way that most stage performers were not. It wasn't simply that jazz musicians heard the reaction of their audience. They *adapted* in response to their audience. This culture of improvisation perfectly fit the overall *consumer* culture of the 1920s. Louis Armstrong listened to what his audience responded to, *and didn't*, and his music improved and evolved. *Quickly.* Think of how similar that strategy is to Clarence Birdseye's experimentation with frozen foods. Or Coco Chanel's experimentation with fashion. Or Alfred Sloan's experimentation with different car makes and models. When recording, Louis Armstrong needed to go by the sheet music in the same way Sloan needed a factory to mass produce Chevrolets. But when Armstrong played live, *improvisation* ruled. In that critical way, jazz culture is consumer culture. It's not the only reason jazz quickly overtook all other American music, but it's one of the most important.[7]

Still, had this been all, jazz would have been notable as a musical innovation. But the 1920s weren't through with jazz just yet. Here's where we get to the "electrification" part.

. . .

The house bands were the mainstays at most of these clubs – the larger ones featured recording-worthy musicians in their own right. Still, the smaller clubs developed new talent and helped meet the demand for performers. (It's not that different from the comedy club scene today.) And yes, some of those top bands would go on multi-city tours. However, to know of one of these acts before the 1920s, you needed to see them perform live. Touring musicians could reach *more* people than they could if they stayed home, but not that many more.

Radio changed all that.

Think about it: If you're a rural kid just moving into St Louis, you

---

[7] Dr. Todd Hostager of Concordia University, Texas, is one of the leading scholars on business improvisational techniques. He studied jazz musicians to learn how they "riffed" off each other in live performances and applied those principles to innovation in other domains.

may have never heard Black music before. You might be intimidated to go downtown to a club and see a live show. But what if you could hear it on the radio? Listening at home was a "safe" way for White kids to get exposed to Black music for the first time. And by the middle of the 1920s, you could even go to the store and take the recording *home* with you (at a price that made sense). Recording technology of the early part of the decade was notably poor, but even so, jazz musicians (ever the improvisers) were among the first to adopt it en mass.[8] By the time Western Electric figured out how to amplify music and transfer the recording to a vinyl disc in 1925, the recording era was born.[9]

Recording did more than simply amplify the jazz audience; it changed the nature of the music itself. Records and radio were intimate, not collective experiences. Before 1925, if you wanted to hear Josephine Baker sing, you needed to see her in person. But with a record, you could listen to her alone in your home.[10] It was as if she was signing to *you, personally*. That emotional connection to the music was as intoxicating as the dance clubs, and the two fed on each other. People who saw a musician play bought their record. Those who bought the records went to see them play. Today, that's so obvious as to seem silly, but it wasn't then.

One of the most unexpected parts of the recording industry was how marketing would impact the course of jazz development. Ensemble performances were popular, of course, but "headliners" (like Louis Armstrong) made promotion easier – audiences could identify with a single performer (and remember them) in a way they simply couldn't connect with a larger group. Again, groups were indeed popular then (and now), but this era saw the rise of individual star jazz performers who could fill clubs, capture listeners, and sell a *lot* of records.

To summarize the story so far, several powerful influences came

---

[8] Louis Armstrong's second wife, Lillian Hardin Armstrong, recalled that he was *not happy* to be positioned 15 feet behind the other performers in King Oliver's Creole Jazz Band during recording sessions. However, given the recording technology in 1923, if he hadn't been, no one else would have been heard. Armstrong's playing was a force of nature.

[9] Credit goes to the engineers at Western Electric for developing the foundation of modern recording technology using amplifiers.

[10] Which was a good thing for American audiences. She spent much of the later 1920s (and her entire career) in Paris.

together at once.

For many of their own reasons, jazz musicians migrated out of their birthplace in New Orleans and resettled in urban centers in the north. A culture of improvisation, adaptation, and responsiveness to the audience mirrored the consumer culture ethos of the time, rapidly elevating jazz above all other music genres. Other societal outsiders used their resources to build clubs and dance halls, which lifted all those groups – Black Americans included – to new levels of prosperity rarely seen before. When Prohibition started, the lure of illegal alcohol gave these clubs (and the music they played) a forbidden appeal. New fashions changed the dress code to something you could dance in. In a sexy way. Listening to sexy music. (And more people were having a lot more sex, with new information on birth control – see Chapter 19.) Technology allowed jazz to reach a wider (and Whiter) audience, which allowed them to "try before they bought."

If you were trying to launch a new product, it would be hard to plan it better.

. . .

We're finally ready to circle back to the Savoy Ballroom in Harlem, New York. In many ways, it was the most famous jazz club of its era alongside its Harlem neighbor, the Cotton Club. However, although they were close geographically and featured many of the same performers over the years, they couldn't have been more different.

Let's start with the Cotton Club. John Arthur Johnson was the first Black heavyweight boxing champion in the United States. In 1920, he parlayed that success into a small supper club he called the "Club Deluxe." It was a high-class affair amid the Harlem Renaissance, but although Johnson was a charismatic presence with a great idea, he wasn't a businessperson. That role would fall to Owen Vincent "Owney" Madden, aka "The Killer," a British-born Irish mobster. Madden bought the club in 1923, refurbished and expanded it, and brought back Johnson to manage it. With free-flowing liquor and top performers, the rechristened Cotton Club packed them in from the entire New York diaspora.[11] If you're imag-

---

11 For much more on the Harlem Renaissance, read historian David Levering Lewis' 1997 book, *When Harlem Was in Vogue*.

ining a set in the *Great Gatsby*, you wouldn't be far off.

The Cotton Club's approach was to provide a safe, high-class environment for *White* patrons to listen to the best jazz music. That's right. The Cotton Club was stage-audience segregated: White audiences (with a few notable exceptions, including Black poet Langston Hughes and celebrities Ethel Waters and Bill Robinson) and Black performers (with a few notable exceptions there too). Promotional materials were *furiously racist* by today's standards...and even pretty racist in the mid-1920s. The Cotton Club promoted an "exotic, jungle" atmosphere, sort of like a performing zoo.[12] But like a zoo, not *too* exotic. Duke Ellington, for example, was expected to perform lighter, more consumable versions of his music, and those (also stunning) contributions are what many people first heard of jazz. Despite that, it was worth it for the performers – they were compensated well – much better than the smaller clubs in the area. Ellington, for his part, signed on as the house band in the late 1920s, still improvising and evolving a lighter jazz style. After the shows, there was no "mixing" of the performers – they often crossed the street to a basement bar for the afterparty, and the White folks went home.

It wouldn't be until 1935 that the Cotton Club finally allowed Black patrons, and five years later, the club would close under pressure from higher rents.

...

There was much that was the same about the Cotton Club and the Savoy Ballroom.

Both were founded at about the same time. The Cotton Club in 1923 (refounded, of course) and the Savoy Ballroom three years later in 1926. On a nice night, you could walk the distance between the two in Harlem. They shared many of the same ensemble groups and individual performers over the years. They were both high-class establishments – not the smoky, seedy places, but buildings with moody lighting, excellent acoustics, and good refreshments (yes, liquor as well – both clubs got in trouble for Prohibition violations). Both were owned – openly or not – by the mob.

---

12   Hughes called the Cotton club "a Jim Crow club for gangsters and monied whites," and compared the experience to visiting a zoo.

Outstanding Black managers operated both – John Arthur Johnson at the Cotton Club and Charles Buchanan at the Savoy Ballroom. And both would become part of the history of the Harlem Renaissance.

But in one key aspect, they differed markedly.

Where the Cotton Club was like a musical "petting zoo" where Whites could look on as Black performers entertained them, the Savoy Ballroom was integrated. In fact, it was one of the first integrated clubs in the United States and certainly the most important. Because while people could listen to jazz on the radio or buy a record of their favorite artist, it was still a segregated experience. White parents might scold their children for listening to Black music, but they didn't need to worry that they might spend meaningful time with them. That sentiment extended to the Irish, Italians, Germans, and Jews. (This was not just common in the southern United States; it was also a feature of northern parents.)

The Savoy Ballroom, by contrast, was a dance hall where all were welcome – the "Home of Happy Feet" – where the only thing that mattered was how well you could dance. It's where swing dancing caught on. It's where the Lindy Hop was invented and refined.[13] Other steps included the Flying Charleston, Jive, Snakehips, Rhumboogie, and variations of the Shimmy and Mambo. And it's where Black and White dancers danced together, many meeting each other for the first time in the great equalizer of dance.

Let's be clear. Spending a night at the Savoy wasn't a utopia. Racism and prejudices still existed. And yes, on most nights the audience was predominantly Black. Despite that, it was the first time people had interacted with people of another race in a way that wasn't cloaked in mistrust and fear. Those people would grow up, and many of them would form the core of the Civil Rights movement a generation later. The experience of choosing who you associate with made more of a difference than they could have ever realized. In stark contrast to the "zoo" atmosphere of the Cotton Club, Langston Hughes called the Savoy "The Heartbeat of Harlem."

The Savoy Ballroom proved more resilient as well. Where the Cotton Club shut its doors in 1940, the Savoy Ballroom kept going strong through the Great Depression, the war years, and into the 1950s, finally

---

13 If you guessed that the "Lindy Hop" was named after aviator Charles Lindbergh, you guessed right.

closing in 1958 as rock and roll – the legacy of jazz – took hold on the airwaves. At best guess, nearly 700,000 people walked through the doors and stepped out onto the integrated floor.

. . .

What jazz teaches us in general and the Savoy Ballroom teaches us specifically is even more obvious now than it was in the 1920s. We can see how much by looking at it with 100 years of distance.

Today, music is a $15 billion annual industry. However, that figure only counts "record sales" (now, mostly streaming). It doesn't include clubs, clothing, and concerts. When you do that, the number *doubles*. Easily. Even more impressive than the raw numbers is the cultural impact. Every popular music genre traces its roots back to jazz – rock and roll, blues, hip-hop, rap, and pop are obvious, but so are less obvious inheritors. One only need to think back to the difference between the stale first rock and roll performances – smiling performers in full suits – and the first time Elvis Presley shook his hips on television. Jazz performance was about energy, joy, excitement – and, most importantly, a shared experience. Successful performers emulated that energy. Sure, some shows and dance clubs remain specific to their audience (race, age, or gender), but most are not. At a live show, you're likely to share that experience with other people.

Coming together to enjoy a show is a choice that consumers freely make with no bigger motive or "conversation" about the grand issues of the day. Of all the difficult legacies of integration, jazz is a happy success story. It can't hurt to look at the sunny side of the street…at least, every once in a while, can it?[14]

. . .

Coda: Gone, but not forgotten.

Over the past five years, a group of people has been trying to resurrect a 21st-century version of the Savoy Ballroom, this time using Virtual Reality. It's not as easy as it looks. The Savoy Ballroom had been demolished

---

14 From the 1959 album, *Sonny Side Up*, by Dizzy Gillespie, Sonny Rollins, and Sonny Stitt.

for over half a century before they picked up the task. Although there were rough floor plans and plenty of photos, there was nothing close enough to an architectural drawing needed to code a VR experience. So, Sharon Davis took it upon herself to figure it out. A swing dancer by trade, she meticulously collected city plans, combed through photos, and did the measurement work necessary to recreate – as close as we're likely to get – what the actual room really looked like.

A few notes: It's smaller than most people remember, especially the dance floor. Two bandstands and a seating area took up a lot of space, which meant the dancing area was crowded – a feature clubs use today to create energy and force people closer together. The bandstand also underwent multiple revisions and color schemes, including the installation of an acoustic metal clamshell. The floors went through multiple replacements as well. (Dancers routinely wore them out.)

On the website, you can watch interviews with people who had been there, see modern dancers learning and teaching the steps, and see photos of dancers and top performers of the era. However, as of this writing, the project is stopped there. You can't put on a Virtual Reality headset and stroll through the club, interact with other patrons, meet Louis Armstrong, listen to the band, or try your feet on a Lindy Hop. It's expensive to get from here to there, and more than just money, the team wants to handle this rebirth in the right way. Visit welcometothesavoy.com for yourself and have a look.

Hopefully, we'll all be able to visit the *Home of Happy Feet* again soon.

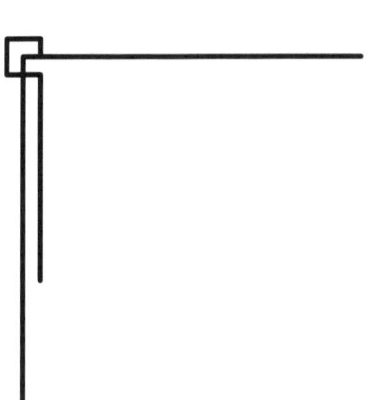

13
SWAMPLAND

To say Charles Ponzi had a spinning moral compass isn't quite right. His moral compass never wavered. It always pointed directly at himself. As it turned out, his sense of direction would serve him...poorly.

During his voyage from Parma, Italy, in 1903, Carlo Pietro Giovanni Guglielmo Tebaldo Ponzi gambled away his life savings. At 21 years old, the young immigrant landed in Boston harbor with the clothes on his back and $2.50 to his name. This inauspicious beginning proved prophetic. Ponzi's first few years in the United States were an utter failure. He couldn't even hold down a restaurant job as a waiter without getting fired for cheating customers. Instead of "heading west, young man" to seek his fortune and escape his poor choices, Ponzi headed north, landing in Montreal, Canada – on the road to hell with all the *worst* intentions.

Like most con artists since the beginning of human civilization, Ponzi was a charmer. He was slim, handsome, well-dressed, and spoke four languages. When fellow Italian immigrant Luigi Zarossi started Banco Zarossi to serve Italian immigrants in Montreal, the young Ponzi seemed a perfect choice to help sell deposit accounts. There, Ponzi saw what it would take to graduate from failed cruise ship gambler and ham sandwich swindler to become the Kleenex of financial crime.[1]

As Ponzi came to learn, the bank was in serious financial trouble. Insolvency wasn't uncommon in an era with far fewer banking regulations and consumer protections than we have now, but it was how Zarossi solved the problem that created a new (and much, much more extensive) problem.[2] Banco Zarossi's pitch to new depositors was simple: His bank would pay double the going rate on deposits – six percent versus the typical three percent. Supercharged by the slick Ponzi and a natural affinity with the local immigrant community, depositors flocked in. Zarossi might have been able to make it work had he been a savvier banker, but he was

---

1 Manufacturer Kimberly-Clark must have mixed feelings that its facial tissues have become genericized to refer to *any* facial tissue brand. Still, it must be an eyelash under a contact lens to have its brand refer to any genericization process, especially one as infamous as this.

2 Banks still get caught doing underhanded things (search for "Wells Fargo account fraud" for a recent example), but that is *nothing* compared to what banks got away with in the 1920s.

not. The only way he could pay interest to *current* depositors was to use the proceeds from *new* depositors. As long as there were enough new customers, all was good. But when the well ran dry…

It didn't take long for the entire house of cards to collapse. Zarossi fled the country. Ponzi (broke, again) forged a check. He was, of course, caught. He went to prison in Canada. After a brief stint in a maple leaf clink, he moved back to the United States…and promptly got caught smuggling immigrants. He went to prison in the United States. Sitting in prison might have been both the best thing that could have happened to Ponzi and the worst. The best was that it kept him away from the public. The worst is that it gave him time to think – about how *not* to get caught the next time.

. . .

In most ways, Carl Graham Fisher wasn't anything like Charles Ponzi. However, in one important way that matters to our story, the fortunes of both men would follow remarkably similar paths.

To automobile enthusiasts, Fisher is a legend. To the rest of us, we need to pause for some brief background. Born in 1874 in Indiana, he began his thrill-seeking career racing bicycles.[3] However, it wouldn't be long until his interest evolved from two to four wheels. In 1904, with a partner, he bought the interest in a patent for acetylene headlamps for automobiles and promptly began manufacturing them. In the early days, nearly every headlight used this technology (electric-powered headlamps would come later). With that money, he founded what is reputed to be the very first automobile dealership in the United States. He also was instrumental in building the very first cross-country highway. No, not the famously numbered Route 66 from Chapter 20, but rather the first transcontinental route from New York to San Francisco, echoing the famous railroad a generation before. Completed in 1913, The 3,000-mile "Lincoln

---

3   Bicycles and bicycle racing were a *much* bigger deal in the late 1800s than people realize. It was the bike riders who first advocated for better roads, not car drivers. Modern motorists often fail to understand the debt they owe cyclists when they want them to "get off our roads!"

Highway" would inspire a flurry of roadbuilding across the country.

If that were all, Fisher would deserve a spot in automotive history, but that *wasn't* all. Not by a long shot. Back home, Fisher never lost the need for speed, and cars could scratch that itch in a way bicycles never could. Not content with owning a successful auto dealership, he used his money to build the Indianapolis Motor Speedway – the first major auto racetrack in the United States. There was only one problem: The track was paved with gravel. *Yeah*. Fast cars were making sharp turns on gravel. (If you thought some people just watched NASCAR races for the chance to see a crash, that's nothing compared with the first races on Fisher's track.) Following numerous fatalities, Fisher lobbied for (and installed) paving bricks to enlarge the track and replace the gravel. That's why they call that track – *to this day* – the "Brickyard" at the Indianapolis 500.[4]

For all his ingenuity, it was *publicity stunts* that made him, like Ponzi, a household name in the 1920s. In one stunt, he hoisted a new car up to the top of a building, *pushed it off said building*, and then drove it away to demonstrate its durability. In another, he attached a hot air balloon to one of his cars and *flew it* over downtown Indianapolis. Follow-up advertising declared: "The Stoddard-Dayton was the first automobile to fly over Indianapolis. It should be your first automobile too."

In each case, however, things weren't quite what they seemed. Take the "flying car," for example. What Fisher *didn't* tell viewers is that the car was an empty shell. It had its engine removed to lighten the load. As people watched the flight, Fisher's team drove an identical car through a backroad to meet up with the airborne car as it landed. Hidden from view, Fisher did the ol' switcheroo and drove the "flying" car back into town.

To summarize, Fisher was a guy who knew how to get things done and attract an audience. He also understood the future. Like Ponzi, he learned to play fast and loose with the facts to make an impact. And he had bigger plans than car dealerships and racetracks. He had eyes on the

---

4 The track has been resurfaced since then, but the name stuck. Reopening on Memorial Day, 1911, over 80,000 spectators paid $1 each to watch the first 500-mile race.

most significant real estate venture since the Oregon Trail: Miami Beach.

. . .

Why anyone would invest money with Charles Ponzi when he started his own company in 1920 seems utterly baffling. However, like all good schemes (including the big one in Florida that we'll discuss shortly), they usually begin with something reasonable and legal.

That was no different here. After a smattering of failed business ventures, Ponzi stumbled on an idea to take advantage of the difference in postal rates between Italy and the United States. The details aren't critical (the technical term is arbitrage), but suffice to say, investors could make handsome profits buying and reselling "International Relay Coupons" that took advantage of war-depressed Italian postage and war-boosted U.S. postage following World War I.[5]

To put the opportunity in perspective, investors might make 5 percent interest on a bank savings account and *50 percent interest* with IRCs. It was a no-brainer for many in the Italian immigrant community in 1920. Ponzi was one of *them*. The situation in their home country was well-known. The arbitrage scheme was (and still is) legal. The 18 initial investors were paid off as promised, making $750 on a $1,250 total investment in the first month. There was just *one little* hitch. Ponzi paid off the *prior* investors with money from *fresh* investors. The returns were so good that most of the next wave of investors were the first wave, with a few new members who heard about it through personal connections. Although wealthier folks would get caught up before the end, note that the initial investors (and, in fact, most investors) were *average* people, not wealthy investors. That'll be important later.

Can you see where this is going? Sure, you can.

The returns were so good that people started piling in to get their share of the action. Within a few months, Ponzi made nearly $1,000,000 *each day* as new investors tripped over themselves to join in. The underlying problem was simple arithmetic. There were not enough IRCs for the number of investor dollars. As journalists and investigators started to do

---

5 To learn more about Ponzi and his scheme, you can hear it directly from the schemer's mouth: *The Rise of Ponzi*, purportedly written by the author, is available in multiple reprints.

the math, they calculated it would take several *Titanic-sized* cruise ships crossing the Atlantic each day to meet investor demand. Yes, Italians send a lot of letters. But no, they don't send that many.

Within a year, the entire scheme collapsed. On November 1, 1920, Ponzi pled guilty to Federal charges and was sent to prison for five years. His investors? They were largely wiped out, eventually receiving about 30 cents on the dollar.

. . .

Scams and scammers are nothing new. We can see examples of such people in all times and places – there's a reason the "Emperor Has No Clothes" and the "Tulip Craze" are universal and cross-cultural cautionary tales. They speak to something deeper in the human experience. Success is hard, and if there is a quicker path to that success, we're listening. Closely.

However, the media and consumer environment created a much wider appreciation and sophistication of these schemes than was possible before. Only so many people in ancient China could ever meet the emperor, and only wealthy Dutch could afford tulip bulbs that cost the equivalent of a house.

We've already talked about Ponzi, but he was hardly the only human mushroom to arise from the dank undergrowth of the 1920s. His contemporary, Leo Koretz, swindled more than $30 million ($400 million in 2020 money) from a few dozen Chicago investors for oil wells. Courtney Chauncey "C.C." Julian took belly-to-belly scamming up a notch by purchasing radio and newspaper ads for another set of non-existent oil wells, eventually soaking 40,000 small investors out of their money.

When we step back, we can start to see the pattern. All scams born in the 1920s shared some key characteristics.

First, the idea should be captivating and exciting – oil wells were the latest thing, as was radio, so you'd commonly see swindles focusing on those new areas. The idea was that people didn't have decades of experience with oil wells and radio stations. They didn't know what they didn't know. That made it easier to concoct a plausible investment story. With the sheer *number* of new technologies – oil wells, radio stations, car dealerships, electrical grids, airplanes, and so many others – crafting a scam was easier than ever.

Second, the potential return on investment can't just be *good*. It needs to be *very good*. Ponzi learned from his "mentor," Luigi Zarossi, that offering six percent instead of the usual three percent was a critical feature. A rule of thumb in scams is that the returns need to be at least double the going rate and, ideally, much more. Recall that Ponzi's IRC scheme delivered ten times the average return.

Third, there is pressure to *act now* before the opportunity disappears. This is FOMO (Fear of Missing Out) at work a hundred years before anyone coined the term. It plays on the psychology of loss aversion and impatience. And indeed, getting in early on a scheme like this *was* the only way to make any money, at least for a while, until it all fell apart. That's because you, as an early investor, would be taking money from new suckers…er…investors.

Fourth, celebrities helped. Celebrities were nearly always some of the first people brought into the scam (or, at least, the first people brought in when the scammer wants to expand quickly); they add a level of credibility and publicity impossible to achieve otherwise. As discussed in Chapter 9, what made celebrities perfect spokespeople for scams was that they were seen as somehow *superhuman* – just like us, but more so. Add to that the rapid expansion of the number of people who became celebrities in the 1920s, and scammers had plenty of candidates to choose from.

Fifth…

Yes, fifth. If you're starting to get nervous about one of your "investments," trust that instinct.

Fifth, investors are made to feel they're part of an elite, exclusive group. Only certain people "can be trusted" to know this stuff. Others haven't caught on yet, but *you* (of course) are one of the smart ones. In a cult-like move, scammers often use this exclusivity to encourage their investors to disassociate with other non-investors, including their friends and family. In the 1920s, scammers would meet their marks in speakeasies, adding the allure of forbidden knowledge and access…and let's not underestimate the role of alcohol in lowering inhibitions and blunting critical thinking.

And finally, here's the test: No scam survives the "look test." As in, *go there and look*. No one from the northeast traveled to Oklahoma to see the oil wells, asked to meet the engineers who built the radio stations, or counted the cars on the fictional dealer's parking lot. Expecting that skepticism, some scammers would trot out one example that they'd take people to see, implying there were "many others" like that one. But most scammers didn't bother because most people didn't ask. If they did, they would see the truth immediately.

So, that's the scammer's formula. Ponzi perfected it – and, as we'll see, many others – took advantage in the 1920s.[6]

If that's all it was, it would have been an odd, disagreeable feature of consumer culture that preyed on the foolish and greedy – a warning to stupid people to be more careful. Sort of like shooting yourself in the foot, not the face. Painful, but not fatal.

What if it didn't always turn out that way? What if a bigger scam didn't simply end with lost savings and injured pride? What if the scam wasn't postal coupons or oil wells? What if the scam was your house? And what if that scam puts the entire consumer economy at risk?

Uh oh.

...

To see this slow-motion car wreck that was the Florida real estate market in all its glory, we need to turn back to Carl Fisher. Of course, Fisher wasn't alone. In this book, *Bubble in the Sun: The Florida Boom of the 1920s and How It Brought on the Great Depression*, historian Christopher Knowlton introduces us to an entire smarmy cast of characters, including other real estate developers George Merrick and Addison Mizner. The title is provocative (and a bit hyperbolic), but it's not unjustified. Ponzi's scheme fell apart in a matter of months, and although painful for those involved, its broader impact was limited. Florida's real estate market would take much longer to implode, and the results would be much more widespread.

Knowlton's book is an excellent resource for understanding the gory details – especially the often-untold stories of the laborers who did all the actual work. However, it's easy to miss the palm tree for the frond. We're going to stick with Fisher's part of the story. To keep our focus and follow the narrative, we'll use the

---

6   The U.S. Securities and Exchange Commission (SEC) has its own version of this formula on its website. It's worth checking out.

same six-step scammer's formula Ponzi so helpfully showed us.

Let's get started.

. . .

First, Miami was *indeed* compelling for several reasons. For anyone who has lived through a brutal northern winter, it's not difficult to understand why. Miami's temperature rarely dips below 50 degrees Fahrenheit, even on the coldest nights. It's hot during the summer, of course – sweltering might be a better word, given the relative humidity – but it's not *desert* hot. In fact, the heat encourages residents to head for the water, which south Florida has in ample supply.

Despite those apparent advantages, Miami faced some serious challenges. Before the 1920s, Miami was a port city (village?) of barely 5,000 people, depending on how you counted. The beaches, such as they were, amounted to strips of sand here and there (showing the area's potential), but primarily featured natural coastal vegetation. Sunbathers don't set out their towels on mangrove roots. What's worse, it was hard to get to. Roads before the 1920s weren't the highways we enjoy today…if they existed at all. Most people came in by boat.

Even Key West was a more prominent attraction. As a port on the tip of Florida Keys, the southernmost city in the continental United States boasted more than 10,000 people, primarily there to support the naval base, fish, write novels, or breed six-toed cats.[7] The railroad out to the final Key was one of the significant unheralded engineering accomplishments of the 20th century, rivaling the challenge of the Panama Canal.[8]

In other words, the area had potential. It didn't take long for Fisher and his contemporaries to work to build the infrastructure and develop the real estate strategy required to unlock that potential. That was Job One. If people couldn't get there, other than by boat, or couldn't stay there, other

---

7   You can visit Earnest Hemingway's house in Key West and meet the famous six-toed cats. So the story goes, they were bred by the Navy because the extra toe would make them better on-ship mousers. Today, they're just fun lap cats, cared for and protected by volunteer retirees.

8   You can still see remnants of the old railroad when you drive U.S. Highway 1 out to Key West.

than in a tent, Miami would only attract the truly wealthy adventurers. (That happened, but it was only a few people.) Florida needed better roads – specifically, a route connecting the northeast to Miami. It also needed hotels – swanky getaways that would serve as the destination for wealthy drivers on a week's vacation.[9] It also needed beaches; what's today the City of Miami Beach was then a marshy mosquito rookery.

Job Two was style. Miami needed its own style, a brand that people would come to recognize in its architecture. Today, that architecture still dominates many parts of the city (or it has been restored to match). Then, plastered pastel stucco was not only climate-appropriate but utterly different than the industrial cities of the north or the palatial estates of the deep south.[10] Fashion followed architecture (see Chapter 22 for more), and it helped that the temperature encouraged light clothing…or, more to the point, much *less* clothing.

Speaking of less clothing, let's discuss Job Three: Entertainment. When you've got Miami's weather, you don't need the theater culture of New York or the power brokers of Washington. You simply walk outside. Ideally, with one of the new "bathing costumes" coming into fashion on Miami's new beaches. When you look at bathing suits around the turn of the century, they were more like bathing *clothes*. Most people remained covered from head to toe. That made some sense in the (often chilly, even in summer) waters around Cape Cod, but those same full-body suits could get you heat stroke in Miami. Naturally, clothes shrunk. Both men and women started showing more skin, and it drove people wild.[11] More skin plus free-flowing (illegal) rum from the Caribbean encouraged a party culture that remains strong more than 100 years later.

In short, Fisher and others lobbied for the basic infrastructure, built the hotels for people to stay in, and encouraged the culture that ensured

---

9 Knowlton's book also covers the need for worker housing and how appalling it truly was.

10 Mizner and Singer were primarily responsible for the Miami style, but Fisher certainly followed suit.

11 If you're thinking bikinis, dial it back. Imagine a modest one-piece bathing suit for women today. Bikinis would come much later.

guests would enjoy themselves.[12] But what happened when people didn't want to leave? That brings us to Job Four: Housing. It's in these new housing developments where our story starts to turn.

The developers focused on two innovations, both critical to what would eventually play out in southern Florida. The first was the idea of the "planned community." All communities are planned to one extent or another, but this concept took it up a notch. Instead of cities growing organically over time as new residents moved in (see, basically every other city to that point), they would sketch out a vision for the city in advance, *before* the first residents moved in – the ideal population, residential areas (each with different income levels), commercial zones, amenities, and transportation. Everyone copied George Merrick's Coral Gables development, including Fisher.

Residents who wanted to move in would need to abide by certain restrictions and purchase their homes and construction from certain builders.[13] Can you guess who owned (or owned interest in) the construction firms? Sure, you can. You can also see the appeal to new residents. The developer could sell a community vision free from a sordid past or messy compromises and mistakes. Buying in was quite compelling, especially when you're struggling to find good real estate in an overcrowded northern city just beginning to offer "suburban" plots.

The second was an adjustment in who he targeted with promotional efforts. At first, Fisher sold his planned community idea to well-off retirees. In a pitch that seems well-worn today, seniors could say goodbye to northern winters and urban stressors and buy a new home in a planned community to spend their golden years in everlasting sunshine. But Fisher was a careful observer of the party culture forming in Miami. These weren't *retirees* falling over drunk and sexing it up on the beaches all night. These were the so-called *nouveau-riche* – people making their fortunes in the consumer product boom of the era (and yes, some – though not as many

---

12   Fisher was in his element here. He understood the need for roads at a deeper level than any of the other major developers.

13   These are usually called "covenants" today. If you own a home in a planned community, you likely signed one.

as you'd think) in the stock market. Fisher put it this way in an interview:

> I was on the wrong track. I had been trying to reach the dead ones. I had been going after the old folks. I saw that what I needed to do was go after the live wires. And the live wires don't want to rest.

In case you missed it so far: Miami had the ideal combination of sun, sex, parties, activities, and housing…and best of all, it was "new," like everything else in the 1920s. All you needed was a car, and you could arrive at the very definition of a booming real estate market.

Fisher's promotional strategy – designed around the planned community and new money investors – set the stage for what was to come.

. . .

The second part of the formula: not just *good* return on investment; *outstanding* returns.

It's important to remember that while we're focusing on Fisher, that's simply out of convenience. We've already mentioned a few of his contemporaries: George Merrick, Addison Cairns Mizner, and Paris Singer. Each was aggressively buying land, creating community plans, and throwing up homes on *both sides* of the Florida peninsula as quickly as possible.[14]

What's important to know at this stage (mainly the early years of the 1920s) is that there was still plenty of "real" demand for property. In short, more people were moving into Florida than there were properties to sell them. By some estimates, more than 7,000 people arrived in the state *daily*. In 1925 alone, Florida gained more than 2.5 *million* new residents. That imbalance of low supply and high demand is an Economics 101 lesson. Prices were going up. Fast.

Fisher told his buyers that his prices would go up (not the *resale* market; *his* prices) by ten percent each year. His buyers, often savvy investors, immediately understood what was *not* being said. The average person might be tempted to think *buy now*, which they did, but investors

---

14 About 350 miles of Everglades wetlands – less generously called "Swampland" – separated the Atlantic and Gulf coastal developments. That little tidbit of geography will become important later.

understood that a commitment to raise prices by ten percent each year was like a guaranteed rate of return. Typical bank interest rates of that time maxed out between three and five percent. Stock market returns might be higher, or they might be much lower. It all depended on the market, and very few people were actually invested in the stock market in the 1920s.[15] Additionally, real estate was (and still is) often considered a safer investment than stocks. The land will always be worth *something*, right? And prices *were* going up everywhere in south Florida. Developers would routinely sell every lot within 24 hours, all paid in cash. Before 1925, that's how it was. People had the money, and they paid in full.

It wouldn't stay that way.

. . .

Third, there is pressure to *act now* before the opportunity disappears.

Until this point, the market was boiling, but it hadn't frothed over and spilled onto the burner. Prices were going up, but they weren't skyrocketing. As we've mentioned, people who wanted to buy property (empty lots or completed homes) could do so, although choice properties were moving fast.

By the middle of the decade, however, things began to change. At first, it was simply the lure of living in south Florida – the weather, the lifestyle, the beautiful people, the easy booze, and the solid investment opportunity open to early buyers. However, unlike a natural hot market that fizzles out, when the scammers enter the fray, they tend to overheat the market. That's precisely what happened.

Fisher and his contemporaries (as well as hundreds of real estate agents) began advertising aggressively in northern newspapers and radio stations. Here's a typical example, published in 1924 by Miami Realtor

---

15   Unlike what you might have been led to believe, stock market participation in the 1920s was not at all as common as it is today. There was no such thing as a 401k, 403b, or other Investment Retirement Account (IRA). Only a tiny percentage of Americans owned stocks, which is why the average person wasn't that impacted by the crash of 1929…at least, not at first.

Henry Sprague regarding his 140-acre plot selling for $68 per acre:

> Wake up—act and buy Tamiami Trail frontage—buy NOW—prices along the Trail are not going down.... I would like to buy it myself, but as I cannot handle it, I am offering it for a quick sale.... This tract should double in value long before it is paid for. If you want this—better bring your checkbook.

It was advertisements like this that served as the ominous, foreboding music in our story. These ads weren't just targeted at wealthy people who could afford to pay cash outright; they targeted people (and banks) that would allow buying "on call" – essentially putting down only a portion of the money to purchase a property.

If that sounds vaguely familiar to what you might have read about stock market meltdowns and other asset bubbles, you're right. Let's say Jane and John Averageworker in Cleveland see Sprague's ad. They'd like to buy in for at least ten acres, but they don't have $680. They've never been to Florida (pay attention to that part), but they've read about it. Regardless of what they think about the morality of the people "down there," Tamiami Trail sure sounds nice. Lots of other people are making money. Why not them?

The issue remains: How do they come up with $680? Here's the trick. They don't have to. They could put down, say, $34 or $68 (about five to ten percent of the total) and take ownership. Yes, the bank (who hasn't seen the property either) still owns 90-95 percent and will ask Jane and John to make interest payments. But here's the trick. If they resell the property before the end-of-term balloon payment comes due (aka "flip" the property), they can pay off the loan and pocket the difference. Besides, we were talking about homeownership, not stock market speculation. Land and homes had tangible value. As the population continued to grow, the demand for homes would always go up. It all made so much sense.

What could possibly go wrong?

As long as prices were going up, nothing. However, the warning signs were there, if either the Averageworkers or the bank that lent them the money would have taken the time to look. Knowlton recalls one investor who started to see the cracks in the façade:

> Shelby finally resolved that she would make a sound, carefully

considered investment. Intrigued by the price and description of one lot, she went to take a look. It turned out to be a rock pit. But in Fort Lauderdale, she passed on another that soon sold for $60,000. A week later, it went for $75,000. Two weeks after that, it sold again for $95,000. If she had bought the binder for $2,500 [purchased on call], she could conceivably have made $35,000 in less than a month. "Terror of an insecure old age suddenly assumed exaggerated proportions," she reported. "Right then and there, I succumbed to the boom bacillus. I would gamble outright. The illusion of investment vanished."

Note a couple of things in that example. The first one you notice is the rapid acceleration in prices. Shelby did well, but that's because she was *on the ground* and *actually went to look* at the properties.

Those that didn't? Well, they often ended up buying "swampland" – land away from the coasts that was nearly impossible to develop (it's an alligator-infested wetland), but happens to sit alongside roads that *connect* separate communities on either side of the peninsula. Shelby knew not to buy that. Jane and John Averageworker in Cleveland did not, and worse, their bank didn't realize that it could turn into an awful loan.

To keep up with demand, Fisher and other developers ran fast and loose with all aspects of their business as the 20s rolled on. (In fact, we *still* don't have accurate records of what happened back then. That's how bad it was.) They knew it was a house of cards and didn't want anyone looking too closely.

That's where the celebrities and publicity stunts came in.

. . .

It was none other than president-elect Warren Harding who kicked off a wild ride of publicity stunts throughout the early 1920s. On a Miami vacation before he took office, Fisher took the opportunity to enlist his small *elephant* as Harding's caddie on the golf course.[16] "I am certain I am going to get a million dollars' worth of advertising out of that elephant,"

---

16   The elephant's name was Rosie. What's "small"? About chest height when Harding was there. She'd grow, however, and be part of plenty of golf stunts (such as teeing off from atop the elephant). Yeah, it's as cruel as you think it is.

Fisher is recorded as saying. Who knows about the "million," but it certainly made headlines.

Remember the new bathing suits? They were like a celebrity in and of themselves. After noticing other people noticing his *wife* Jane on the beach in her form-fitting, sockless bathing suit, most men of the time would have been angry. Not Fisher.

> "By God, Jane, you've started something!" he exclaimed. "Why, damn it, I've been trying for months to think up an idea for advertising the Beach nationally. We'll get the prettiest girls we can find and put them in the goddamnest tightest and shortest bathing suits and no stockings or swimming shoes either. We'll have their pictures taken and send them all over the goddamn country as 'the Bathing Beauties of Miami Beach.'"

Not to be outdone, other developers paid a swimmer (Olympian Helen Wainwright) $10,000 to swim around Davis Islands – presumably in a similarly form-fitting costume. They'd bring in tennis professionals to give lessons. Golf pros, too, though it's unclear if more circus animals were involved. Closer to Fisher's heart, Miami Beach featured auto races, speedboat races, barnstorming exhibitions, and flights to show investors the islands from the air.[17] Developers from Tampa and Orlando knew Miami had the big draw, so they'd station buses at the ready to whisk potential buyers across the swamps to *their* developments. Even noted bible-thumper William Jennings Bryan (see Chapter 11) got into the act, talking up one of Merrick's properties.

Supporting this elephant-fueled rave of public relations were *quite literally* tens of thousands of classified advertisements placed in newspapers all over the country. The *Miami Herald* alone ran more than 600,000 of them. What was the average person *supposed* to think? It sure seemed like an exclusive club.

. . .

What made it even more exclusive was a change in Florida law – supported

---

[17] Today, we see overhead shots all the time; think of how compelling those photos would be in 1925.

and lobbied for by the developers.

In 1924, the Florida legislature made an important change to the state's constitution. It abolished the state income tax *and* inheritance tax – the first state in the nation to do so – to lure more wealthy people to the state (or at least lure away their "tax" residence). Unsurprisingly, it worked.[18] Not only were you a landowner in the sunniest state in the nation with the best-looking beaches, the most fun activities, the fanciest homes, and the sexiest people, you were wise to move there. You could *save money* in the long run by leaving a "high tax" northern state.

Plenty of people (rightly and wrongly) blame the ubiquitous advertising and publicity stunts as the best way to create a psychological air of exclusivity. Or that rich people attract other rich people. Or other not-rich people want to feel like rich people. Or that plenty of people want to take rich people's money. That's all true to an extent. But savvy politicians would beg to differ: *Money talks.* And there was a lot of money to be had (and saved) in Florida if you were smart enough to play your political cards right.

. . .

The gambling analogy is quite apt for the last step in the scammer's process: The "hold card" was that no one was looking at what was really going on. We've already seen signs of that.

By 1925, it was challenging to source construction materials and nearly as difficult to find the labor to build homes once you did. Not only did that force delays, but it also led to property values stagnating. The *New York Times* called it a "lull" in the Florida housing market, but it started to worry developers, and it *really* started to worry the banks.[19]

---

18 It's still working. Net incoming migration to Florida in 2022 was the highest of any state.

19 From an article in *Forbes* magazine in 1925: "Florida has made money for those who had money, and is making money for those who have money. But victims of the get-rich-quick mania who are sending money to Florida or going to Florida to buy lots in expectation of reselling them overnight at a dazzling profit will be disappointed. Brains, effort, and foresight have yielded, and are yielding, many fortunes in Florida, but blind speculation is little likely to reap anything but loss and sorrow. Investigate before you invest.... Even the stock market has not boiled as violently as the land boom. Watch your step!"

Well, perhaps "worry" is the wrong word. Researching the era himself (and fighting through notably poor records, even by 1920s standards), banking historian Raymond Vickers found that *90 percent* of the Florida banks that failed in the later crash were guilty of fraud. In other words, the bankers were in on it too. If they were worried, it was probably about going to prison.

Northern banks may not have been defrauding their customers, but because they didn't do enough due diligence, their balance sheets were exposed – *very exposed* – to even a slight uptick in defaults. Remember, in the Ponzi scheme, you always need new investors to pay off the ones who came before (and cash out). If you leave early, you could cash in. But if you got greedy…

Everyone got greedy.

In retrospect, the first auctions that failed to command the asking prices should have been the warning klaxon. A legitimately hot housing market had devolved into a bubble. A disaster waiting to happen. A Ponzi scheme. A house of cards ready to topple in the slightest breeze. You could have chosen any of those metaphors, but the last might have been best.

The breeze was coming.

...

On the night of September 17, 1926, the breeze finally came, south Florida style.

The hurricane that arrived that fall wasn't a monster by today's standards. It didn't need to be. Developers had removed much of the protective natural barrier to storm surges, replacing vegetation with sand. Beach sand…doesn't make a very good dyke. Wind-driven rain toppled poorly-rooted trees and ripped away poorly-built homes, especially those hastily constructed – let's call them what they were – *shacks* used by work crews. In the end, the modest hurricane would result in damage estimated at $500 million ($6.9 billion today). It was worse than the San Francisco earthquake 20 years before and *still* one of the most expensive disasters in U.S. history.

It was the sort of bad news that could break through the public consciousness in a way that dire pronouncements about financial balance sheets could never match. The media, as it does, began to pile on. People started pulling out of contracts. Northern banks started calling loans. Many banks in Florida simply folded. Developers lowered prices. It was so bad for many banks that they remained severely weakened years later when the stock market crashed in 1929.[20]

As the Florida housing bubble burst, there was no end of hand-wringing and moralizing about what went wrong. Knowlton pins part of the blame on the hubris and poor moral character of the key developers:

> Three of them—Fisher, Merrick, and Davis—had one other failing in common: they were prone to what the judge in the Davis divorce proceedings labeled "habitual intemperance." As the decade progressed, each developed a serious drinking problem. (Addison Mizner's vice was food.) Prohibition made little difference in their drinking habits. In fact, if there was any place during the Prohibition years where the Volstead Act was laxly enforced, it was in Florida.

In other words, the major developers were so busy getting drunk and fornicating that they weren't paying attention to their businesses. Knowlton continues to lay it on thick, and not unjustifiably so. He details environmental problems, the shockingly large wealth gap on display, poisonous racism (bad, even by 1920s standards), greedy real estate agents, and lying advertisers – all willing to bilk good people out of their hard-earned money to sell them a piece of swamp along a highway in the Everglades. Additionally, the flurry of building coincided with the rapid growth (and overgrowth) of suburbs throughout the country. When the Florida bubble popped, so did dozens of other smaller ones. Home construction wouldn't recover 1926 levels until 1950, more than 24 years later.

Overall, consumers usually make smart choices, especially when making individual decisions in a normal market. But the Florida housing bubble was nothing like a normal market. Ponzi schemes create a psychological gravity that's hard to escape, even when you know what to look for. If we're being generous, we can thank Ponzi, his fellow scammers, and the Florida real estate developers of the 1920s for teaching the consumer economy how to recognize a bad deal. However, it's hard to imagine the

---

20 Another 1928 hurricane didn't help. It scored a direct hit on Palm Beach and dashed hopes of a quick recovery developers might have been harboring.

proud owner of ten acres of a swamp with only alligators as neighbors thought they learned a good lesson.

If it looks too good to be true, it probably is.

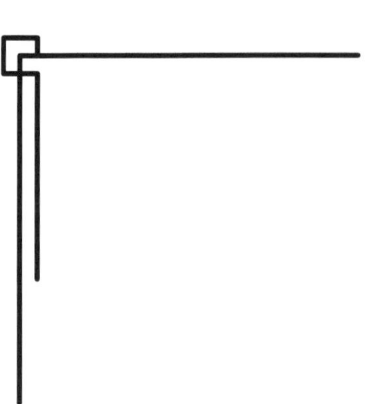

14
CHANGING THE GAME

> It was a one-man station, and that one man was me.
> – *Judith Waller*

The station was WMAQ in Chicago. The "man" was Judith Cary Waller, more affectionately known as the "First Lady of Radio."[1] The problem (and opportunity) were simple: How do you operate a commercial radio station? As in, one that makes money. It's unclear if Waller chummed around with goat herder and surgeon Dr. John Romulus Brinkley (who we met in Chapter 8). Still, she seemed able to dream up a more sustainable business model than promoting quack medical procedures to pay the station's bills. (Goats everywhere breathed a collective sigh of relief.)

Waller, an alumnus of the spectacular J. Walter Thompson advertising agency, wanted to work in print *journalism*, not broadcast radio. She saw herself more like the famous investigative reporter Ida Tarbell and less like the equally-prominent advertising copywriter Helen Lansdowne (who we'll meet in Chapter 17). Long story short, Waller crossed paths with newspaper owner Walter Strong during a European trip and got up the courage to ask him for a job. His response probably wasn't what she was hoping for. Strong mentioned that he had just bought a radio station in Chicago, and if she was interested, she could manage *that*.

Here's where Waller demonstrated *true* courage: She admitted she didn't know what a radio station *was*. Strong, also showing uncharacteristic humility (a good sign of a successful leader), admitted that *he didn't either*. However, anyone (especially a woman in the 1920s) who had the guts to walk up to a newspaper executive and ask for a job was the kind of person he wanted to help him figure it out.

Perhaps as expected, the situation at WMAQ in the spring of 1922 was...not ready for prime time.

Waller walked in to find a filthy dump of an office building with a couple of lonely staffers. The mess she could clean. That wasn't the biggest problem. The vexing issue was that the radio station's broadcasting power was a paltry 100 watts. Not *kilowatts* or *megawatts*. Watts. To put that in more practical terms, she might have been better off with a megaphone

---

[1] Waller isn't the only female broadcaster to earn that honorific, but she certainly was the first. You can read more about Margaret McBride in the 1950s on the Library of Congress website.

on top of a tall building. That said, the station's paltry broadcasting power didn't really matter; they had little (nearly nothing) to broadcast. In a final indignity, the station had no way to make money besides asking Strong (and the newspaper) to keep writing checks to cover its operating expenses. WMAQ was bleeding cash – a vanity project – and would surely be closed soon.

Waller would not be defeated, but she did need to improvise. *Quickly.*

Of all the station's problems (and we won't get into the antiquated state of equipment or the working environment even neutered goats wouldn't accept), the most critical issue was a lack of programming. No one would pay for advertising on a station no one listened to. Filling time was job one.

She convinced musicians to play on the air to generate excitement for their live performances (affordable vinyl LPs were years in the future). That helped. She cajoled the University of Chicago to air educational lectures. That helped too. She included storytime for kids. Children's programming is always good business. She negotiated the rights to broadcast college football. Football isn't a great "radio" sport – nothing like baseball (more on that shortly) – but it was a start. Most obviously (in retrospect, at least) was creating one of the nation's first radio news programs – *Daily News* – which doubtlessly pleased both Waller and her newspaper owner. In short, Waller's answer to anything that would fill time was "yes, please." She had 24 hours of potential broadcast time to fill. Any idea was a good idea.

Waller not only had ideas; she delivered. With the increased publicity and popularity of the station, she convinced the LaSalle Hotel to install the WMAQ tower on top of their 23-story building. Along with a new 500-kilowatt transmitter, the taller perch increased her broadcasting power by at least an order of magnitude.

But Waller noticed something more important. Through careful and continued observation, she understood that musicians playing on the radio drove traffic to their concerts. Lectures on the radio filled live classrooms. Storytime for kids not only sold books, but it also kept moms tuned to their radios each day. College football games kept alums connected to their alma mater, even when they couldn't attend. In other words, although it didn't replace being in-person, *over-the-air* experiences fed a desire for *in-person* experiences. Brinkley and his goats might have figured out how to charge for advertising on the radio, but it was Waller who figured out how to keep people interested *between* the ads.

If that's all Waller accomplished, she would have earned her place in broadcast royalty. But that wasn't it. It was what would happen *next* that would change the sports experience forever.

After hearing from a friend that her son was disappointed he couldn't attend Chicago Cubs baseball games due to an illness, Waller had another idea. In 1924, she approached Cubs' majority owner William Wrigley.[2] Would he be interested in broadcasting Cubs games on WMAQ?

The Cubs…weren't very good that year. Or, frankly, in the years before that year.[3] Would anyone want to *listen* to a team they didn't feel was good enough to see in person? Ticket sales were about as strong as Cubs' batters, but Waller had a solid case to make. She had seen for herself how a broader radio audience could boost ticket sales.

Wrigley, for his part, saw Waller's experience, genius, and grit immediately.[4] The Cubs would be on the radio in a *big way*. It changed everything about modern sports.

. . .

In 1920, it wasn't obvious that baseball would be "America's pastime," that it would come to dominate radio sports broadcasting, or that the combination of baseball and radio would change the nature of sports itself. To understand why, we need to turn the clock back to the beginning of the

---

[2] If you checked Wikipedia as of early 2023, it says "1925." This is one of the many minor errors I've worked to correct during the course of writing this book. I trust James Robert Walker's recounting and research of this incident in *Crack of the Bat: A History of Baseball on the Radio* to get that date correct.

[3] The truth hurts, Cubs fans. From 1920 to 1925, the Cubs hovered around a .500 record each season.

[4] Waller admitted (much later) that she wondered if he would be amused that a woman would ask just as much as she wondered if the idea had any appeal to him. Wrigley, for his part, was a consummate innovator and visionary. He had built his chewing gum business by responding to consumer demand, and he knew a good idea when he saw (or in this case, heard) one.

century and learn (just a little) about the so-called "Dead Ball Era."

(Not an auspicious beginning, is it?)

Baseball generates more than its fair number of statistical historians. It's one of those few sports that collect oodles of data about all aspects of play – not just the wins and losses, but also pitches, hits, swings, fouls, and fielding performance from *every* individual player. According to the data people, there was an anomaly in hitting and scoring performance from 1900 to 1919.[5] Put simply: *The scores were much lower.*

Why was that? Data historians point to a few possible root causes.

The first was the *foul-strike* rule. If you watch (or play) baseball today, you're familiar with this one, but it wasn't always that way. The rule states that a foul ball counts as a strike to the batter *unless* the batter already has two strikes. Before 1900, a batter could whack away at the ball with abandon without those errant hits counting against the strike count. Only *swings and misses* were counted as strikes. That rule change made batters more cautious, waiting for better pitches before taking a swing. Naturally, fewer hits meant lower scores.

The second was the ball itself. That may seem minor, but during a modern major league game, the ball gets replaced *multiple times*. For example, watch the switcheroo when a slider pitch goes a little too low and hits the dirt in front of the home plate. The catcher will absently hand the ball to the umpire, who will replace the ball immediately before the catcher returns it to the pitcher. Something about the aerodynamics and the spin of a scuffed ball makes it harder to hit. Pitchers knew this, of course. They'd *purposefully* scuff the ball, spit on the ball, rub the ball – whatever it took to make the ball *even harder* to hit. When batters struggle, the logic follows that you'll get fewer hits and lower-scoring games.

The final reason was the parks themselves. It can be hard to understand that parks were actually *bigger* in the 1920s. They weren't bigger for *fans*. They were bigger to *play in*.[6] Larger (and more inconsistently sized) playing fields meant home runs were harder to hit. More in-field hits

---

5   Examining the records, there's a definite decline during those years, but it's really two declines with a bit of improvement in the middle years. Talk to a baseball statistician if you'd like to know more (or if you're having trouble getting to sleep).

6   Today's baseball stadiums hold many more fans – nearly 43,000 on average according to Major League Baseball (MLB) data.

naturally lead to fewer scored runs. (When a ball is hit "out of the park," they almost always mean "into the stands" where the audience sits. In that case, all runners on base score with no possibility a fielder can tag them out.)

Teams and hitters responded to these situations by hitting balls low, short, and in the dirt. A fly ball could be caught – and often was – calling the batter out immediately. (Let's not talk about sacrifice flies, okay?) The idea was simple: *Get on base by any means necessary.* This was the golden era of ground balls, bunts, and, most importantly, base stealing. This Darwinian process favored lithe, fast runners, not big, powerful hitters. Baseball was a patient, tense game with a ton of strategy…but not much excitement.

Without going deep into the statistics (which baseball fans love to do), batter productivity – measured by the complex, multi-factor metric "slugging percentage" – suffered dramatically during this era. For the uninitiated, a better way to explain the situation is simply to look at the number of home runs scored during a season. Today, a "big slugger" will routinely hit over 30 home runs. In the Dead Ball Era, a *good* hitter got 10. In fact, one of the greatest hitters of that era, Cactus Gavvy Cravath, only hit 19.[7] Perhaps even more telling, games routinely scored fewer than four runs *in total*, from *both* teams.

All that said, watching baseball in person *could be exciting*…if you were watching in the park. (Remember, this was the era before video cameras and jumbotrons.) Unfortunately, it was tough to see the finesse of the fielders and the speed of the base runners unless you had great seats.

If baseball was tough to watch in person, it was *horrible* to listen to on the radio. If that was going to change, *baseball* needed to change. The change happened at just about the time Waller was figuring out how to fill airtime on WMAQ.

...

What ended the Dead Ball Era? Baseball historians are like regular historians, only more so. They *love* to argue. It's part of the sport for them. In

---

[7] You can see the number of home runs explode after this era; remains high today. More of a mix of 1, 2, 3, and home runs.

short, you won't get a definitive answer, and we won't struggle through a complete analysis of the pros and cons here. We'll list just a few of the high points. If you want more, read *Tales from the Deadball Era: Ty Cobb, Home Run Baker, Shoeless Joe Jackson, and the Wildest Times in Baseball History*, by Mark Halfron, or talk to any baseball geek.[8]

In other words, there's no shortage of answers. Here are the most popular.

In 1920, owners switched the yarn that wraps the inner core of the baseball. Why? Ever since the league changed from a *rubber* core to a *cork* core in 1911, the ball was less "lively" and resulted in lower-scoring games. The owners had a direct incentive to boost hitting – more hits meant more runs scored. More runs scored meant more excitement. More excitement meant more ticket sales.

However, the league disputes this claim, arguing that there was no statistically significant difference between the two balls in play. As for excitement? Halfron recounts stories of baseball games of that era that remind you more of *hockey games* today. You went to a fight, and a baseball game broke out. Fans would routinely assault players and umpires. Players would jump into the stands to assault fans. An air of "rowdiness" pervaded baseball, but it was not a brand of exciting that lent itself to radio.

Another explanation puts the blame on pitchers – the so-called shine ball, emery ball, and spitball were wicked challenging to hit (or at least, to hit *well* or *far*). As those pitches and techniques were outlawed, batters responded with better numbers.

However, that's hard to reconcile as well. The MLB allowed pitchers specializing in those throws to continue using them well into the 1920s. The last pitcher to throw a spitball licked up his ball and sent it over the plate in *1934*. Altered balls seem unlikely as a root cause, although removing them from the equation probably helped.

Speaking of cleaner balls, it took the death of a player to get more baseballs placed in play during a game. With only one ball in play during the entire game, the ball would travel erratically, soften up as the game went on, and become challenging to see as it got dirty (especially at twilight). Cleveland Indians shortstop Ray Chapman took a (fatal) ball to the

---

8   The book is a real eye-opener on that era in baseball. It was a dirty, raw sport with fixed games, gambling, and fighting.

head in August of 1920. After that, the new rule stated that the ball must be replaced whenever it got dirty.

Fresh baseballs might have had something to do with it, but if that were true, statisticians would see more home runs hit in earlier innings than later ones. That didn't seem to be the case. There was likely some impact, but it's difficult to tease out how much.

Was it smaller ballparks? Maybe, but there weren't good records (or measurements) on ballpark dimensions during that era, so it's hard to know. A ballpark rule change probably helped a little. The new rule stated that if a ball was hit over the fence in fair territory, but landed in foul territory, it still counted as "fair."

In short, all of those factors probably had *some impact* on the end of the Dead Ball Era. But that's a statistical way to look at the problem. For the purposes of *our story*, we're looking at the end of the dead ball *narrative*. When do people *think* the Dead Ball Era ended? When did they start thinking about baseball differently? There's no question about the inflection point. From a narrative and commercial perspective, the most significant change was Babe Ruth.

. . .

George Herman "Babe" Ruth, aka the "Bambino," aka the "Sultan of Swat," started his professional baseball career as a pitcher. During his stint in the minor leagues with the Baltimore Orioles, Ruth *loved* to hit, but pitchers only occasionally showed up in the game in a rotation. The reason is pretty simple: Pitchers need the rest. Along with the catcher, they are the only position to be involved in every play; and unlike the catcher, the pitcher is throwing full out on every pitch. It's a lot of work.

Ruth would get his wish. He made his way to the major leagues as an outfielder for the Boston Red Sox. After a series of poor management decisions immortalized as the "curse of the Bambino," Ruth was traded to the New York Yankees.[9] The rest, as they say, was baseball history.

In the early 1920s, the New York media (harsh as it often can be)

---

9   We're glossing over a huge part of the story, and it's a source of endless debate among baseball fans, but it's not core to the story here. The important part is that Ruth ended up in New York – the most powerful, trendsetting media market in the United States.

described Ruth as a "piano on toothpicks." That was an unkind, but not entirely wrong, way to describe Ruth's physique. Observers today accustomed to modern athletes are often shocked to see pictures of Ruth from this era. He sported a massive barrel-chested torso supported by spindly legs and tiny wrists. One would not have guessed just by looking at him that Ruth would be the one to utterly demolish batting records, put an end to the Dead Ball Era, and revitalize baseball.

Ruth was *clearly* not in shape when he arrived in New York. Although he *was* developing as a hitter, his trainers understood that he wouldn't make it as a player long-term if he didn't take better care of himself. After a disappointing 1925 season where his performance nearly *halved*, Ruth spent the 1925-1926 offseason at the gym. It worked. Ruth's 1926 performance bounced back to his 1924 levels, and 1927 was even better. That was the famous 60-home run season – a record that would not fall until Roger Maris one-upped him in 1961.[10]

Ruth's improved performance allowed Yankees' managers to build a team around him. Alongside future hall-of-fame players Tony Lazzeri and Lou Gehrig (who were both young at the time), Ruth anchored the so-called "Murderer's Row" for the Yankees in the back half of the 1920s – not a reference to any mob connections, but rather their ability to murder the professional careers of opposing pitchers. During the 1920s, the Yankees appeared in six World Series and won three.[11]

There's plenty more on the baseball history of that era's Yankees, generally, and Ruth in particular. If you're interested, pick up a copy of Jane Levy's book, *The Big Fella: Babe Ruth and the World He Created*. On-field performance aside, the real twist in the story here isn't necessarily Ruth's play; it was *the man himself*. Ruth was a great player, but he certainly wasn't the *best* player – even on his Yankees teams. However, he *was* the most famous player. Even a century later, he remains one of the top ten

---

10 We're going to *purposefully* ignore the so-called "steroid era" in the early 1990s. In many fans' minds, the few players who topped Ruth and Maris have an asterisk behind their records.

11 That famous "called shot" – the one where Ruth pointed to deep center field as if to indicate where he would hit his home run? That wasn't until the 1932 World Series against the Chicago Cubs.

most famous sports players of all time. Why is that?

What Ruth did *off the field* became a crucial part of his story.

What were the stories? Let's get specific. In those days, players would share hotel rooms when they traveled from city to city. Anyone who roomed with Ruth…roomed with his suitcase. The Bambino was on the town, spending the night with any woman who would sleep with him, and plenty did. Sometimes, more than one per night. He drank – openly and regularly – during Prohibition. Like many other celebrities of that era (see Chapter 9), Ruth was a larger-than-life figure who knew how to cultivate the media.

Even Yankees management couldn't fully reign him in. He'd get in shape, but he *loved* the lifestyle…and one aspect of it in particular. As Ruth put it:

> I'll promise to go easier on drinking and to get to bed earlier, but not for you, $50,000, or two-hundred-and-fifty-thousand dollars. I will not give up women. They're too much fun.

It's easy to say that Ruth was famous only because he was so good on the field. Fans were interested in him because of his performance. Yes, there's more than a little truth to that. Ruth did indeed perform well, but that can't be the only explanation. Ruth's performance struggled at many points, most notably in the early 1920s and later in his career as his habits (and inevitable age) caught up with him.

But the baseball historians we've mentioned point to something more. They argue Ruth was a breath of fresh air that the country needed after not only the Dead Ball Era, but also after the trauma of World War I, the shock of the 1918 flu pandemic, and the brief (but harsh) economic downturn of 1920-1921. Ruth came along at just the right time not only to make baseball exciting, but also to give people something positive – and frankly, less serious – to think about than those things. America needed a break, and Ruth would give it to them. Put simply, Ruth was *interesting*.

Historian Glenn Stout probably put it best:

Ruth was New York incarnate—uncouth and raw, flamboyant and flashy, oversized, out of scale, and absolutely unstoppable.

Ruth was the very first sports player to have a *brand*, not just a career.[12]

He certainly was larger than life, but as you might be able to guess by now, Ruth's biggest direct impact on sports was off the field and far beyond New York. It's time to turn the radio back on.

...

In his book, *Crack of the Bat: A History of Baseball on the Radio*, historian James Walker details the first experience putting baseball on the radio.

It was only months after KDKA in Pittsburgh announced a "play by play" of the presidential results where Republican Warren Harding defeated Democrat James Cox. This was the first time the American public understood the drama radio could add to a live contest. The natural next step was the World Series of baseball. Even better, the 1921 World Series featured two New York teams – the Giants and the Yankees – which guaranteed a big audience. The storyline proved compelling as well: The Giants were still practicing the "inside game" of the Dead Ball Era, and the Yankees were relying on power-hitting behind Babe Ruth. Although the Yankees' approach ultimately would win out later in the decade, the Giants took the series.

The 1921 series marked a fascinating transitional era for baseball fans, but for our purposes here, they're more interesting because they marked the beginning of radio broadcasting in baseball. It was not what you might think. The 1921 series was more like a call-in show from the field rather than a live broadcast. The announcers, famed broadcasters Grantland Rice of WJZ and Tommy Cowan of KDKA, weren't physically

---

12   What about the "Baby Ruth" candy bar? The Curtiss Candy Company (with headquarters coincidentally down the street from Wrigley Field, claimed that it was named after President Grover Cleveland's daughter, Ruth Cleveland. That's feasible, of course, but doesn't seem likely. Cleveland hadn't been in office for over two decades, and his baby daughter had been dead nearly that long. Doesn't it seem suspicious that they launched the candy bar in 1921, just as Babe Ruth's popularity was on the rise, and concocted that story to avoid paying royalties? Sure, it does.

present at Polo Grounds.[13] The reason was simple: You needed broadcast equipment installed at the field, and there was none. It meant that a guy on the telephone in the stands called a guy in the announcers' booth to recreate the events in the game that he couldn't directly see – sort of like a game of "telephone" – but with a lot more people.[14] It was clunky, odd, and…strangely compelling.

Why? Remember, this is 1921, not 2021. Only so many people could fit into the stands at Polo Grounds. Newspapers would publish results – sometimes quite quickly – but even the fastest writers couldn't relay the game *immediately as it was happening*. Instead of 50,000 people knowing what happened and five million waiting until later that evening, all five million people could follow the game live. Walker might have phrased it best:

> Writing can produce expressions that are timeless, but radio can always communicate them in less time.

The broadcaster needed to be more than a good newspaper writer. Most writers of that era hated broadcasting because, frankly, they weren't very good at it. Writers, especially newspaper writers, are quick with a turn of phrase, but they need time to come up with just the right words. Broadcasters needed to develop a "live" style of calling balls, strikes, pitches, and plays on the field. Some of that language adapted well from the printed page; others did not. Something about an announcer yelling, *"Steee-rike one"* or, *"That ball's going…Going…GOING…it's outta here!"* that simply doesn't work on the printed page. Broadcasters lived – and called games – in the moment.

The immediacy of the game that the announcers could deliver *was* important. However, radio brought something else.

For the 1923 World Series, radio took it up a notch and called the

---

13 Polo Grounds in New York hosted all the games for that series – the Giants and the Yankees alternated who would be considered the "home" team.

14 For clarity, Rice was the guy on the telephone and directly broadcast on KDKA, but think about it for a second. Imagine your radio announcer calling the game from a cell phone at the field. The quality would be…not great.

game directly from the stands.[15] Obviously, that cut out the *man in the middle*, but it was more than that. The title of Walker's book should give you a clue: People could *hear* the "crack of the bat," the yells of the vendors, the roar of the crowd – it was a soundscape that radio of that time wasn't quite good enough to filter out. To turn a more modern phrase; the *bug* was a *feature*. Most people had never been to a game, but by listening to baseball on the radio, they could see it in their mind's eye. It made people want to see the game for themselves. Think of it like getting a sample of a new flavor of ice cream at the grocery store. It makes you want to buy the entire tub.

The soundscape of the game had appeal, but only to a point. When you consider the slow, deliberate cadence of a baseball game – the time for a pitcher to warm up, a batter to approach the plate, or changing sides during the top and bottom of an inning – the game features a challenge to radio broadcasters: *dead air*. You can't create a fully immersive experience dependent on random vendors screaming "COLD BEEEEEEER!" into the stands. Earlier broadcasters solved the problem by retelling the story of the game after the fact – the game was over, but the broadcast would be like a theatrical performance of the game that was. That…wasn't as compelling. The 1923 World Series would be more than simply the first game broadcast directly from the field; it would also transform the dead air problem into one of the most compelling aspects of the game.

Broadcaster Graham McNamee became the first true *color commentator*. During the 1923 World Series, he provided insights on pitching and batting strategy, how the players might be approaching the situation, and the stakes of a particular play before the batter walked up to the plate. But more than that, he'd fill the time *between* the plays with notes about the game, facts about the ballpark, how the weather felt for the players, the mood of the crowd, and personal notes about the players. Not only did color commentary help people understand the strategy and flow of the game in a way that the statistics and individual plays could not, but McNamee's context also helped put people *there*, at the game. It made listening to the game not just a substitute for being there, but also a unique

---

15 The 1922 World Series was (more or less) a radio repeat of the 1921 event.

experience in and of itself.

And what's a good source of color commentary? You guessed it – the most colorful baseball player of that age. Babe Ruth.

Despite the success of baseball on the radio, many newspapers (and owners, by the way) on the East Coast weren't that interested in extending radio coverage to regular season games. There was a technology investment that seemed worth it for the "big game," but not *everyday* games. With East Coast *population* density came a density in the number of teams. The Giants and the Yankees didn't have to worry about making fans in Massachusetts. New England had plenty of its own teams. They usually didn't struggle to fill the stands.

The Chicago Cubs, playing in the new Wrigley Field, had no such benefits. They needed a different solution. Waller would take lessons from the first few World Series contests and redefine sports forever.

...

Advertising educational and musical programs on the air taught Waller that radio broadcasts would drive in-person ticket sales. But it was more than that. Evening games reached a balanced audience, but they were primarily a male-dominated affair. By contrast, Waller understood that *day games* could reach children and women at home. She worked to tailor her station's advertising approach based on day parts – advertising home products during the early games and more men's products during the night games.

What's more, the day games on the radio gave moms something to listen to *with* their children – both boys and girls – which made them excited to talk about it with other kids on the playground, their moms at home (who also became interested in the game), and their dad when he got home. It encouraged kids to go out and play the game in the streets and fields in the neighborhood. It drove moms into the day game stands as an activity with their kids. More than anything, it drove revenue for the radio station and ticket sales for Wrigley.

However, we're not *fully* considering geography, and we should. Although the mass migration to the cities was well underway by the 1920s, nearly half of the population remained in rural communities. Unlike the tight population densities of the east coast teams, the western teams (Chicago and St. Louis *were* considered "west" at that time) relied on radio to reach their broad, rural audiences. In other words, Waller's strategy ensured that it wasn't just the kids in Chicago who grew up listening to the Cubs and becoming fans – she broadcast to kids as far away as Indiana, Wisconsin, and Iowa.

That's all theoretical. What was the *evidence* that Waller's strategy worked? Let's look at the numbers.[16]

Of the 16 teams of the MLB in 1920, the Chicago Cubs attracted about 481,000 fans to their home games during the regular season. However, their crosstown neighbors, the White Sox, drew in nearly double that number. The New York teams, triple. At least they weren't struggling to attract fans as badly as the Boston Braves, whose regular-season attendance couldn't top 200,000. However, that was little consolation to Wrigley, which is likely why he willingly agreed to Waller's proposal.

Put simply, the impact of radio was *striking*. By 1926 – the first full season of radio broadcasts for Cubs home games, stadium attendance topped 885,000, second only to the Yankees at just over a million. By 1929, as New York attendance stagnated, the Cubs pulled in nearly *1.5 million* fans to Wrigley Field. To put that in perspective, regular season attendance for *all MLB teams* in 1929 reached 9.5 million. Cubs' attendance dwarfed every other club. In a statistic that would have made Wrigley proud, his stadium brought in 500,000 *more fans* than the Yankees. Waller's strategy of broadcasting *all* regular season home games, and not just the World Series, certainly drove that positive feedback loop in attendance.

(It probably didn't hurt Wrigley's chewing gum business, either.)

To summarize: Waller made the turnstile clink.

. . .

Beyond driving stadium attendance, why was the marriage of radio and baseball so fruitful?

Consumers love new things, and new technology tends to draw our attention. Certainly, it helped that radio was the new thing. However, the

---

[16] Baseball inspires more statistics than any other sport. Check out BallparksOfBaseball.com to dive deeper into this data.

allure would fade quickly if that's all it was.

It also helped that programming staff at radio stations needed to fill time. As we discussed in Chapter 8, stations have – theoretically, at least – 24 hours to fill. The more programming they have, the more potential advertising they can sell alongside it. Waller certainly understood that, but she also knew that the advertising question was moot if consumers didn't *listen* to the radio. Who wants to advertise on a radio program no one listens to? What's *on* the radio had better be compelling.

Conveniently, baseball became compelling just about that same time. We've talked about the end of the Dead Ball Era and the magnetic appeal of Babe Ruth. Both those things helped. More hits created more drama that mirrored the drama in Ruth's personal life. Ruth was just as exciting off the field as he was on the field. He made people want to tune in.

Who would tune in? We've talked about moms and kids during the day – which might have surprised you – but we failed to mention something else that might have slipped by. Baseball played a *lot* of games during its regular season (it still does), and it plays them multiple times of the day and throughout the week. That's in sharp contrast to "Sundays" for American football or "Saturdays" for college sports. Baseball's scheduling variety provided radio broadcasters with plenty of compelling programming throughout the week.

Baseball games were also cheap to broadcast, at least after the initial investment in the equipment at the stadium. Advertisers liked them too. Sports games (especially close ones) tend to keep people glued to the radio, even during sponsorship breaks. Remember, revenue minus cost equals profit. Sports, and especially baseball, were *hugely* profitable for early radio stations.

Of course, radio drove stadium ticket sales. But more than that, a broader geographic fan base would grow as those areas grew. The bigger the fan base, the more merchandising opportunities presented themselves. It also gave people a reason to buy radios. Radio manufacturers loved baseball too.

In between batters, commentators could create a storyline, filling airtime with chatter that would keep people glued to the radio – sometimes even angry at it – from hundreds of miles away. As Walker mentioned in the title of his book, there is just something about the *soundscape* of baseball. When you heard the crack of the bat, you knew something exciting would happen.

All these factors combined to draw people into baseball in a way they were not involved in almost any other sport. Kids would play baseball in the street.[17] Adults would bet on games. Women would listen at home. Employers would buy a radio so that workers could listen on the job. People would tune in at cafes, on the street, and on the farm.

Radio made baseball America's pastime. The combination was, *perhaps*, the most compelling consumer product of the 1920s.

. . .

The lasting impact of the marriage of baseball and radio speaks for itself.

The sports industry in the United States – including only the major professional franchises – topped $77 billion in 2020, according to research firm PwC. That number breaks down into four categories, all in about equal proportion: gate revenues, media rights, sponsorships, and merchandising. That $77 billion doesn't count sports tourism – people traveling from other areas (and countries) to watch a sports game. According to Grandview Research, that's another $50 billion. Sports equipment? $66 billion.[18] Add in another $3 to $5 billion in sports-themed video games.

Better than $200 billion in direct revenue doesn't account for NASCAR and other racing leagues. It doesn't include college sports. And it doesn't include the "sports-like," scripted wrestling leagues such as the WWE. That $200 billion also doesn't account for the influence of sports on fashion – especially shoes, but also on so-called "athleisure" clothing.

Consumer appetite for sports drama is nearly limitless, but the most exciting segment might be so-called "fantasy" sports. It accounts for (only) about $8 billion in the United States, but that number is hardly representative of its influence. In a fantasy sport, fans choose players from multiple teams for their own "dream team" and then see how those players perform during the regular season. Sometimes, fans play for their enjoyment; sometimes, they play in an office tournament; or sometimes, they join up

---

17 Babe Ruth, for his part, was a huge proponent of encouraging kids to play.

18 The total is $86 billion, but that includes home fitness equipment, which isn't really what we're getting at here.

with friends to create an ad hoc league of their own.

The technology seems very *information age*, but it's not. Baseball fans have been collecting that data for over 100 years, so it's only natural that statisticians often conclude that they can manage a team better than *professionals*. Entrepreneur Dick Seitz started the first accepted fantasy baseball league in 1951. He called it the APBA (American Professional Baseball Association), and he built on the earlier idea of All-Star Baseball in the 1940s.[19] *That idea* is almost certainly the brainchild of fans in the late 1920s and 1930s. In other words, kids who grew up listening to baseball games – and Ruth's antics – on the radio.

It all comes back to Waller – a woman with the guts to take on a challenge no one understood, create the modern radio station, create the soundscape for one of the most storied ballparks in the world, and transform the business of sports while she was at it. What do you think? Would Waller have drafted Babe Ruth onto her fantasy team? You bet she would have.

---

19 Not to be confused with the professional league founded in 2005 as an alternative to the MLB.

15
MARKETER IN CHIEF

> One story tells of a bet made between two men, one of whom was to sit next to the president at a large dinner, that he would not say three words during the entire meal. Towards the end of the evening, getting desperate because Mr. Coolidge had not yet spoken at all, the man next him told of the bet, ending: "He bet ten dollars you wouldn't say three words, but I bet you would." Mr. Coolidge, according to the story, considered the matter for some moments, then turned a little towards his companion. "You lose," he said.
> – From a 1925 story in McClure's Magazine titled, "The President!: A Study of Calvin Coolidge."

Like many of the best stories about presidents and celebrities, this one isn't true.[1] There are no fewer than eight versions of this story. Sometimes, the bettor is a "society" woman. Sometimes, a frustrated "high official" in government. Sometimes, the foil of the story is a foreign dignitary. Although the story is apocryphal, the sentiment is not. Calvin Coolidge wasn't your typical glad-handing politician. He was careful, deliberate – and, if his biographers are to be believed – a little sullen, and perhaps even what we might call mildly depressed.[2] Yes, he could be disarming and warm in private, but he clammed up in large group settings.

One would think a guy like this would be the *last person* to earn a spot on the 1920 ticket alongside Warren Harding. After Harding died unexpectedly in office, Coolidge would be the last person anyone would think could win the presidency in his own right less than two years later.

Yet, that's precisely what happened.

To understand why we need to take a quick step back.

Calvin Coolidge was an Amherst graduate and true, blue-blood Republican Yankee. He was careful, deliberate, and patient. Coolidge was content to rise through the ranks of Republican politics, biding his time, and taking the proper steps in the established sequence. He served as the Mayor of Northampton in Massachusetts before becoming governor in 1919. All seemed to be going well, if uneventfully. Without the intervention of fate

---

[1] Garson O'Toole is one of the best "quote investigators" out there. It's a fun historical niche. Pick up his book, *Hemingway Didn't Say That: The Truth Behind Familiar Quotations*.

[2] Which is completely understandable given the circumstances of his son's death while Coolidge was in the White House.

that year, that might have been as far as Coolidge ever rose.³

Like most critical infrastructure workers today, police had limited options in 1919 to walk off the job. That summer, in response to rising living costs and stagnant wages, the Boston police force went on strike. Perhaps predictably, as the police refused to patrol, Boston erupted in riots, looting, and lawlessness. Although the worst impact was felt only in a few neighborhoods, the psychological impact (and call for the mayor to act) was swift. However, the mayor finally called in the National Guard after the *second* night of rioting.

Then, as now, the National Guard is under the direction of the governor, not the mayor. Although the mayor made the request, Governor Coolidge publicly took command of the situation, deliberately usurping the mayor, and settled the matter. In the public's eye, Coolidge brought law and order back to Boston, not the mayor.

In a few days, Calvin Coolidge went from a second-tier, country club Republican to the most talked about Governor in the United States. Even President Wilson (a Democrat) commended Coolidge for his decisive action.

As good as the publicity was for Coolidge, public memories are fleeting. Governors in Massachusetts (at the time) served only two-year terms. Coolidge might not even be safe during the next state election, much less ready for elevation to a national nomination.

Working against him, Coolidge had a reputation for a cold demeanor and curt public statements. He wasn't exactly unfriendly, but he wasn't naturally warm or easygoing. Despite that drawback, the press seemed to like him. Coolidge treated reporters well and could be disarming (and

---

3   Calvin Coolidge is one of 18 presidents who wrote autobiographies or memoirs. There's a Wikipedia page devoted to it. For a broader view, try Amity Shlaes' 2013 biography, *Coolidge*, or Charles Johnson's *Why Coolidge Matters*. Both of them would tell you that this chapter shortchanges Coolidge and his accomplishments, and that's a fair criticism. However, this is a chapter about presidential *marketing*, not presidential politics. Read their books for more. They're both worth your time.

even charming) in one-on-one interactions.

How did this person become president?

Let's ask Bruce Barton.

. . .

Barton is the most influential person of the 1920s you've never heard of. Without him, there would be no President Coolidge.

Barton grew up in Oak Park, Illinois. He was an ambitious midwestern kid who went east and graduated from Amherst College in 1907. As it turns out, that's the same college Coolidge attended. That connection is why Barton agreed to meet Coolidge more than a decade later.

Like many advertising professionals of that era, Barton went through a period of self-doubt and intellectual wandering early in his professional career. America's rural, hardscrabble roots enchanted him, but he couldn't resist the newness and potential of the new century. He couldn't resolve that conflict in his mind, and he struggled to find his place as the 1910s progressed. The Great War (World War I) galvanized his purpose.

Advertising was a new field. If you were to ask most people in 1917 if they considered Barton's profession "professional," they would have laughed in your face. Advertising was promotion – filled with the likes of P.T. Barnum and innumerable snake oil peddlers. The only purpose of advertising was to trick good people into doing something or buying a product they otherwise wouldn't.

The war would change that forever. President Woodrow Wilson saw the potential of advertising when he created the Committee on Public Information, a group tasked with creating and distributing war propaganda in the United States. The CPI hired young advertising professionals like Barton to concoct a positive impression of the country's purpose in the war in the public mind…and specifically, to sell war bonds. Advertising had never been used in this way, and it was a stunning success. There would be no going back.

After the war, when he received the call about a Massachusetts Governor (and fellow Amherst alum) who needed some "polishing up" to get him ready to compete for the 1920 Presidential nomination, Barton agreed to meet him. Although reluctant at first (Coolidge had a reputation for being cold, unyielding, and quite the opposite of what any advertising executive would want in a client[4]), Barton would quickly change his mind after spending time with the not-so-quiet and taciturn Coolidge. This was one of the most important meetings ever held in the history of politics and advertising. What happened next changed everything.

...

As we've mentioned, Americans have short political memories. The shine on Coolidge had already begun to wear off as the race for the Republican nomination for president heated up. In addition, plenty of high-profile Republicans angled for the spot, including Warren Harding and Hebert Hoover. Coolidge was a minnow in a shark pond. He had two choices: Get out or get eaten. Barton helped Coolidge choose a third option: Switch species from minnow to remora, attaching yourself to the underbelly of the biggest shark.

Understanding how Barton pulled it off means understanding the "consumers" who would need to "buy" this new product.

First were the convention delegates. Ultimately, they were the only group that mattered in a nominating convention. They numbered in the few hundreds, with a smattering of aides and hangers-on. Of those, a far smaller number would be the power brokers, meeting behind closed doors to decide which candidate names were placed in contention. Would they remember Coolidge between stogies and scotches?

The national press might be able to help with that. Positive press coverage could make the difference in how delegates (and the general public) viewed a candidate. It was a toss-up which situation was more challenging – that the national press knew you (and had an opinion you may need to change) or that they didn't know you (and you needed to craft an initial opinion). Coolidge was a bit of both, but he was largely unknown outside the northeast.

Finally, obviously, was the broader (national) voting public. Neither

---

4   Bruce Barton founded the ad agency Barton, Durstine & Osborn (BDO) in 1919, eventually becoming Batten, Barton, Durstine & Osborn (BBDO), which remains a force in the advertising world as of this writing (now part of the Omnicom Group.) He is personally credited with naming General Motors and General Electric, and designing the "GE" circular logo. The story of him "creating" the Betty Crocker character, however, is not true. (See Chapter 15 for more about Betty's true parents.)

delegates nor the press would care much for someone the voting public didn't know or care about. Coolidge might have a reputation in the northeast, but that halo didn't glow far beyond Yankee country. Furthermore, his stance against the police union put him at odds with any labor voters or sympathizers. That might not be much of a hindrance at the business-friendly *Republican* convention, but nominators weren't dumb. They knew their candidate needed to appeal to swing voters in the general election.

Let's be clear. A presidential nomination wasn't quite what the Coolidge camp hoped for; that was unrealistic. However, keeping in line with Coolidge's climb-the-ladder history, getting his name in the mix was the logical first step. The convention was unlikely to nominate him, but the new president (should the Republican win) might nominate Coolidge for an influential cabinet post. For that, Coolidge needed to make a good showing with delegates at the convention.

Coolidge had money (financed through the J.P. Morgan organization, among others), so the budget wasn't a concern. He also had a compelling story to tell from the Boston Police Strike, at least with those voters swayed by the first Soviet "Red Scare" following the Bolshevik Revolution a few years prior.[5]

Coolidge was known for aloofness and silence, but *his wife* was gracious and gregarious. Perhaps she could help reach a new group of female voters? Women's suffrage meant that a vast new group would vote, for the first time, in the 1920 election.[6] However, no one had experience with female voting patterns at the national level. What issues would play? Which would not?

---

5   The first "red scare" followed the Russian Revolution in 1917. The next would follow the end of World War II and the beginning of the Cold War. Most people are familiar with only the second.

6   Fifteen states (mostly west of the Mississippi River) allowed women to vote prior to nationwide suffrage, so voting patterns weren't completely unknown.

That's the situation in a nutshell. Coolidge had a shot, but it was a long shot. Barton had his work cut out for him.

...

Although Barton discovered that Coolidge was, in fact, a warm and gracious person who cared deeply about what people thought of him, that knowledge required personal, one-on-one effort. In a mass communication campaign, that simply wasn't going to be feasible. There wasn't time for Coolidge to shake every hand. It was only a few weeks before the convention.

Barton decided to employ a time-tested strategy: turn a perceived liability into an advantage, explicitly promoting Coolidge's stern reputation as something to be admired, not scorned.

> [Calvin Coolidge] seems cut from granite: one could almost strike sparks with such a name, like a flint.
> – Bruce Barton, in a sort of "advertising tagline" for the future president

To understand the creative appeal, simply say the name "Calvin Coolidge" out loud – the hard "C" sounds in each name, two rolling syllables in each – and the word "cool" baked right in.[7]

Barton recognized the need for a mass market appeal, using his public relations skills to get articles placed in the major magazines of the time. He made sure the submitted photos of Coolidge showed him in business clothes, a bit less formal than was the custom with politicians, indicating that he was ready to roll up his sleeves and get to work rather than simply make dry speeches. Photography also played to Coolidge's strengths. He could write well, but he was a dry speaker. In those days, magazines were booming, meaning that his written words (albeit with some of Barton's flourishes) could reach further than speeches. To drive that point home, take a look at another one of Barton's lines:

It sometimes seems as if this silent majority had no spokesman. But

---

7   At the time, this was only a synonym for "cold," but it would begin to become a synonym for "trendy" and "stylish" from here on out.

Coolidge belongs with that crowd: He lives like them, he works like them, and understands.[8]

But more than simply reaching a mass audience, Barton first recognized what product marketers already knew: Individual audiences had unique concerns. The candidate needed "features" that appealed to specific "buyers." Coolidge was a product to be packaged and marketed. Barton recognized three key audience segments and tailored Coolidge's appeal to each one.

First were traditional values voters. For them, Coolidge was the law-and-order candidate that would speak for the silent majority of hard-working, everyday Americans who might identify with their heritage (Irish, German, or Italian) but were *American* first. In speeches (that Barton wrote), Coolidge focused on assimilation and was against "hyphenated" Americans of any stripe.

Second were Black voters, especially in the north, but also in areas of the south. For that group, the message was not what you might think. Coolidge (again, using Barton's carefully crafted speeches) provided a stern, almost fatherly message. Success was their responsibility to attain. Merely 50 years of freedom was a short time to expect all the benefits of White society. It may seem patronizing in the extreme, and a speech more aimed at assuaging the guilt of White Americans. But that's a revisionist interpretation of the feelings of White Americans that largely didn't exist at the time. White voters weren't overly concerned with the issues of Black voters in 1919. More than that, the response in the Black community was decidedly *favorable*. Black voters felt Coolidge was the first politician who wasn't pandering for their votes or simply lying to them. His honesty was refreshing and (as the reports from the time demonstrate) welcomed.

Third was women voters. Barton went beyond speeches here, arranging for publishing articles profiling Coolidge (and his wife and family) directly in women's magazines. Barton's message was surgical: He played on women's traditional role as nurturers of the home, reminding them that they had more to fear from a breakdown in law and order than men. The veiled threat was that they and their children were at risk. The message

---

8   Nope, that wasn't Richard Nixon's catchphrase. He stole it from Barton and Coolidge.

sold very well.

In each of these publications and with each audience, Barton introduced one of the most important innovations in advertising to that point: contradiction advertising.[9] Here's how it works. Barton understood that Americans hearkened back to a traditional, simpler time – yet also wanted the new, the bold, and the exciting. He felt it himself. He saw that he could sell factory-made furniture by promoting it with "traditional craftsmanship" messages. Canned goods would sell better if the words "old-fashioned cooking" were on the label. If you're scratching your head, you're not alone. This strategy makes no rational sense. It's a contradiction, but something about it appeals to our emotional desires – a yearning to have our cake and eat it too. Barton saw the same potential in Coolidge, the brand. Coolidge became the ridiculous-sounding "Contemporary Forefather." Predictably and counterintuitively, it was a hit.

The stage was set before the convention, but name awareness and slick positioning wouldn't mean squat if delegates didn't put Coolidge's name into contention. What happened next was sheer creative brilliance.

Pre-convention discussions with delegates found that many of them could recognize Coolidge if prompted, but that they didn't spontaneously include his name among the top contenders.[10] In other words, Coolidge was on their minds, but not top of mind. That wouldn't do.

To elevate Coolidge, Barton arranged for spontaneous-seeming letters to pour in from all parts of the country. (Simply getting support from the northeast wouldn't be enough.) Today, we call that strategy "astroturfing," where paid promoters mimic the appearance of grassroots support. In 1919, no one had seen it before; there was no reason to believe this wasn't authentic support for Coolidge. Based on the articles in major magazines, it was not an unreasonable assumption.

Editors began to assign reporters to interview this new candidate. Barton was happy to supply specific times and locations where Coolidge would be available (spontaneously, of course) during a walk about town.

---

9   Academics call it the "Collapse of Meaning" strategy or "Reason Why" advertising. Those make even less sense than "Contradiction" advertising.

10 Being able to select a brand name from a list is called "aided recall" in the research business. Coming up with the name on your own is called "unaided recall," and it makes advertisers cry tears of joy.

And, of course, Barton planted the questions and scripted Coolidge's responses. Good progress, but not enough.

How to address the final problem? Many of the delegates now knew about Coolidge, and perhaps they even had a favorable impression, but the masses were not the ones deciding the names in contention; the backroom power brokers were. How could Barton get their attention? Solution: Use the support of the masses to make the dog wag the tail.

Coolidge was a prolific writer, albeit a bit stale at times. Barton repackaged a previously written collection of Coolidge essays and speeches (with the bland title "Bay State Orations"), editing them into snappier and shorter excerpts. Barton retitled it "Have Faith in Massachusetts" (from a memorable line in one essay), printing it in a tiny black book that could fit in a standard men's shirt pocket.[11] He made sure every delegate had one on their way in the door.

As the convention droned (and the big wigs were hashing out the nominees behind closed doors), bored attendees started reaching into their pockets and reading the little black book. Although the convention settled on Warren Harding as its nominee for President, delegates deadlocked on the Vice-Presidential nomination. Multiple names floated in the air. None landed. An exasperated crowd (probably also with some

---

11   Hmm. When you look at the actual book, it's about the size of a mass-market paperback with a hard cover – a little more than six inches tall and at least one inch thick. That's a bit large to fit in a shirt pocket – an inside jacket pocket was more like it. Perhaps Barton had some smaller copies made for the convention? If he did, I couldn't find one. Only a handful of original print copies survive, available from thrift and historical booksellers.

nudging from a Barton plant in the group), began yelling, *COOLIDGE!*

The chant quickly spread. The convention had its pick for Vice President. The rest was history. The pair would win easily in the November election.[12]

. . .

Let's fast-forward 28 months.

Warren Harding was dead. Calvin Coolidge was president.

Although Harding was quite popular during his term in office and continued to be in the days and weeks immediately following his death, it didn't take long for his administration's scandals to catch up with him.[13] In less than two years, Americans would go back to the polls.

It wasn't obvious that Coolidge was the best choice. Herbert Hoover was not only a rising star among Republicans, but also enjoyed broad popular support from both parties.[14] Voters would quickly form an opinion about Coolidge, and there was no time to waste.

With the dirt barely settled on Harding's grave, Barton jumped into action. His first task was another opportunity to transform a liability into a strength. Coolidge wasn't "accidental" or a "caretaker" – he was precisely the person for the job. He was cool (get it?) under pressure. His calm demeanor was what the country needed after years of war, disease, and scandal. The public was ready for calm. Barton sensed it and tuned Coolidge's public statements appropriately. The strategy worked. With the immediate crisis behind them, Coolidge and Barton could turn their attention to the 1924 election.

Winning a general election required more than stability; it required inspiration. How was Coolidge, a person not known for showy displays of

---

12 Analysts of the time would say that the American public wanted "normalcy" after years of war and pandemic. The Democratic candidates (even with up-and-comer Franklin Roosevelt as the VP on the ticket) were the underdogs. Wilson (the incumbent Democrat) was not only unpopular, but he was also essentially housebound after a stroke. He couldn't play an active role in campaigning.

13 If you're interested, read more about the Teapot Dome scandal.

14 Herbert Hoover was a behind-the-scenes figure in many of the stories in this book, especially automobile regulations, home mortgages, and motion picture film promotion.

emotion, going to pull it off? Barton knew Coolidge was brilliant one-on-one, but general elections were mass-market affairs, weren't they? Not so much. At least not anymore. 1924 was the first radio election.

Most people think it was Franklin Roosevelt who first used "Fireside Chats" to connect with everyday people. They're simply not reading their history. It was Coolidge (at Barton's urging) who used radio broadcasts to bring his message directly into people's living rooms. Barton dispensed with the highbrow speeches (Coolidge wasn't good at them anyway) and pioneered a more casual approach.

It was Barton who coached Coolidge into using "I" and "you" instead of "the President" and "the American people." That was a critical change. Holding the listener's attention required a personal touch, which Barton knew from his experience advertising consumer products on the radio. On the radio, if people weren't interested in what you had to say, they simply walked out of the room, and you would never know it.

The impact was palpable. People felt as if Coolidge was sitting in the living room with them.

To boost his relatability, Barton steered Coolidge away from abstractions and policy discussions, replacing them with simple narratives, examples, anecdotes, and personal stories. In a short time, Coolidge didn't seem so cold and aloof. People were surprised. *They liked Coolidge.*

Although radio was growing fast, it couldn't be everywhere and didn't reach everyone.

When Coolidge couldn't be on the radio (in your living room), he could pose for a photograph. That was the only problem with Barton's articles: People didn't read them. They were great for name awareness, but Coolidge didn't need name awareness any longer. Voters knew who he was. In addition to the audience-targeted articles, Barton focused on the Coolidge "image" – quite literally. If Coolidge needed to dress up as a cowboy for a Western audience, he dressed up as a cowboy. For a business publication, Coolidge would wear his business suit. If Barton wanted to reach farmers, Coolidge would wear overalls. His political opponents lampooned Coolidge for dressing up in "costume" for the press, but that's not how the American public saw it. They saw someone who respected them and valued them enough to dress like them. The image of belonging was more important than the substance of his policies.

Barton was so impressed by the power of radio and photography to reach broad audiences that he did away with most of the door-to-door campaign activities. (In later years, campaign strategists would resurrect and improve these tactics, but at the time, they were ineffective money pits for lazy patronage job seekers.)

Barton also was the first campaign manager to take a strategic look at the electoral map, counting states instead of voters. Why campaign in Massachusetts? It's already won. It didn't matter if you won by one vote; a simple majority carried the electoral votes. The opposite strategy held with Georgia. It's already lost. It didn't matter if you lost by one vote; a simple minority ceded the electoral votes to your opponent. He was the first to recognize that a small number of swing voters in those "doubtful states" (as he called them) were the key to the election.

Again, Barton reached into his advertising psychology hat and pulled out a solution. He would begin the summer projecting confidence that the election was already won, but as summer turned to fall, he would change the tone. What if Coolidge didn't win? What would happen to all that prosperity if the opponent won? There were "troubling signs" that the opponent was "gaining ground." The psychology was simple: Fear is a better short-term motivator than optimism. And "short term" is the game's name on the approach to Election Day.[15]

One last thing. Barton struck, perhaps, the most ingenious and long-lasting innovations in a long list of political innovations: the marriage of business culture and Protestant Christianity. To do that, he cast Jesus in the role of a successful corporate manager, guiding and organizing his Disciples to create a powerful enterprise of truth and goodness. The repositioning of the church's mission served to sanctify business activity as a modern way to spread goodness and prosperity into society at large. Now that Barton reconciled faith and business, many Protestant Christians could ally (without guilt) with the Republican party, ingraining a pro-business and pro-prosperity message into thousands of churches and millions of sermons. In Barton's words:

---

15 See Chapter 18 for more explanation of Timestyle.

All business is his Father's business. All work is worship. All useful service, prayer.[16]

Democrat John Davis didn't stand a chance in 1924. Coolidge won convincingly: 382 to 136 electoral votes.

. . .

Coolidge won the presidency. Barton won presidential marketing. How many innovations did Barton introduce in a six-month period, all adapted seamlessly from consumer culture? Let's count them.

He planted stories favorable to Coolidge in major magazines to boost name awareness and, later, to craft a brand image through photography. Candidates from then on would use variations on that technique. Later, they'd create the "media" by publishing their own books (though primarily through ghostwriters).

If the media wasn't fast enough, Barton created support out of thin air. Organizations and politicians of all stripes still use astroturfing to fake grassroots, popular support today – more often using social media and bots than form letters and postage stamps.

Barton capitalized on lingering fear of lawlessness and immigration to make "law and order" and "America first" the first persistent wedge issues. He understood you could never entirely eliminate criminality or completely cut off immigration. Yes, prohibition and suffrage motivated voters (as we saw in Chapter 5), but they were essentially complete once passed. By contrast, Barton could use these new wedge issues to whip up favorable public sentiment on demand.

Which voters cared most about wedge issues? The "silent majority," of course – those people "fed up with politics as usual" and who needed someone to "fight for *them*" in Washington. If not the silent majority, perhaps "soccer moms," "the Black vote," or "Evangelicals" could push

---

16 Barton wrote two well-known books, *The Man Nobody Knew* (about Jesus) and *The Book Nobody Knew* (about the Bible). His biographer, Richard Fried, titled his book (cleverly), *The Man Everybody Knew: Bruce Barton and the Making of Modern America*. As of this writing, the book had four reviews on Amazon. It's worth more than that. Pick it up.

your candidate over the edge. Barton pioneered all those segmentation strategies.

Working within the party system and major media was ideal. Still, if the party or papers wouldn't go along, advertisers like Barton were comfortable taking their "product" direct to the "consumer," bypassing the power structure or manipulating it for their ends. Donald Trump's candidacy and presidency in 2016 took predictable pages from that playbook.

When we think about the political marketing of the 20th century, we don't often think of Coolidge, and we certainly don't think of Bruce Barton. But Franklin Roosevelt wasn't the first president to use the radio; John Kennedy wasn't the first president to craft a visual image; Ronald Reagan wasn't the first to put America first. They all owe their *marketing* success to Barton.

It was a change in culture that could not have happened before the 1920s without the training in consumerism that voters were getting in their daily lives. They were ready. Barton transformed American politics from civic virtue to consumer choice. Politicians were the products. Legislation was a service. Votes were the price you paid.

All that other stuff? That's "just marketing."

16
FIVE-CENT TRIP TO HELL

Our silent film opens with small-town Remember "Mem" Steddon on a train to Los Angeles with her worldly new husband, Owen Scudder.

Everything seems the perfect picture of a whirlwind marital bliss, but there's a nervousness in Mem's eyes. When the train stops for water in the California desert, she seizes the opportunity to rabbit, disappearing into the landscape. In a few moments, the train resumes its westward trek. You might expect her new beau to halt the train and lead a search party into the hardscrabble wilderness, but he does nothing.

"Why didn't he tell the conductor and stop the train?" the title card on the screen asks. (Remember, this is a silent film.[1]) But the pregnant question goes unanswered.

Mem quickly regrets her ill-planned escape. Wandering through the desert, albeit with perfect hair and makeup, she comes across an Arab riding a camel. No, Mem wasn't hallucinating from lack of water; this "Arab" is an actor on location filming a movie. (Yes, this is a movie within a movie. It's all very satirical, as we'll see.) Rescued but trapped on set, Mem accepts an offer to play a bit part in the movie to earn her keep during filming. As it turns out, she seems to have a knack for cinema.

Meanwhile, we check in with the dastardly Mr. Scudder. Mem was right to be nervous. He's been playing the "sweet-talk her, marry her, take out life insurance on her, and murder her" game. Eventually, he ends up in London, where he meets his comeuppance: a "Black Widow" playing the same game. Barely escaping with his life, Owen returns to the United States in search of Mem.

Let's hit the fast-forward button. In a combination of lucky breaks and hard work, Mem ends up landing ever-better roles until she's a major Hollywood star. Skip forward a few more years, and who comes back into the picture? Owen! The same schmuck who left her to die in the desert is now jealous of her stardom (and her *pair* of gentleman suitors), and he wants her back. Is it a love…square? Two guys. Plus her. Plus Owen. A long triangle simply wouldn't shape up.

The film's climax involves a circus tent, a lightning strike, a panicked blaze, and a wind machine propeller blade inching its way toward a trapped

---

1 Cinematographer John Mescall creates this conflict and foreshadowing with costume, gestures, and expressions alone. Actors were *exceptionally* talented in the 1920s.

Mem. Finally realizing the error of his ways, Owen saves Mem from the spinning blades of death in time's nick, only to be mortally wounded. In his dying moments, he admits to Mem that they were never truly married, making her free to choose a more deserving suitor.

Only moments removed from her horrifying near-death experience, the director asks Mem if she can continue shooting scenes. An actress now forged in the crucible, she stoically agrees. *The show must go on.*

That's the gist of the plot of the 1923 silent film, *Souls for Sale*, by Rupert Hughes. A trusting, innocent small-town girl marries a conniving, manipulative big-city boy. Eventually, that naive young woman grows up, makes a name for herself, and earns a better "Happily Ever After." The movie even features big-name cameos from Charlie Chaplin (a name that still rings a bell 100 years later), Erich von Stroheim, Barbara La Marr, Jean Hersholt, Chester Conklin, and Claire Windsor (names that usually don't).

It sounds like the kind of movie Hollywood might make to shamelessly capitalize on the country's mood (specifically, its newly-empowered half) after the passage of the 19th amendment.

Reviewing the rediscovered copy of the film in 2009, critic Roger Ebert called it "a prime example of the mid-range entertainment Hollywood was producing so skillfully at the time." Not exactly a ringing endorsement to rush out and see the movie, is it?[2] Little wonder film-goers weren't pining for archivists to dig this movie out of the lost-and-found bin for more than 70 years.

Though to see this as a milquetoast, sappy, forgettable female empowerment flick trying to exploit the mood of the early 1920s misses the real drama. The film gives us a clue; we might miss it, but viewers of that era would not. The real drama was behind the camera.

. . .

---

2   Chaz Ebert maintains the website for her late husband, Roger, who died in 2013. Since then, it's grown beyond an archive of his reviews, expanding with fresh criticism of modern films from various authors.

To get a better sense of the audience Hughes had in mind, we need the book version.[3] It explores motivations and rounds out two-dimensional characters in a way its movie adaptation could not. Specifically, Hughes focuses on Mem's home life *before* she finds herself on the train to perdition.

In Hughes' book, Mem leaves her pious, rural Indiana family to seek fame and fortune in Hollywood as a movie star. Her devout father disapproves, but she goes anyway after a trite argument contrasting the chaste religious life and a hedonistic Tinseltown den of sin. In addition to bouncing from casting calls, whirlwind affairs, love triangles, to propeller deaths, Mem uses her time in Hollywood to compare and contrast the church life of her upbringing with the glamour life she discovered in Hollywood.

Yes, the Hollywood versions of people were, on the whole, sleeker and sexier versions of her Indiana peers, but that's where the *differences* stopped. Hollywood had affairs, scandals, addictions, abuse, and broken relationships. However, so did her hometown – the church elders, business leaders, and community pillars all succumbed to the same temptations. They were just better at hiding it from public consumption.

In the end, Mem realizes that people are people – wherever they are – and they might as well be free to live out their lives without the cluck-clucking of crusty older men and women who hid their sins under a cloak of righteousness. Hollywood could be a nasty place, but at least they weren't hypocrites. Predictably, her father sees the error of his ways and respects his daughter's choice and new morality.

Yawn.

At least the movie version had an exciting climax. The book was a plodding, anti-moralistic satire.

What was Hughes' beef with the godly set? It all boiled down to the hypocrisy he saw in American culture – the same hypocrisy he tried to show in *Souls for Sale*. "Religion is the refuge of bigots and idiots," he liked to write. And he wrote a lot – not just screenplays and books, but dozens of shorter pamphlets.[4]

In his writings, Hughes noted that civilizations fought against

---

[3] Both the book and the film are now considered public domain. You can watch or read them for yourself.

[4] The pamphlet was the 1920s version of the blog or vlog.

Christianity in its early days – most notably the Greeks and Romans – when they discovered that this new religion was less about piousness and helping the less fortunate, and more about power and restricting the daily pleasures of the average person. In his mind, the powerful would do what the powerful had always done: make different rules for the masses than for themselves.

He didn't need to search far for his evidence. Hughes saw no correlation between church attendance on Sunday and good behavior the other six days of the week. Of course, some people acted in line with their beliefs, but they were the exception, not the rule. The church (any church) was simply another social organization – like the Freemasons or a sports club – and certainly not worthy of the social standing and deference it received.

Hughes (smartly) didn't want to touch the anti-religious angle in the movie, instead choosing to rewrite this slightly-botched coming-of-age story as a dramedy. At least that would appeal to a broader audience of newly-voting female moviegoers. People went to the movies for an escape, not a sermon. They could get plenty of those in church.

Souls for Sale was the kind of book only a culture warrior would write in 1923, and that's precisely who Hughes was. He was on the front lines of a new battle between Middle American conservatism and the emerging hedonistic self-expression of Hollywood. Up until the 1920s, it had been a one-sided fight: The moralists had the upper hand over the modernists.[5] But with the advent of mass media – radio, and especially motion pictures – the modernists could finally fight back on a grand scale.

Not only could Hollywood use the power of storytelling to make this clear, but it could also paint a new vision of a "life of sun and pleasure" that was at odds with the church's restrictions and delayed gratifications. Hollywood could offer heaven *now*, not after a lifetime of sacrifice and good works. In essence, Hollywood was setting up a rival religion. Instead of parishioners attending church, it would offer consumers a trip to the

---

5   Scholars talk about this as the conflict between traditional "Victorian" and Christian morality and the concept of "modernity" and self-actualization. If you're familiar with the debate, you're more informed than most. We won't use the high-brow, academic language here. It defeats the purpose, as you'll see.

movie theater. People were free to choose which one they liked better.

If that's true, why would Hughes be so critical of *Hollywood's* scandals? Moviegoers would have recognized the themes in *Souls for Sale* – especially the salaciousness and abuse. Hughes treated them as a *satire*, not as an *exposé*. He poked fun at Hollywood's scandals so they wouldn't seem so egregious or offensive.

But not everyone was laughing, and they had some reason not to. It's about time we looked closely at some of those scandals.

. . .

Hollywood didn't take long to start feeling the impacts of a hedonistic approach to life.

One of the most notable was the so-called "Arbuckle" scandal. On September 11, 1921, silent film comedy star Roscoe Conkling "Fatty" Arbuckle and two male friends sloshed it up at a drunken hotel party in San Fransisco. Partying with the group was hotel guest and struggling actress Virginia Rappe who, as the police reports would have it, died the next day after falling ill. Medical examiners would identify the cause of death as peritonitis due to sexual trauma.[6] The rapist? It seemed clear that it was Arbuckle.

As a made-for-media scandal, it had everything: glamorous hotel, illegal booze (this *was* the Prohibition era, by the way), A-list movie stars, a struggling (innocent) actress just trying to make a name for herself, and a suspicious death. Amping up the sensationalism in story after story, the *San Francisco Examiner* and the *Los Angeles Examiner* painted Arbuckle as a violent sexual predator – doubly shocking because of his nice-guy comedy image.

Arbuckle eventually won acquittal on the charges after seven months of trials on three manslaughter charges that ended in hung juries. Drunken parties with blacked-out (or high) guests don't turn out credible witnesses – a disturbing trend that, sadly, continues. Arbuckle might have won acquittal, but no one thought he was innocent. His career never recovered. The only "winners" were William Randolph Hearst's media empire.

---

6   No, you don't want to know more.

The scandal sold a *lot* of papers.

Sadly, this wasn't the only scandal.[7]

1920 to 1924 was a rough stretch for the young film industry. Olive Thomas – star of *The Flapper*, and the image of stylish women most people picture when they think of the 1920s – died of a drug overdose just months before Arbuckle met Rappe. Or consider the unsolved murder of William Desmond Taylor, who was found dead and shot in the back by an unknown assailant in February 1922. Handlers tried to clean up the scene, trying to learn a lesson from the Arbuckle debacle, which destroyed evidence police needed to piece together what happened. Who left those empty bottles of alcohol and slinky nighties all over the floor? Was Taylor caught in a love triangle? Was he secretly gay? Bisexual? A member of a drug and sex cult? In a show of chutzpah shocking even by today's standards, Hearst reporters (along with some thug friends in the mob) kidnapped Taylor's gay Black driver to try to threaten him into confessing. You could hardly make this stuff up.

The subplots in *Souls for Sale* don't seem so "sub" now, do they?

However, there's a big difference between church scandals and Hollywood scandals. Indiscretions (or worse) in a church may never see the light of day. By contrast, Hollywood *relied on* publicity for its livelihood. That bright spotlight would give religious leaders (hypocrites though they may be) a chance to thump their bibles furiously. The problem was the nature of publicity itself. Hollywood is a publicity machine; its job is to bring attention to its productions and the actors people want to see. In the 1920s, that also meant the allure of the southern California lifestyle. That's great when things are all sunny smiles and big premiers, but you can't turn off the cameras when sordid things happen. Unlike a middle-American church that could keep its sins confined to the confessional, Hollywood could not. And the media was all too interested in making its own movie, feeding the outrage machine to sell newspapers and radio airtime.

Hughes might be right about the hypocrisy, but most people would not see it that way. When you only see one side of an argument, it shouldn't

---

7   Independent historian James Stewart recounts this scandal-plagued era quite well. His book, *Mystery at the Blue Sea Cottage*, recounts the suspicious death of dancer Frieda "Fritzie" Mann in San Diego in 1923. It's a well-researched and fascinating look at the dark side of Hollywood's early days.

surprise us when most people think that's the *only* side. As good as Hollywood's publicity machine was (and is), it could not prevent cultural commentators from writing their own script of what happened in the 1920s.

. . .

According to public moralists and armchair sociologists, Hollywood history follows a predictable descent into debauchery.

In Hollywood's virginal early days, silent films were quaint, engaging, and virtuous. But Hollywood would rot from the inside out without the guiding hand of God (god? gods?) and traditional moral guideposts. That's why scandals festered in the shadows – sex parties, drug-fueled orgies, alcohol, and crime. Worse, the children (children!) who plugged their hard-earned coins into "Nickelodeons" were unwittingly supporting this depravity, taking their own "five-cent trip to hell." If that wasn't bad enough, once engineers figured out how to sync sound with moving pictures, the number of movie theaters exploded in the United States, infiltrating not only the dens of sin in the big cities (with "scary" immigrants), but also wholesome, unassuming, and unprepared small towns. As the number of theaters increased, people stopped attending church services. No, it didn't happen all at once, but the decline was immediate, and the root cause was crystal clear.

The net effect was that morality slipped through the hands of church elders, classroom teachers, homemakers, and community fathers. Now it was in the hands of blow-snorting actors, sexually-deviant directors, and money-grabbing producers.[8] And this new Hollywood religion was commercial, not spiritual. They were in league with all the companies tricking you into buying things you "didn't need" – like refrigerators, radios, ovens, and cars.

Don't believe the evidence? Just look around you! Movie screens featured larger-than-life, beautiful women wearing glamorous androgynous clothing, smoking cigarettes, swearing, driving cars, and carrying barely-disguised hip flasks. Those so-called "flappers" (see Chapter 22) were invading small towns. They demanded to be heard – first at the voting

---

8   And yes, this was a commonly-held anti-Semitic trope. The image that Hollywood was "controlled" by Jewish people started in the 1920s.

booth and then (gasp!) at home. They wanted to orgasm during sex... just like *men*. My god, when will this end?! How much more proof do you need?

If you think clickbait is an invention of the 2020s, you would be (very sadly) mistaken. Articles and pamphlets by the thousands spouted all this nonsense in the 1920s.

Where did people get these ideas? It might be from this guy: Robert T. Handy. He wrote *The American Religious Depression, 1925-1935* in the 1960s. He argued that Christianity began to decline in the middle of the 1920s as consumer culture took off. Handy and his contemporaries believed that the 1929 stock market crash and resulting Great Depression would repudiate that culture and guide people back to the flock – sort of like the Biblical tale of Sodom and Gomorrah.

But it didn't.

To their credit, Handy and other scholars were quick to blame themselves and the church, not Hollywood. Organized religion simply wasn't as compelling to the average person once they've seen movies and experienced the joys of consumer culture. If churches preached as they did in the 1890s as they did in the late 1920s, it's no surprise that religion faded from public life. How could your local church choir compete with a movie show tune? How compelling was eternal bliss after death when consumer culture could offer marvelous electronics and entertainment today?

Religion needed to up its game. Handy wasn't advocating changing core aspects of faith; he wanted to make the church relatable to the challenges people face *now*. They might not be starving for food, goods, and entertainment, but they were starving for meaning and purpose. The church needed to focus on the "eternal" truths and make those relevant for the new "consumer," not just the "flock" and "parishioner." People had more choices now. If the church didn't adapt and show its value in this new culture, consumers simply wouldn't buy it. And a business without customers won't be in business for long.

Handy and his academic contemporaries might sound more thoughtful than most of the punditocracy (thank goodness), but were they any more correct in their assessment of the situation than Hughes and the Hollywood elite?

...

Let's step away from the moralizing on both sides for a minute. Was Hughes right? Or was Handy right? What hard evidence can we find?

First, let's have a look at movie attendance over the 1920s. At the beginning of the decade (the first data available begins in 1922), Americans visited theaters about 40 million times each week. That same year, the country's population was about 110 million people. Doing some simple math, you get a ratio of about four visits per week to the theater for every 11 people. But when you consider that for a moment, that's not the right way to look at it. Then, as now, some people love going to the movies, and others never go at all. In addition, in 1922, theaters were not evenly distributed across the country (though they tended to be concentrated in population centers.) In other words, theater attendance was widespread but certainly not universal.

In the silent film era, up to about 1927, theater attendance *did* outpace population growth, but not spectacularly. With a U.S. population reaching nearly 120 million, theater attendance had grown to about 50 million weekly admissions. In other words, the population grew by about 10 percent, and theater attendance rose by double that, or 20 percent.

We can see clearly from the data that the early days of Hollywood did not seem impacted by scandals. If drunken sex parties turned people off, that disgust didn't show up at the box office. (If you're starting to understand the difference between what people say they do and what they *actually* do as a crucial part of consumer culture, you are beginning to catch on.)

But the most significant change, by far, came with synchronized sound. Silent movies had sound but were limited to music and cue cards. Synchronized sound meant that the audience could hear the actors talking. That was a huge deal, and people loved it.

U.S. population continued to grow in the 1920s, but the growth rate flattened by the decade's end, edging up only a couple of percentage points per year. By contrast, theater attendance spiked during that time.

By 1929, theater attendance reached over 100 million visits per week. By 1932, that number would peak (for all time, so far, by the way) at 110 million weekly visits. That meant, on average, that each person in the United States went to the movies each week.[9]

Those data seem to support Hughes: Consumers preferred the movie theater to the church. Or at least they went just as often – Saturday to the movies; Sunday to church.

. . .

However, a careful observer would ask the obvious follow-up questions: Did movie theater attendance come at the expense of church attendance? Did Americans swap one preacher for another? Was Handy correct that the church lost its relevance to the average person?

Let's use additional hard evidence to answer those questions.

First, let's take a look at church membership. That number includes people who identify as belonging to any church. However, in the United States, that meant (primarily) one of a variety of Christian denominations with a much smaller mix of Jewish, Muslim, and other faiths. According to Gallup, which began collecting reliable data in 1938, formal church membership hovered at about 75 percent throughout most of the 20th century, only beginning its decline in the 1990s. As of 2020, that number has dipped to 47 percent. Earlier (though less reliable) data showed church attendance falling from 90 percent to 75 percent from 1880 to 1930. In other words, there is some evidence of a decline in church membership, but it certainly didn't correlate with movie theater attendance.

But church *membership* isn't the same as church *attendance*. People could remain local church members and simply attend less frequently. As movie attendance increased, did people attend church less frequently? Short answer: No. The data here are remarkably consistent throughout the 20th century: About four in ten people attend church weekly. That number edged up in the 1950s to five in ten before restablizing in the

---

[9] According to the International Motion Picture Almanac, theater attendance feel throughout the 1950s and 1960s as television caught on, bottoming out in the 1970s at about 20 million visits per week. That number remains low – about 30 million visits per week by 2000 – or about one-third of the peak in the late 1920s and early 1930s.

1960s. That bears out with the experience of pastors. They'll tell you that their membership is routinely about two to two and a half times weekly attendance. There are plenty of reasons for this – personal issues, illness, travel, or simply lacking a perceived desire or need. However, there is no correlation between church and movie theater attendance.

Perhaps Handy was trying to deflect blame for church scandals of the 1960s by hearkening back to an earlier time when it all started to go downhill. Unfortunately, the evidence doesn't support the conclusion that there was any sort of religious depression to coincide with the economic depression any more than Hollywood was the root cause of a cultural turn away from the church.

In other words, Hughes and Handy were *both wrong*. People weren't choosing between the church and the movie theater. They choose both.

All that other stuff about the culture war? Most Americans grabbed their popcorn, sat back, and let people like Hughes and Handy entertain them.

. . .

In the past 100 years, not much has changed.

Feeling tremendous pressure to clean up its act, the movie industry consolidated. With that consolidation came the agreement to self-police content and avoid additional scrutiny. (It's much easier with a handful of major film studios than it is with dozens.) Gone were the edgier movies of the 1920s, replaced with *Miracle on 34th Street* and *Gone with the Wind* in the 1930s. In the Great Depression and War Years, the biggest swear word was "damn," and married couples slept in different beds. Hollywood stars were still pretty, but they kept the themes decidedly PG.

In this, the church thought it had won, and to an extent, perhaps it had. But the tension never went away. Hollywood, ever seeking audiences hungry for entertainment, understood that edginess sells. As the 1960s and 1970s progressed, movies began to change. Moralists didn't have nearly the trouble with violence as they did with sex, so actors in westerns, space operas, and war movies blew each other away with gusto. If Hollywood did push the boundary, there would be protests from the usual quarters (which usually boosted ticket sales), and the studios would dial it back for a while. It was like a game of cat and mouse where the cat was lazy, asleep, or couldn't see very well. Hollywood will find a way to make that movie if it sells tickets.

But Hollywood also felt (and continues to feel) that it is the champion of progressive culture, free from the church's restrictions. Sometimes, studio executives and movie stars privately (and lately, not so privately) lampoon middle-American "bumpkins" for not being as tuned into the world as they are. Over the decades, Hollywood has pushed the boundaries on what messages it shows on screen. Filmmakers, often deeply committed progressives themselves, *want* to make viewers uncomfortable. In these cases, however, it's not the church that gets in the way; it's the moviegoer. Consumers tell Hollywood, in no uncertain terms, what they're ready for and what they're not. Go too far, and the movie bombs at the box office.

For his part, Hughes had a tough relationship with Hollywood. Despite attempts to revitalize his legacy, there was a reason his work was lost and forgotten for nearly 70 years. (An archivist happened across a busted-up copy of *Souls for Sale* cleaning a storage room. It very nearly ended up in the trash.) Even amateur historian James Kemm – Hughes' cousin – couldn't manage to save his reputation.[10] This line comes at the end of a scathing 2009 review:

> History's verdicts are often unfair, but despite Kemm's best, belabored efforts to resurrect Cousin Rupert's reputation, he's arguing a losing case.[11]

Being a commentator and satirist is difficult and thankless. Only authors like Mark Twain can pull off immortality, and that's saying something. That's why we've gone to such great lengths here to explain the context – *satire requires context*; otherwise, it's not satirical. Without setting the scene, *Souls for Sale* (the book and the movie) are clunky and forgettable. It's why political and topical comedy ages so poorly. (If you doubt

---

10 It would have been better to focus on his groundbreaking, multipart book on George Washington. Or perhaps his belief that technocrats should guide society and the economy…but he was somehow against socialism and communism…sort of like planned capitalism? It was weird.

11 You can read the Kirkus review of *Rupert Hughes, Hollywood Legend,* on its website. It's…not kind.

that, watch a political satire from even a decade ago.)

For their part, consumers simply respond to their options. They're content to consider what both churches and movie theaters offer (and now, a broader definition of Hollywood to include a wider variety of full-length and short-film creators) and choose for themselves what they like. They want the tension, the drama, and the scandals – not just on screen, but from commentators and pundits as well. Consumers love the show. It's not a game of cat and mouse. The cat and mouse are both dolls on the consumer's marionette.

That's perhaps one of the most important points to understand about consumer culture in the 1920s and its enduring legacy. Consumer culture is not a *tradeoff* culture. It is an *abundance* culture. When presented with two options – church or movies – consumers of the 1920s, and consumers of today, don't choose. They want it all.

The price of the trip to hell might have gone up, but consumers have always been willing to pay it.

17
MAD WOMEN

Proctor & Gamble corporate offices. Cincinnati, Ohio. 1911.

Helen Lansdowne must have been nervous.

There she was, reviewing her notes and sweating it out, about to walk into a room of executives to present her ideas for the advertising campaign for a new P&G innovation. Even a century ago, this was a company already known for its skill in developing consumer products. But this time was different. They were going out on a limb by hiring New York-based advertising agency J. Walter Thompson and trusting their most significant product launch that year to a woman who had yet to turn 30.

What was the innovation? A little background is needed.

Since the invention of the Cotton Gin by Eli Whitney in 1793, cotton harvests mushroomed.[1] The end of the Civil War and changing economics of southern plantations after emancipation led to further mechanization and ever-more efficient yields. A *lot* of cotton was being produced. And that meant, somewhat naturally, a *lot* of cotton seeds. If someone could figure out something (profitable) to do with the leftover seeds, farmers wouldn't need to plow cash back into the ground.

P&G found an answer. Their engineers solved the problem of processing cotton seeds into cottonseed oil that *didn't* smell rancid.[2] The resulting thick, white goo didn't taste like much (anything, really), but it could serve as the fat in all sorts of cooking and baking. What's more, unlike butter, it could stay on the shelf at room temperature for months without spoiling, and unlike animal fats and lard, it had a neutral taste. They even came up with a catchy name for it: "Crisco," after its first candidate, "Crispo," was rejected because a potato chip company came up with that first. (In fairness, they should have seen that coming.)

The problem was that people had prior opinions about cottonseed oil – specifically, the opinion that it smelled like a raccoon defecated in a gym sock.

---

1   Patented in 1794, Eli Whitney's cotton gin received number 72-X. It sort of makes you curious about patents 1 through 71, doesn't it?

2   That was a big win, by the way. The process is called hydrogenation, and basically involves getting water molecules to bond inside the lipid (fat) molecule chains. Hydrogenation is common in processed foods today. Just look at many labels in the grocery store and you'll see some version of it.

The thought of baking a pie crust with cottonseed oil was…unappetizing.

The all-male P&G answer to that smelly misconception was to tout this innovation as a "scientific discovery," focusing on the hydrogenation process and the broader benefits of industrialized food processing. That would surely convince the woman of the house to stock their pantries with this strange white glop. Wouldn't it? Let's just say Lansdowne had different ideas. She shared her ideas in the form of an instructive story.

Imagine a young woman in her home raising two young children. A few years back, she moved from her parent's rural homestead to an apartment in the city with her new husband in hopes of better career opportunities. Away from the maternal support structure in her mother's kitchen, this young woman was on her own. She could send a letter asking mom for advice, but it might take weeks to get a response. Telegraphs are a bit quicker, but they were expensive. Her parents didn't have a telephone, and to be fair, she couldn't afford one either.

Like her mother (and her mother before her), she cooks with lard and butter. She knows from experience that those options are finicky and expensive. Make the wrong choice, and the resulting pie crust or pastry might not taste as you expect. At the local market, she sees a new product. Unlike butter and lard, it's not refrigerated. "Huh," she wonders. "How do they do that?" The clerk tells her that it's a new type of shelf-stable shortening that she can use as a substitute for fats like butter and lard. It's cheaper than either one, can stay good for months on the shelf, and it's made from vegetables.

She still has questions. Does she substitute this new product for the same quantity of butter or lard in her recipes? Does it alter the baking time? How will it change the taste? If not, will she need to add more salt or seasonings? She knows how to use butter and lard. She's never heard of this stuff. Most women would have a look, think it over, and then put the tub of Crisco back on the shelf.[3] Lansdowne probably let that sink in

---

3   Many retail stores of the era better resembled a modern deli, with products displayed behind glass or on a wall behind a clerk. Sears was an early pioneer of the "unaided" shopping experience. We learned about that in Chapter 6. Although you probably would have asked a clerk to see the product, and handed it back to him or her when you decided against it, modern readers wouldn't quite get the reference because unaided shopping is the norm today.

before continuing with her (better) story.

Our young woman sees a Crisco advertisement *before* she heads to the grocery store. Instead of touting its "scientific" appeal, the headline reads, "Tested Crisco Recipes – The Absolutely New Product for Frying, For Shortening, For Cake Making." This new ad acknowledges her hesitation by clarifying how she'll use this new product. Additional written copy in the ad explains what the product is and, more importantly, how to use it. It even contains a full recipe she can try at home. And here's the best part: For only a couple of stamps, the good folks at P&G would send her a sample of Crisco *and a recipe book* to get her started.[4]

Lansdowne explained that most people – especially homemakers – didn't care as much about science, innovation, or industrial processes as much as they cared that the product *worked* as expected. Our young woman simply needed instruction on how to use it because her mother wasn't around to ask.

The result? In less than eight years, Crisco sales increased by 1,000 percent.

We can't know what the grizzly, old men in the P&G board room thought about women in general, but the results spoke for themselves. Helen Lansdowne made it rain. She would meet with the Board of Directors at least four more times in the coming years – the first woman to do so. They understood that women might lack power in the boardroom (there were no women on the P&G board for decades to come), and they had not (yet) received any national political power (and wouldn't until August 1920, when the Nineteenth amendment went into effect), but they controlled the purse strings in the home.[5] If P&G wanted to sell more hydrogenated vegetable fat, it had better recognize the "feminine"

---

4 *The Mirror Makers: A History of American Advertising and Its Creators*, by Stephen R. Fox, includes this among dozens of anecdotes from the early days of advertising. It's worth the read, even for laypeople.

5 You may read articles from historians claiming that women *didn't really* have that kind of purchasing power and that it's more a case a revisionism to assign a stronger role to women than they actually had. What historians miss here is the difference between a "buyer" and an "influencer" in the transaction. Yes, the husband might write the check, but his wife made the decision. (Sorry historians, not even a first-year advertising student would make this mistake.)

approach.

What follows is more than a story of processed food and the rise of the modern advertising agency. It's the story of how expert copywriters – many of the best ones, women – borrowed from Old Testament prophets and the Sermon on the Mount to create a new type of faith in consumer products. This is the story of a new kind of preacher, and it will challenge your Mad "Men" perception of modern advertising.

. . .

There was a time when advertising was not considered a reputable profession.

Stop laughing.

Are you done?

Okay, can we move on?

Great.

Advertisers before the 1900s were "tolerated" at best, and it's not hard to understand why. Most people lay the blame on showmen and hucksters like P.T. Barnum. His circuses traded on many things – exploitation, animal abuse, and shock value – just to name a few. But his most significant innovations weren't cruelty and hyperbole; Barnum's most ingenious discovery was the importance of running an advertising operation like you'd run any modern factory.

To look only at the dark side of the circus era (which is the trendy view now, more than a century later) is to miss the point of how difficult it was to make it all work. Barnum faced all the challenges of a modern railroad (the prime method of transportation) along with the added pressures of protecting a hyper-trained performer workforce, coordinating an untrained labor force in each new town, transporting and caring for exotic animals (allowing them to die assuredly was *not* the idea), and critically, ensuring people would come out to see the fruits of all that labor.

These were the days before mass media in their current form, and besides, newspapers were not known for creating excitement.[6] What's

---

6 This was still before the so-called "Yellow Journalism" era and the birth of sensational headlines to sell newspapers. If you're interested in learning more about that, find books about the run-up to the Spanish-American War in 1898.

more, the circus train visited not only the big metropolises but also specialized in bringing entertainment to small-town, rural America.[7] You could get away with a lackluster promotional effort in New York City and still draw a good crowd. You might also get away with it in Columbus, Ohio. *Maybe*. But do a poor job getting the word out in rural Minnesota, and no one would show up when you rolled into Winona. To make a buck in a town with a few thousand people, almost every living soul needed to come out to see your rolling menagerie.

Barnum ran his advertising department like Ford would produce Model Ts decades later. Days before a show, teams of promoters scouted the next town down the tracks. Some would visit the local chamber of commerce to get the business community on board. Others would canvas the churches. Still more would begin to recruit and train short-term laborers to assemble needed temporary infrastructure. All this would help give the townsfolk a direct incentive to talk up the circus to everyone within earshot. But the most critical task was to plaster every surface with colorful, vivid posters so that people knew what to expect – not just from the performances, but also from the sideshows and vendors.

Imagine Disneyland 100 years before Disneyland. On wheels. In some ways, more creepy. In other ways, less. That's the idea.

For people in small towns along the circus route, it was the most excitement they were likely to get all year. Remember, these were the days before the internet, before television, and even before radio. Living in small-town America was pretty dull by today's standards. Yes, you might be able to watch a theater performance, but only the largest cities could support putting on a play. Most rural townspeople would never see one. Yes, the Sears catalog was starting to filter new products into rural America, but most people couldn't afford much of what they saw. A circus offered a shared experience the entire year revolved around – like Christmas in July. The circus coming to town was a huge event well into the 20th century for many small towns until television put a final nail in the trap door coffin in the 1960s. Talk to someone in the Baby Boomer

---

7   The Ringling Brothers (and their circus) hailed from Baraboo, Wisconsin. If you're interested in circus history, check out the Circus World Museum. Baraboo is about three hours from Chicago by car.

generation from a small town. They'll tell you.

Let's recap. Advertising was associated with freakshows, animal acts, scams preying on small-minded people, and rural towns. But behind the curtain, advertising was evolving into *marketing* – a broader concept that involved defining what made a compelling product, setting the right price, and coordinating complex logistics – not simply coming up with snappy slogans.[8]

Before the 1920s, advertisers were all dressed up with no place to go. There simply weren't that many products to sell, and most consumers didn't have that much money to buy them. For example, if you wanted a sewing machine (one of the first consumer products in the late 1800s), only a couple of companies made them, and only then, one or two models. You probably bought it from a traveling salesperson.

The consumer revolution changed everything. Advertising would be ready.

. . .

Despite the ill will, advertising as a business was doing pretty well.

From the end of the Civil War until the end of the 19th century, the advertising industry had grown tenfold from $50 million annually to over $500 million. However, the raw dollar amount doesn't tell you much when considering inflation and population growth over that time. A better measure is the proportion of total economic activity, which we usually measure in Gross Domestic Product (GDP). Rerun the math, and we learn that for every $100 of economic activity, businesses spent $0.70 on advertising at the end of the Civil War. By 1900, they were spending $3.00.

Advertising would grow faster from there.

Before 1900, the driving factors for increased investment in promoting your goods were (a) the industrial revolution, increasing the output of consumer products, agricultural output, transportation, and entertainment, (b) a massive influx of immigration that swelled the potential customer base, and (c) most of those people living in cramped cities where it

---

8 To be fair, it wasn't until 1917 that the word "marketing" even appeared in a college textbook in its modern form. If you're curious, search for Ralph Starr Butler's "Marketing Methods" college textbook.

was easier to use the available mass media of the day to deliver messages. However, manufacturers weren't content to rely solely on print advertisements in newspapers. They hired legions of salespeople to hit the streets – quite literally, to go door-to-door. Where traveling salespeople were impractical, Sears launched its catalog business, using the postal service to target America's still-vast rural population.

But more than anything else, the experience of World War I showed business leaders advertising's true potential. In the wartime crucible of President Woodrow Wilson's Committee on Public Information (CPI), a generation of young professionals learned how to use mass communication to change opinions about U.S. involvement in the war, and more importantly for Wilson, to compel action to buy war bonds by the millions.[9]

Once the war ended, those now-savvy professionals needed work, and the business community was more than happy to snap them up. Would there have been an advertising industry had it not been for the war? Clearly, yes. Would it have been ready for prime time? No, probably not.

. . .

With that in mind, we can pick up where we left off with the cooking grease monkeys at P&G and why they would trust Helen Lansdowne to save them from themselves.

We can't talk about advertising in the 1920s without talking about J. Walter Thompson – not the founder himself, but the advertising agency. By the time we get to this point in the story, Thompson had sold his namesake advertising agency to Stanley Resor. If you're picturing a 1920s version of Don Draper from *Mad Men*, you will be disappointed (pleased?). Resor was straight-laced, analytical, and a skilled manager. He also was just about the perfect person to help JWT face down the coming cultural upheaval – to not just survive, but thrive in it – and redefine what a company was and what it could accomplish in the process.

Resor sidestepped the first challenge: the image of the profession itself.

---

9 Wilson also signed the Sedition Act of 1918, which curtailed free speech during the war. It wasn't a token gesture designed for its "chilling" effect. People went to jail, including socialist firebrand Eugene Debs.

That ship had sailed, and for any business leader that mattered, *advertising* mattered. It was as simple as that. If any ad agency executive cared what the general public thought, they got over it. That said, Resor realized that touting the agency's methods and practices didn't make good public relations – a practice that continues today. Ad people were an insular bunch.

Ad agencies couldn't hide from the second problem: *data*. Today, it's difficult to imagine a world in which you simply didn't know where all the gas stations were. Or grocery stores. Or bike manufacturers. Or… anything. Seriously. Think for a moment about how vexing a problem that would be. Let's say you're a manufacturer of gas pumps. Your target market, one would hope, would be the growing number of gas stations. *But you have no idea where they are.* Yes, you could travel around town and create a list, but that was slow, expensive, and you probably missed most of them. Or you could try to comb through publicly-available tax filings. That's not much better. In a fast-growing market, your information would be at least a year old. And that's *business* information. *Consumer* information and preferences (the gas buyers at those gas stations) were even harder to come by. Trying to collect data in those days was like removing a sliver wearing mittens.

Most business leaders before the 1920s didn't try. They could get away with making advertising decisions based on gut, instinct, and "local" knowledge. However, as companies grew and competitors multiplied, they simply couldn't keep up.

Frustrated that available data could no longer meet client needs, Resor did what any forward thinking leader did in the 1920s: he built it himself. In 1920, he commissioned the landmark study, "Population and its Distribution," with a simple goal: list all retail establishments (hardware stores, grocery, drug, clothing, etc.) by national location. The resulting book spanned 218 pages for $2.50 – or under $40 in 2020 money. More than 2,000 companies bought one.

In 1922, he went one step further, hiring Paul Cherington out of Harvard to become Director of Research. Through the rest of the decade (until specialist research firms took up the job), JWT would conduct innumerable public opinion surveys to serve existing clients and win new ones. They compiled the first retail trade data from virtually nothing: Who bought what, where, and why? Where were the retail locations? What could you expect to sell? Seasonally? Where were there gaps? Where was your competition? What was the ratio of retail locations and options (and product sets) by population center? JWT had the best data in town…and its pick of the best clients. Then, as now, to the data goes the spoils.

However, as ingenious as it was to build the best database in town, nothing stopped other advertising agencies from compiling their own lists and doing their own opinion surveys. Many did. As we've learned, there was plenty of leftover government-trained talent.

The bigger issue was the nature of consumer products themselves.

First off, there were a lot *more* of them. The 1920s was the first time most people could buy a clothes-washing machine, refrigerator, dishwasher, or garbage disposal. This isn't a complete list, but it's a telling list. Notice something? They're all *home* conveniences. And when we think about the master of the home in the 1920s, we're talking about a *mistress*.

Women decided what products made their way into the home and which did not.[10] The home was *their* domain – partly by religion, partly by custom, and partly by default. That meant women made the decisions on a wide variety of new products on offer – appliances, yes, but also foods (like our Crisco example), clothing (which we'll talk about in Chapter 22), entertainment (mostly radio), and children's products (which will get full attention in Chapter 25). Automobiles are the consumer product most people associate with the 1920s – and yes, it was a big purchase – but *most* of the new goodies on offer would end up in the kitchen, bedroom, bathroom, or living room, not the garage. That meant *women* controlled *most* consumer spending.

That realization put Resor (and most companies of the era) in a bind. They were, on the whole, sausage fests. We might chide the men of the P&G research department for how they wanted to handle marketing for Crisco, but most ad agencies of the day were no better. You can see plenty of advertising of the era touting "scientific" food, the wattage of the toaster heating elements, or the horsepower of the sewing machine. The mistress of the house didn't care about those things, and the ads weren't working.

Manufacturers were desperate to appeal to women. Ad agencies, ever the opportunists, wanted to be the first to fill the need, but the trouble was too many penises walking around and not enough vaginas. And simply

---

10   Or "influenced." The distinction hardly matters.

adding token vaginas wasn't going to cut it. To truly make an impact, these women would need to be commanding presences inside the agency with the power to make *real* decisions.

To his credit, Resor was a humble leader who believed in data *and* personal experience. If you worked on the Yuban coffee account, you spent time making coffee with customers in their kitchens. If you worked on the Ford account, you spent time at the dealership selling cars. If you worked on the Little Leather Library account, you spent time door-to-door selling books.[11] If you wanted to market a new sewing machine, but your copywriter's genitalia meant he had probably never sat behind one, you needed a woman. Data could only tell you so much.

What would happen when you gave one of the most brilliant people of the age free reign to make decisions?

Helen Lansdowne would write the consumer bible.

. . .

A SKIN YOU LOVE TO TOUCH

You, too, can have its charm if you will begin the following treatment tonight:

Just before retiring, lather your wash cloth with Woodbury's Facial Soap and warm water. Apply it to your face and distribute the lather thoroughly. Now with the tips of your fingers work this cleansing, antiseptic lather into your skin, always with an outward and upward motion. Rinse with warm water, then with cold – the colder the better. Finish by rubbing your face for a few minutes with a *piece of ice*. Use this treatment *persistently* and in ten days or two weeks your skin should show a marked improvement – a promise of that greater loveliness which the daily use of Woodbury's always brings.

Send now for this beautiful picture

This new painting of "A Skin You Love to Touch," by Mary Greene Blumenschein has been reproduced in nine colors, 15x19 inches, by

---

11 It's part of what made the Book of the Month Club so effective. In Chapter 10, we meet another JWT alum and BOTM Club founder, Harry Scherman.

a new and beautiful process. No printing or advertising appears on it. Just send us your name and address with 10c in stamps or coin, and we will mail you the picture, together with a cake of Woodbury's Facial Soap large enough for a week of the "skin you love to touch" treatment given here. Write today! Address: The Andrew Jergens Co., 230 Spring Grove Avenue, Cincinnati, Ohio. If you live in Canada, for picture and sample address The Andrew Jergens Co., Ltd., 230 Sherbrooke Street, Perth, Ontario, Canada.

25c a cake. Get a cake today.
For sale by dealers everywhere throughout the U.S. and Canada.

It really is a beautiful painting, and it's an integral part of the first in a series of print advertisements for Woodbury's Facial Soap (this one from 1911) written by Helen Lansdowne.[12] *Advertising Age* calls this one of the top 100 campaigns *of all time*, which, when stacked up against "Think Small" from Volkswagen and "1984" from Apple Computer, says something about its quality and effectiveness.

Why was it so good? A few reasons.

First, it showed a clear vision of what you would achieve if you used the product. In this case, the painting focuses on a young woman with perfect skin being caressed by a gentleman suitor. (He's shown behind her – she's the star of this show.) The image is powerful, but the written copy makes the goal clear: *skin you love to touch.*

Beyond the image and the headline, the ad provides clear instructions on achieving the desired objective. Each word is descriptive. You can picture in your mind's eye precisely how to apply the soap, how to remove it, how to use hot and cold water, how to use ice, and finally, when you can expect results. The language is almost…*sensual.* That's no accident. Lansdowne understood the power of careful word choice to paint a mental picture. To drive the point home, the ad made a nearly irresistible case to try it for yourself. Who wants to send away for a bar of soap, even if you call it a "cake?" Add a 15x19-inch print of the painting shown in the advertisement, something you could frame and display in your home, and you've got a winner.

---

12 Note the gender of the artist. Lansdowne was an ardent feminist who actively supported other women.

The results, like Crisco's, were outstanding. Those ads sold a lot of soap.[13]

The campaign ran for decades. Later ads teased sexuality even more overtly with headlines that included "TNT for Two," "Appointment for Love," "Miracle at Midnight," "Contact," and "Sudden Storm." You'd have to be a eunuch (or dead) not to feel the sexual tension.

But there's a deeper reason this ad campaign was successful. Lansdowne was telling a *story* – specifically, an *instructional* story with a moral: Use this product and follow these specific instructions, and you will succeed in romance. Authors in the romance genre call this type of story arc the "HEA" or "Happily Ever After." The characters in the story might face challenges and experience conflict, but in the end, they will find a way to make it work. It's one of the ways romance differs from drama. Dramatic stories can be downers. Romance novels *never* are. That's what makes them so enduringly popular.[14]

There's another word for an instructional story that you might be more familiar with: a *parable*.

The HEA isn't the only parable to come of age in the 1920s. Let's look at a few others. You'll likely see echoes of these stories in advertisements you recognize today.

In the 1920s, as more people moved to the city, your personal appearance as well as the appearance of your home and its entryway, became the object of increasing scrutiny. In contrast to the reality of rural, small-town life, where everyone knew you from an early age, urban life featured first meetings at random times. That meant you could be judged, for the first

---

13   Personal hygiene was a "ripe" area for innovation in the 1920s. For more, look to the fascinating story of Edna Meloney. Her father created one of the first antiperspirants to stop his hands from sweating during long surgeries. Before she turned 18, she had set up a company to market her product – Odor-Oh-No – to society women. At first, she recruited women to sell door-to-door. After a couple of false starts, she hired JWT to create advertising campaigns to help teach people how (and why) to use this new product. Sadly, like Lansdowne, no one has written a biography about her story, which means the only place you'll read about it is from writers who use her story to show how advertisers "tricked" people into thinking they smelled bad. That's a shame. She deserves much more than that. Her story of entrepreneurship is inspiring. It's almost certain she met Lansdowne, although she didn't work on Meloney's account.

14   Romance novels outsell every other fiction category in the bookstore by a margin of two to one.

time, at *any time*. And hence, you need to be prepared because *you never get a second chance to make a first impression*. Today, we remember that slogan for another P&G product (a dandruff shampoo), but advertisers used different versions of that same parable to sell lawnmowers, home furnishings, cleaning products, and wardrobes. The lesson was clear: You had better buy now to be ready whenever that moment came.

Or consider the number of new products on offer for the first time in the 1920s. Until then, only the wealthy could afford an automobile or a refrigerator. Their high prices and scarce availability gave them an allure of desirability. As these products proliferated, advertisers needed to be careful not to cheapen the experience of owning something previously fancy. Well, now, *every man was a "king" and every woman a "queen" in their own castle* – an idea so powerful because it trades on the independent homesteader image of Americans, even though their "castle" might amount only to a cheap tenement flat in Brooklyn.

Were all those "new" products *really* a good thing? Did they somehow take us away from our "traditional" values? Did they make us less masculine? Less feminine? Less *human*? Would our lives be better if we *returned to nature* – an ancestral time when we hunted our food and built our own shelters? In the 1920s, the rebellion against "soft" foods helped sell oodles of *crunchy* Post cereals, and today forms the basis for the appeal of the "paleo" diet.

Even if you appreciated previously-luxury products and accepted modern conveniences for their own sake, you still might be concerned about the pervasive influence of consumer culture and how it might impact your children. How could parents encourage children to do the right thing when they hadn't yet mastered being "consumers" themselves? Campbell's Soup solved the problem by reminding parents that children would not only eat their vegetables, but like doing it too. It's the same "constructive play" idea that Lego and other educational toys would use in later decades.

You get the idea. Happily Ever After, You Never Get a Second Chance to Make a First Impression, Your Home Is Your Castle, Getting Back to Your Roots, and the Innocence of Youth were all *parables* – instructional stories with a moral (and commercial) lesson. Together, they would form a new religious text for modern life. It was more than an instruction manual but perhaps something less than a consumer bible; Lansdowne and her colleagues didn't see themselves quite as priestesses of a new religion.[15] Still, they certainly understood the need to find universal storylines they could bend and refashion to fit the needs of their clients.

There's just something about how humans respond to stories. The first person to write the new storybook would win. And win, JWT did, with a unique combination of science and storytelling. Lansdowne was as intuitive and demanding as Resor was analytical and accommodating. People liked Resor. People respected Lansdowne.

Together (and yes, eventually, Resor and Lansdowne did get married and had their own HEA), they created a new type of organization. It wasn't a *scientific* organization, though it used data. And no, it wasn't a *creative* organization, though it used storytelling and art. They created the template for the *innovation* organization – a unique mix of right-brain and left-brain thinking where each side enhanced the other in a one plus one equals three equation.

The results speak for themselves.

During the 1920s, JWT billings grew from $10.7 million in 1922 to $37.5 million by 1929. Since then, the agency has produced groundbreaking work for clients as diverse as Kraft cheese, Ford automobiles, Kodak cameras, and the U.S. Marine Corps.

. . .

A bit of caution is warranted here.

Let's not imagine that the advertising world of the 1920s was a post-gender, egalitarian work utopia. JWT organized a "Ladies Department" to handle accounts and products that needed a "feminine" perspective. It's unclear how much influence the department had outside of these accounts, but knowing Lansdowne and her position in the company, that influence was not zero. But whereas male employees rotated through different assignments before settling into their best fit within the

---

15 The title (and to be fair, the writing) is academically opaque, but *Advertising the American Dream: Making Way for Modernity, 1920-1940*, by Roland Marchand, is a worthwhile read if you want to go deeper. Watch out for any book that uses the word "modernity" as a theme. You'll need a dictionary to power through it.

organization, women stayed in their place.

The only reason women were respected to the extent they were was a combination of Resor's support, Lansdowne's force of will, and the resulting culture of innovation. You don't critique what works. But despite unmistakable results, it would take decades for women to begin to catch up – they remain underrepresented in advertising today, making up only 42 percent of all ad agency employees in 2021.[16]

It's also true that the advertising industry caught a fair (and unfair) share of the blame for convincing people that processed foods were better than their "natural" counterparts. Crisco is the poster child example of this. Part of Lansdowne's brilliance involved shifting the discussion away from the "hydrogenation" scientific language to the customer- and outcome-focused language of the brand itself – *don't trust the science, trust the brand, and trust what it delivers for you*. That approach helped encourage a greater importance of brands generally.

Brands are a shorthand way for us not to be paralyzed by every possible consumer decision. As complexity increased, it was (and continues to be) impossible for everyone to know everything. Could you imagine the research needed to make an informed decision on every grocery store purchase? How about just *one* item in your shopping basket? You'd never leave.

We'll meet Stuart Chase in Chapter 26, where we'll talk more about consumer reviews, but brands still command a lion's share of sales in every category they appear. Yes, generics and store brands appeal to a few people, but even "store brands" have a brand. The brand is the store.

But blaming the advertising industry for paying attention to customer desires is like blaming a shark for eating a fish. They're just doing shark stuff. Brands (and the advertisers who create and nurture them) are powerful because they serve a clear need.

How much need, exactly?

In raw dollar terms, the advertising industry earned nearly $150 billion in fees alone in 2021. Fees for placing those ads in various media

---

16 That data comes from the U.S. Bureau of Labor Statistics, which may be a bit misleading. "Advertising" employment is more than simply the classic "Advertising Agencies" you might be envisioning. That said, when you move from "employees" to "managers," the gender gap remains stubborn.

added another $300 billion. Sure, the mix of media is different today than it was in the 1920s – digital takes the lion's share today – but radio advertising still accounts for $11 billion, and P&G remains one of the biggest advertisers overall.[17]

Advertising might look like a big number, but when you compare it to overall economic activity (GDP) at about $21 trillion, it's not. It hovers around 1-2 percent. That's not much different than the 1920s, if not a little smaller in percentage terms. However, that tiny sliver belies advertising's actual influence on the economy.

If you believe advertising's trade group (and I'd recommend you take their findings with a dollop of Crisco), advertising contributes more than $6-7 trillion in economic activity (both directly and indirectly), or nearly 20% of all GDP, and employs more than 20 million people.[18] Even if we split the difference – 1-2 percent of direct spending to 20 percent of influenced economic activity – advertising ranks right up there with "healthcare" and "manufacturing" in terms of the total impact on our daily lives.

But all this discussion of the role of women in the workplace, the power of brands, and economic impact somehow makes the point and misses the point. There is something deeply *human* about storytelling – something so powerful that it can create opportunities for the disadvantaged, help us reduce complexity in our lives, and build the largest economy the world has ever seen.

For her part, Helen Lansdowne earned the #14 spot on Advertising Age's list of the top 100 advertisers of the 20th century. She was inducted (posthumously) into the Advertising Hall of Fame in 1967. On January 3, 1964, when she passed away at the age of 77, the *New York Herald Tribune* eulogized her as the "Greatest Copywriter" in the advertising industry.[19]

With what we know now, we can do one better. Helen Lansdowne was the "Greatest Storyteller" of her generation.

---

17 Amazon was the #1 advertiser in 2020, with Facebook and Google close behind.

18 The Association of National Advertisers (ANA) and The Advertising Coalition commissioned the study in 2014. They have a reason to exaggerate advertising's impact. Hence, the grain of salt.

19 Why has no one written a biography about her? Seriously.

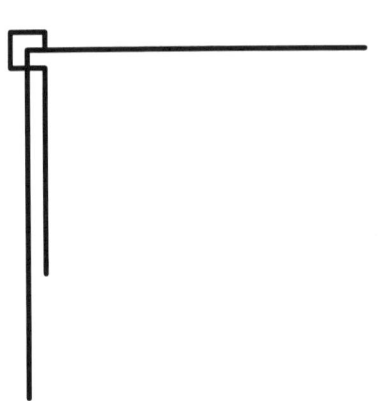

18
THE SENSEMAKERS

> T I M E is interested—not in how much it includes between its cover—but in HOW MUCH IT GETS OFF ITS PAGES INTO THE MINDS OF ITS READERS.
> – *from the first investor pitch for* Time *magazine*[1]

Imagine yourself as one of 46 former Yale classmates of Briton Hadden and Henry Luce. You remembered those two from your college days, and you knew they chummed around together, but you probably hadn't thought about them much in the past couple of years. As you walked down the hall to meet them, what might have been going through your mind?

Was Hadden still binge drinking? Nights on the town with Hadden were fun, but did he have what it takes to start a new business? Did Luce still have that chip on his shoulder? Nights on the town with Luce were *not* as fun; he was smart, yes, but also irritating and exhausting.

Now they were waiting in your office, and they had a pitch for a new business venture to share with you. At the end of it, you knew they would ask you to write them a check. They wanted investors. That much was certain. But regardless of your misgivings and questions, Yale is Yale. If a member of The Order wants to meet, you meet.[2] That's just how it is.

After a few pleasantries, Hadden took the lead. "People talk too much about what they don't know," he remarked. (No argument there.) He continued with an example that would have been top of mind for every business-savvy up-and-comer at the time – war debt from the recently-ended Great War. Everyone seemed to have an opinion, but very few knew what the deeper issues were or what to do about them.

Newspapers were little help, Hadden continued. They tended to cover discrete events – a speech from the president, the signing of a treaty, or an economic report. But if you missed a day, it was hard to catch up and even harder to connect one piece of information to the next. Moreover, even the *New York Times* was just a *regional* paper, read by mostly New

---

1   Yes, the title of this chapter is written in "Timestyle."

2   Both Briton and Luce were members of Yale's not-so-secret "Skull and Bones" society. It's sort of like the secret menu at In-N-Out Burger, but much less delicious and far more snobby.

Yorkers.³ Even then, most New Yorkers claimed they read the paper, but they internalized very little. Having a copy of today's paper under your arm was a status symbol – a corporate fashion accessory – not a source of knowledge or understanding. At least the *Times* has (reasonably) competent journalists. In other areas of the country, with far less reporting talent, people might be better off if they read nothing at all.

"What about getting news on the radio?" Radio was the big thing everyone was talking about.

Fuhgeddaboudit, Hadden scoffed. At least with the newspaper, you can return to it later, even if most people don't bother. Given the time slots available and the lack of professional broadcasters in the early 1920s, radio was hopeless as a source of solid journalism.

"Okay, but what about movie newsreels?" Movies were big too, and in the 1920s, they featured short newscasts instead of previews.

How much could you learn in five minutes while you waited for Charlie Chaplin? Besides, most guys hoped the "bank was open" with their ladyfriend when the lights went down.⁴ (Hadden had the reputation as quite the ladies' man, so his remark would have seemed in character.) Hadden volunteered the next question: *What about magazines?* Sure, magazines had wide audiences, but they focused on culture, entertainment, and homemaking, not serious news.

It wasn't just that people didn't have a place to make sense of the world around them; the world was racing away from them. People were awash in new product advertisements, world news, cultural upheaval, and celebrity gossip everywhere they looked. The pace of change was accelerating so rapidly that many simply gave up. The true problem wasn't information – there was actually *too much* information. The problem was not enough *context*. There was no *one* place where people could go to get informed about the day's news. No one could make sense of it all. The solution they proposed was an entirely new media creation: the "news magazine." It would filter out the week's noise and give readers just what

---

3   That was true until quite recently. In the 1920s, the *NYT* was only big in NYC.

4   The "bank is open/closed" is not a euphemism for sexual intercourse, though one could be forgiven for thinking so. It was slang in the 1920s for kissing or making out. Did a trip to the bank sometimes lead to a "deposit" or a "withdrawal" at evening's end? Perhaps, though probably (hopefully) not in the theater itself.

they needed to know and why they needed to know it.

Hadden was good. He was convincing. But his Yale classmates weren't stupid.

"What about the *Literary Digest* magazine? Don't they summarize the news every week, just like you're proposing?"

This was the opening Luce was waiting for. He was the quiet one. The analyst. And the quiet ones are *always* the most dangerous. When he smelled blood, he was the shark you never saw coming.

Luce pulled a copy of the *Literary Digest* from his case.

The *Literary Digest* is a joke, Luce spat. It simply grabs the stupidest stories from the country's worst backcountry newspapers and bumpkin reporters. No one takes it seriously. It's a way for "sophisticated" people to laugh at what some hillbilly in Alabama thinks about the pig controversy at his county fair last week.

As the fellow member of the Skull and Bones laughed knowingly, Luce would pounce.

This 'joke,' Luce would point out, is the *second highest circulation magazine in the country*, right behind the *Saturday Evening Post*. He leaned in. Think about what we could achieve with our news magazine that would take that strategy to its logical conclusion? What if we could merge the popularity of quick-hitting, lively gossip with hard-hitting, deep analysis of the issues?

Hadden might be the charmer, but Luce was the closer. It was like thunder and lightning, and they awed people with their combined force of will. Their former classmates might keep asking questions, but they weren't skeptical. They were almost begging Luce to explain it to them.

"What does the business model look like?" they'd probe, in typical Yale fashion.

It was almost reflexive. They knew the answer would be good, and it was. It was *very* good. Luce and Hadden were too smart not to have thought this through. Journalism is difficult and expensive. Hundreds of people beat the street for hours each day simply to cobble together the basic facts ahead of horrifying-tight daily deadlines – for some papers, *twice* daily. Reporters had no time to collect their thoughts, analyze the facts, *and* write to explain and provide context. They were writing just to report. They were constantly moving on to the next story.

Their "news magazine" would fill in that missing context, and *only* that missing context. Instead of scrambling after stories and doing the dirty work of reporting, fact-checking, and hounding, their editorial team would review the week's news and write the connective tissue between the stories. Yes, they'd have to pay for good writers and editors, but that was nothing compared to the expense of field journalists. They were outsourcing the hard and expensive work and paying only the cost of buying a copy of their newspapers. They would buy journalist talent for *pennies*, not salaries.[5] Better yet, no one cares where the information came from. People don't care about sources and methods. They *value* whoever makes sense of it for them. That's what people were willing to pay for.

Once thoroughly starstruck, Hadden would step back with the verbal face slap to bring potential investors back around: Reading the *New York Times* makes you feel dumb. Reading *Time* magazine will make you feel smart. What would you rather subscribe to?

The only question remaining: How many zeros need to be on the check?

Meetings like this raised $85,675 from sixty-nine friends and acquaintances, most of whom were Yale alumni. That's a little more than $1 million today. It was plenty of money to start a journalistic revolution.

. . .

Yes, the pitch was good. It was notably better than most new business venture presentations, then or now, you're likely to see. And yes, the two young men (barely 25 years old) could benefit from a built-in network of wealthy Yale alums, especially the exclusive Skull and Bones Society – sort of an uber-Yale. Heeding the patriotic call to service in the Great War, both entered officer training, though neither would serve in any meaningful capacity. But despite all those advantages, they were indeed special. And despite those surface similarities, Briton Hadden and Henry Luce were about as different as two people could be.

Hadden grew up in New York during the painful birth of sensational journalism. Also called "yellow" journalism, his formative years saw Joseph Pulitzer and William Randolph Hearst do battle with

---

5   The technical name for that business practice is "cost externalization," which gives capitalists financial erections not to be believed.

ever-more-outrageous headlines and armies of newsies hawking papers on every corner. In this case, the competition was a Darwinian evolution in reverse – a downward spiral in quality reporting as the competition required increasing volumes of poorly researched but emotionally amplified stories. For every groundbreaking exposé from Ida Tarbell, there were dozens of slap-together stories of celebrity exploits and sports contests. New York was drowning in journalistic trash.

Biographer Isaiah Wilner notes that the journalistic turmoil of 1920s New York deeply influenced Hadden. Even with the intellectual energy of a young man, Hadden could recognize that the sheer volume of information made it impossible for one person to make sense of it all, and Hadden was unusually intellectually energetic. Even in an era known for its wild personalities, Hadden stood out. He loathed the pretentious elites he read about in the papers, somehow forgetting that as a Yale graduate, he certainly qualified as one of them. He was creative, amusing his friends with made-up games and crazy adventures. In his student newspaper days at Yale, he'd turn his pungent pen on authority figures of all types. Hadden relished bringing the high and mighty down a peg.

But Hadden's satire came with a purpose. He used it like a comedian pokes fun at situations and people: to get at the underlying truth. Where a comedian would stretch the truth to make a point, Hadden believed in letting the facts do the heavy lifting, using the satirical edge on the facts as the twist of the verbal knife in the belly. He loved eccentrics and weirdos, mostly because he was one. He drank hard, partied constantly, and slept around. He brought the new magazine the rebellious spark that every entrepreneurial venture needs. He understood that the greatest sin wasn't offending someone; it was being ignored. And Hadden was pathologically incapable of being boring.

For two young men who shared so many experiences, it's hard to picture a different person than Henry Luce. Hadden's partner in this new venture was born and grew up in rural China, the son of Christian missionary parents.

It was a...bad time to be a Western missionary in China. It was barely a generation after the so-called "Opium Wars" of the middle of the 19th century, in which British forces crushed opposition and forcibly opened trade. Tensions remained high. In 1900, the Society of the Righteous and Harmonious Fists staged a rebellion in northern and western China to oppose outside influence – Western power in Europe and the United States, yes, but also nearby Japan. At issue was the opening of trading with China in general and the poor terms of those trades specifically.

The "Boxers," as they came to be known, paid particular attention to Christian missionaries.[6] They saw them as the vanguard of changing Chinese culture into Western culture. (Japan was troublesome too, but that was more of an Asian ethnic conflict.) Suffice it to say, Luce had seen quite a bit of the world – surviving an uprising where he very nearly could have been killed – before he was sent off to boarding school in New York at age 15. As it turned out, that was the same boarding school Hadden would attend.

Luce grew up indoctrinated in the belief that combining Christian values and American business capitalism was the key to improving living conditions worldwide. In time, Luce would evangelize that message in the pages of his new magazine. But that was all in the future. First, Luce needed to make a name for himself in the big city – a place as different than rural China as it was possible to be. It wouldn't be easy.

It wasn't his academic skill. Privately tutored until he arrived in New York, Luce was clearly "brilliant," as his later classmates would attest. However, his upbringing on the other side of the world deprived him of the social skills that came so easily to Hadden. Luce spent his years in school perpetually frustrated that high society couldn't see his genius. He would have to get by on raw talent and determination – a big chip to carry on such young shoulders.

Perhaps Hadden and Luce saw something each needed in the other. Luce needed Hadden's creative spark and his easy manner with others. Hadden needed Luce's raw skill and ruthless execution. They were both among the best journalists the 1920s would produce, and by a strange twist of historical fate, they both found themselves at the same school at the same time.

. . .

---

6 They were named "Boxers" for their exercise routine, which they believed would protect them against modern bullets. It did not.

It's difficult for modern audiences to understand how different 1923 was from just ten years before. The transition from the teens to the twenties defies hyperbolic description, but perhaps the most significant change was the nature of *information* itself.

News outlets – both printed media like newspapers and magazines, and fledgling radio broadcast media – competed with each other in a positive (negative?) feedback loop to "fill space" in their pages and "fill time" on their airwaves. Economic pressures led to much of that space and time being filled with celebrity, sports, and opinion content, which is cheaper than fact-based research and reporting. It helps that it's also trendy and easy to consume. That meant the average person who couldn't give a rip about politics and foreign affairs could pick up a copy of the newspaper to read about their local sports team or indulge in a bit of celebrity gossip. More content meant a larger audience. A larger audience meant more revenue.

That was true in print, but it was especially true on the air. As we saw in more detail in Chapter 8, there was no practical reason a radio station couldn't broadcast 24 hours per day. It didn't take long for long stretches of "dead air" to fill with cheap, easy-to-produce, syndicated programming. As the 24 hours filled, radio stations learned they could shorten the time slots. Instead of turning off listeners, it had the opposite effect. More programming variety attracted a wider group of listeners. The net effect was an ever-shortening programming window. In the early days of radio, programs might be hours long. By the end of the decade, a news report might only last 90 seconds.

If new information from print and radio was a river, advertising was the flood. Today, we tend to see only the frothy top layer of advertising – the exact message that will trigger us to buy one product over another. That's because, 100 years after the first mass-produced radio left off the RCA assembly line, we all know what a radio is. The same goes for most other products we find around the home. But in the 1920s, advertisers needed to explain these new-fangled things, how they worked, and what you might do with them. Then *and only then* could they convince you to buy one. In practical terms, when you see radio sets advertised in that era, you see a stunning variety of messages – that they transmitted their signal through the air, that they ran on electricity, that you might use it to listen to music, and that perhaps you'd take one along to the beach – to say nothing about the prices, where to buy one, and the comparative benefits of competing models.

Hadden and Luce were correct. Life in the 1920s was intellectually exhausting. The average person had no way to make sense of it all. In that deluge of facts, those who *could* make sense of it saw an immediate advantage: Knowledge equaled status.

That's something their Yale buddies would have understood instantly. Although more people attended college after the war (often with government help), an undergraduate degree wasn't a prerequisite for the desire for influence. However, what passed for "facts" in the *New York Times* or on radio station KDKA was a torrent of unconnected tidbits, like jumbled puzzle pieces on a table. Whoever could help people assemble the picture would win.

...

Though several biographies chart the rise of *Time* magazine in its early days, Isaiah Wilner's *The Man Time Forgot: A Tale of Genius, Betrayal, and the Creation of Time Magazine*, comes the closest to the truth about that first chaotic decade with both Luce and Hadden at the helm. You'll read about the new business pitch summarized at the beginning of this chapter. Or how the magazine's original name was "Facts" until, uncharacteristically, it was Luce with the creative insight to change the name to "Time." (Facts were the problem; *Time* was the solution, as well as the primary reader benefit. *Time* gave its readers more time. It was very clever.) You'll experience the turbulent early days of Hadden's manic episodes and Luce's ruthless management style. Wilner also details the high-drama of an ill-fated move to Cleveland to be more centrally located in the country (one of Luce's less-than-insightful moves), and a middle-of-the-night move back to New York City (which was Hadden's doing, and it probably saved the business.)

It's a fascinating history of a classic media startup, but ultimately, it isn't as relevant to consumer culture as the innovations the team produced. *Time* literally created the times…or at least, how people thought about them.

If complexity was the major problem with the news (and information in general), then simplification would be the critical innovation. As Luce would put it:

> The one great thing was simplification. Simplification by organization, simplification by condensation, and also simplification by just being damn well simple.

The first task was the presentation of complex information itself. As *information* delivery machines, newspapers function quite well. As *understanding* delivery machines, they're like eating soup with a fork: ill-suited for the task and deeply infuriating. It's not hard to understand why. Newspapers report the news as soon as practicable after it happens. Space may not be *theoretically* limited, and papers would grow in sports and celebrity news coverage, but it was limited in practice. Printing costs, available advertising revenue, and the willingness of customers to pay at the newsstand set a cap on the reasonable length of any newspaper. In a practical example, if a new bill just passed Congress, there was precious little time to talk about what came before, what might happen after, and what it all meant in the grand scheme. The newspaper could cover what happened – who voted for and who against, and perhaps sprinkle in a few quotes – but that was it. The average reader would be left wondering why this new legislation was relevant to them. Newspapers march ever forward. If you don't keep up, you're left behind.

Time would solve that problem, paradoxically, by going slower. Instead of trying to keep up with the daily grind of daily reporting, *Time* staff would collect the day's newspapers from New York City and around the world. (This was more convenient in New York than it was in Cleveland, to Hadden's operational credit.) Laying all the newspapers in front of them, they would tell the bigger picture – not so much the *what*, the *how*, and the *who*, but the *why*, the *so what*, and the *what now*. In other words, *analysis* instead of reporting. Of course, that meant the *Time* editorial team – in the beginning, primarily Hadden and Luce – would need to be up on all the major events. This is where their experience working together, their shared love of journalism, their Yale education, a worldly perspective (especially from Luce), and their outstanding intellect truly shined.

What made *Time* so special is that Hadden and Luce understood national and world events so well that they could distill thousands of words of reporting into a handful of short paragraphs. Instead of the "inverted pyramid" journalistic style, where the most important information came first and was often devoid of context, *Time* would tell short stories like a comedian would tell a good joke: The "punchline" came at the end, and only after the appropriate setup. The magazine's weekly format and short summaries allowed *Time* to pack hundreds of news items in as few as 30 newsstand pages.

The New York journalistic elite hated being reduced to a pithy few paragraphs, but the average reader loved it. They couldn't get enough. Even better (at least for the Yale buddies who pitched in the money) was that the business model worked. Maintaining a cadre of reporters wasn't only expensive; it required connections to the halls of power. Those connections were difficult, took years, and could be lost with a retirement. But once they published what they knew in the newspaper, anyone could buy those years of experience and connections for, quite literally, pennies. *Time* would allow the newspapers to absorb the costs of recruiting, training, and maintaining talent, and the magazine would read it, summarize it, and repackage it for sale...all at a fraction of the cost.

But that's abstract. How did all this work in practice? *The State of Tennessee v. John Thomas Scopes*, more commonly known as the Scopes Monkey Trial, in the summer of 1925 provided the opportunity for the *Time* approach to shine. Although we covered the trial and its impact in greater detail in Chapter 11, the trial had all the trappings of the first "made for media" legal event – colorful characters, dramatic dialog, an epic battle between science and religion, and guiding (or protecting) the minds of children.

Journalists covered every aspect of the trial in spectacular detail, generating tens of thousands of words per day in multi-part summaries in the next day's newspaper or (for the first time) live commentary and coverage on the radio. It was the first "trial of the century," and people were captivated. It was Hadden and Luce's moment. As Hadden liked to say, "you can never be too obvious." They knew people simply couldn't consume, much less interpret, the flood of facts coming across the wire from Tennessee. Not only was it simply too much information, most people didn't have the legal training to know what was going on. But readers didn't just need to know what was happening; they begged to know what to think about it. Here's how *Time* described the backdrop to the trial, and its protagonist, John Thomas Scopes:

> [Scopes is the] alleged violator of the state's anti-evolution law, bewildered instrument of Science and Faith which have accidentally chosen Dayton as their battleground and in whose wake has come the usual camp-following of freaks, fakes, mountebanks and parasites of publicity.

Hadden and Luce didn't need to sweat it out in tiny, forlorn Dayton, Tennessee, to pass judgment on what was happening. The trial was a circus – obvious in retrospect to anyone there – but it was *Time* that would name the elephant in the tent.

All this "creative summarizing" makes an awkward point about journalistic objectivity. It's impossible to inject context without injecting judgment. *Time* would need to evaluate facts, emphasize some, and omit others. But how would they do that consistently?

The innovation *Time* might be best known for is the iconic "Timestyle" – mostly an invention of Hadden, but enthusiastically championed by Luce as well – an acerbic, irreverent take on the news that ruffled serious journalists (but that readers adored). We've already seen some examples of that. During the Scopes trial, *Time* called the journalists who covered the trial "camp followers," "freaks," and "fakes." Did readers know what a "mountcbank" was?[7] Nope. But that was part of Hadden's charm. A word choice was never so obtuse or clever that the average reader couldn't guess the meaning from context (or simply look it up), but it made reading an adventure. In other words, *Time* wasn't just simplified; it was funified.

The unofficial stylebook features several other jolly good rules. Writing must be entertaining and use witty phrase turns. Oh, and it's not "turns of phrase," just like "time's nick" is not the "nick of time." If covering a famous person (which *Time*, especially Hadden, relished bringing down a

---

7   Mountebanks: a person who deceives others, especially in order to trick them out of their money; a charlatan. Thank you, Oxford English Dictionary. We can get that answer correct during the next trivia night at the bar.

peg), the writer must use a middle name or nickname. For example, auto tycoon Walter Chrysler went by…well, Walter Chrysler. His middle name was Percy, and he *hated* it. Hadden insisted on using his middle name and would often *only* use that name in writing. Secretary of Commerce (and later President) Herbert Hoover was the "Beaver Man" – industrious, round, buck-toothed, busy…but not inspiring. In its tinkering with the English language, *Time* coined the words "tycoon" (used above), "socialite," "guesstimate," "televangelist," and "pundit." It was even the first to use the iconic "World War II" in print. Inverted sentences, *Time* wrote, decades before a certain little green sage spoke them in a famous space opera. Even spelling rules weren't sacrosanct. A 1925 headline read: "Klu Klux Klan in Kolorado." In telling the story of the lowest hate in the highest state, *Time* writers would invert the inverted pyramid, focusing on storytelling rather than firehosing information. The buildup created emotion and suspense, which made sense because people could have already read the "facts" elsewhere.

In other words, *Time* invented Timestyle to operationalize perspective-giving.

All this isn't to imply that Hadden and Luce dispensed with *all* original fact-finding. They'd hire sleuths – often women – not only because they were cheaper than men but because they could get their hands on information without raising suspicion. For example, in 1929, their team discovered the precise location of the first lady's bathtub inside the White House. Of course, "serious" journalists wouldn't consider this "serious" journalism (and it wasn't), but readers *loved* those often irrelevant but always irreverent details.

However, that sort of digging could make enemies – not just of people in power, but indignant readers who felt *Time* should keep out of Mrs. Coolidge's private bathroom.

So what happened when *Time* received angry letters excoriating the editors? Did they bury the screeds in a "letter to the editor" and let it rest? Or maintain a policy to only correct factual errors, as big papers were known to do? Or ignore them and keep the inflammatory content out? No. None of those approaches would work for *Time*. The new magazine traded in snappy, punchy, and sometimes insulting opinions. They were bound to upset people. So they did what no other publication had done to that point:

They published their critics. And sometimes, the editors would retort.[8]

For example, in a July 18, 1925 article, Horace Elmer Wood II takes issue with *Time* editors categorizing a tapir as a "pig." It ends with:

> As a matter of fact, the closest living relatives of the tapir are the horse and the rhinoceros.

Many letters were printed as is, with no response. Not this tasty morsel, however:

> As everyone knows, a tapir is no pig. Nor did TIME say that it was. The word (pig) indicated merely that tapir meat much resembles pig in taste.

It was typical of *Time* to turn a clumsy cladistics science lecture into a culinary comparison.

Tasty tapirs are one thing, but Hadden and Luce published all manner of letters, many of which were much less flattering – not only to the writing but to the advertisers too. More than once, the team had to remind grumpy CEOs that by courting controversy, *Time* increased its readership. Increased readership meant more people saw their ads. The more people saw their ads, the more people bought their product. So, suck it up, buttercup.

Perhaps the most persistent critique was that the magazine played "fast and loose with the facts." However, that scurrilous editorial ethos played well with the so-called "hipflask generation," who were all too happy to rebel against stupid rules and crusty cultural paragons. (During the 1920s, the magazine often featured a "Prohibition" section filled with unflattering exploits of government agents.)

Even past issues are shockingly readable and fun today, forcing you to look up the occasional word (which, paradoxically, made readers feel smart, not dumb). *Time* included a quick summary at the end of each issue in two parts – *Point with Pride*, and *View with Alarm* – in case those tidbits didn't get their due elsewhere. But the bulk of the magazine was

---

8   The *Time* archives are fantastic. They are super readable. You can find this one by searching the vault for the July 27, 1925 edition, page 21.

tasty tapir meaty, covering everything you'd need in a full intellectual meal: national news, foreign news, music, theater, books, education, arts, sports (even obscure stuff), aeronautics (new!), radio (new!), business, religion, medicine, celebritics, law, curiosities, and even a news quiz game – all in less than 30 pages. You could read it in about an hour because no story spanned more than a handful of paragraphs. It was fun (mostly because of Hadden) and ruthlessly edited (mostly because of Luce).

It wasn't just what the reader could read that made *Time* special. Hadden and Luce created the modern "media kit" – a now-common explanation to advertisers of who reads the publication (aka demographics), circulation numbers, and advertising rates. They advised advertisers that full-page ads didn't perform as well as half- or third-page ads that contained copy. (People spent more time reading those pages and routinely skipped full-page promotions.) They also offered advertisers better rates to buy ads in bulk and spread out insertions over time. (Advertisers were just beginning to learn that repetition was critical to long-term success.) The timing (ha!) was perfect – advertisers needed new places to promote their products, and they needed better information on who was reading so they could outflank the increasing competition. All this seems pedestrian today. In the 1920s, it was revolutionary.

. . .

The first issue of *Time* magazine, published on March 3, 1923, was a logistical disaster. Many of the 1,000 or so initial subscribers got nothing. Others received multiple copies. Despite those hiccups, the team sorted all those issues soon enough. By the end of its second year, *Time* boasted over 17,000 subscribers and made its first small profit. The format would evolve, with 1927 seeing the introduction of the iconic red border (which helped the magazine stand out on the newsstand), color advertising on the inside covers, and the first "Man of the Year" capitalizing on Charles Lindbergh's celebrity (see Chapter 9 for more).

The road from here is one part extraordinary and one part heartbreaking.

First, the transformational part. *Time* created the "commentary" genre, helping people make sense of the flood of information coming their way. In that, it was spectacularly popular. By 1927, circulation has grown by an order of magnitude to 175,000. By most measures, it was the most influential publication in the United States for decades, reaching 4.2 million subscribers by its peak in 1990.

Even those numbers understate its legacy. The same creative genius that birthed *Time* expanded into pictorial essays with *Life* magazine in 1936.[9] Luce believed pictures could often tell the story better than words, and millions of returning veterans from World War II would agree. In 1954, the company launched *Sports Illustrated*, the first publication to do for sports coverage what *Time* did for news. Even people uninterested in athletics could become engrossed in its storylines.[10]

But it was *Fortune* magazine, launched in 1929, that truly showed the break between Hadden and Luce. A business-focused publication, *Fortune* would make the opaque commercial world clear for the average person for the first time. For Luce, it was a natural evolution. From his earliest evangelizing in China, he believed the American industrial system and the Christian Jesus were the world's twin saviors. Luce would use his influence with *Time* and *Fortune* to spread the American gospel far and wide. But Hadden detested business culture, and especially business leaders. He hated prostituting his talent to help people who already knew how to sell. Sadly, by the end of 1928, Hadden was in no shape to argue. His lifestyle had caught up with him, and an unlucky nasty strep infection proved fatal in February 1929.

Within two weeks, Luce removed Hadden's name from the *Time* masthead. *Fortune* launched before the dirt was settled on Hadden's grave. In the following decades, Luce gave over 400 speeches. He mentioned Briton Hadden four times. Luce didn't forget Hadden. Luce *erased* him.

Nearly 100 years later, *Time* magazine is a shadow of its former self. Since the 1970s, it has been more neutral and centrist, but that's when other media were picking up the acerbic, tell-you-what-to-think ball and running with it. Left-leaning public radio took off about this time. Right-wing talk radio got its start not long after in the early 1980s. The model was, essentially, the *Time*

---

9 A magazine titled "Life" had been circulating since 1883, but by the 1920s, it was bankrupt. There wasn't much about the prior magazine that survived the transition. Luce simply bought the name.

10 There's evidence Hadden had these two publications in mind from the beginning.

model: Don't report the news; tell people what to think about it.

Although media outlets across the ideological spectrum will occasionally conduct deep reporting, the most popular content is *commentary*. Even professional journalists are increasingly moving toward an advocacy approach in their coverage. Why? It's easy to blame social media algorithms for prioritizing sensational coverage, click-bait headlines, and opinion-spouting over fact-reporting. But they wouldn't exist if we didn't want them. As consumers, we're struggling with the same problem our great-grandparents faced 100 years ago: too much information and not enough *Time*.

PART 3
THE LITTLE BLACK DRESS

HOW CONSUMERS LEARNED TO CHOOSE THEIR IDENTITIES.

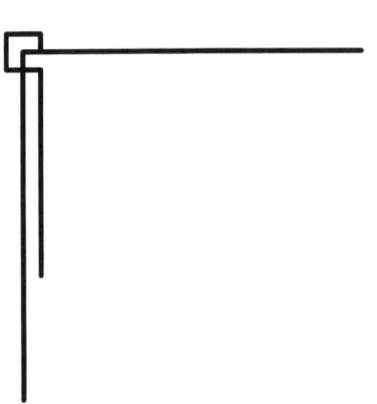

19
FAMILY FOR SALE

To say Margaret Sanger was controversial in the 1920s is an understatement. To say Margaret Sanger remains controversial *100 years later* is also an understatement.

That's rare in historical terms. Most people who were deeply controversial in their time go through multiple reinterpretations as the decades pass. Many times, those revisions trend in a more favorable direction. Just think of the "historical arsonist" Genghis Khan.[1] For hundreds of years after the Mongols exploded onto the scene in the 14th century, Southeast Asians, Arabs, Europeans, and everyone in between were united in their utter loathing (and justifiable fear) of the most successful conqueror in world history. But fast forward to the 20th century, and the Great Khan has been re-imagined as a change agent, burning away the dead brush of stagnant civilizations and ushering in the first (safe) overland global trade network.

Perhaps Sanger only needs a few more centuries to pass before she's remembered universally more favorably? That's tough to say. She's best known for her tireless advocacy of women's rights – specifically, their *reproductive rights* – which got her into trouble with the Victorian and religious power structures of the day.

On one side of the ledger, she was a nurse who witnessed firsthand the frightening lack of knowledge women had of their bodies. Physicians (primarily men) knew barely more. Many of their medical practices were little evolved from their 2,000 year old Greek versions. Aristotle was a lot of things, but a knowledgeable doctor about women's anatomy was not one of them.

In 1916, she published "What Every Girl Should Know," a no-nonsense guide to female anatomy, menstruation, masturbation, sexual impulses, pregnancy, miscarriages, and sexually transmitted diseases.[2] The book is stunning for its boldness and clarity. Many other books of the era (especially advertisements) cloaked sexual functions in euphemisms and

---

1   History podcaster Dan Carlin may not have been the first to coin this term, but he's done more than anyone else to popularize it. He completed a marathon podcast series titled "Wrath of the Khans" that's well worth the $1.00 per episode he asks for it.

2   This work, among others, was digitized by Google and is available free online.

polite language. Not this one.

Sanger believed that if women had the information they needed, they could make better decisions for themselves and their daughters:

> A woman does not need to be a college graduate, with a special degree in the study of botany, before she can tell her child the beautiful truth of its birth. But she does need to clear her own mind of prudishness, and to understand that the procreative act is natural, clean, and healthful.

In other words, moms might be squeamish about saying the words "vagina," "orgasm," "penis," and "semen," but if they didn't speak up, their daughters would (literally and figuratively) grope around in the dark. Often, they'd learn too late that they should have insisted on a condom if they didn't want to get pregnant.

We'll explore what made Sanger's direct approach so effective shortly, but we need to explore the other side of the ledger before we can do that.

There's evidence Sanger was both a eugenicist and a racist – not the closeted, wink-wink, nod-nod, dog-whistle kind – the *public* kind. In that, she was very much in line with the prevailing thinking of the time. Several prominent thinkers and scientists worried about race purity and believed different races were inherently superior or inferior.[3] There's even evidence she encouraged abortion among Black mothers for precisely this reason. We'll discuss the actual evidence (or lack thereof) for those conclusions, but if you want to demonize Sanger, you'll be able to find plenty of ammunition.

However, falling down the rabbit hole of Sanger's personal and political views blinds us to the actual consumer innovation she created. Sanger rewrote the vocabulary of awkward discussions into plain language. She confronted the moral and legal authorities of her time, putting her life and freedom on the line to provide women access to contraception. Almost

---

3   The idea of race didn't simply involve the terms White, Asian, Hispanic, or Black that we might use today. "Theorists" of that era constructed a complex hierarchy of the "White" race where Northern Europeans and Anglo-Saxons sat at the top, Southern Europeans in the middle, and Eastern Europeans at the bottom. Oh, and the Irish. They hated the Irish. One senses the feeling was mutual.

singlehandedly, she birthed the market for sexual products and services.

Unlike most consumer markets, nearly *every* American will purchase contraceptives at some point during their lifetime. (Often, several times.) You ought to know how she did it.

...

The 1920s were an odd time socially and politically. This decade was the height of the so-called "Progressive Era" in the United States, where many intellectuals and activists saw a much more significant role for government intervention and social engineering.[4] Before we can understand Sanger's work – and, more importantly, what it meant for consumer culture – we must step back into her world.

The era's politics were just as complex as they are today, perhaps more so. *Both political parties* featured progressives and feminist members. Left-leaning activists could join thriving communist, socialist, or labor parties spurred on by the fledgling Soviet Union. Right-wingers swooned over Benito Mussolini and his growing fascist regime in Italy. Even a handful of late-1800s anarchists remained active. Think of it as political spaghetti…that was dropped on the floor.

In this saucy social mess, it's easy for modern commentators to conflate Sanger's political beliefs with her activist work to build a market for sexual products and services. In some ways, of course, her feminist perspective influenced her actions. And yes, she leaned toward the trendy 1920s version of socialism, but we're not here to discuss political science. It's helpful to set aside the rhetoric and focus a little closer to the day-to-day reality of most people.

Scholars attempting to find connections between the era's sweeping social movements and the realities of daily life often point to first-wave feminism. That movement certainly played a part in highlighting women's issues and led directly to the Nineteenth Amendment to the U.S.

---

4 People often mistake FDR's interventions in the economy during the Great Depression of the 1930s as the beginning of a more prominent government role in everyday life. They were very much a continuation of ideas starting three decades earlier.

Constitution, granting women the right to vote in Federal elections.[5] But again, there was a difference between activist rhetoric (which sometimes featured an angry, militant tinge) and most women's day-to-day lives. It's clear from the direct, firsthand evidence that most women wanted *both* the specific rewards (and challenges) of family life *and* expanded voting rights.

Others point out that this was an era of vicious religious anger, mostly against Catholics and Jews from their Protestant counterparts. They explain the rise in birth control discussions, products, and services as a way for Protestants to differentiate from (and attack) Catholics in their midst. They add that because immigration was higher in the preceding decades from primarily-Catholic southern and eastern Europe, birth control was a wedge issue to use politically. However, that's an odd reading of history. It was primarily *Protestant* leaders and government officials who created and enforced the so-called Comstock Laws that prevented the sale of "lewd" materials — which, at the time, included all birth control products. More to the point, people of all religions routinely ignored such laws.

More modern scholars (primarily in the past ten years) have attempted to overlay another dimension onto the family planning and birth control discussion: race. They point to massive gaps between Black and White Americans in their knowledge of and access to birth control. Additionally, they point to feminists (like Sanger) who perpetuated ideas of racial hierarchy and *operationalized them* by "encouraging" Black women to abort babies in higher numbers. Although there is evidence Sanger held these views, it's a stretch to claim she had a master plan in mind to harm people of other races. The more straightforward interpretation is that she advocated for spreading information to *all communities* because she felt Black mothers (and, to be fair, other White immigrant mothers) needed it the most.

Observers at the time, however, were smarter than that. Political journalist Walter Lippmann summed up the personal relevance of birth

---

5   Many states allowed women to vote well in advance of this. The first of which was Wyoming in 1869.

control (and the irrelevance of politics) this way:[6]

> It is possible for a man to be a socialist or an individualist without ever having to make one responsible decision in which his theories play any part. But when he thinks about divorce and contraception, continence and license, monogamy, prostitution, and sexual experience outside of marriage, are matters that are bound at some point in his life to affect his happiness immediately and directly.

Historian Trent MacNamara cites these (and many other) sources in his tour-de-force takedown of our collective misconceptions of the role of government, religious institutions, and the various -isms that dominated public discourse in the 1920s.[7] He points out that journalists and historians tend to focus more on what public figures say and write because that information is easier to get. Sneaking into the bedrooms of average Americans to see if hubby wore a condom or wifey douched post-coitus was…more challenging, and hence, usually ignored. In other words, unless we move beyond the moral pronouncements and use the available data (including birth rates and advertisements) to infer behavior, we can't get an accurate picture of the monumental changes happening at the bed-sheet level.

To do that, MacNamara examined that data in detail. The conventional wisdom holds that as people moved from the country to the cities in the early 20th century, family sizes shrunk as people no longer needed children to work on farms. Parents could then devote more attention to each remaining child, slowly changing the zeitgeist of child-rearing from "farm hand" to "cherished legacy." (We'll examine that in more detail in Chapter 25.) And while that line of reasoning seems to make sense, it's not supported by the data. *Averages hide the truth.*

Some immigrant families were large, but family size had shrunk since

---

[6] Most famous for coining the term "Cold War" to describe the state of affairs between the United States and the Soviet Union after World War II.

[7] His book, *Birth Control and American Modernity: A History of Popular Ideas*, is not only a challenging read but also challenging to find. That's unfortunate, because it's an example of outstanding scholarship. The best books ask questions no one thought to ask and use evidence no one thought to consider. It's worth more than the one review on Amazon it currently has. Buy a copy and give it a review.

farm machinery became popular in the mid-1800s. Contrary to popular belief, children were not necessarily profitable on farms in the early 1900s, especially the smaller ones. (When you consider the economic implications, it is not surprising that it was the *men* who thought most about birth control before the 1920s.) At least on the farm, you'd have the space. In a tiny apartment in the city? Not so much.

Yes, religious beliefs and government policies played a role, but the data show that both those explanations fail to explain shrinking family size better than growing economic opportunity. In MacNamara's most memorable observation in his entire book, driven by a deep quantitative analysis of statistical tables, *in a battle between a baby and a Ford, the Ford usually won.*

Sanger intuitively understood MacNamara's conclusions from her experience as a nurse. While she was an active feminist and socialist, those movements meant less to her strategy than the realities of intimate decisions between two people and their individual economic circumstances. Those people didn't need to know where the next workers' rally was being held; they needed to know how a condom worked.

...

Unlike her pontificating contemporaries, Sanger moved from her comfortable suburban New York neighborhood into the city proper to be closer to work – not to the fancy neighborhoods, but to the slums of the East Side, filled with immigrant mothers and their children.

What she saw there horrified her. Yes, she helped women in childbirth, but all too often, she treated women suffering the aftereffects of botched home abortions. When questioned about birth control practices, they'd share their "old country" techniques involving lying on your side, talismans, and varying herbal remedies. Most were ineffective but harmless. Some were ineffective but *deadly.*

Sanger wanted to share better information with her patients. However, because of the existing Comstock Laws, printed information was either nonexistent or filled with euphemisms that those without a command of the English language couldn't easily grasp. She knew that her wealthier patients (sometimes) had access to better information, but not always. Newly-arrived immigrants were simply lost.

In one particular incident Sanger would retell in speeches years later, she was called to the apartment of a "Sadie Sachs" who was desperately ill from an abortion she attempted to perform herself. After she and the attending physician had stabilized the patient, Sadie (obviously a pseudonym) asked the doctor what she could do to prevent getting pregnant in the future. Sanger recalls the male doctor's flippant response:

> You want your cake while you eat it too, do you? Well, it can't be done. I'll tell you the only sure thing to do…tell Jake to sleep on the roof.

Were the specifics of her story embellished? Perhaps. However, the story is representative of the attitudes of many physicians of the time – nearly all men – who had little respect for home birth control remedies and even less respect for immigrant mothers.

As her socialist friends railed against the violent and crowded conditions of the slums in abstract terms, Sanger saw the very personal struggles of families – especially women – in their most intimate moments. Sanger wasn't a talker; Sanger was a doer. She witnessed firsthand that the most significant issue was a lack of good information, and providing that information – in the most direct terms – would become her life's work.

. . .

Okay. That's it. No more talking *around* sex; we need to talk *about* sex – Sanger style.

What follows won't cloak the sex act in cute metaphors or loving language. Although we might not blanch at Sanger's directness, people of the 1920s certainly did. For many, this was the first time they would have seen this information. We could explore plenty of primary sources, but we'll focus on two: "Family Limitation," published in 1914, and "What Every Girl Should Know," released two years later. They helped demonstrate an evolution in Sanger's approach as her work became more widely known.

Sanger begins her first 16-page pamphlet directly. She makes it clear that women are ultimately responsible for family planning because they will bear the child and assume the primary responsibility for childcare. The book's introduction immediately instructs women to begin tracking their menstrual cycle proactively: *Don't wait to see that you don't (menstruate); make it your duty to see that you do.* She recommends writing it down rather than relying on memory. Only with that knowledge, can women begin to take control of their sexual lives.

> Don't be over sentimental about this important phase of hygiene. The fact is that unless you prevent the male sperm from entering the womb, you are going to become pregnant.

It's also notable that she recasts the doctor's advice from "tell Jake to sleep on the roof" to "prevent the male sperm from entering the womb." The doctor's version is a sly nod toward curtailing Jake's horniness. In her version, the advice is clearer: Don't let Jake's sperm into your vagina. There's no ambiguity there.

Once women had started counting days, the next thing they needed to do to prevent unwanted pregnancy was to remove any semen from the vaginal area. In this pamphlet, that meant douching. From here, Sanger doesn't hold back. She provides suggestions for multiple formulations, including Chinosol (her preferred method – with instructions on how to get tablets directly from the German manufacturer), Lysol (not the brand you're thinking of), Bichloride of Mercury (which she recommends strongly against, hopefully for obvious poisonous reasons), Potassium Permanganate (with a warning that it can stain), Boric Acid ("not very reliable"), a Salt Solution (the easiest to have on hand), and a Vinegar Solution (again, widespread), among several others, each with detailed recipes and shopping lists to take to your local pharmacy. Those instructions also included anatomical drawings to help guide women as they used their fingers to really get up in there and extract all the semen they could. They look like modern anatomical drawings in any high school biology textbook today, but in 1914, they were revolutionary.

Only after Sanger describes methods women can use on their own does she discuss the male partner's role. She explains how to use a condom properly but admits that these may be unavailable, accidentally break, be worn improperly...or, let's be frank, men may not want to wear them. In the final case, she warns against relying on the practice of "coitus interruptus," otherwise known as "pulling out" before ejaculation. Although it can work in theory, it takes significant self-control from the male partner, which may not work every time. (See previous instructions to douche post-coitus.) Other contraception methods – sponges and diaphragms – also received some limited attention.

What's remarkable about this document, aside from its plain language, is that it extends birth control beyond the mechanics of pregnancy prevention and explores the reasons for doing so.[8] Sanger reminds women that they don't want to be "burdened down with several unwished for children, helpless, starved, shoddily clothed, dragging at your skirt, yourself a dragged-out shadow of the woman you once were." However, you didn't need to adopt this nihilistic view of motherhood to benefit from Sanger's message. On the positive side of the ledger, she also discusses why effective birth control – and the required communication between partners – would lead to greater sexual enjoyment. For example, she reminds men that achieving orgasm first (or not "together") often prevents women from achieving sexual satisfaction because his limp penis is…not up to finishing the task. She reminds men that when they wonder why their partner has turned "cold" toward sex, that's often the cause. Additionally, Sanger reminds men and women that *not* worrying about pregnancy allows women to relax more during sex and increases the chances they will be able to climax faster.

Today, you'll likely read similar advice (in varying degrees of directness) in multiple popular sources. In 1914, that level of specificity was utterly unheard of. Even 100 years later, if you ignore a few specifics, the information presented in this packed, 16-page document is surprisingly accurate. It's even more remarkable when you realize this might have been the first time many women had access to this information.

---

[8] Sanger mentions preventing unwanted births as one way to prevent human exploitation by capitalists and militarists. However, that's not only more a statement of the times she lived in but also a bit ignored by her readers. They wanted to prevent pregnancy for reasons other than the rise of the global proletariat.

This pamphlet confirmed that there was plenty of pent-up consumer demand for practical information about sex, and Sanger was ready to keep supplying it.

. . .

Two years later, Sanger took it up a notch with the 91-page "What Every Girl Should Know" – perhaps her most famous work. Aside from simply a five-fold expansion, the book marked an evolution in her approach in several ways.

First, perhaps most importantly, the book covers the entire female lifecycle, not just conception and pregnancy. Chapter titles include Girlhood, Puberty, Sexual Impulse, Reproduction, Some of the Consequences of Ignorance and Silence (mostly about venereal diseases; we'll get to that in a moment), and Menopause. A more apt title for the book might have been "What Every *Woman* Should Know." Still, Sanger was explicit in her desire to catch girls early – to provide correct information at the beginning rather than correct misinformation later.

Much of the information in this longer book is (still considered) factual and noncontroversial, like the first pamphlet. However, a few areas brought Sanger into conflict with the authorities of the time *and* might make even modern readers a bit uncomfortable, albeit for different reasons.

Let's begin with her in-depth discussion of the sexual impulse for women. As you'll recall, Sanger discussed the female orgasm in her first pamphlet, but only concerning the act of sexual intercourse with a male partner. In her 1916 book, she expands that notion to include self-pleasuring and masturbation. This may shock those who have lionized Sanger as a paragon of female empowerment; like many of her contemporaries, she links masturbation (even healthy exploration of the body) with depravity, disease, and psychological disorders. She felt it was her duty to inform girls as early as possible about the dangers of this behavior *before* the impulse strikes them or before other girls begin talking about it "on the playground." At best, masturbation will prevent the adult from the "natural" performance of the sex act. At worst, girls could become prostitutes.

In one particularly poignant scene – and odd, considering the titular subject of the book – she describes treating a *boy* she identifies as a chronic masturbator, describing this as her most revolting experience as a clinician. Remember, this is from a nurse who has treated tuberculosis, smallpox, and measles. She had delivered stillborn babies. *This* is the most revolting experience. It tells you something about the prevailing wisdom of the time and the enduring popularity of the Victorian anti-masturbation ideal.

She contrasts the urge to self-satisfy with the "normal" sexual impulse, especially in the difference between infatuation and long-term love. On the surface, that seems reasonable, but it's clear that her version of that relationship is one of finding the ideal partner (to be clear, a man), getting married, settling down, and raising a family. Straying from this path led to destructive ends: prostitution on one end and denying yourself the joy of motherhood on the other.

In short, Sanger wasn't throwing the Victorian ideal of the baby out with the bathwater; she was telling women they should have an equal say in when to fill up the tub.

The second area that didn't get much attention in Sanger's first pamphlet was venereal disease. She begins this chapter by refuting the prevailing myth that once a boy reaches puberty, he needs to "get a woman" to "use his organs" and "sow his wild oats" lest he become permanently sexually stunted. Sanger cites her experience that many young men who undergo this right of passage contract venereal disease during this time. If they're fortunate enough *not* to have this experience, their risk of contracting venereal disease later in life decreases. However, the real issue for girls and women is that their partners are likely to spread those diseases to them when they have sex – even if they wait for marriage. The risks to women are more than the pain and discomfort of the disease itself, but the additional risks to fertility, pregnancy, and childbirth.

In that section, she encourages doctors (many of which are beginning to see the light) that a man's diagnosis should not be kept secret from his spouse, as was the common practice of the time:

> Women should protest against the so-called medical secret, which decrees that they be kept in ignorance where their health and life are directly concerned.

Again, Sanger focuses on *information* as the critical weapon and *ignorance* as the enemy.

While it's not necessary for the context of this book to explore her detailed descriptions of various diseases, remember, these are the days long before sex education became common in schools. It's unlikely girls and boys (not to mention their parents) would have had access to this level of information outside of a doctor's office. By then, it would be too late.

It was this last chapter on sexually transmitted diseases that started to grab *wanted* attention.

. . .

It may not have *felt like* wanted attention, but one suspects from Sanger's writing and speeches that she began to court controversy as a way to amplify her message. But that's for later. Let's focus on the immediate aftermath of her 1916 book and the opening of the first-ever family planning and birth control clinic in Brooklyn, New York, that same year.

The gist of the Comstock Laws was that they set rules on what you could and could not send through the mail. They covered offensive and explicit material of all types. Sanger's vivid descriptions of venereal disease and female climaxing certainly fit the bill, as well as the sale of contraceptive products.

Nine days after her clinic opened, Sanger and an associate were arrested and fined.[9] Long story short, she would not agree to more lenient sentencing if she stopped providing sexual information and contraceptive products. In a statement in another ruling against her, a trial judge declared that women did not have "the right to copulate with a feeling of security that there will be no resulting conception." For asserting that women indeed had a right to copulate pleasurably, Sanger spent time in jail, in a workhouse, and even was forced to leave the country for a time.

The net result was different from what the judge had in mind.

The media attention cast light on Sanger's work in a way that wouldn't have been the case otherwise. The public loves a juicy, lurid story, and this

---

9   Said associate and Sanger's younger sister, Ethel Byrne, went on a hunger strike in protest and was force-fed, the first woman to be so treated in American custody.

one had it all. More than that, what Sanger was advocating made sense to people. More people read her books as cases wound their way through the courts. As more people read her books, more people demanded the types of products and services they learned about. They were already comfortable ignoring the Comstock Laws, just as they were comfortable flouting Prohibition Laws that just went into effect (see Chapter 5), so rubber runners became almost as common as rum runners along the Canadian border.[10]

In 1918, Judge Frederick E. Crane of the New York Court of Appeals ruled that doctors could prescribe contraception, but it would hardly matter. It was like handing out condoms after the orgy...or whatever your favorite sexual metaphor might be.

. . .

That last part is a crucial point. Although Sanger's feminist and socialist ideals – as well as her personal experience as a healthcare professional – drove her personally, they don't provide the best explanation for why the market for birth control exploded in the 1920s. From her writings, Sanger likely would have bristled at the notion that she enabled a *consumer* revolution in sexual freedom, but let's examine the evidence from a consumer-first perspective.

First, Sanger's core message was empowerment and enjoyment of the sexual experience through better knowledge. By allowing people to decide for themselves (rather than have authorities or men or the church decide for them), the average person can make better choices about when, how, and why to engage in sex. It wasn't Sanger or some government "Department of Reproduction" deciding for you. Choosing for yourself is part of *consumer* culture.

Second, wealthy people might be able to flout the law, as they did with alcohol during that era, but at-risk people she met in the slums wouldn't be able to do that. Sanger realized there were more viable long-term strategies than smuggling rubbers across the border. Building a market economy for sexual products likely wasn't her motivation to martyr herself in

---

10 Sanger's second husband, Noah Slee, smuggled diaphragms into New York through Canada in boxes labeled "3-In-One Oil " and became a successful legal manufacturer of contraceptives in the United States.

court. However, it motivated entrepreneurs to lobby the government to loosen restrictions to satisfy the market for satisfaction. Enabling open market competition is a *consumer* value.

Third, Sanger realized that people needed more than medical facts; they needed a *shared language* for sexual behaviors, services, and products. Much of the language of the time was cloaked in euphemism and sly asides. Unclear language led to confusion and misinformation – people who don't know what to call a condom can't decide to use one, can they? And even if they wanted one, would they know what to ask for at the store? Sanger's bold, direct use of language – for example, popularizing the term "birth control" as opposed to the more milquetoast "family limitation" – empowered both women and men. Creating the language for products and services builds *consumer* confidence.

And finally, Sanger wasn't content with simply providing information. She would give the means to act on that information. One of the key complaints about her Brooklyn clinic was that it distributed contraceptive products, not just pamphlets and advice. Like getting a sample at the grocery store, once people tried these products (and experienced their benefits), they wanted them again. Sanger's efforts created the demand for diaphragms, condoms, douches, and other protections. Giving people a product or service they can buy at the store creates *consumer* demand.

. . .

As we've mentioned, Sanger's legacy isn't universally positive. We're sidestepping much of that legacy here to make a point: Our political leanings and culture wars skew our perception of history, focusing on the foam and not the beer.

Is it fair to criticize her for taking advantage of anti-Catholic sentiment (and the church's opposition to birth control) to nudge Protestant officials to support birth control availability? Is it fair to read her 1920 follow-up book, "Women and the New Race," as a roadmap to implement eugenics and racist views? Is it fair to view her creation of the American Birth Control League (and later, Planned Parenthood) as responsible for millions of abortions?

If you're interested in diving into that legacy, you'll find plenty of company. But be warned, most books on the subject have an ax to grind

– one way or the other. Unless you set that aside, as difficult as that might be, it's nearly impossible to see the long-term impact.

And that impact is crystal clear.

By the end of the 1920s, Sanger's efforts had convinced two-thirds of all women and 40 percent of all men that birth control was a legitimate option for adults to take control of their sexual lives. She taught women (and men) about contraception in a way that they would see the consumer benefits for their own sexual lives. There would have been no widespread adoption of "the pill" in the 1960s without Sanger. In the intervening 100 years, the market for contraception products passed $7 billion annually in the United States alone. Survey data from the U.S. Centers for Disease Control and Prevention show that essentially all women will use some form of birth control at some point in their adult lives. Read that again: *all women*. If that isn't a successful consumer product introduction, it's hard to say what it would be.

Margaret Sanger was a feminist, a socialist, and a radical. She was also (perhaps unintentionally) a market maker – the Henry Ford of sexual freedom.

20
HOW YOU GOT YOUR KICKS

On May 26, 1928, fifty-five sweaty skeletons shambled their way into Madison Square Garden.

Despite their sorry state, they weren't quite finished with C.C. Pyle's 3,422-mile Great Transcontinental Footrace, also painfully and appropriately known as the "Bunion Derby." Finalists ran the final 20-mile indignity by circling the Garden's 1/10-mile track *two hundred times*.

Most of the 257 competitors who set off from California in March took the "rabbit" approach.[1] Given the climate and terrain immediately east of the starting gate, one struggles to imagine a more foolish strategy. Seventy-five runners called it quits before sunset on the first day. (Early stops along the way included the Mohave Desert and the Dead Mountains. They're not named that because of the pretty flowers.) The field continued to dwindle throughout the dusty fields of the vast middle west. Only ninety-nine made it to Chicago, the symbolic halfway point.

The winner (survivor?) was a 20-year-old, part-Cherokee farm boy named Andy Payne. He clocked the best time at 573 hours, 4 minutes, or just shy of 24 *days* of elapsed time from Los Angeles to New York. His tortoise-like victory proved the adage: Slow and steady wins the race. Payne speed-walked the U.S.A. instead of running it. Smart kid.

You'd think an epic cross-country footrace charting the nation's brand new "Mother Road" (much of which remained *unpaved* during the race) would generate more excitement in New York. You would be wrong. Runners nearly outnumbered spectators when they finally panted their way across the finish line.[2] The final indignity must have been hearing the applause from a couple of dozen spectators echo through an empty stadium.

The big idea was to promote the completed-but-not-yet-fully-paved Route 60. *Whoops*. Route 62. *Dammit!* Route 66. (Road numbering is a whole other story. We'll get to that later.) Cy Avery and other boosters had worked like dogs for years to get this route to pass through several towns

---

1   There's some debate about precisely how many runners started the race – the number ranges from 199 to 257. It's not important. If you're lucky, you can even find a biopic from the Sundance film festival about winner Andy Payne and his experience in the race.

2   Payne probably came away happy, though. He came away with the $25,000 grand prize. That's over $427,000 in 2022 money. Not bad for a farm boy, huh?

in Oklahoma on its journey cross-country. He had faced delays, grifters, and racists along the way. Avery stuck with it because he knew each little town along the route would benefit handsomely from the expected traffic along the best new route from Chicago to Los Angeles.

No one at the time could have foreseen the migrations of the Great Depression and the Hippie Counterculture along the length of America's highway. But Avery knew that the automobile was the next big thing. He had a feeling people would use it to get out and explore the country. His job was to ensure every wanderluster would need to stop off in Tulsa for a meal and a bed.

C.C. Pyle counted on Avery's boosterism to look past the scruffy bits of his so-called "plan." Along the route, Pyle hoped to recoup the considerable expenses that included a traveling coffee truck, field hospital, advertising, and even a fancy red tour bus,[3] by cajoling towns along the route to pitch in for expenses and charging spectators to pay to watch the race.

Somewhat predictably, the race was a complete, unmitigated disaster from the starting bomb.[4] At least, that's what the newly-formed Route 66 Association thought. Pyle was the P.T. Barnum of his time – a showman and promoter of the first order. Unfortunately, he wasn't much of a cross-country race organizer. To call the footrace a trainwreck is to mix metaphors, but the word choice is apt.

Pyle made his first mistake before anyone started running. He scheduled about 50 miles of progress each day. That *might* be fine on paved concrete,[5] but unpaved gravel, sand, and mud? Route 66 was a runners' hellscape. Worse, at least from the sponsors' perspective, was that Pyle's ad campaign didn't mention the Route 66 Association. That's like forgetting to put the bowtie on the front of a Chevrolet – it's one of the seven deadly

---

3   The runners had tents and slop. Pyle slept in the nice bus and gourmet meals. I suspect the runners would have killed him in his sleep had they had any energy left at the end of the day.

4   Yes, an actual bomb. Pyle had a flare for the dramatic, but one wonders whether a cannon would have done just as well.

5   They're lucky they didn't have much asphalt. It would have been a smoldering death trap for dehydrated runners.

sins of marketing.⁶ But the most significant unforced error: Pyle failed to secure firm commitments from all those teeny towns along the way *before* runners started west. Had he done that, he would have learned that although a few would pony up (another mixed metaphor, sorry), most were too small to either cover expenses out of pocket or be able to attract enough curious onlookers willing to pay.

By the time Pyle and his bedraggled menagerie reached Chicago, he was expecting to collect the $60,000 promised by Avery and the other Route 66 boosters, but they were so peeved that they refused to pay him. The money was running out. The bank repossessed his red tour bus. Although all parties eventually came to terms, the Bunion Derby was a boondoggle of the first order. Avery worried aloud that the reputation of the Mother Road would never recover.

(Hint: It would.)

. . .

People love to watch a trainwreck.

Cy Avery should have known that, but he was earnest in the way all midwesterners are. As finances deteriorated and runners collapsed, Americans were drawn into the debacle. No, there might not have been many people who would turn out in New York to watch runners struggle through the gates. Still, media coverage blossomed during the spring of 1928, calling attention to the (shockingly poor) state of the roads in general and making a case for their improvement. It also, quite literally, put towns along the route on the map. That included Avery's hometown of Tulsa, but also Santa Fe, Flagstaff, Albuquerque, and Santa Monica.

The names of those not-so-little-anymore towns hint at the more profound truth. The idea of the automobile as something more than simply a mode of transportation derives from its midwestern roots – a culture not imported from Europe, New York, or California – but homegrown on the vast open prairie.

With its swarming crowds and choked streets, east coast culture created *collective* transportation culture: subways, trains, and ferries. This

---

6   Or *"logos obliviate"* – an unforgivable curse for Muggle marketers.

culture valued shared transportation experiences and created an etiquette all its own. How much room should you leave between passengers? When should you give away your seat to an older person? What types of food and drink are okay? How drunk is too drunk? Should you defecate in the corner? Those sorts of things. Even 100 years after Henry Ford popularized the automobile, east coast metropolises still make driving akin to the tenth circle of Dante's inferno. But alas, some guy might be masturbating in the seat next to you on the subway, but at least you'll get to work on time. So, worth it. Right?

What we think of as "car central" in southern California today is an invention of the post-war era: drive-in restaurants, fast food, drive-in theaters, muffler modifications, and low-rider customizations. All those things remain part of that culture today. But remember, in 1920, Los Angeles county zoned more farmland than housing tracts. LA's half-million people had a lot of room to move around. By comparison, New York City crammed in ten times as many people in a fraction of the land area.

No, car culture is *midwest* culture. There's a reason Henry Ford found his footing in Michigan and not Massachusetts. It was the midwesterners who wrote the first traffic rules.[7] It was the midwesterners who stayed in new "motor hotels" (motels). It was the midwesterners who grabbed a meal at greasy-spoon diners. It was the midwesterners who invented the roadside attraction.[8] And it was the midwesterners who built the first truck stops. Despite all that, to think of car culture as a network of roads and kitschy new businesses misses the point.

To understand the story of what the automobile *truly* means to Americans, we need to get to know Cy Avery, the unique features and geography of the inland ocean of grass, and why he was willing to go to such

---

[7] Herbert Hoover played a big role here. We think of him today as something of a bumbler as president, but that's not how people saw him at the time. As the first ever Secretary of Commerce, he took an active role in public-private partnerships to lay the groundwork for the growth of new industries in the 1920s.

[8] Ever been to the Corn Palace in Mitchell, South Dakota?

lengths to create the self-service version of the transcontinental railroad.

...

Simply charting the growth in the number of automobiles in the United States doesn't tell the whole story. A better way to understand this explosion of popularity is to look at the number of cars *per capita*. In 1900, only 11 cars hit the roads for every 100,000 people, meaning there were only about 8,500 cars in the entire country. That same year, America boasted an equine population of about 2.5 million animals. Do the math, and horses outnumbered cars 300 to one.[9] Fast forward ten years and the number of cars per capita increased *46 times* to just over five per *thousand* people.[10] By 1920, that number had jumped again to 87 cars per 1,000 people. By 1930, nearly *one in four* Americans owned a car, bringing the overall number of vehicles on the roads to more than 26 million.[11]

It was one of the fastest adoptions of new technology in history to that point, and its impact cannot be understated. Most of that impact didn't (at first) involve wanderlust, drive-ins, and backseat nookie. It was much more pedestrian than that. The growth in automobiles showcased a stunning problem with *infrastructure*.

Until the 1900s, the best roads were *Roman* – as in the turn of the millennium Roman Empire. To be fair, those were good roads – transformative, really – by ancient standards. They allowed the Romans to move soldiers and equipment over vast distances faster than their Mediterranean rivals.

The best modern analog to a Roman road circa 1920 was made of

---

9   Does it make a bit more sense now why the part of the car that holds the steering, wheel, gauges, entertainment center, and the glove box is called a "dashboard?" In carriage days, a piece of wood protected riders from mud kicked up from horse hooves as they ran.

10 Fun fact: America was still home to over two million horses until the end of World War II, when cars (and mostly tractors) finally took over most agricultural work that horses used to do. You can still find about a half million horses today in the United States today, mostly for pleasure riding and ranch work.

11 The Model T had much to do with that growth, accounting for 15 million of the 26 million (or so) cars on the road by 1930. The overall figures come from the "Transportation Energy Data Book: Edition 36.2" from Oak Ridge National Laboratory.

paving stones. They're durable but require constant maintenance to fill in the chips, cracks, and holes. When you're traveling a few miles per hour in a horse and wagon, a 15-inch hole in the road is an annoyance. That same hole can be fatal when you're speeding along at 50 miles per hour in a car or truck.

One of the things that made the Roman roads so spectacular was the Empire's commitment to maintaining them. Then, as now, maintenance was spectacularly *expensive*, and when the Empire crumbled, so did the roads. They were so expensive that most post-Roman civilizations didn't bother. As late as 1904, the federal government estimated that the United States had 108,283 miles of gravel roads, 38,622 miles of composition roads (stone, shell, sand, etc.), and 1,997,908 miles of dirt roads.[12] When we use the word "road" to describe American roads in the first decades of the 20th century, we mean…basically…dirt. Only a smattering of roads used new-fangled materials like concrete and asphalt. Big cities like Paris, Long Island, and Washington D.C. showcased a handful of pretty, paved boulevards, but that was it.

Blame radio (in part, at least) for creating the demand. People in the country heard exciting stories about what was happening in the big cities and wanted to be a part of it. For their part, people in the cities wanted to see some of those National Parks that Teddy Roosevelt talked up for themselves. It was natural for them to want to get "outdoors" at a time when most city dwellers lived in overcrowded, dirty tenements. Others saw cars as a way to escape brutal northern winters and soak up some sun in Florida. (We met the first "snowbirds" in Chapter 13.) However, all those dreams were easier said than done in 1920. Traveling by car was an adventure of mechanical breakdowns, unmarked "roads," and lawlessness. Americans demanded better.

The problems with American roads in the 1920s were the same issues that confronted the Romans two millennia before: Who would pay to build them? And once they were built, who would pay to maintain them?

Responsive to voter demand (and sensing an opportunity to be rewarded for meeting that demand), both major political parties introduced a "road plank" in their party platforms. Each called for significant

---

12 This comes from federal government data published for the Louisiana Purchase Exposition in St. Louis in 1904.

levels of government support. The differences simply amounted to how many dollars would be spent and how those dollars would be allocated.

President Woodrow Wilson (a Democrat) was an ardent advocate of good roads and made them a party platform priority in 1916, writing:

> The happiness, comfort and prosperity of rural life, and the development of the city, are alike conserved by the construction of public highways. We, therefore, favor national aid in the construction of post roads and roads for military purposes.[13]

The Federal Highway Act of 1916, signed by Wilson, and the follow-on Federal Highway Act of 1921, signed by his Republican successor Warren Harding, created the model for highway funding we still use today – a federal/state partnership with a 50/50 co-investment of funds that pitted states against each other to compete for matching dollars.

Democrats liked the infrastructure investments for their collective good. Roads had the potential to improve the quality of life for citizens in the midwest and west. There, the distances were so great that there was no way for any single company or town to pay for hundreds of miles of "in-between" roads. Republicans liked roads for their economic impact. They reduced the transportation cost burden on businesses and allowed them to free up capital for product and service improvements. Both made the *realpolitik* calculation that good roads were a winning issue at the polls.

That focus on state-by-state competition led directly to boosters advocating for their own little corners of the country – to connect smaller communities to the rest of the American economic engine.

The boosterest booster of all was Cy Avery.

. . .

It's one thing for politicians to slap each other on the back after they've signed new legislation. If you're lucky, you might get handed the pen. That's great, but building roads gets "dirty" quickly. For the practical

---

13 From the Democratic Party platform, adopted in St. Louis, Missouri, during its 1916 convention.

matters of financing and building roads, you need people like Cy Avery working on the ground level.

Oklahoma was lucky to have him. Avery was a business renaissance man who happened to be the right person at the right time to take advantage of new business opportunities in the 1910s and 1920s. But remember, just because the opportunities are there doesn't mean they'll turn into anything. You can't be afraid of hard work and taking risks. In the gumption department, Avery was in his element. He remained flexible as conditions evolved, and he followed the money.

Avery's early career as an insurance agent gave him a unique perspective on the new oil prospecting rigs he was insuring. They weren't profitable *yet*, but as the demand for refined oil products like gasoline expanded, he knew that oil would be a big thing. That wasn't a stunning insight at the time, but being an insurance agent gave him the specific facts he needed to know where precisely to invest for maximum effect. It wasn't long before he started his own oil and gas investment company. Not unpredictably, it did well. He used that money to buy ranch land and raise cattle – another big thing that wasn't a stunning insight, but again, knowledge of the specific opportunities in the region made the difference. With the money from insurance, oil, and cattle, Avery invested in restaurants, hotels, and other amenities in the Tulsa area.

Again and again, it was the knowledge that made the difference. How do you get it when very little is published, and everything is new? *Personal relationships.* Luckily, Avery "never met a man he didn't like." He was the kind of person who knew everyone, was invited to everything, and got the first call when someone needed advice. Put simply: Cy Avery was in the middle of everything. Over the coming years, he would ensure that Tulsa would be in the middle of the newest and biggest cross-country road.

. . .

To paraphrase the modern saying, *Mo' cars. Mo' problems.* Cy Avery was the type to add, *Mo' problems, Mo' opportunities.*

Despite the national call for more roads, it wasn't obvious that the main east-west artery would go through Oklahoma. The original route would leave Chicago, head west through Kansas, and only turn north once it reached Utah. Then, it would snake through the high desert to Las

Vegas and finally cross to Los Angeles. Obviously, for Avery, that needed to change.

Luckily (unluckily?), the Rocky Mountains present a significant natural barrier to any transcontinental road. They don't call them "rocky" because they're grassy and idyllic. It's one of the most rugged mountain ranges in the world, with peaks averaging more than 14,000 feet above sea level. But it's not that high *everywhere*. There are places you could cross the divide with a lot less effort than others. That original route through Kansas and Utah? Avery convinced federal planners that it would be *much easier* to turn south earlier – through St. Louis, Missouri, and into Oklahoma in a sort of diagonal path – instead of heading west from Chicago. After crossing into Tulsa, the route could take the (much easier) due west path through the desert states of (west) Texas, New Mexico, and Arizona.

Once Avery convinced federal planners to alter the route through Oklahoma, he needed to find a way to pay for it. In practical terms, that meant many of the roads in the original path were…well, the best way to put it is "less than ideal." Road designers today tend to avoid steep grades and sharp curves. That makes the roads both safer and more fuel efficient. (If you've ever made good time on an interstate versus white-knuckling it on a winding hilly road, you get the idea.) However, there simply wasn't enough money to pay for the road construction itself (in 1921, the cost had ballooned to $35,000 per mile or more than a *half-million dollars* per mile in 2020 money) *and* pay landowners for rights-of-way through their property that would have allowed straighter and gentler roads. Avery had to live with those design flaws and advocate for improvements later.

Avery also worked to ensure as many roads as possible *weren't made* of sand, gravel, or dirt. Concrete was best. Asphalt was acceptable. But in the end, he needed to settle for the fact that any road was better than no road. The net effect was that roads varied widely in condition and pavement, tending better the closer you got to major population centers. (Remember the partially-paved conditions for the runners? That's why Route 66 was such a mess.)

Why was Avery so insistent on grades, curves, and road materials? It all comes down to the maintenance of what planners of the time called "four-season" roads.

As we've noted, weather on the Great Plains can change dramatically and quickly. Anyone living in the area today understands the frustrating reality of the four seasons: Fall, Winter, Spring, and Road Construction. Water is the underlying problem, primarily in its ice and snow varieties. As it freezes, it expands. As it thaws, it contracts. Water will sneak in and break it apart if there's any crack in the road (and there are always cracks in the road).

If the new east-west road would boast "5,000 cars a day," as Avery predicted, it needed to be open and passable all year. That meant bricks were out. Roads built with pavers have built-in cracks. Sand and gravel turned into a quagmire in the spring. Dirt roads? Driving your car over the scrubland *next to the road* would be easier. At least there, you'd have a few plants to hold back the mud. That's why concrete and asphalt were (and still are) preferred. They can take Mother Nature's punishment better than anything else.

Higher-tech materials meant more expensive roads. However, as experience taught maintenance crews, building the road was the easy part. Keeping roads passable 365 days each year was the real challenge, and challenges cost money. The only way to address that issue was a reliable tax base which could only come from more people living in the area. (Federal matching funds helped build roads. It didn't do quite as much to maintain them.) For more people to live in the area, they needed to be able to make a livelihood.

The economic development challenge is where Avery's broader experience paid off. He knew (from personal experience and investment) that some jobs could come from hotels, restaurants, filling stations, and mechanic shops. The existing roads in the early 1920s were so bad that people carried an entire range of spare parts and impromptu camping equipment. Roads were inconsistently (and often not) marked. Getting lost was a right of passage. Driving was an adventure. To attract a more casual brand of adventurer, Avery needed to make driving through Oklahoma a little less dodgy. That's why he fought so hard for the "Wisconsin plan" that assigned standard numbering: even numbers for primarily east-west roads and odd numbers for north-south routes. More on that in a minute.

That said, tourist economies are fragile economies – any sustainable tax base for road maintenance needed to include more than just enough money to maintain roads. Growing families required a full range of infrastructure (schools, water, sewer, safety) to build a lasting community.

Good roads also meant faster access to the other goods and services that cars and trucks could carry along the route. All those shiny new consumer goods and fashions people read about in the catalogs and magazines could not be had in days, not weeks. On the flip side, goods and services that people produced in those towns along the road could get to market faster – not just farm goods, but lots of other stuff too, including oil and related products. New businesses could be encouraged to relocate to places with good transportation because their transportation costs would be lower, and they could count on an eager workforce. Even an out-of-the-way city like Tulsa could enjoy the benefits of dense, east coast metros. Families could make a home on the prairie while still feeling connected to the rest of the country.

Finally, Avery was comfortable with the bare-knuckle blood sport politics of the Jim Crow south. The road issue was so complex that individual localities with sparse populations simply couldn't manage it, but that didn't mean they did *want* to. The 1916 and 1921 Acts provided some money, and every local two-bit politician wanted a piece of it. If cajoled and managed, they might slow progress, but progress would come. Left alone, however, Avery knew the engine of progress would seize up.[14]

. . .

The few biographies of Avery that you might find, including Susan Croce Kelly's *The Father of Route 66: The Story of Cy Avery*, delve into the fascinating detail about the final decision on the number "66" and Avery's role in creating the iconic "shield" graphic that still depicts all U.S. highways.[15] For all his effort, it's worth letting Avery have his moment. Let's watch the final act.

On April 30, 1926, Avery sent a telegram to federal highway planners.

---

14   He never was able to mollify the KKK. They hated him because he wouldn't bow to their pressure. Avery wanted the economic tide to lift all boats. The KKK only wanted to lift the boats painted white.

15   Kelly also wrote "Route 66" – a pictorial love letter to the highway and well worth the money for a coffee table copy. The political details about the numbering system and legislative actions are necessary, but tedious. We'll skip them here. Her books make it *barely* tolerable. It's not her fault.

Here's what it read:

> Regarding Chicago Los Angeles Road, if California, Arizona, New Mexico, Texas and Illinois will accept Sixty Six instead of Sixty we are willing to agree to this change. We prefer Sixty Six to Sixty Two.

It was more important that the road went straight through the heart of Tulsa. It didn't matter quite so much precisely what number it carried. That said, there were better numbers than others. The first thing to understand is that there were a *lot* of roads being planned – not just out west but in the more densely populated east as well. Planners didn't want to give a north-south route the number "51" and have its east-west counterpart in the same geographic area the number "50" if they could avoid it. (That would get confusing in a hurry.) The net result was a jigsaw puzzle of possible combinations, drawn by hand, and argued by political appointees. Imagine 24 kittens trying to play with the same ball of yarn.

As one of those feisty kitties, Avery was in the thick of it – whether as a formal state representative from Oklahoma or a "private citizen." (In fact, one could argue that he was more effective unofficially than officially). During one auspicious meeting, the association president doodled his idea for a distinctive marker for the highway signs. Reportedly, he handed it to Avery, who – knowing the critical influence skill of "improving" on an idea rather than challenging it – made a few "changes" to the sketch. A unanimous vote on an envelope sketch sealed the deal on one of the most iconic images of Americana.

Let's let Avery take the victory lap on Route 66:

> This road of ours is the shortest . . . to Southern California. There is already a tremendous traffic volume and it will increase rapidly when the national highways are designated. Auto tourists will say take National Highway 66 in the east and follow it all the way: there will be no chance of getting lost. Naturally it will be the best road . . . it will get the business.

When Avery said "best," he was being serious, not literal. Other roads might have better construction materials, gentler grades, or straiter straightaways. Route 66 would be the best for none of those reasons.

. . .

Avery's enthusiastic boosterism for Route 66 was more than simply motivated self-interest. He understood something lurking in American consumer psychology biting for the chance to get behind the wheel and see the country.

The road trip would become the ultimate *American* adventure. And no, it had nothing to do with inevitable mechanical breakdowns of early cars and impromptu required roadside camping trips.

Driving is an individual experience rather than a collective act. In the automobile age, you could plan your adventure with your family, friends, or more to the point, all by yourself. On a train, you could get across the country since the end of the Civil War, but you had to do it with at least a few dozen strangers, and usually many more.

Driving is an adventure on *your* timeline. Since the beginning of the railroad and steamship age, you needed to check the schedule if you wanted to get somewhere. You only could go *when* they were going, not just *where* they were going. If operators canceled a train departure or didn't stop where you wanted, you were out of luck. With your car, you choose when to leave.

Driving is the first time the average person could choose their own adventure. On a train, promoters would work hard to sell you on the destination and your itinerary. (That still happens with cruises today.) In your car, you set the agenda. Sometimes, you had a plan. Perhaps a guidebook showed some crazy roadside attractions you wanted to check out. But more often than not, you only had a vague idea of what you wanted to do. There is something about not knowing where you would eat, what you would see, where you would sleep, or what was over that next hill.

The biggest draw for all the carefully planned infrastructure from Cy Avery and others was the knowledge that you could go on your adventure and then come home safely. Unlike the one-way trip in covered wagons (where, if video games are to be believed, you may very well die of dysentery), the same Mother Road would guide you back home. Avery's vision was the perfect expression of wanderlust – safe in the knowledge that if you fell in love with California (or any place along the way), you could stay. Or not. It was up to you. That psychological safety allowed Americans to experience freedom and adventure they hadn't known before.

When people think of the Great American Roadtrip, the iconography of Route 66 comes to mind. Route 66 (and the vast midwest and west in general) spawned folk music and songs of the open road for generations. In the 1930s, it served as the migration route out of the dust bowl plains to greener pastures (and a new life, and hopefully work) elsewhere. After World War II, it was the migration route to California, transforming Los Angeles from a third-tier backwater into a continental counterweight to New York. During the 1960s, it smelled distinctly of…"grass."

Even today, in an age of easy air travel, tens of thousands of people still converge on a tiny town in the foothills of the Rocky Mountains – riding their motorcycles, sometimes for days, on a pilgrimage to Sturgis, South Dakota, each August. Beginning in 1938 with a few riders of Indian brand motorcycles, the annual Sturgis Motorcycle Rally essentially birthed the Harley Davidson brand and the mythology that goes with it. The event has drawn over 500,000 people each year for decades, generating nearly $1 billion in economic activity for a town in the middle of nowhere with fewer than 7,000 souls in the off-season.

A rally of more than half a million people may seem an odd legacy for Route 66. Still, when you take away the specific route and the details of any particular road and explore the cultural impact, that's precisely what it is. Sturgis may be a group experience, but each person makes the journey as an individual. The rally has a schedule, but you come and go as you please. You decide where you'd like to go along the way. East coast visitors might stop in the Great Smoky Mountains on their journey west. On the ride north, people from Texas may visit Mark Twain's Mississippi river valley towns. West coast visitors will take their time crossing the Rockies. Sturgis is the ultimate choose-your-own-adventure, and its enduring success owes everything to the idea of Route 66, not the road itself.

But even if you never participate in a motorcycle rally, Route 66 created the idea – that little feeling of wanderlust – embedded in American consumer culture. More than anyone else, we have a midwesterner to thank for that.

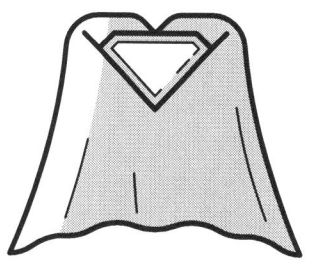

21
ALL-NATURAL INGREDIENTS. ARTIFICIAL PEOPLE.

The advertising department at Washburn-Crosby Company, the forerunner of today's General Mills, had a problem. A good sort of problem, as problems go, but a problem nonetheless.

Even before the 1920s, the Minneapolis-based advertising team at Washburn could out-market just about any consumer packaged goods competitor on the planet. But this time, they had out-marketed *themselves*. The idea seemed simple: a mail-away. Readers needed to remove the page from the *Saturday Evening Post*, cut out 20 scrambled pieces of a picture puzzle, reassemble them into the finished image, and mail in their entry. Within a few weeks, they'd receive a pin cushion embossed with the Gold Medal Flour logo.

Given the technical challenge involved, one suspects that mom gave the puzzle to her kids to finish while she did something productive. However, completing the puzzle turned out to be a bit *too easy*. Just over 30,000 people responded within a matter of weeks.

Can you imagine the overflowing mail room in Minneapolis? Do the rough math, and you'll get 312 cubic feet of envelopes, or about the volume of a small bedroom stuffed with contest entries top to bottom. *Oy*. That might have been more entries than the crack marketing team at Washburn had in mind, but no matter. Just drop a little pincushion into a box, slap on a couple of stamps, and be done with it. About 30,000 sewing kits would remind their owners to use Gold Medal Flour every time they sat down to mend a shirt or reattach a button. In Marketing 101, they call that "a win."

The "problem" was the notes that came along with the entries. Mostly, they asked about baking and cooking, but some touched on more…personal issues. (Think advice column stuff.)

The marketing department was already *good*. They pioneered the "kitchen test" idea, putting their flour up against their competitors, with a money-back guarantee as an incentive. Because of their success, Minneapolis earned a reputation as the "Mill City" in the decades following the end of the Civil War. The city was the most prolific food marketing center in the world; the Mini-Apple[1] would also incubate pantry icons

---

1 New York City is the "Big Apple." The "Mini-Apple" is one-part cute pun and one-part inferiority complex.

Pillsbury, Land O'Lakes, Hormel, Post, Kemps, Old Dutch, and Cargill. What made the marketing department *great* is what happened next.

The marketing team decided to create a person out of thin air who would respond to the letters.[2] She would be the archetypal homemaker – intelligent, thoughtful, friendly, patient, but also a bit no-nonsense. She would dispense with personal advice crafted by the team of culinary experts with good ol' common sense Minnesota wisdom.

She wouldn't be the first character created solely for advertising purposes. "Uncle Ben" and "Aunt Jemima" predated her creation by a few decades,[3] but she would be unique. Unlike her predecessors, Washburn's character didn't begin life as a visual image. She wouldn't have a "face" until she turned 15 years old. No, this character was something more than that. She wasn't a mascot or a minstrel. She responded to you individually. You felt like you knew her.

The story of her creation and evolution is more than a story of a genius marketing department responding to new opportunities and new delivery mediums. It's the story of what marketing can be at its best – creating a deeper connection between a company, its products, and its customers.

To read her fan mail is to come to an odd (and perhaps, uncomfortable) realization about modern consumer culture: A fictional person was more real to more people than most of the real people in this book.

She would sign her name, *Betty Crocker*.

. . .

Let's back up a step. Why would the good folks in the Washburn marketing department decide to create a "fake" person to respond to contest entries? Wouldn't a "real" person do just as well? Plenty of other companies

---

[2] If you search for this on Google, you're likely to come across the apocryphal story that advertising icon Bruce Barton (who we met in Chapter 15) created Betty Crocker. The archivists at General Mills disagree. Their records show that Barton and his firm, BBDO, were involved in later advertising campaigns, but that he did not create the character.

[3] Using the term "Uncle" and "Aunt" was *not* a show of respect to Black people of this era. People (largely, but not exclusively in the South) used those titles specifically to *avoid* using "Sir" and "Ma'am." Those terms of respect were meant only for Whites. Every Black person was an Uncle or Aunt, no matter their station in life.

used spokespeople in their advertising. That seems like the cheaper and easier option.

Not always. Unfortunately, "real" people are no end of trouble.

It should go without saying, but you can't control what real people do or say in their free time. If that were the case, Subway Restaurants wouldn't have allowed former spokesperson Jared Fogle within 500 yards of a school. *Oh, but they try.* Modern endorsement deals feature all kinds of provisions on what people do and say. For example, if you're a Nike-sponsored athlete, god help you if they see a photo of you sporting Adidas kicks. Despite the admonishments, however, behavior is notoriously hard to police in today's social media environment. There have been many high-profile cases where people have done or said something that reflects poorly on the brand, though rarely as severe as Fogle's 2015 conviction for child sex trafficking.

Things were a bit simpler, and a bit more complicated, in the Roaring 20s. On the one hand, endorsers of the 1920s had fewer media opportunities to flub up. Finding Babe Ruth passed out drunk in a New York bar didn't hurt sales of his namesake candy bar. (Who knows how that would go over in an era of smartphone video.) On the other hand, endorsement contracts were far less sophisticated. An off comment from the Babe to a *Times* reporter could still mean trouble for the sponsor.

Marketers tend to overthink the risk and overestimate the impact on their brand from a spokesperson's snafu, but "real human" issues can prove a distraction that pulls them away from the critical thing: selling more of what that person is endorsing. Charles Lindbergh (Chapter 9) got into trouble for his antiwar and (purported, but not fully true) Nazi sympathies. However, the spokesperson doesn't need to be a celebrity. "Average" people get into plenty of trouble as well, and they often have less experience in adeptly handling the media. The underlying benefit of using a spokesperson is a double-edged sword. The more a person's face is associated with a product or service, the more people associate good *or bad* things with them.

In short, people are risky.

Even if they do nothing wrong, real people have another troublesome characteristic. They might get sick. They might want to quit. They will eventually die. In the latter case, you could consider converting the "real" spokesperson into a more-immortal caricature – Colonel Sanders comes to mind – but that's tricky (not to mention a bit creepy). People can, in fact, tell the difference between real people and cartoons.

What's more, you may simply want to go in a different direction with your marketing and decide to let the spokesperson go. The problem is that people will still remember they were a spokesperson – memories built over time can be hard to disassociate. Think of an athlete that switches shoe brands. Once you've let that person go, they're usually free to pick up another sponsor, and that sponsor may be a direct competitor. Most sponsorship contracts explicitly lock out former sponsors for a defined length of time, but enforcing a lawsuit could have the perverse result of giving publicity to a spokesperson who doesn't work for you any longer.

What else could you try?

Henry Ford gives us a notable example from that era: Use the founder's name not only as the company namesake, but also as the official spokesperson. That's great if everything is going well, but if the company's fortunes falter, the founder's reputation can also falter. (In other words, the risk runs both ways.) And that's assuming Ford doesn't let his ego get the better of him and starts trying to control his workers' personal lives to create a "model" society. (He did that, and more.) Walt Disney, who founded his namesake company in 1926, ran into the same problems. In extreme cases, the board of directors of a publicly-traded company can fire the founder (Apple's Steve Jobs comes to mind). However, boards are loathe to do that. It risks creating a sympathetic figure in the public eye.

Another path is to choose another person from history or mythology as a symbolic stand-in. Tesla and Nike are good examples, though they face their own problems. First, you need to educate people on who and what they are, and second, you'd better hope against hope that no one looks *too* closely at the fact Nikola Tesla was a weirdo, and Greek gods did bizarre, pervy stuff.

Failing that, you can draw up your own mascot. Usually, these animals are cartoons that symbolize some aspect of the brand.[4] The "black cat" from Eveready batteries with the nine lives, or the "When it rains, it

---

4   Though they don't need to be. Some brands (especially pet foods) choose live animals as mascots. In that case, it's wise to choose a breed that's not *too* distinctive for what should be obvious "circle of life" reasons.

pours" girl from Morton salt,[5] or whatever the Green Giant is. The benefits are clear. You won't find the Green Giant passed out behind an adult bookstore.

By contrast, a wholly *invented* person is an empty container you can fill only with the traits and characteristics you want them to have. They say precisely what you want them to say. They do precisely what you want them to do. They go where precisely where you want them to go. They're caricatures of real people – think McDonald's Ronald or Progressive's Flo – but they still have much of the relatability of real people. They have all the benefits of celebrity endorsements and cartoonish mascots with none of the drawbacks.

Invented people also conferred *trademark* legal protection on the company. In 1893, struggling pancake flour miller R.T. Davis hired former slave Nancy Green to portray Aunt Jemima at events, on product packaging, and in advertising. It didn't take long before Green turned around Davis' fortunes and spawned a raft of imitators. Davis sued, eventually winning a landmark case in intellectual property law. In the so-called "Aunt Jemima Doctrine," the courts ruled that the image of a real person hired to play a commercial character would carry the same protection as a brand name, logo, or distinctive packaging. Washburn's marketing staff certainly understood the situation (they competed with that brand) and its implications.

Of course, the downside of creating your own "real" person is that they take a lot of time and investment. You can endow them with the perfect character traits, but that doesn't mean people know who they are. It takes time for consumers to get to know this new person, and the strategy is not without its risks. Just because the invented person will never engage in salacious nightlife doesn't mean that the marketing department won't make a mistake. If you instruct them to say something dumb, they say it. It becomes part of that person's history in a way that an ineffective advertisement does not.

People are personal.

In other words, should you choose to go down this road, you must

---

[5] Originally, the slogan was meant to indicate the quality of the salt. Specifically, that it would continue to pour from the nozzle even in damp weather. That's fair. But in 100 years, do you think they could have designed a metal spout that *didn't* break your fingernail to pry it open?

think hard about scripting this person's (so-called) life. If you don't, you lose all the benefits. Betty Crocker needed to proceed carefully. Let's see how she did it.

...

Women of the 1920s needed help.

As young people and families moved from farms to cities, they lacked the family support system that their mothers and mother's mothers had relied on for generations. (Let's be clear, although men cooked, we're mostly talking about daughters and mothers.) That meant they couldn't rely on the recipes and on-the-oven training that their mothers might have provided a generation ago. That's the odd paradox: Although cities pack in more people per square mile, they offer fewer meaningful connections. Those changing demographics drove the advertising approach for products like P&G's Crisco (we met *Mad Woman* Helen Lansdowne in Chapter 17). Daughters needed surrogate mothers and grandmothers in the kitchen, and Betty Crocker could be that person.

That said, the early days of Betty Crocker followed a more conventional script.

Washburn pioneered the "money back" guarantee, encouraging homemakers to try the product in their kitchens and see for themselves. But as we've already mentioned, there was the awkward possibility that without a bit of help, the test…well, let's be charitable…might not go well.[6] So naturally, Betty Crocker started helping with recipes.

In 1926, Betty Crocker "asked" readers to spend $0.70 for a set of endorsed recipes housed in a cute recipe holder. She "wrote" cookbooks as well. Of course, whatever the format, those recipes featured Washburn (later, General Mills) products. Those recipe boxes and cookbooks were designed to mimic what they might see in their grandmother's kitchen. But more than a simple rehash of hand-me-down recipes, Washburn invested in a full test kitchen in Minneapolis to validate, improve, and

---

6   For example, substituting salt for sugar. If you watch baking shows on television, you know this happens. It's easier than you think to make the mistake, and the results are just as terrible as you can imagine.

invent new ones.[7]

Betty Crocker was on her way to becoming a surrogate matriarch. The only thing missing now was seeing (or hearing) her in action.

. . .

Women of the 1920s weren't the only ones undergoing a transformation. Their kitchens were as well.

Not only were many young women separated from their families, but they also owned a menagerie of gadgets in their kitchens that their mothers would not recognize – electric mixers, toasters, gas ranges, electric ovens, coffee makers, and refrigerators – just to name a few. New technology utterly transformed the kitchen in the 1920s. Wood, coal, and elbow grease were out. Gas, electric, and power tools were in. Recipe cards and cookbooks could describe ingredients and provide proportions, but they could do little to help women understand how to incorporate new appliances into the cooking process.

For that, Betty Crocker went on the road. *Literally.* In cities across the country, she performed live cooking demonstrations using the newest gadgets and recipes. You might be wondering: *Hey, wait a second. Betty Crocker isn't even a real person. She was just a signature on a card.* The marketing department hired a series of real people to fan out and give the demonstrations. Think of it like a kitchen version of sitting on Santa's lap. Did people realize this Betty Crocker wasn't the "real" Betty Crocker? *Hmm.* Some people certainly did. Others? Perhaps not so much.

A group photo of the "Betty Crockers" from the era shows 30 women with stunningly similar bobs, shiny red lipstick, crisp collared shirts, spotless aprons, perfect smiles, and all "agelessly 32 years old." The photo isn't half as creepy as it might seem. The Bettys seem genuinely happy to be there. During the 1920s, this platoon of kitchen soldiers fanned out across the country, visiting dozens of cities and conducting thousands of

---

7   It still exists, by the way.

standing-room-only demonstrations to rapt audiences.[8]

Despite recruiting, training, and deploying a small Betty army, there was only so much ground they could cover and only so many people they could meet in person. Betty Crocker needed *mass media*. And luckily, the 1920s had just such a thing. As Forbes magazine would reflect in 1945, "the radio made Betty Crocker." So long as there were enough Bettys who sounded about the same – sound quality on the radios of that era wasn't so good – she could reach an audience of *millions*, not merely hundreds or thousands.[9]

Betty Crocker developed an online persona, not unlike a modern-day Dr. Ruth Westheimer. She was direct, but she didn't come off as cold. Her advice was no-nonsense but delivered with a soft touch. Starting in the mid-1920s, Betty Crocker hosted on-air cooking classes reaching an audience of over *30 million* people of a total U.S. population of only about 116 million. By contrast, the premier homemaking magazine of the day, *Ladies Home Journal*, where she also appeared, reached only 2.4 million.

Her catchphrases would become icons: "I bid you welcome to our circle" invited listeners into the kitchen with her. "You can do it, and I can help you," predated Home Depot's snappier version decades later. "I believe homemaking is a noble and challenging career," was a winning aspiration decades before anyone "started with *why?*"[10]

Other brands may have tried to copy her success, but no one had Betty Crocker's reach or name recognition. In just one record of local broadcasts, the NBC radio affiliate ran the "Betty Crocker Cooking

---

8   Photos of the audience show women of *all* ages, not just those starting out in life. And surprisingly, many men as well. One might be tempted to think they were "dragged along" by their wives or ogling the Bettys, but it's hard to fake genuine interest, and these men were clearly engaged in the cooking demonstrations.

9   It helped that Washburn-Crosby Company purchased floundering Minneapolis radio station WLAG and renamed it WCCO. When you think about it, the call sign change made sense. Did the company's investment in the station in 1922 prompt the marketing department to give Betty Crocker some (at least, discounted) airtime? One would think so. Then, as now, it pays to own media.

10 The entire eight statements of the "I believe" Homemaker's Creed are inspiring in their entirety. You can read them on the Betty Crocker website. Do you think that's where Simon Sinek came up with his pop business psychology claim to fame? We should ask his grandmother.

School of the Air" twice each week from 10:30-11:00 am, from 1926 to 1936, and averaged 15 million listeners per episode. Do the math. That's nearly *eight billion* listener hours. Billion. With a "B."

Continuing to run up the score while they were ahead, Washburn created the Betty Crocker Cooking School. If you submitted your kitchen "report" to "Betty" for grading, you'd become an official graduate. According to General Mill's archives, 238 people did so in the first year, ranging in age from 16 to 82. Eventually, *millions* would graduate over two decades, including a fair number of men.[11]

All at the same time, Betty Crocker (her team) continued to answer questions and letters from fans. The more people who "saw" "her" or "heard" "her," the more they wanted to connect with her. In one telling piece of fan mail, Lillean Dennick of Ruffsdale, Pennsylvania, wrote:

> I look forward to your cooking school as much as my husband looks forward to the hunting season, a man who lives every day in the year 'til the season comes. Now my husband and son eat almost everything I prepare. In my last sack of Gold Medal Flour there was a recipe for cinnamon coffee cake and I made it for dinner and I'll tell you it was delicious. When I make something good, my husband says, 'I bet Betty Crocker told you how to make that.'

Or how about Mrs. J.W. Rich of Houston, Texas:

> I always listen to your broadcasts whenever I can and I've been so very interested to hear about those contended husbands. My husband thinks I am a wonderful cook and every time he gets to raving about it, I tell him, 'Betty Crocker,' ought to hear him, for he is the most contented husband I ever heard about. We have been married 45 years last September and we are more in love with each other all the time.

In these and hundreds of other letters, it's clear that Betty Crocker meant a lot to people. That connection wasn't lost on the Washburn

---

11 As the Great Depression took hold, many men needed to switch roles with their wives when she was able to find work and he could not. Betty Crocker's advice for men in the kitchen reflected this reality in her implacable, non-nonsense style. Men grew to love her as much as women did.

marketing department. If your grandmother told you to buy something, wouldn't you? You would.[12] As the 1920s went on, Betty Crocker filled (at least part of) that role. In practical terms, if Betty Crocker had a product to sell, women of the 1920s were buying it, and Betty Crocker sold *everything* in the kitchen.

Betty Crocker would aid the war effort in the early 1940s, teaching homemakers how to do more with less, use vegetables from "Victory Gardens," and make the most out of ration coupons. She would record audio recipes for blind cooks, believing "everyone can cook" a century before Pixar made a movie about a rat becoming a French chef. In 1949, Betty Crocker was one of the first television personalities, adding a powerful new dimension to her radio career. That program ran for two decades. Nationwide baking contests, sponsored by Betty Crocker, ran into the 1970s and created the template for the modern *Great British Bake Off*, among dozens of other programs. Her cookbooks remain in print *today*, over 100 years later. Though most people visit the online version, you can still subscribe to a Betty Crocker magazine. Her name and face are a staple of dozens of baking products on grocery store shelves. Hers was the first "Chex Mix" recipe. Her "Hamburger Helper" was the first time many children played a role in meal preparation. When planning the all-American Thanksgiving meal, it's Betty Crocker who planned the menu.

Although she's had several voices and multiple faces, her "official" portrait has evolved over the years to match prevailing styles and trends. On October 21, 2021, Betty Crocker turned 100 years old.

...

Since the 1920s, research on commercial "mascots" has shown, rather convincingly, that they work. A series of studies from Cornell University showed brands that used mascots were 37 percent more likely to increase sales and 30 percent more likely to increase profits. And that seems reasonable. It's easier to connect with a character (even a cartoon version) than the very best brand name or logo.

Walk down the aisles of your local grocery store, and you can't miss

---

12 Anyone with a midwestern grandmother understands this. Defy them at your peril.

them. Nearly every brand features some sort of mascot, though most of them are *obviously* fake. No one believes the Kool-Aid man could be a real…person? Do they? Deducing the Gordon's Fisherman identity is a bit trickier. Paul Newman only looks fake. (He was, indeed, a real person.) That same research showed that 21 percent of mascots are based on humans, a number that presumably (and inexplicably) includes the Kool-Aid Man; 19 percent are birds, which makes sense, they're attractive; 16 percent are domesticated animals, primarily cats and dogs, especially in the pet aisle; and anthropomorphized vegetables bringing up the rear at 2 percent.

Since the 1920s, we've seen an explosion in character icons in product and service marketing, including the Pillsbury Doughboy, Chester Cheetah, the Energizer Bunny, Tony the Tiger, Mr. Clean, the Michelin Man, Mr. Peanut, Flo from Progressive, Captain Morgan, the M&Ms, and the Geico Gecko. Even non-profits get into the game. Think McGruff the Crime Dog and Smokey, the Bear. *Remember… Only YOU Can Prevent Forest Fires.* It's unclear what category the Green Giant belongs to. Animal? Vegetable? Pituitary Glands? He's another midwestern invention, "born" in 1928. McDonald's restaurants feature an entire cast of characters. Ronald the clown (sort of) makes sense. The Hamburglar? Okay. But what, precisely, is a "Grimace?"

When we leave the physical world and go online, every social media company or software platform seems to have some cute cartoony icon. It's almost like they come as a package with Series A venture capital funding. Here's a check for $2 million…and your green owl mascot.

Despite (or perhaps, because of) their weirdness, mascots work. People relate to them, and we buy what they're selling.

In an era of augmented and virtual reality, we should expect to see even more opportunities for characters to prove very real to us. It's already happened in expansive online role-playing worlds, where real humans pay real money for virtual goods and imaginary relationships.

However, to see Betty Crocker simply as a mascot misses the point. She was, and still is, so much more to people than merely the food industry's most effective pitchwoman. Although she sold through a carefully crafted artificial presence, her creators knew there was more to it than that. Maybe it was the letters they received. Maybe it was the popularity of the radio programs. Maybe it was the fixed attention of her audience at a live cooking demonstration. But maybe it was an understanding of something a little… *more*.

As people became more urbanized, they tended to become less *traditionally* religious. That is, less religious in the Judeo-Christian singular God sense of the word. However, they still wanted something akin to what the Greeks thought of as gods. Their concept of the gods was more like "superhumans" – just like us, but more so. Zeus wasn't just jealous; he was epically jealous. Artemis (Mars) wasn't just violent; he was bloodthirsty. Aphrodite wasn't just beautiful; she was mesmerizing.

That psychology probably explains the enduring popularity of celebrities (which we discussed more in Chapter 9) and the enduring appeal of comic book characters and their blockbuster movies.

In many ways, Betty Crocker was our very first superhero. *Betty Crocker wasn't just a good cook; she was our matriarch.*

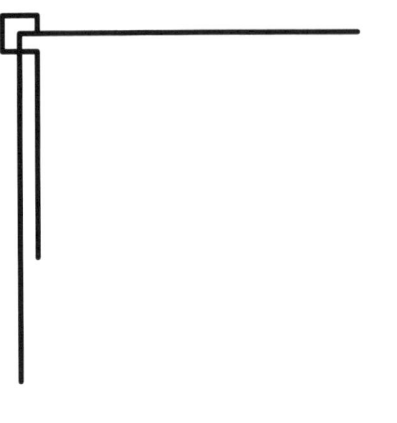

22
DEMOCRATIZING FASHION

If you believe cunnilingus and fellatio are inventions of the sexual revolution of the 1960s, what follows might come as a bit of a shock.

Let's start with the survey data.[1] In 1900, 14 percent of women reported having sex before marriage. By 1920, 39 percent mounted before matrimony. In those same studies, more than twice as many women reported achieving orgasm during sex. Bottom line: Women were having (much) more sex and *enjoying it*. (One presumes the men also enjoyed sex, but no one really doubted that.)

Remember, this is *survey data* – it's what people *reported* was going on. Sexual habits are notoriously difficult to get people to be honest about. A general rule of thumb is to *double* the number of people saying they're doing something randy unless you have complex statistical controls in place. If we use that heuristic, a *majority* of young people were having sex before they got married.

Why did everyone start getting so lucky in the 1920s? A few reasons.

First, people were a lot closer together. Between 1860 and 1920, the number of people in the United States living in cities with populations over 8,000 jumped from 6.2 million to 54.3 million. What's more, it was the farmer's *daughter*, not the farmer's son, who was most likely to leave the homestead.[2] In the first sexual revolution, population density provided its own gravity. You can't bump uglies if you can't bump into anyone. What's more, larger cities also offer a level of anonymity. Anyone from a small town can attest to the reality of nosy neighbors reporting back on your every move.

When our young woman moved into the city (usually alone), she needed some way to make a living. By 1929, *one in four* women was employed outside the home nationwide, including 50 percent of all single women and a much higher percentage of all women who lived in cities. *A girl's gotta eat, right?* Although she might not have much *extra* money, she alone decided how to spend it. Predictably, entertainment venues of all

---

1   Historian Joshua Zeitz shares these, and many other, statistics about American's sexual habits in the 1920s in his book, *Flapper: A Madcap Story of Sex, Style, Celebrity, and the Women Who Made America Modern*. We'll come back to his work later in this chapter.

2   You can hardly blame her. You probably weren't going to inherit anything with a gaggle of brothers in your way. The data comes from U.S. Census Bureau.

types sprang up to meet the demand.

If you were going to be wing-to-wing with a flock of people (and potential mating partners), your plumage better look good, you had better smell nice, and you had better know how to play the game.

The Tunnel of Love wasn't just a ride at Coney Island, folks. That embroidered, black, floor-length dress wasn't going to work. If your new beau had to spend 15 minutes unlacing your corset, that was 14 *more minutes* than it took to get through the ride. Body odor? Forget about it! What did the boys want? Not the subservient, chaste farmer's daughter; that's for sure. They wanted sassy and seductive, not meek and simple. If our gal needed some help in the plumage department, she was about to get it.

This was the era young people – and more to the point, young *consumers* – and even more to the point, young *women* – began driving the fashion world. As we've seen, we can't talk about fashion without talking about sex. And we can't talk about fashion without talking about Gabrielle Bonheur "Coco" Chanel.

. . .

Fashion is a complete sensory experience. Fashion is more than how you look; it's about how you *smell*, how you *sound* when you talk, the *feel* of your clothing, and even how you *taste* (breath mints and chewing gum became popular at about this time). That's important to remember as we tell the story of the birth of consumer fashion in the 1920s. Although we'll focus (primarily) on how people chose to *look*, Chanel is just as famous for her fragrance (Chanel No. 5) as she is for her clothing.

However, more than the sensory experience, fashion is a *state of being* – it's about how you act, carry yourself, and interact with others. Fashion is a representation of our identity – or at least, the identity we wish to present to others. That's important too. That's why it's important to talk about Chanel as a full person – her personality, her drive, and her energy – not just her clothing. If we choose not to discuss the complete person, we wouldn't be discussing *fashion* in its broader sense. More than that, it wouldn't be fair to her legacy. However, before we can talk about the specifics of Chanel's innovation, we need to step back *before* her era to understand a bit more about what getting dressed was like.

It's funny how surviving photographs shape our perception of the past. The world before the 1920s was a pretty drab place for most people, but not for the reason you might think. In that era, photos (such as they were) couldn't show color. It's better to examine the *paintings* from the 18th and 19th centuries to understand the wide variety of colors and patterns in clothing before the modern era.

Paintings of people parading around France, England, Germany, and Italy show vibrant colors and stunning variety. The women wore elaborate, billowing dresses complete with their own scaffolding – and up-dos to match. Even blemishes became opportunities for fashionable embellishments. Because smallpox remained endemic until the 20th century, many high-born types sported ugly pock-marks on their faces.[3] Stylists of the time turned lemons into lemonade by adding tiny "patches" in the shape of stars, hearts, and moons over the scars. It's really quite striking. And this wasn't simply a woman's game; even the men were pretty.

That said, we need to remember that being well-coiffed was a privilege of the wealthy.[4] No peasant woman was wearing a metal-framed crinoline and whalebone corset to milk her family's cows, no matter how much support her girls upstairs needed. Everyday women and men typically owned one set of clothes for casual use, with perhaps a Sunday-best outfit that made an appearance at weddings and funerals. (Often yours, in both cases.) Natural fabrics and simple dyes were the most common by necessity. Most wore black, white, and gray fabrics or natural linens and leather.

However, as the Industrial Revolution upended clothing manufacturing, all that started to change. Mass production was coming to clothing and jewelry, just like everything else. Now, the average middle-class family could afford *multiple* outfits of clothing designed specifically for different occasions. Additionally, the advent of durable plastics and other synthetic materials expanded the possibilities of jewelry production from *precious* metals and stones to *non-precious*, but still attractive, versions of the same

---

3   Smallpox was a cruel disease in that its worst lesions often targeted the extremities.

4   There's an entire grievance subculture around corsets and how they crushed internal organs, restricted breathing, and led to the (mis)diagnosis of "fainting spells" in women. There's some truth to that, but not as much as you think. Much of the hoopla is the result of our historical "wealth bias." What survives are the tales from rich people, not regular people.

thing.⁵ Obviously, that made it cheaper to *own* clothes, but it didn't say anything about *what clothes* you would own. However, the decisions at play at the beginning of the 1920s were more significant than all that. As we've discussed, the social structure was changing – especially in the cities – and *women* were taking the lead.

Women would look different, yes, but they would also *act* differently. Women of the 1920s were, for the first time, choosing their own identities. The first one many would choose for themselves would be the *flapper*.

. . .

When you ask people 100 years later what comes to mind when they hear the term *flapper*, they'll describe what the style looked like. The iconic image is a young woman with a knee-length, slightly boxy dress, a short hairstyle (often a curly mop of hair or straight hair curled around the ears), a few pieces of oversized costume jewelry, a cute hat worn at a jaunty angle, and sensible shoes.

Mostly, however, you can tell by her *eyes*. The flapper is always smiling, yes, but smiles can be faked. You know it when you see one; the smile doesn't touch the eyes. Flappers weren't fakers. What defined a flapper was a genuine verve for life, and everyone could tell. Their positive energy was infectious.

Even the dictionary definitions of the word give us a clue that the true nature of the flapper was a *combination* of outward appearance and inner attitude – the broader definition of fashion, not the narrower one. As early as 1922, "flapper" had entered the lexicon. Here's how the Webster Collegiate Dictionary defined it:

> A young girl, esp. one somewhat daring in conduct, speech and dress.⁶

---

5   For more on the backstory of fashion jewelry (more than we can go into here), pick up a copy of *Adorning Fashion: The History of Costume Jewellery to Modern Times*, by Deanna Farneti Cera. For more on the science of plastics that made this possible, look up inventor John Hyatt. He created the process for making celluloid, the first artificial plastic, in the late 1860s while searching for a substitute for ivory for making billiard balls.

6   Oxford commas weren't popular in that era.

It bears a moment to tease apart each word in that definition because they'll give us signposts as we continue. The first is "young girl." Ignore the "girl" part; that's simply an archaic way to refer to a young *woman*. Flappers weren't elementary schoolers or pre-teens. Although teenage girls certainly began to adopt aspects of flapper culture, young women in their twenties drove this trend. The 1920s marked the first time *young adult* consumers drove the fashion industry, not older buyers.

The second phrase of note is "somewhat daring." Daring implies that a flapper challenged the conventional wisdom and behavioral norms… but not *too much*. Although we'll see aspects of flapper culture that started to cross the line into self-destructive behavior (especially among the Hollywood and literary vanguards), *most* flappers were content to bend the rules, not break them. They were exercising their freedom to pursue happiness within the system, not outside it.

Finally, note the three words that define what flappers were daring about: *conduct, speech, and dress*. Only the final word mentions outward appearance. The true definition of a flapper was how she *acted*, not what she *looked like*. Yes, fashion involves clothing choices, but fashion is more than that. Fashion is about what those clothes *say about you* and how you interact with the world. That is the critical difference between fashion before the consumer revolution of the 1920s and fashion after it.

In his book, *Flapper: A Madcap Story of Sex, Style, Celebrity, and the Women Who Made America Modern*, historian Joshua Zeitz leans into the more salacious details of the iconic flappers of the 1920s as well as adds depth and color to Webster's (admittedly dry) definition. A flapper is sexy, flirty, and a bit mischievous. She has a zest for life that's obvious to everyone around her. She lives for the joy of the moment. You might see her at a club or a speakeasy (see Chapter 5 or Chapter 12 for more). You'll often see her with *other women* rather than random men; the 1920s is the origin of the "girls' night out." That's not to say she wasn't interested in meeting men (or women, for that matter), but first and foremost, going out was a chance to see and be seen.[7]

However, that's abstract. Where did people of the 1920s get their

---

7   Seriously. Do a Google Image search for "flapper" and you'll notice the same thing. Most of the images are of women with other women. That's not an artifact of photography of that era; it's trying to tell us something about the culture.

ideas for how the flapper would act or what she would wear?

They might read about her in one of F. Scott Fitzgerald's books – or, more likely – in one of his many short stories and essays. A struggling writer from St. Paul, Minnesota, Fitzgerald eventually fell head over heels for (what would become, in his writing) the archetypal flapper: Zelda Sayre. Sayre was a certified wild child who not only cultivated that image in the media, but (uncharacteristically for a flapper) also *lived it* in person. Both attractive young people, she and Fitz would often find themselves stumbling out of a speakeasy, falling over drunk in some wealthy family's pool, or in bed with some random man (or woman, or both).[8]

Fitzgerald's work provided a blueprint for the flapper lifestyle. His short stories centered around joyrides (no one knew what to do in a car; they were new), necking (exactly what it sounds like; this was all about kissing the neck), petting (stroking or touching each other; it didn't involve dogs and cats), smoking and drinking, applying makeup (again, this was new for many women), and hairstyles (mothers weren't much help with these new, shorter do's). Note that Fitzgerald wasn't talking about sex *exactly*. He strongly implied it, readers absolutely inferred it, and he never denied it, but he didn't come out and *say* it.

For its part, the media (as it does) grabbed onto that implication and inference and ran with it for all it was worth. Fitzgerald and Sayre participated in this orgy of attention lustily. They were some of the first modern celebrities (see Chapter 9), and they had an intuitive sense of cultivating the media for their own gain. Of course, this meant that the image of the flapper in the media was a young woman falling over drunk, having sex with random strangers, swearing like a sailor, and speaking her mind any chance she got. Fitzgerald and Sayre certainly lived up to that portrayal, even if most flappers did not.

Reading about flappers was all well and good, but the 1920s was the dawn of the *visual* age as well – the movie age. Young women out on the

---

8   Many other famous men and women would follow this formula in the coming decades: Attract scandal, especially of the sexual kind, to create media interest. The reality was as true then as it is now: Sex sells.

town could also see the vision of the flapper larger than life on the big screen.

...

Who's the archetypal "black and white" female movie star people picture in their minds?

It's probably Vivien Leigh playing southern belle Scarlett O'Hara in *Gone with the Wind*. If you asked most people when that film was made, they might say "the 1920s." However, that's incorrect. *Gone with the Wind* was completed in 1939 and released in 1940 – nearly 20 years after the silent movie era began in Hollywood. Contrary to the image many people hold, female film stars of the earlier period were *not* meek and petulant damsels.

We could choose several stars to highlight the transition from silent films to "talkies," but perhaps Louis Brooks is the best focal point for our purposes. After starring in some lighthearted silent comedies, she broke into serious filmmaking with what is considered her best work: *Beggars of Life*. The themes in that film would be difficult to watch *today* – a fact that often changes people's perceptions of the innocence of the "earlier time." Without going into the details, *Beggars of Life* is a story of a young woman from the country who kills her abusive father. Finding herself penniless and chased by police, she decided to "ride the rails" dressed as a man. (Her iconic curled bob hairstyle helped her pull off the look.) Somewhat predictably, she's discovered on the train, but she manages to hold her own in a group of rough men. Deciding to cast her lot with one of the men she meets, Brooks' character evades the police and escapes to freedom in Canada.

The tragic movie parallels Brooks' life in several ways. During the filming, she had a one-night stand with a stuntman. After their encounter, he spread the rumor on set that she picked up a venereal disease from a one-night stand the *weekend before* with the film's producer. (She was married at the time. Her husband was…not pleased, to say the least.) She was also reported to have had a one-night stand with Greta Garbo, who Brooks called a "masculine, but gentle lover." She loved sex with men *and women* and wasn't afraid to say so. People flocked to see her movies in the 1920s, but she struggled with the negative media attention. By the end of the decade, she had escaped the American media's sexual obsession by continuing her film career in Europe. However, if the media thought that chasing her out of the United States would reduce her popularity, they were wrong. She was the first in a long line of A-list female actresses.[9]

The question is: How closely did the flapper image match the *actual* flapper lifestyle? The answer: Yes, *sort of*. Did flappers drink? Yes. Were they sometimes drunk? Yes, but less often than you might think. Did they have sex? Yes, but most of the time, what happened in the backseat of the car was something short of the full act. Did flappers speak their minds? Oh, yes. That's something they were more comfortable doing than any of the other stuff.

But what's important to understand is the difference between the *image* of the flapper and the *reality* of that identity that women adopted. By dressing a certain way, a flapper could have those "naughty" associations without *actually doing* all those things. She *could* do them, but she didn't need to. The *image* was enough. Flappers could live vicariously through Sayre and Brooks, adopting the parts of their behavior they liked, trying what they were curious about, and leaving everyone else with the mystery of which was which.

The image of the flapper gave women a new type of role model and templates for a different way to act in society, but it didn't give them much they could *buy*. And remember, the "look" was the critical part of adopting the flapper identity – however *you* chose to embrace it.

This is where Coco Chanel comes in.

. . .

Chanel began her career at the most logical intersection of what makes fashion fashionable. She had two jobs: By day, she was a seamstress, understanding the mechanics of fabrics, thread, stitching, buttons, patterns, and embellishments. By night, she was a cabaret singer and dancer in Paris. For the uninitiated, that's a tougher job than it seems, and Chanel had one of the toughest jobs in a tough business. So-called *poseuses* (literally translated as "exhibitionists") entertained the crowd between acts. That

---

9   In 1982, Brooks published a memoir of sorts, titled *Lulu in Hollywood*. In it, she recounts these stories (true, false, or a mix of both) as well as her struggle to make a living after she fell from her film career peak.

not only taught her how clothing *functioned* (or failed to) on stage, but it also showed her how people *reacted* to fashion. In a performance, the costume is part of the show. The two cannot be separated.[10]

Stories of her early life weren't just embellished; they were *purposefully* vague and mysterious. Chanel understood from her days entertaining military types at the cabaret that fashion was as much about the backstory and performance as it was about patterns and fabrics. That said, Chanel's life was exotic, even by flapper standards. Historian Rhonda Garelick details this time in Chanel's life quite well in her excellent biography, *Mademoiselle: Coco Chanel and the Pulse of History*. We won't dive into her on-again/off-again affairs other than to say that the public perception of being a mistress didn't concern her in the slightest. In one particular reminiscence that sums up Chanel's attitude to sleeping with two married men at the same time, she was smitten that "two gentlemen were outbidding for my hot little body."[11]

Were the stories about Chanel true? False? Embellished? Somewhere in between? Does it matter? Actually, the *question* matters, not the answer.[12] The mystery provided an allure that catapulted the ambitious Chanel from a clothing tinkerer into a fashion icon.

She spent the years before the 1920s opening her first boutiques and experimenting with new types of fabrics – simpler, humbler options that steered away from the glamorous and complex French fashion of that era. Instead of lace and silk, she used jersey and tricot. At the time, that's what *men's underwear* was made from. (One thinks Chanel might have been

---

10 Chanel acquired her nickname "Coco" about this time. In a pattern that would define her, she left the origin a bit of a mystery – comfortable with multiple versions of the story floating about. It could have been a nickname given by her father, a play on words in a performance, or a shortened form of the French word "cocette" – a "kept" woman.

11 Rumor has it that the shape of the bottle for the iconic Chanel No. 5 came from one of the military canteens a lover carried.

12 Her *true* backstory, such that we can tell, is pretty sad. She was abandoned as a child and orphaned – a shameful situation in France at that era. It's not surprising that she obfuscated it. She understood fashion's potential to provide people (including, most importantly, her) a way to create a fresh identity. You're also likely to read stuff about affairs with Nazi generals during the German occupation of France during World War II. Unsurprisingly, the current Chanel organization disputes these characterizations, but from what we know, Chanel wasn't shy about taking a lover.

familiar with those fabrics. Who's to say where inspiration should come from, huh?)

She also experimented with models walking the boulevards parading her fashions for others to see – sort of like walking billboards. Modeling is underrated by those out of the fashion industry; they think it's vain and shallow. But thought of a different way, a model is *quite literally* a demonstration – a "try before you buy." The consumer gets to see that clothing on someone else and, ideally, on someone you *want to be like*. Chanel wanted you to imagine yourself in her clothing, and the best way to do that was to find beautiful people to walk around in it.

Chanel was also the first person to *popularize* costume jewelry. Yes, making jewelry from non-precious versions of metals and gemstones was possible, but they were *copies*, not statements in their own right. Chanel saw it differently. Copying precious metal and gem designs was *limiting*. There was no reason a piece of jewelry couldn't be designed to specifically complement a particular dress, pair of shoes, or elegant hat. Chanel made costume jewelry that wasn't a substitute for the real thing, but rather a real thing in and of itself. Chanel's approach caught fire quickly. Within only a few years, she was able to pay back her early financiers and investors and step out entirely on her own.[13]

...

In 1926, the American edition of *Vogue* magazine published an image of Chanel's "little black dress." Although Chanel had introduced the dress in France before the 1920s, this was the first time it showed up so prominently in the United States.

It was solid black, sat just below knee length, had a high neckline, and featured long sleeves. For the modern viewer, it's probably not what you would expect. It had a thinner silhouette than its more contemporary version, and it showed surprisingly little skin. However, the key elements were there. And remember, what we picture in our minds shows our *recency* bias. Plenty of dresses today take inspiration from Chanel's work. In the 1920s, this was a radical departure from its predecessors'

---

13 It's not entirely clear when Chanel designed her iconic logo featuring interlocking Cs, but she is reported to have designed it herself. It's been in use continually for over 100 years.

billowing, structured gowns and minuscule waistlines that sported a rainbow of pastel shades and floral prints. The little black dress was elegant in its *simplicity*.

The magazine dubbed it the *garçonne* look, literally translated as "little boy" or "tomboy," which seemed appropriate compared to what came before. Critics of the time (older men, but not exclusively older men) were…unimpressed. Here's a typical critique:

> No more bosom, no more stomach, no more rump. Feminine fashion of this moment in the 20th century will lop off everything.

It didn't help that *other* Chanel fashions amplified this trend toward androgyny and masculinity. Her designs featured ties, high-fitting trousers (pants on women!), and suits that mimicked menswear. She designed them to fit deliberately oversized on smaller female frames.

Vogue, however, understood what Chanel was getting at. It reminded them of the Ford Model T – in 1926, at the peak of its popularity. They noticed that the automobile's strong lines, black color, and sleek design bore a striking resemblance to this new woman riding in (or driving) it. Massive, flowing dresses might have worked well for a horse and buggy era, but this was a new time. Fashion was changing to match. And just like the Ford Model T, Chanel made her little black dress *affordable* and *practical*. Much of that had to do with the materials chosen. She picked more durable fabrics for daywear, like wool, and more elegant fabrics for eveningwear, like satin or velvet. Most importantly, all of them were cheaper than embroidered silks.[14]

However, fashion wasn't all about going "out on the town." As more women worked outside the home – especially in the cities – they needed a professional wardrobe. Being on constant display meant staying up-to-date on trends to create a positive professional impression. Big fancy dresses weren't going to work. A more…well, let's say…*masculine* approach was more practical. In those days, office culture *was* masculine.

---

14 A note about bras. Although not Chanel's invention, her fashions popularized the brasserie over the corset. Both do the same job, but the bra is more flexible and minimal than the corset. It's easy to put on, and more to the point made at the beginning of the chapter, it's easier to take off.

Chanel's inspiration meant those clothes were both practical and feminine, no matter what a crusty old journalist might say. The twenty-somethings of the 1920s weren't listening to the editors of the *New York Times*; they were listening to the editors of *Vogue*.

The appearance of the little black dress in *Vogue* had one other significant effect: Like putting gas in the tank of a Model T, consumer culture would fuel the fashion engine.

. . .

New York may have set the trends in the United States for fashion (although, to this day, it still follows Paris), but it didn't take long for the American commercial machinery to catch on.

Chanel's fashions (and copies thereof) started appearing in other magazines. As we saw in Chapter 7, "housekeeping" magazines devoted significant portions of their publications to highlighting the latest dresses. By the time the late 1920s rolled around, those patterns had changed markedly. Gone was any pretense of the era of fashion that was – big dresses and complex embroidery. "In" were shorter dresses, varying necklines, and boxier forms that mirrored Chanel's. More than that, many women of that era still *made* their own clothes, and the new fashions were easier to copy than earlier designs. Twenty-somethings might be heading to the department store to pick up their dresses, but thirty and forty-somethings often made them at home. The net result was the same. As Zeitz put it: "Fashion doesn't exist until it's on the streets."

To that point, how long did this *diffusion* take from the haute couture of New York to the pedestrian walkways of Muncie, Indiana, or Duluth, Minnesota? You might be surprised by the answer: about 18-24 months. In other words, it takes about the same amount of time *today* – 100 years later with overnight shipping and 3D-printed jewelry. That tells us that the *idea* of fashion has a power – and a deliberate path to acceptance – that is not necessarily dependent on any modern technology.

You might think that Chanel would have bristled at the idea of other designers copying her fashions, adapting them, and earning their own living. Yes, she was an ambitious businessperson, but her higher purpose was clear: "I am for the women." Her mission was more than simply selling clothing or bottling scents – what traditionally counts as "fashion" in most people's minds. Her view was the broader vision of fashion we discussed earlier; it was the entire experience, the identity of the person wearing it. Through fashion choices, a woman could create the image *she* wanted, independent of her upbringing, societal expectations, or "station" in life. *That* was the ultimate expression of consumer choice. Chanel gave women a powerful tool to express themselves.

...

Criticism of Chanel's work and influence came from the usual corners. We've already talked about the dirty older men who wanted to see more "bosoms" and "rumps." We've hinted at society elites who loved Chanel's fashion…until they saw "lower class" women wearing it. But perhaps the most vigorous and persistent critique came from a most unexpected place: *feminists.*

First-wave feminists were protesting and *sometimes getting jailed* promoting suffrage (the right to vote, which they achieved with the passage of the Nineteenth Amendment) and demanding equal treatment with men. These were big, serious issues. The flapper lifestyle was anything but serious. As described by Fitzgerald and shown on screen by Brooks – but perhaps most personified by Chanel – the flapper channeled the idea of freedom through consumer choices: Not just what to wear, but also what entertainment to enjoy, where to dance, what to drink, and who to sleep with. They weren't as concerned about equality in the *theoretical* and *principled* sense; they exercised their freedom in everyday decisions. Women were voting with their wallets.

Yes, there was an overlap between the two groups, but there's a case to be made that between the feminists and the flappers, the *flappers* saw more immediate, practical benefits in exercising their choices. As the 1920s ended and the 1930s began, the American economy spiraled into the Great Depression. For many historians, the end of the Roaring 20s was a return to "decency," "morals," and "frugality." Although it's a common misperception that people moped around for ten years, people *did* need to tighten their economic belts. In that, flapper fashion proved remarkably resilient. Remember, it was cheaper to buy and easier to wear – perfect for a time of economic challenge. Regardless of the economic mood, *fashion* was here to stay.

...

By 2021, the global fashion industry topped $1.5 *trillion* (with a "T"), with the United States portion of that market approaching $294 billion. In comparison, that's nearly half the size of the U.S. *automobile* market. In other words, U.S. consumers spend about half as much on clothing as they do on cars. (It's doubtful that Henry Ford *or* Coco Chanel would have predicted that.) Although women's clothing makes up about 60 percent of that total, men have also jumped into the fashion pool. Menswear eventually adopted Chanel's strategy of simpler clothing with more durable, flexible fabrics. Think about it. Sportswear is to men's suits what the little black dress was to flowing gowns: a more practical alternative. Golfwear is just as acceptable in the boardroom as a three-piece suit; in fact, likely more so. Odd though it may seem, a polo shirt and khakis were *Chanel's* inspiration.

However, sales numbers and industry strategy only tell part of the story. You only need to compare photographs of crowds in the 1910s to a similar group in the 1950s and another in the 2010s. Try it sometime. (Crowds at sports stadiums are a great example, and the photos are easy to find.) In the earlier pictures, you're struck by the *sameness* in appearance. The men all seem to be wearing the same clothes – almost like a uniform of blandness. The women do as well. There might be a fun hat in the crowd or a colorful pattern, but women's clothes all were quite similar, especially for anyone who *didn't* have the money to buy anything nicer.

Fast forward to the 1950s, and the scene changes *dramatically*. The men still look…well, like men of a much earlier generation. The styles may have updated a bit, but they're still monochromatic. The women, however, are not. They sport various styles that are common today – not the specific styles themselves (especially hairstyles), but the variety of *different* styles of hair, makeup, clothing, and jewelry.

Wind the clock forward again past the turn of the new century, and *both* women *and* men show remarkable variety. Some men still sport elegant suits, but many will dispense with the tie. Some wear a sport shirt and jeans. Many wear fashion inspired by urban music – bold colors, patterns, and designs. Some are practical. Many are not. So-called "athleisure" clothing is typical throughout.

However, as we've learned here, the *look* is not the point. Fashion is about *identity*; it's about the image we want to present to the world. That's Coco Chanel's true legacy. She gave each of us the freedom to decide that for ourselves.

23
BUYING A BETTER YOU

> Every day, in every way, I'm getting better and better.
> – Émile Coué de la Châtaigneraie, French psychologist and pharmacist[1]

Since 1995, Amazon has published a list of its 100 top-selling books each year. The *New York Times* and *Wall Street Journal* (among others) also publish their lists, but Amazon doesn't editorialize its rankings. Sell enough books, and you make Amazon's list. By contrast, the good folks at the *Times* and *Journal* judge what books "deserve" to be on their lists, and they don't tend to like self-help books. It's easy to see why. Self-help would consistently crowd out the top spots if their lists included those titles. What's nice about Amazon's list is that it gives us a better idea of what people are *actually* buying, not what elite editors *think* people should be buying.

In 2021, James Clear's *Atomic Habits* captured the #1 spot on Amazon's best-seller list. *The Four Agreements* from Don Miguel Ruiz grabbed #3. Self-help books nabbed 20 of the top 100 spots overall – a list that *still includes* Dale Carnegie's classic, *How to Win Friends & Influence People*, and Napoleon Hill's, *Think and Grow Rich*, both originally published during the Great Depression (1936 and 1937, respectively).[2]

And 2021 wasn't a fluke. For the past 100 years, despite raising the ire of snobby Manhattanites, Americans have bought self-help books in spectacular numbers. There's a saying in the publishing business: If it weren't for self-help books in the nonfiction section and romance novels across the aisle in fiction, there would be no publishing industry.[3] Self-help books routinely outsell all other nonfiction genres *combined*. They're so popular that

---

1 In 1920, Coué's published, *Self-Mastery Through Conscious Autosuggestion,* in French. An English translation followed two years later. You can find both on Google Books for free.

2 Have you ever heard the phrase, "If you can conceive it, believe it, you can achieve it?" It's a required chant in karate schools everywhere.

3 Romance novel readers are notoriously voracious consumers of content. Many can consume hundreds of books each year. That popularity has spawned a mind-blowing number of sub-genres, including (and this is not a joke) Amish vampires, NASCAR romance, mermaids, gargoyles, cavemen, alien abductions, shape-shifters (e.g., werewolves, werebears, weredeer, werehorses, etc.), and paranormal pregnancies. Don't you want to meet an Amish vampire?

it's difficult to imagine a modern bookstore (bricks or clicks) without them.

If you've ever heard "if you can conceive and believe it, then you can achieve it," wondered why there are seven habits of highly effective people, or danced like no one was watching at a Tony Robbins seminar, you've got Émile Coué to thank.

Or to blame?

In the spirit of the self-help industry, go ahead and judge for yourself!

. . .

When most people ask about the uniquely American self-help phenomenon (especially people outside the United States), they answer with some combination of "city on the hill" American exceptionalism or the "rugged individualism" myth built into the country's origin story. Those might be table-setters, but they don't quite explain why the 1920s laid out such a lavish buffet for the movement's growth and the industry that supports it.

We get our first hint at a better answer by looking into medical treatments of the time. That's important because it's when people feel at their most vulnerable and powerless. What could doctors offer around the turn of the last century?

Here's a hint: *Life imitates art.*

> Sherlock Holmes took his bottle from the corner of the mantel-piece and his hypodermic syringe from its neat morocco case. With his long, white, nervous fingers he adjusted the delicate needle, and rolled back his left shirt-cuff. For some little time his eyes rested thoughtfully upon the sinewy forearm and wrist all dotted and scarred with innumerable puncture-marks. Finally he thrust the sharp point home, pressed down the tiny piston, and sank back into the velvet-lined arm-chair with a long sigh of satisfaction.
>
> "Which is it to-day," [Watson] asked. "Morphine or cocaine?"

[Holmes] raised his head languidly from the old black-letter volume which he had opened. "It is cocaine," he said; "a seven-per-cent solution. Would you care to try it?"

– Excerpt from the opening scene of *The Sign of Four*, by Sir Arthur Conan Doyle, 1890

If we wanted to understand the prevailing view of medical treatments around the turn of the century, you could do worse than the world's greatest detective.[4] You could even buy cocaine in cough drops for children, though (perhaps fortunately), this was the early days of food and drug regulation in the United States. Many of those formulations did not contain what their labels promised.

Medical science was just shifting from a loose apprenticeship system for new "doctors" to providing rigorous training in the scientific method, and the transition wasn't smooth. Consequently, medical doctors didn't have the respect they would earn later. That's not *only because* of rampant quackery but, paradoxically, perhaps because of scientific rigor. "Real" doctors couldn't do much for the average person in the early 1920s. At least the quacks could lie to them. When you're in pain, lies sound better than the truth. That's just human nature. (Strategic "lying" will play a significant role in this story. Stay tuned.)

These are the days of the very first anesthetics – nitrous oxide and sulfuric ether – which were not that effective but certainly were welcomed by patients in dental clinics. Dentists were among the earliest adopters of *anything* that wasn't opium or shots of liquor; you can't really "bite down" on anything at the dentist. Necessity is the mother of invention, right? Doctors wielded preciously few weapons outside of a dental chair to fight disease. They could offer vaccinations against smallpox and understood the basics of mosquito control to fend off yellow fever and malaria. Still, polio, measles, and cancers were all outside their (current) areas of

---

4   In later writing, Doyle wrote storylines where Holmes eventually learned to manage his addiction.

expertise.[5] Doctors were at the stage in scientific development where they knew what caused many diseases, but they could do little to treat them. In 1918, doctors could offer little more than palliative care during the worst months of the flu pandemic.

And that's when we're talking about *physical* conditions. People with psychological disorders were ignored (if they were lucky) or institutionalized (if they were not). Given the options available, is it surprising people took matters into their own hands?

It's especially not surprising when you consider a new crop of role models – amazing people who transformed the world a generation before. Along with the fictional Brit, Sherlock Holmes, Americans had their own heroes – and *they* were real. Industrial titans Rockefeller, Carnegie, Vanderbilt, Hill, and Edison showed what everyday people could do with grit, determination, and unapologetic ruthlessness.

Ida Tarbell wrote *The History of the Standard Oil Company* in 1904, detailing the excesses of the Robber Baron era. And yes, those excesses created the moral weight behind the Progressive movement in the United States. However, for the average person, the details were muddy – both the "good" things and the "bad" things the barons did both qualified as "great" things.[6] Or, more to the point, all publicity is good publicity, given enough time.

The new business leaders of this era – Ford, Durant, Chanel, and others – catalyzed attention and reflection on the *previous* generation. What was it about those previously-successful people that made them successful today? It wasn't only business leaders who asked those questions; the average consumer did too, both of them carrying the hope of capturing some measure of that success.

---

5   Early versions of the smallpox vaccine amounted to transferring the live virus from a person with a *mild* infection to an uninfected person hoping that the resulting infection would also be mild. It didn't always work out that way. Later, doctors also discovered that the less-dangerous cowpox virus conferred immunity to human smallpox, so they switched. For malaria, the only treatment was quinine, derived from Peruvian tree bark. It's still a front-line treatment today. Yellow fever had no effective treatment.

6   There is a certain universal appeal to this concept, well put in J.K. Rowling's description of her iconic baddie, Voldemort, in the *Harry Potter* book series.

All the ingredients were there. Americans just needed someone to come along with the recipe.

...

If you want the best recipes, it's probably a good idea to ask a French person.

Émile Coué worked as an apothecary in Troyes, France – a small community about 100 miles (150 kilometers) east of Paris. He originally dreamed of a career as an analytical chemist, but family financial trouble pushed him into the more practical (and less academic) branch of applied chemistry, what we'd today call *pharmacy*. In those days, mixing medications was as much art and alchemy as it was science and procedure. However, Coué was a scientist at heart. During his 28-year career in practice (from 1882 to 1910), he couldn't help but notice something surprising.

When he would deliver a formulation along with a gentle, positive statement about its quality or efficacy, those patients would indeed report feeling better and healing faster. More often than not, they were confident that the medication "worked" for them. *Hmm*. It didn't take him long to craft a simple experiment and observe the results. For some patients, he'd make a positive comment. For others, he would not. To anyone familiar with the "placebo effect," Coué's findings should not come as a shock.

A term dating from the late 1700s, "placebo" was a derogatory term for medications or treatments that focused on pleasing, rather than healing, the patient. Coué certainly would have been aware of the definition, so it's not surprising he noticed its effects. In fact, most of what Coué offered was a placebo. (To be fair, all other pharmacists fell into that same bucket.) Hallucinogens and opioids made patients feel better – at least for a while. We've hinted at cocaine and opium as treatments for a variety of ailments, and those were indeed common. Other concoctions featured inert metal powders, like gold and silver, and toxic heavy metals, like arsenic and mercury. Gold and silver tended to make people feel like they were feeling better because they seemed ritzy. Arsenic and mercury…not so much.[7] But they were *all* placebos.

Coué did not know why human psychology has a mysterious effect on certain conditions in our bodies; he simply knew that placebos could work. We can, quite literally, will ourselves into feeling better. The effect has limits, of course. No matter how much a doctor tells you that your arm is not broken, a shard of bone sticking out of your skin likely will convince you otherwise. However, the placebo effect *can* impact how much pain you perceive from that injury based on what the doctor tells you – especially if you consider that person an authority figure. Bottom line: It's complicated, but it works.

Coué almost certainly knew that many of his formulations had little (or no) clinical effect and that most (if not all) recovery was simply the patient's body healing on its own. However, the positive psychological impact…was interesting. What Coué did next would change our perception of what the average person could will into being.

...

In 1920, Coué published his groundbreaking book, *Self-Mastery Through Conscious Autosuggestion*, in Europe. An English translation followed two years later. The book would be the culmination of his life's work. (He died four years later at age 69.) His disciples would carry his message to the United States (and beyond), but it's worth exploring his core ideas in some detail. You'll likely find them oddly familiar.

Coué's basic idea is straightforward: You can direct your subconscious mind toward achieving your goals by repeating specific words and phrases. His most famous phrase – *Every day, in every way, I'm getting better and better.* – is perhaps the best example, though plenty of options can work

---

7   If you're curious about the history of heavy metals in medical treatment, you can follow the Lewis & Clark trail. In that era, doctors treated venereal disease in men by inserting liquid mercury into the patient's urethra. As the men urinated along the way, that mercury found its way into the soil, where it remains today.

for individual circumstances.[8] If you've heard Henry Ford's oft-quoted – "Whether you think you can, or you think you can't, you're right!" – or one of its innumerable variations stenciled on the walls of karate studios, now you know who popularized the idea.[9] Though it seems easy, success with "conscious autosuggestion" requires following some guidelines.

First, you must reject the idea that "willpower" is somehow the source of correcting problem behaviors or achieving goals. You may take the actions – for example, making ten door-to-door sales calls – but your heart won't be in it. Your mind will see any negative feedback as confirmation that your actions aren't working. Coué learned in his practice treating thousands of patients that if they didn't believe, *deep down*, that they would get better, find love, or start that business, they simply wouldn't, no matter what phrase they repeated.

Instead, the better tactic involves simply resetting your brain's default mode. Coué describes it as having two brains – a conscious and a subconscious mind. The salesperson struggling through ten door slams is making a *conscious* error. He's overthinking it. Actually, the trouble is that he's thinking about it at all. Repeating targeted phrases is more like getting a song stuck in your head. You want that "melody" to play in your mind even when (*especially when*) you're not consciously aware of it. In a sense, you're reprogramming your mind as if it were a moist computer.

Second, you must choose your phrase carefully. You're looking to shift your mindset, not to articulate a specific goal. Our salespeople should not repeat, *I will make ten sales calls today*, or even *my sales calls will be successful*. Rather, he should say something like, *I am excited to meet people today*. Did you notice the difference? Making ten sales calls is too specific. What if you cannot complete them? Fail too many times, and your subconscious brain will lose confidence. The same goes for hoping for "successful" sales calls. As any salesperson knows, you might go through prolonged

---

8   The original French was: *Tous les jours à tous points de vue je vais de mieux en mieux.* You don't need to understand French to hear the change. You can listen to Coué say it in his own voice on his Wikipedia page. His speaking style is energetic and lively, but he drones noticeably when he gets to this phrase. It's quite striking.

9   A 1947 *Reader's Digest* article attributed this quote to Henry Ford, but there is no other evidence that he actually said it or wrote it. That said, when you read biographies of Ford, the sentiment fits.

droughts due to random chance. That's why the third phrase is best. Over the long term, successful salespeople love meeting other people. It doesn't matter if they close any particular sale; their energy is infectious. That enthusiastic mindset will set the baseline expectation – the default mode in the brain – and allow the conscious mind and its higher-order rational thought process to fill in the details as the situation develops in real time. Coué found that in conflicts between will and imagination, imagination *always* wins. You're simply training your imagination strategically.

To skeptics, this sounds a lot like hypnosis. In the popular view of hypnosis, practitioners place people into a trance where the (usually charismatic and ungodly attractive) person dupes simpletons into believing they're an elephant. Coué's treatment was not hypnosis; he created a clinical treatment using the placebo effect. His patients were fully conscious while learning and repeating the words and phrases. The therapist simply guided the process. To work, it was critical that the patient *actively believed and accepted* the process.

Coué's practice (and his book) articulated four general rules.[10]

The first is the "Law of Concentrated Attention." What you focus on becomes more prominent in your mind. Anyone worried about the results of a lab test from their doctor knows this rule intimately. Or, less ominously, try *not* to think of a blue elephant. You can't *not* think of one, can you? Advertisers learned to use that same tactic as a priming effect. For example, if you're interested in a new car, your mind seems to "seek out" automobile advertising.

The second is the "The Law of Auxiliary Emotion." We're likelier to stick to an idea if it's teamed with a powerful emotion or physical action. Does that work by engaging more areas in the brain? Maybe. Millions of horny teenagers don't need a reminder that strong feelings have a way of capturing the mind. In Coué's practice, he often asked people to close their eyes and fall backward to link strong emotions (fear and relief) to their experience. So, yeah. Blame Coué for all those trust falls you endured in summer camp or corporate retreats.

The third is the "The Law of Reversed Effort." If we're not careful, we can program precisely the *opposite* of what we want. Remember that

---

10 Although the term "rules" did not appear in Coué's original work (others added them later), it's a helpful way to understand his general principles.

salesperson? If he's not careful, he can accidentally begin repeating to himself – *I'll get the door slammed in my face* – creating a self-fulfilling prophecy. Worse, negative phrases tend to be stickier than positive ones. Coué suggests creating effortless, positive phrases that focus on *your* actions and thoughts, not the responses of others. That's why "being excited to meet people" was the best phrase to repeat. It is entirely within the salesperson's control. Even if a prospect rejects the sales offer, our salesperson could still be excited to meet people.

The fourth and final law is "The Law of Subconscious Teleology." In short, your *conscious* brain will figure out how to get what your *subconscious* brain wants. If our salesperson intends to enjoy this meeting with a potential customer, his conscious brain will look for ways to accomplish that goal.

A trained practitioner can help guide you, but the core idea remains: You control your destiny by shaping your thoughts. It's that easy.

. . .

Modern readers of the book, including most physicians, might be skeptical of some (or all) of what was just described. However, as long as serious mental illness doesn't go undiagnosed or treated, Coué's advice is, at worst, harmless. However, we must explore some of Coué's more problematic chapters to understand why his work was so influential.

There's a particular passage near the beginning of the book where Coué states that he successfully treated a young boy who continually had fantasies of stabbing his brother. That would be bad. If he had grown up without those thoughts redirected, they could have led to "unconscionable" actions. (Luckily, Coué reported the treatment was indeed successful.) Thankfully, other examples are less...stabby. But that doesn't mean Coué didn't veer off the road for purely psychological ailments and suggest conscious autosuggestion for treatment for physical conditions as well. Many of the testimonials in the book retell "cures" for a wide variety of medical conditions. Today, very few disciples of Coué venture into this realm, but in the 1920s, it was commonplace. That shouldn't surprise us, given what we know of the effectiveness of medical doctors in that era. Coué simply told stories that would resonate with his audience.

Coué devotes a full 40 percent of his book to patient stories, all under the chapter heading: "What suggestion has done: Observations of some remarkable cures."[11]

Here is just a sampling: A Mrs. D of Troyes (France), 30 years of age, was cured of tuberculosis. Mrs. Z seemed to have the same thing, although Coué calls it simply a "congestion of the lungs" (which also could describe TB, but let's not quibble). Miss M.D. found her asthma cure. Mrs. Hazot, 48, left bronchitis behind. Mr. X, a professor, healed his larynx, though it wasn't clear what was wrong with it in the first place. Further examples go on for 16 pages and include "cures" for conditions as varied as "womb trouble" (nope, you don't want to know), paralysis, abscesses, kidney disease, ulcers, and heart disease.

A trained scientist (or healthy skeptic) can recognize the problem immediately. No, it's not that Coué's treatments don't work; it's that you don't *know* if they work. Those patients may have recovered independently with no treatment. Coué included no control group in his study to test for that possibility. But more than that, he only included *successful* results. A valid scientific study must include both successful and unsuccessful outcomes. Coué's presentation leaves the reader with the impression that his methods work 100 percent of the time. That is why it worked (and continues to work) so well.

There's an old saying in marketing: If word-of-mouth were perfect, there would be no need to advertise. We trust people "like us" in situations "like ours" more than we ever trust salespeople or ads. However, the reality is that our social networks are limited. That remains true today, even with the wide use of social media, but it was especially true in the 1920s. Coué needed to use testimonials as a proxy for genuine word-of-mouth to reach a broader audience.

That's why Coué was so careful to include patients of all ages, including children, young adults, and older people (though "older" meant people in their 40s and 50s in the 1920s). Each testimonial would include a brief, clinical-sounding biographical sketch, a discussion of prior treatments by other "doctors," remarks about how ineffective they were, a description of his treatment, and finally, the miraculous result. Although most medical practitioners of the era used testimonials of some kind in their advertising,

---

11 Modern copies of Coué's work include all kinds of extra content that would not have appeared at the time. The original is more like a pamphlet than a book.

Coué was the first to use this deliberate format. By sharing a few dozen case histories, rather than a single quick example, patients surely could find one that sounded like them. That was the idea.

Using patient stories is not necessarily unethical. People want to hear stories from people like them, and it can comfort patients to know that they aren't the first to go through this ordeal. To be fair, many of the era's established medical treatments (bloodletting, opioids, shock treatments, etc.) did more harm than good. It's not unreasonable to consider Coué *ethical* for his time for discouraging people from considering those treatments.

But we're not here to debate medical ethics. Personal agency is a core tenant of consumer culture. Coué's true innovation was to give patients control over their health, just as they were learning in all other aspects of their lives. His work may have been popular in Europe, but it found fertile ground in the United States. Self-determination and conscious autosuggestion were like invasive species with no competition in their new home.

. . .

The clever use of personal anecdotes cloaked in the mythology of self-determination of the American psyche partially explains why Coué's self-help bible caught on, but only partially. To understand the more profound reason, we must look at the book's other half. It's a how-to guide for self-help *practitioners*.

When you read the book as Coué wrote it (not how it is described here), instructions for his disciples immediately follow a basic introduction and high-level description of the autosuggestion method. The order of the content in the book suggests Coué's primary audience was not the general public, but others who would further his message in their own practice. By the time Coué published his book, he may have known he was near the end of his life. He was passionate that his ideas would not pass away with him, and to ensure that, he needed to create a legacy. With his book, Coué succeeded. Self-helpers still preach from his bible today.

Coué's techniques center on building trust between the practitioner and patient. As we've discussed, the method can backfire without the certainty trust creates in the patient's mind.

Coué reminds practitioners to focus on a single objective with the patient – an objective that the patient can fully internalize. Coué advises starting small and building confidence over time if the goal is too big. He also discourages using praise *or* reproach – either positive or negative feedback. It's not about validation or punishment. Autosuggestion works by convincing the patient that what will happen in the future is a preordained fact, not something given to chance. Therefore, positive feedback is unwarranted. (You knew it would happen, didn't you?) When it doesn't, negative feedback risks creating bitterness with the practitioner. (It simply didn't happen *yet*.)

Should the patient doubt you, Coué gives his disciples the same advice: *Don't create your own negative autosuggestion; it will become a self-fulfilling prophecy.* Given time, patients will come around. To build that trust, Coué detailed several trust-building experiments (like the "trust fall" described earlier) to use before suggesting a word or phrase for the patient to repeat. Trust the practitioner. Believe in the process. The result will take care of itself.

The result certainly took care of itself for Coué. In a positive feedback loop for his followers, the more people who used Coué's methods in their practice, the more exposure Coué's book would get, and the more people would seek out a practitioner using Coué's methods.

Coué not only created the self-help movement, but he also created the self-help *industry*.

. . .

One of the first disciples – Peter to Coué's Jesus – was Charles Baudouin. He did more than anyone else to popularize Coué's work and bring it to the United States. If you read biographies or books about Coué, they usually include quite a bit of original writing from Baudouin. He worked to professionalize autosuggestion, making it easier for others to go into practice for themselves. Much of what we see in self-help over the coming decades are modern interpretations of the original.

Napoleon Hill's *Think and Grow Rich*, published at the height of the Great Depression, is a business-centric version of Coué's work. It focuses on the success of Carnegie, Ford, and other industrial titans – merging Coué's concepts with strategic biographical narratives to create a roadmap the average person could follow to (presumably their level of) success.

Whether readers have been successful can be debated, but Hill's success is not in doubt. His book has sold over 20 million copies and remains one of the Top 10 best-selling books of all time.

A couple of decades later, in 1952, Norman Vincent Peale wrote, *The Power of Positive Thinking*. Peale was a Christian minister who leaned on the concept of "faith" to supercharge Coué's work for a Christian audience, though millions of non-believers also took Peale's lessons to heart. Al Franken's iconic television character "Stuart Smalley" could have been signing directly from Peale's hymnal with the affirmation: *I'm good enough. I'm smart enough. And doggone it, people like me.* You know you're successful when you get a parody.

Fellow evangelical Dr. Robert Schuller's "Hour of Power" television program ran *uninterrupted* from 1970 until he died in 2010 – a full 40 years of the same basic idea of salvation through positive affirmation in a belief in a higher power. Now hosted by his grandson, the show is still airing as of 2022. Hilary Hinton "Zig" Ziglar was born just as Coué's work landed on U.S. shores. Ziglar inspired generations of salespeople with over 30 books and countless in-person appearances. His heir, Tony Robbins, continues to go strong – expounding a message of "peak performance" through self-improvement to tens of millions worldwide. But being a self-improvement guru isn't a male-only field. Rhonda Byrne wrote *The Secret* in 2006, quickly outselling Hill with over 30 million copies in 50 languages.[12] Brene Brown, Cheryl Sandburg, and Marie Kondo follow the same trail. They encourage you to "dare to lead," "lean in," and "spark joy."

We're leaving out *hundreds* of others. Their methods might differ, but they do so only in style, audience, focal point, and business model. But they are all Coué's protégés.

. . .

Self-help holds a special place in the American heart, but how big of a place?

In 2020, the "self-help" industry earned $10.4 billion, mainly from book sales and seminar tickets. The "professional help" industry

---

12 Be careful of what you read on Wikipedia. The entry for this book claims it was inspired by *The Science of Getting Rich* by Wallace Wattles in 1910. But Wattles focused on willpower, whereas Coué argued against it.

– psychology and counseling – was worth $30 billion during the same time. However, that doesn't mean Americans trust "professional" help three times as much. Remember that the latter figure includes insurance-adjusted premiums, time-intensive 1:1 counseling sessions, and (often) expensive pharmaceuticals. When you adjust for medical inflation, just as many people are helping themselves as getting help from a professional.

To those who pooh-pooh people who dance at a Tony Robbins seminar or purge their closets to find joy, is their message any different than what you might hear at your local health club? By joining this gym, *you* can create *your* best life. Forget genetics, diet, or environment. Yes, *you* can become a yoga goddess! Even the critics of (unrealistic) gym messaging use Coué's strategy. Do you think six-pack abs are a sign of cultural and gender oppression? You can join the "body positive" movement! Boys, are you laughing right now? You shouldn't be. How many of you own a waxed and polished pickup truck, complete with a scratch-proof bedliner to…affirm your masculinity? How many of you own a belching motorcycle and dress up in pristine leather costumes to join hundreds of others on a road trip to the middle of nowhere to…show your individuality?

Home improvement stores are more prevalent in the United States than anywhere else because…you can do it, and we can help. The most popular athletic company in the world dropped the word "you" entirely. It's implied that *you* just did it.

Most self-help is positive, but Coué's creation can be dangerous in the wrong hands.

One of the critical ways conspiracy theories gain so much traction is that they rely on *you* to do *your* own research. Of course, the propagators plant plenty of signs leading you down the rabbit hole.[13] Unlike therapists, psychologists, and psychiatrists, Coué's disciples value charisma over credentials. The self-help industry still relies on personal testimonials (occasionally from famous people) and tends to resist controlled experiments. And sometimes, they still step over the medical line and recommend "mind over matter" cures to real physical illnesses and diseases.

---

13 There are so many examples – from UFO sightings, to the "truth" behind the JFK assassination, to the 9/11 "inside job," to QAnon.

But despite the criticism, Americans gorge themselves on self-help in the same way they crave the newest thing, seek the best experiences, and demand more, bigger, faster, and better! No one is going to hand you those things. *You* need to get them for *yourself.*

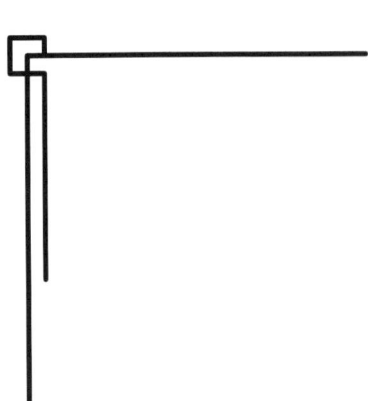

24
CAPITALISM WITHOUT THE CAPITALISTS

I magine that you and your spouse have decided to move your family from your parent's rural farming community to one of the big cities. Some version of that story played out so many times during the 1920s that we could pick just about any city as our setting, but let's choose Raleigh.

You were a blacksmith in rural North Carolina, and there's plenty of work as a skilled laborer in your adopted hometown. Luckily, Raleigh is large enough for a Black community to exist.[1] Although racism is rampant (even in the north, but especially in the Jim Crow south), you can make a living *largely* free from physical and emotional harm, especially if you stuck to Black neighborhoods and business districts.

The problem is that you need to learn more about how the modern *economic* world works.

You don't have enough money stashed away from what your parents could provide to purchase a home, and the rental flat you're staying in now won't be appropriate for a soon-to-be family. You need a home. A home costs money. And because you don't have enough money to buy one, you need a loan. In fact, you need to borrow money for just about everything – a home, appliances, an automobile, and baby clothes. You name it.

Everyone seems to want to lend you money, but you're smart enough to understand that borrowing $100 today and paying back $180 at the end of the year isn't a good deal.[2] That is, if the bank would deal with you *at all*. Department stores might, but their interest rates were even higher. Your wages were good, but you knew that if you weren't careful, you'd be in debt forever. You read about that in *The Jungle*.[3] You knew the risks. The bottom line is that you need a crash course in financial literacy. But who would teach you?

Banks had little incentive to educate consumers so long as they kept depositing money. Department stores had even less motivation. A loan

---

1   Why we chose North Carolina in this example will become important later, especially if you happened to be Black.

2   There was no "revolving credit" (aka credit cards) as we understand it today.

3   The book tracks the story of a fictional immigrant arriving in the meatpacking district of Chicago, but the example resonated with a broad set of Americans.

shark? Let's say that mob enforcers were not hired for their classroom etiquette. However, because you lived in Raleigh and happened to be a tradesperson, you might have a different option. (Even if – *especially if* – you were a minority.) It was a special place with a mission to help people like you get loans at reasonable rates and – *this is the crucial part* – get the education you need. Their logic was simple: If you weren't a savvy consumer with good money skills, you were a poor credit risk. This wasn't charity; it was education.

You could choose a credit union.

. . .

There are two people more responsible than anyone else for the growth of credit unions in the 1920s: Edward Filene and Roy Bergengren. Yes, there were lots of people that helped along the way, but this is a story of what a little money and a lot of effort can accomplish when they work together.

Let's talk about the money first. Edward Filene was the son of Filene's department store founder William. Along with his brother Abraham Lincoln Filene, Edward took the initial idea for the department store in 1881 and ran with it. Fast forward to 1921, and Edward Filene was wealthy enough to be better known for his philanthropy work in the Boston area than he was as a retailing magnate.

Along with Massachusetts banker Pierre Jay, Filene (always referring to Edward from now on) lobbied for the first credit union legislation in the state in 1908.[4] That strategy was critical. Credit unions could only take deposits or lend money with a legal framework, either at the state or the federal level. Filene's standing in the community made it happen locally, but subsequent laws would get harder to pass in other states. However, that foothold in the northeast was a vital example he could point to

---

4   St. Mary's Bank of Manchester, New Hampshire, is generally accepted as the first credit union in the United States, founded in early 1908. Filene took advantage of the momentum to lobby for a credit union law in Massachusetts.

as proof that the credit union was workable in the United States system.[5]

Although we'll follow Roy Bergengren's story from here on out, remember that Filene was always in the background, providing funding and encouragement. Bergengren would do all the groundwork. Today, we sometimes think that it's all "big money" that decides things. And yes, that's true to an extent. It was true in the 1920s as well. But lots of people have money, and lots of people have interests, and often, they're in conflict. However, anyone who understands lobbying a legislature knows that it's an often-thankless job – twisting arms, counting votes, managing legislative calendars, and schmoozing power brokers. It's not simply that Bergengren needed to convince enough legislators in a state to support credit unions; he needed to blunt counter-lobbying efforts from banks who didn't want the competition. In other words, Filene's money was necessary, but it wasn't sufficient.

Bergengren was just the right person for the job. He was a glad-hander's glad-hander. Unlike many social butterflies, however, he was also relentless and focused. Bergengren met Filene when he was looking for a new job in 1921. The two hit it off almost immediately, and a classic mentor/student relationship quickly developed. The student's first challenge: Change the laws in every state in the union to allow credit unions to operate. He was a missionary on a one-man crusade of his own design, with only the support and counsel of the aging Filene to guide him along the way. (Bergengren would have no staff to speak of until 1928.)

To understand the passion that would drive a young man to invest nearly a decade of his life in this cause, we need to understand what makes a credit union unique.

. . .

Let's back up a step. What the heck is a credit union? And how is it different than a bank? If we don't understand that, it's hard to understand why

---

5 That's because if people knew about credit unions, they thought of the *German* examples from the 1800s. Filene's German heritage was the wellspring of the idea – it was born of Old-World trade guilds. However, telling people your idea was "German" inspired in the 1920s, just after World War I, was…less than an effective persuasion strategy.

Bergengren would spend years living out of a suitcase.

We'll begin with the formal definition of a credit union from its national association. Although the national organization didn't exist in Bergengren's day, its definition still applies:

> Credit unions are not-for-profit organizations that exist to serve their members. Like banks, credit unions accept deposits, make loans and provide a wide array of other financial services. But as member-owned and cooperative institutions, credit unions provide a safe place to save and borrow at reasonable rates.

In other words, a credit union is the same as a bank, with one critical difference: *ownership*. In a credit union, the people who deposit the money own the organization, not an outside investor and corporation. As such, they tend to be small, nimble, and responsive to their *members'* needs. A credit union doesn't have outside investors. Every investor is also a *stake*holder, not just a *share*holder. Every member has a stake in the outcome, and that changes the organization's entire reason for being.

Let's get practical. What would you do differently if *you* owned a financial institution that lent money? First, you'd want to make sure you were making good investments. If a member makes poor financial decisions, it hurts you *personally* as a member of that credit union. That's why credit unions focus so much on consumer financial education – they have to. *It's their money.* As such, a credit union isn't a financial institution at its core; it is an *educational* institution. However, unlike a school, these lessons happened to real people, in real life, and had real consequences.

Who were those people, exactly? As we've mentioned, there are plenty of flavors of credit unions, and they're usually based on "affinities" of some type. The most common type is an *employer* credit union. In other words, employees of a big company form a credit union to serve other employees of that big company. To be a member, obviously, you need to work at the company (or *ha*ve worked for it at some point). It's easy to understand who's in and who's out.

Moreover, members know the other members, often personally and quite well, because they've worked together for years. As you might guess, it's easier to assess credit risks that way. If you know Frank from accounting is a putz, you'll be more careful. Other credit union types include trade groups – plumbers, electricians, carpenters, and the like. Still others form from religious groups, veterans' organizations, small communities, and some colleges. The big idea is that some common thread holds them together, giving them a meaningful basis to personalize the financial experience rather than relying solely on a bank's depersonalized heuristics. Credit unions used financial metrics, of course, but they could move beyond them. That was especially important for the people we highlighted earlier – those shut out of the banking system due to religion, national origin, or race.

Okay, now that we know how banks and credit unions differ, what's the big deal? Why was this a *crusade* for Bergengren and not just a lobbying effort? What was unique about the financial system in 1921 that made it such a crucial time to provide American consumers with this option?

. . .

> Economic democracy is attained by applying the principles of political democracy to the affairs of the marketplace.
> – *Roy Bergengren, 1921*

Like many books from this era, Bergengren's biography of the credit union movement has been out of print for a long time.[6] That's unfortunate. Bergengren's book not only catalogs the minutia of his state-by-state push to get new laws passed, but along the way, he helps us understand the philosophy of *economic democracy* so central to the credit union ethos. We'll get to the legislative details soon enough, but they're less important to our story than *why* a credit union exists. We'll linger there first.

As much manifesto as it is a timeline, Bergengren begins the book… at the beginning. What was it like for the average person to ask for a loan in the early 1920s? Ever heard of the word "usury?" Quite literally from the Latin root *to use*, usury referred to the loan-sharkishly high interest rates borrowers would be asked to pay for the privilege of getting some of the bank's money. Annualized rates of 50, 100, or even 200 percent were

---

6 Old book treasure hunters should search for the 1952 edition of *Crusade: The Fight for Economic Democracy in North America, 1921-1945*. In fact, one of the only copies left is housed in a historical center library in St. Paul, Minnesota.

common. Bergengren even cites a particularly Great White-sized rate of 3,400 percent. To put Jaws in perspective, if you borrowed $10,000 for a used car at 3,400 percent interest, you'd pay more in your *monthly* payment than the loan amount.[7]

If we take it up a level, the credit union is a very *American* idea. Bergengren reasoned that if America was controlled *politically* by individual democracy, wealth should be managed similarly. Why was that important for Bergengren? The end of the Civil War saw the beginnings of the Industrial Revolution. Up until that point, the American economy was controlled by individual farmers and small businesses. (Even the most prominent businesses before the Civil War would be considered, most generously, mid-sized companies today.) In that America, economic democracy worked pretty well. That doesn't mean there weren't problems, but there were many more direct linkages between your stuff and who made your stuff.[8]

Industrialization and railroads changed all that. The back half of the 1800s gave us many of the names we recognize: Rockefeller, Morgan, Vanderbilt, and Hill. Depending on who you ask, they were industrial powerhouses that transformed American living standards; or they were Robber Barons who lied, cheated, and stole to amass unjustified fortunes. They were probably some of both. The key issue from an economic democracy perspective is that American commercial life didn't work as well with such a vast gap between the wealthy and everyone else. To carry the political example forward, it would be like saying one person in town had 10,000 votes, and everyone else had one vote each. Not very fair, huh? That's the gist of the economic relationship Bergengren wanted to rebalance.

---

7 That's why you need to take Bergengren's example with a grain of salt water. These were super short-term loans – as in days, not months or years. Regardless, 3,400 percent *is* high.

8 Historians, if this sounds a lot like the idea behind the Roman Republic, you're correct. The founders studied classical literature, especially Republican Rome, as a model for the fledgling United States. That's why our upper legislative house is called the Senate.

The basic idea of the credit union is that a group of people can organize cooperatively, pool their individual savings and, from the pool, take care of their own credit needs without usury.

When Bergengren said "groups," he meant those who had been largely shut out of the financial system. They included Black descendants of enslaved people, newly arrived ethnic groups, and tradespeople. With financing (and, more importantly, financial *education*), these groups could fully participate in commercial life. In practical terms, they would be able to buy homes, cars, appliances, and all the other wonders they saw advertised. Lack of financing limited their ability to choose. However, a level playing field *did not* mean socialism. Filene and Bergengren were clear about that:

When people depend too much on the government, they become subjects of the government rather than masters of it.

Nor did they view the credit union as a public/private partnership or quasi-governmental agency. The credit union was a *third* way. The private sector (and by that, they meant the banking system) was good for many things. It could leverage vast private capital to fund business innovation and expansion. The profit incentive was supremely well-tailored to do that. However, the profit incentive has its downside as well. Banks would only fund loans with a strong profit motive; the more risk they took, the higher the interest rate. At some point, borrowing became unattainable for the average person.

The public sector was good for other things. Governments could put vast public capital to work on infrastructure, defense, and social programs that didn't make sense for (or were beyond the scope of) any private enterprise. On the other hand, government programs could be bureaucratic, slow, and (on occasion) quite wasteful.

The credit union filled the gap between them. It would serve those people or businesses that were too small or presented too much risk that the banks would not serve and the government could not fully understand. To do that, a credit union would take advantage of the power of *many* individuals – but not *too many* – to provide that service. It hearkened back to a simpler tradition in American life. Credit unions were like the first fire brigades established to serve the common good in a challenging, frontier existence. It was almost a "second" American revolution, and the symbolism wasn't lost on Bergengren as he lobbied state legislatures.

Filene's motto for the credit union movement was "not for profit, not for charity, but for service." Bergengren certainly agreed with his mentor, but he was keen to be more practical. He pushed back against the Darwinian "survival of the fittest" mantra so prevalent in the business dogma of the era and instead advocated "stronger together." However, he was also smart enough to realize that togetherness had limits; that's why affinity was so important. The credit union recognized the limitations of collective identification and used it to the movement's advantage. Plumbers understood other plumbers. Lutherans understood Lutherans. Black people understood Black people. When you put the three together, however, you lost that advantage.

Lastly, the credit union movement was spiritual but not religious. Every credit union was formed on core values of honesty, loyalty, tolerance, unselfishness, truthfulness, sympathy, faith, and goodwill – *not* exploitation, graft, snobbery, false advertisements, broken promises, arrogance, cruelty, and selfish leadership. In that, the credit union was more than a financier *or* school. It was a philosophy. A way of life. A practical channel for idealism.

That was Bergengren's crusade. Now, let's see how he did it.

...

The road ahead was not easy.

Massachusetts wasn't the first state to allow credit unions, but it was part of only a handful of states with a "good" law. Others included New York (1913), Rhode Island (1914), North Carolina (1915), and a handful of smaller states. However, some states *had* credit union laws on the books, but there were so restrictive and antiquated that it would have been better to start from a clean slate. Laws in Wisconsin and Texas (1913), Oregon, South Carolina, and Utah (1915), and Nebraska (1919) needed significant reworking.

In short, Bergengren's task was threefold: First, get good laws on the books in those states that didn't have them. Second, fix the bad laws that prevented the credit union movement from taking root. And third – and this was an important objective – encourage new credit unions to organize in those states as quickly as possible. A law was no good if no one used it. Worse, some people (bankers, especially) might use that lull to nudge a good law in a bad direction in subsequent legislative sessions.

In one telling example, Bergengren discovered that new credit unions were acting *too much* like banks. Some credit unions were turning down the same loans that nearby banks rejected without providing the education their members needed to *become* credit-worthy. In short, it wasn't that the credit union should be making a bad loan, but rather that they had a bigger responsibility to make the lender ready for that loan. There's a difference. A bank wouldn't do that. A credit union must. Otherwise, why bother?

Beyond those tactical objectives sat the true goal: a *national* credit union organization chartered on federal law. As Bergengren put it:

> Bring the total of credit unions to the point where it would be possible to organize self-sustaining state leagues of credit unions until a credit union national association should be possible.

Before that could happen, Bergengren needed to put up or shut up. In 1921, he and Filene formed the Credit Union National Extension Bureau to crystallize all lobbying activities. Despite that, remember, this was *one guy* crisscrossing the country lobbying for credit union laws. He had no staff. It was just him. That said, Filene's encouragement proved invaluable. Filene's money allowed Bergengren to make one essential investment in 1924: *The Bridge*. This magazine helped him communicate with local organizers, set messaging strategies, and exchange successful techniques.

. . .

Bergengren's chapters read like a travel log: state after state, railroads, and cars, meetings upon meetings within other meetings. Many successes and some stubborn failures. Bergengren found some of his most fertile ground in the culturally-similar areas of the Midwest – fixing the laws in Wisconsin and Nebraska, and getting news laws passed in Minnesota, Iowa, and Ohio.[9]

Perhaps his greatest achievement, however, was promoting successful credit unions in the south, building on the North Carolina example. Filene and Bergengren weren't content with an intellectual opposition to the racism they saw, nor did they believe in making communities dependent on the generosity of others. Bergengren called the credit union movement for Black communities "a democracy of deeds, not of affirmations." By 1926, over 90 credit unions were catering to the Black community in North Carolina alone, which "probably accomplished more than all the debates in Congress."

What were the specific accomplishments? Let's take this example for *only* postal credit unions. In April 1925, postal workers could choose from 36 chartered credit unions. Collectively, those 36 credit unions served 5,087 members with assets of $166,390. They had made 3,756 loans valued at $283,684. One year later, 48 postal credit unions served 9,726 members, with loan values topping $1 million. A little more than a year after *that*, the number of credit unions nearly doubled to 83, and the amount of money lent tripled to over $3 million on over 30,000 individual loans.[10] If you do the math, the average loan value was about $100. A modest sum (even in 1927), but enough to buy a used car, a new refrigerator, or build a modest addition to your home.

Despite those successes, Bergengren couldn't get credit union laws passed in 10 states, primarily holdouts in the northeast and west: Connecticut, Delaware, Vermont, Maine, Idaho, New Mexico, Nevada, North

---

9   In his book, *American Nations: A History of the Eleven Rival Regional Cultures of North America*, Colin Woodard makes the case that cultural similarities are more important than state boundaries when understanding American culture. Part of his thesis is that the Northeast and Midwest are *culturally* similar and hence, will lead to similar approaches to problems.

10 This example comes from Bergengren's book on page 116 under the heading, "Gladden our 1927 Christmas." It's pretty clear he took this effort personally.

Dakota, South Dakota, and Wyoming.

That's why the *national* credit union law was so important.

...

There's an old saying in banking: When you owe the bank $1 million, the bank owns you. But when you owe the bank $100 million, you own the bank. In a nutshell, that's the position the banks found themselves in at the outset of the Great Depression in the early 1930s. In short, we can paraphrase the old saying: When one bank customer gets into financial trouble, the bank owns them. When all the bank's customers get into financial trouble, they own the bank. Or, more to the point, the bank fails. Lots of them did.

Credit unions also failed, but not surprisingly, not nearly as many. The reasons are simple, and we already know them. Credit unions understood their customers. If you had a membership full of plumbers, you understood the market demand for plumbing services. Credit union executives could plan for changes in ways general-purpose banks could not.

Additionally, credit union members tended to save more and borrow less because of their focus on education. That's not to say that the Great Depression didn't sting, but it wasn't the same. That's why Bergengren – in a rare rebuke to Filene – rejected his mentor's advice to ask the Roosevelt administration for $100 million in assistance to stabilize the credit unions' financial position.

> To [Bergengren], it meant destroying the vital principle of the whole movement by converting a community enterprise into an agency of the government. To teach people how to help themselves was more important by far in times of depression than at any other time.

Instead, the duo seized the initiative to lobby for the ultimate prize: a national credit union law. In 1934, they succeeded.[11]

Over the intervening decades, credit unions have not only changed the financial landscape for American consumers, but the idea of an affinity-based alternative has spread globally. By 2018, over 274 million people worldwide were members of a credit union, with 40 million people added since 2016. In a population of about 3.8 billion adults, that's roughly 7 percent of *all* financial relationships.

More telling, during the financial crisis of 2007-2008 (the so-called "Great Recession"), credit unions outperformed commercial banks again. In a not-so-surprising rhyme of history, commercial banks were five times as likely to engage in risky subprime lending and two and a half times as likely to fail than a comparable credit union. In fact, credit unions came out of the crisis *stronger*. They doubled lending between 2008 and 2016 (from $30 billion to $60 billion in the United States) while small business lending dropped by roughly $100 billion overall.[12]

Again, not surprisingly, people trust credit unions more than banks. According to a 2018 credit union survey, public trust in credit unions is double that of comparable banks – 60 percent to 30 percent – and small businesses are 80 percent less likely to be dissatisfied with their credit union than with a bank.[13]

As of 2020, credit unions hold about 4,800 charters in the United States. The largest is the Navy Federal Credit Union, both in terms of members (primarily former military) and total assets. It traces its history to the same time FDR was inking federal credit union legislation, and today has assets of over $150 billion and members of all service branches. In total, credit unions manage about $2.14 trillion in total depositor

---

11 For his part, Bergengren thought they should have started at the federal level, but Filene won *that* debate. Filene reasoned that the 1920s administrations of Harding, Coolidge, and Hoover would have been less receptive. That's hard to say. Harding might have gone along. Coolidge probably wouldn't have. But Hoover probably would have.

12 This data comes from the Small Business Administration. The SBA isn't the only source of small business loans (credit cards are a big one), but *banks* administer SBA loans so that they can track that data.

13 Always take industry data with a grain of salt, but from anecdotal experience, this seems about right.

assets. To put that into perspective, commercial banks (including retail banking, investment banking, and business banking) control about $7.77 trillion of U.S. assets. The rough math tells you that about one in four dollars deposited is with a credit union.

However, what's more important than the 27 percent figure (which can vary from year to year) is the influence credit unions have had on the entire financial industry – mainly for the better. Banks always know, deep down, that consumers have another choice. In this case, the tail truly can wag the dog.

The verdict, 100 years on? It seems Bergengren's crusade certainly reached its promised land, even if he wasn't there to see it.

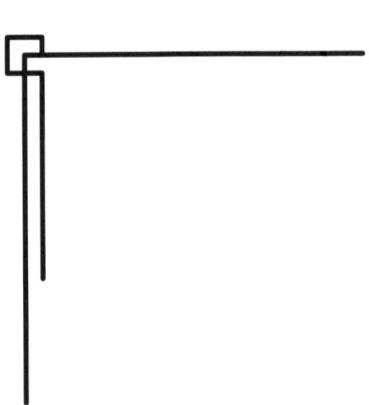

25
"PLEASE, CAN I..."

> As soon as a child begins asking for money for his personal needs it is time to place him on an allowance. He should buy his own pencils and notebooks and pay his own carfares, pay for his school lunches and clubs.
> – from *Child Training*, by Angelo Patri, 1922[1]

Don't get hung up on the pronouns. By "he" and "his," Angelo Patri didn't mean only boys.[2] Pronouns were a matter of convenience and standard practice of the day, though later in this chapter, he separates unique advice for boys (setting business arrangements for payment for chores before performing them) and girls (receiving training in accounting because they would control household finances). That's not what's important to this story.

What's truly remarkable about Angelo Patri's 1922 book is that it includes a chapter on consumerism *at all*. Notice that he wasn't asking: "Should children become consumers?" He added one critical word that changed the entire nature of the discussion: "*How* should children become consumers?" In a decade full of burning questions, this one might have been shining the brightest. People were searching for answers, and Patri seemed like just the man for the job.

Patri hailed from the Palermo region and rose through the teacher's ranks to become the first Italian immigrant to become a principal in a major metropolitan district. Out of his office in New York, he wrote the wildly read syndicated column "Our Children." He was the 1920s version

---

1 Like many books of this era, it's out of print. Luckily, the Internet Archive digitized it. The PDF version is a scanned copy, so you can read it exactly how parents would have read it. What you notice there that you wouldn't in a "text" version is how the publisher uses clear space between each short chapter to make the content easier to consume for busy parents.

2 His name sounds like it derives from the word "Patriarch," but it doesn't. Angelo's surname was Petraglia, the equivalent of "Peter" in Italian. Like many immigrants (the author's great-grandparents included), Patri's family shortened its surname to make it more "American" and easier to pronounce.

of Dr. Benjamin Spock.³ As an immigrant, he had a unique perspective on the unique challenges facing kids moving away from "traditional" homes and into the big cities. Italian parents read his columns, of course, but so did Irish parents, German parents, African parents – in fact, any parent within earshot. It didn't hurt his image that, as an Italian, his persona carried a little Mafioso malice. Maybe Angelo Patri was more like Vito Corleone than Dr. Spock? No matter. When the Godfather spoke, you listened.

Patri's advice seems modern and sensible even 100 years later: Parents should set their child's allowance *slightly more* than the child's financial needs. This encourages freedom of choice and, specifically, the freedom to make (small) mistakes. During a weekly financial report, parents were to review spending – not to scold or nag – but to question and coach. A punitive approach would only encourage children to withhold information. Additionally, the child must not be allowed to borrow money because doing so would encourage "living beyond their means" – a cardinal financial sin. In his writing, Patri tried to channel Victorian moralism and recast Ben Franklin's thrift for a new generation of consumers.

It didn't work. Why? The children's *parents* weren't following Patri's advice. Most families lived beyond their means. Many husbands and wives fought about money. Most of them borrowed to afford luxuries they couldn't get otherwise. Anyone with children knows that they're not dumb – quite the opposite. They're keen observers of adult behavior. They mimic what parents *do*, not what parents *say*.

Advertisers sure knew it. It didn't take long for businesses to realize the direct impact of children's buying power and their indirect impact (influence) on household purchases and to begin targeting them directly with promotional messages. Advertising trade groups of the time recognized the three most powerful words in all sales straight from children's mouths: *"Please, can I?"*

You might be tempted to believe that if advertisers could persuade their *parents* with relative ease, their children should be a piece of cake.

---

3   And if you don't know who *that* is (or think it has something to do with *Star Trek*), you were probably born after 1980. His first book, the 1946 first edition of *The Common Sense Book of Baby and Child Care*, sold nearly 500,000 copies in its first week. You can find the 10th edition on Amazon today. Dr. Benjamin Spock sold more than 50,000,000 books during his lifetime, and remains a best-selling author more than two decades after his death in 1998.

Compared to adults, children were naive, simple-minded, and easily manipulated.

As it turns out, the true experts in a child's consumer behavior weren't adults.

. . .

The 1920s was a challenging decade to raise children. Parents of any age often struggle to understand cultural changes, often lacking the basic understanding they need to make good decisions about those products and services for their children. In the 1950s, it was rock and roll music. In the 1980s, it was video games. In the 2000s, it was the internet and social media. And while those were significant cultural shifts, they were nothing compared to the cultural upheaval and sheer amount of "new" on offer in the 1920s. (Reflect on what you've already read in this book. Now imagine being a parent during that time.)

The demographic makeup during that time is even more difficult to grasp for modern readers. About 30 percent of *all Americans* were under 15 in 1920. If you add in young adults (under 25 years old), that number approaches 50 percent. In other words, *half* of all people were *young*. The reasons for this first baby boom are much more varied than its second iteration in the 1950s. The end of the First World War had something to do with it, just like the urge to procreate at the end of the second.[4] Prosperous post-war economies tend to lead to more children.

Additionally (and a bit sadly), people didn't live as long. According to statistical records, average life expectancy in the United States was about 54 years in 1920 and 58 years by 1930.[5] Considering the average lifespan, it's not so odd to see half the population under 25; it's about what you'd expect. However, the biggest single driver of the young population

---

[4] Post-war demographic bumps tend to happen a bit later than you'd think. An economic recession often follows demobilization, which was true after both World Wars.

[5] If you look at the old charts published by the CDC, they don't always show the population "under five." For our purposes, infants and toddlers aren't quite "consumers" until they can begin to influence decisions of their own volition, which happens a bit later. Five years old isn't a magic number, as many parents of three and four-year-olds fighting through the grocery store can attest, but it's as good as any.

was immigration. Over the preceding two decades, people arriving in the United States had the large families they were accustomed to in Europe – primarily Italian, Irish, and German – but many other smaller ethnic groups too.

This mix of factors led to the most dynamic melting pot of young people (in proportion to the total population) that America had ever seen. Given the dynamic nature and cultural upheaval in 1920s America, it's little surprise there was so much demand for advice about how to (properly) raise children. Our new friend Angelo was only one of many. Let's visit the bookstore to get a sense of the advice on offer to parents.

You may be familiar with this gem: "A penny saved is a penny earned." On the shelf next to Patri was none other than Benjamin Franklin. In contrast to Patri's lessons on how to train children to be good stewards of their resources with allowances and freedom, Franklin (and the Victorians who followed him) preached a child-rearing gospel of thrift and industry. In this church, spending was discouraged. Spending beyond your means wasn't just a poor financial decision; it was a moral failing – an evil, a sin.

But it was more than just being careful with money. Franklin preached stoicism in the face of monetary hardship: "Rather go to bed without dinner than to rise in debt." It was almost a pride in poverty: "Having been poor is no shame. Being ashamed of it is." Given those pearls of wisdom, is his child-reading advice any surprise?

> Educate your children to self-control, to the habit of holding passion and prejudice and evil tendencies subject to an upright and reasoning will, and you have done much to abolish misery from their future and crimes from society.[6]

In contrast to Patri's advice, Victorian-era children harbored "evil tendencies" that needed "self-control" to "abolish misery." Not a very empowered view of childhood, is it? It wasn't very effective either. As we've discussed several times in this book, moralists grasp their pearls, but the

---

6   There is no shortage of places to find original quotes from Benjamin Franklin, but be careful. Many are paraphrased, mis-attributed, or incorrect. The best place is Franklin's own words in his *Autobiography*, though you can find several other reputable books of Franklin quotes.

average person asks where they can buy them. Although this sentiment pervades much of the literature of the time, it was clear parents weren't heeding the advice any more than their Victorian-era fore-bearers did.

Many wealthy Victorians (Franklin included), who were comfortable doling out admonitions to less-well-off parents, rarely took their own advice. It's hard to take advice from hypocrites drowning in debt, isn't it? It's even harder when that advice was better suited to the simpler 1800s than the fast-changing 1900s. The number of products on offer was simply too great, and the messages were too compelling. In practical terms, when confronted with moral indignation or a new refrigerator, the refrigerator wins every time. More than that, with many parents living in cities, they were away from those "simpler" moral influences (their parents back on the farm). Additionally, immigrants (especially second generation) actively wanted to split with the "old ways" of frugality in their newly adopted home. To be fair, many parents wanted to become "American," which meant spending like Americans.

If old-school moralism wasn't going to help parents raise kids, perhaps *new* moralists were the answer.

Socialists, Communists, and Marxists enjoyed a "peak proletariat" popularity in the 1920s. They argued, with varying degrees of intensity, that capitalistic corporations were corrupting the "goods" economy to enslave the working classes in a desire for unimportant things instead of owning the means of production (aka factories, distribution networks, etc.) for themselves. Using their trained and devious lackeys (advertising folk), they created a grand conspiracy of distraction that channeled and amplified personal insecurities to keep the masses suckling at Henry Ford's teet. Driven by irrational desire, consumers would endure the horrors of wage slavery – meek and powerless.

If that all sounds a bit hyperbolic, you're right. Historians don't find much evidence for corporations going out of their way to establish social controls on their workers or customers.[7] Predictably, the primary evidence

---

7 Henry Ford was a notable exception, and that's where the popular misconception comes from. He was obsessed with his workers' personal habits, including alcohol consumption, church attendance, and civic engagement. He had…let's just say, strong opinions on the "correct" behaviors. Despite his efforts, he was wildly unsuccessful. He knew how to manufacture cars, but he often failed to understand human behavior.

shows they were more concerned with meeting fickle consumer demands, lowering input costs, growing market share, and outmaneuvering other companies trying to do the same. The most we can say about companies attempting social control was their lobbying efforts for favorable government regulations.

Another argument was that businesses were trying to rationalize and create demand because they had so much surplus that their super-efficient factories could produce. Although that might have some truth at the macroeconomic level, it's certainly not true for individual firms. It's an odd reading of that history from historians who have never run a business. Businesses can produce as much as they want, but if no one buys it, they'll have a warehouse full of unsold merchandise. The industrial revolution was over. The *consumer revolution* of the 1920s gave much more power to individual choices, and those new buyers were much savvier than the Marxists gave them credit for.

Even worker conditions were improving. Ford had something to do with this (to his credit), but organizations competing for talent tended to drive down worker hours and increase pay.[8] These new moralists might have had a point in the 1880s, but by the 1920s, power had shifted, and the old class warfare arguments seemed stale and irrelevant in the "roaring" decade. Despite the revisionist historians who like to claim the 1920s were prosperous only for the privileged few, the data don't support that assertion. The decade represents one of the most equal distributions of wealth in American history.

And finally, despite an increase in advertising directed at children (as we'll explore in more detail shortly), evidence that businesses were working to "indoctrinate" children to become mindless consumers, ever-loyal to that company's brands strains credulity. Quantitative data is limited on what parents and children thought during that era, but the best evidence is that sources of influence shifted as family sizes shrunk because of the mass migration from rural to urban areas. Most people attribute the "nuclear family" to the post-atomic-bomb era of the 1950s, but smaller families more closely aligned with the *discovery* of nuclear mechanics in the 1920s

---

8   Secretary of State Herbert Hoover (a Progressive *Republican*) had a strong hand in this. He helped the steel industry negotiate an 8-hour workday with its labor force when it walked off the job in protest of 12, 16, or even 24-hour shifts.

than their application in weapons in later decades. Smaller families meant a stronger role for parents (rather than grandparents and extended families) and an even more prominent role for a child's peer group.

That insight about the growing influence of peer groups leads to a more reasonable place to look for guidance on educating children: schools. Universal compulsory attendance in the school system was reasonably new, and many schools of that era struggled with chronic underfunding.[9] However, a fatter budget probably wouldn't have helped. Also, educators (often, parents themselves) didn't know any better than parents how to teach children about money and consumer choices. In some schools, banking institutions stepped in to provide a savings curriculum and a semblance of a financial relationship. For example, the schools would create "forced" savings accounts to which children contributed. They'd earn (a tiny amount) of interest while learning the value of saving money, setting goals, and compounding interest. In some cases, that goal was an identified bigger purchase – say, a bicycle – instead of gum or candy that they presumably wanted now. In other cases, banks offered children's accounts alongside accounts for parents, involving parents directly in the business relationship.[10]

Did it work? You be the judge. Historian Lisa Jacobson quotes this young student's typical response when asked why he isn't keen on participating in the school's banking program:

> My father advises me to save [ten cents a day], but I say what's the use? I have all I need.

Evidence shows that savings accounts at schools aimed for 100 percent compliance but rarely, if ever, achieved it. Part of the reason seems to be a mismatch between the educational need and curriculum structure.

---

9   It wasn't until 1918 that Mississippi became the final state to enact a compulsory, universal public education attendance law. (Massachusetts was the first, in 1852.) Interestingly, an Oregon law was ruled unconstitutional by the *United States Supreme Court in Pierce v. Society of Sisters*, determining that "a child is not a mere creature of the state." This case essentially codified the dual role of public and private education in the United States.

10   Advocates charged, not without merit, that savings accounts for children were simply a marketing scheme. They were correct then, and they are correct now.

At their core, these "lessons" were reheated versions of Victorian thrift casseroles with a little Patri seasoning sprinkled on top. The finished dish simply wasn't that appetizing. Worse, children found this sort of forced delayed gratification infuriating. They saw their parents getting the new thing they wanted, or if they didn't have the money on hand, the credit they needed to consummate the purchase. Children wanted that same freedom.

Children wanted to know *how* to buy what they wanted, not *if* or *when* they should buy it. And if no one would teach them, they'd learn it on their own.

Let's find out how they did it.

...

There's preciously little direct research evidence on children's buying habits in the 1920s. It would be decades before scholars started examining patterns. And frankly, by that point, the Rubicon had been crossed. So, how are we supposed to learn how children internalized consumer culture?

The best way is to observe their behavior *indirectly*, by watching how *advertisers* worked to understand and reach them with promotional messaging. What makes advertisers unique in this regard is their incentive structure and feedback loop. In other words, if something isn't working, they'll quit doing it and try something else. Child psychologists and other moralists (right wing or left wing) have an odd tendency to keep offering useless advice well past the point anyone is listening. By contrast, throughout the 1920s, we can see direct evidence of a growing sophistication of marketing and advertising approaches to children.

> A railway promoter, confessing his reliance upon children to win "the undivided attention of an adult audience," told his advertising colleagues that "the oft-repeated, 'please can I?' of the child often outsells more mature forms of salesmanship."

Advertisers began where you think they might: Children were seen as influencers on their parent's buying activities. For example, a mom at home might be trying to get their children to eat more vegetables, more nutritional foods, or more food in general (malnutrition was the issue in those days). As we've already mentioned, with smaller family sizes and fewer outside influences, parents gave children more latitude in family decisions. (After all, many advertisers were, in fact, parents themselves, not evil Beelzebubs.) In other words, children were a pathway to their mother's pocketbooks. Early advertising targeting children featured primarily products for the home – food, cooking, gadgets, and educational toys.

In one typical example, a full-page advertisement for the soft drink brand 7-Up featured the headline, "We have the youngest customers in the business," and showed a mother giving her toddler his own glass bottle to drink. The ad copy goes on to remind mom that, unlike other soft drink brands, 7-Up lists all its ingredients and that she could "feel good about" the decision to allow her child to drink it.[11]

In short, the strategy began by focusing on mothers (and sometimes fathers as well) to aid the development and well-being of their children. It didn't take long, however, for advertising to begin addressing children directly. In this next evolution, children were to repeat the messages they saw – simple arguments advertisers knew would help convince a predisposed mom to buy that toy (or that soup) at the store. A classic example comes from the now-defunct soap brand Vinolia. Its advertising told children what to say: "Mother, Mother! Fido ate my soap. And it was Vinolia!" or "If I must be washed, wash me with Vinolia." The company's strategy contrasted sharply with Lifebouy (another leading brand of the time), which focused more on mothers and the value of "keeping your family clean." Brands like Vinolia saw an opportunity to sidestep the in-depth appeals and rationalizations of adults and influence purchases by giving children simple messages to repeat to their parents.

Advertising would evolve quickly from here. In some cases, the company would bypass mom's approval entirely and encourage the children to ask for a product by name, presumably, until mom's resistance wore down and they bought it. That was especially popular with toys – Daisy brand

---

11   It wasn't until 1966 that manufacturers were finally *required* to list all the ingredients in their products, and not until the 1990s was the non-ubiquitous "Nutrition Facts" label introduced. Until then, it was *caveat emptor*. You can read more about the history of food labeling in "Front-of-Package Nutrition Rating Systems and Symbols: Phase I Report," published by the National Institutes of Health: National Library of Medicine.

rifles and "Teddy" bear dolls feature prominently, though they were hardly the only ones.[12]

The next evolutionary step was natural – children would eventually become adults. Therefore, it was important to build brand loyalty early. What beer would you drink? What razor would you use? What car would you drive? If advertisers could build loyalty with children, so the logic went, they could lock in future customers.

One of the first brands to use this strategy nationally was the Chrysler Motor Company. It gave away nearly 150,000 miniature replicas of its sleek DeSoto Airflow sedan. The sharp blue toy with the oversized white-wall wheels was a favorite among boys of the 1920s…with the not-so-subtle goal of convincing their parents that the new "streamlined" body style wasn't so radical after all…and the even less subtle goal of convincing the boys that "streamlining" was the way of the future. The Model T defined *every car's* archetypal shape in the 1920s, but the Airflow was a preview of what was to come in the late 1920s and 1930s – precisely when those boys would be buying *their* first car.[13]

However, it was more than simply automobiles. As we've mentioned several times in this book, the number of new gadgets on offer exploded during the 1920s, and parents (then and now) aren't exactly the most "up on the new stuff" as their kids are. In a brilliant early strategy that combined a child's toy with educational content, Kodak developed a program where local salespeople would invite neighborhood children to an in-store demonstration of their new Kodatoy movie projector. They taught kids to use it and, more to the point, subsidized the cost of buying one and taking it home. The objective was simple: "Create an active salesman in each home" – the kids would teach their parents, who would, in turn, go and purchase the (much more expensive) real thing.

A careful observer will notice this next evolutionary step was simply

---

12 The "Teddy Bear" dates back to 1902 and opportunistic Brooklyn candy store owners Morris and Rose Michtom. They saw a political cartoon from Clifford Berryman in the *Washington Post* that featured the president refusing to shoot a bear on a hunting trip. You can read more about it (and see the cartoon that inspired the uniquely-American stuffed animal) on the National Park Service website.

13 As of January, 2023, you could buy your own vintage example from eBay seller "havoverf" for $375. It's pretty beat up, but still recognizable.

an influence strategy under a different guise. Yes, kids got to play with toy cars or movie projectors, but the true objective was an adult purchase. The next step was obvious: Target children with products made exclusively for them – snacks, candy, toys, bicycles, and clothing.

As we've already mentioned, the number of children spending a significant part of their day outside the home (in formal school and unstructured play) increased. That meant peer groups were gaining in influence, and perhaps none more so than the Girl Scouts and Boy Scouts organizations – both founded only the decade before.[14] Each organization quickly accepted advertisers to support donations from volunteers and fees from activities and dues. Both published magazines with content explicitly designed for children – some of the first publications to do so. These children-centric delivery channels also spurred the growth and sophistication of advertising efforts for children. For the first time, it wasn't trying to influence mom or dad. These were ads for kids, with products kids could buy – with their own allowance money – or by asking mom and dad for help.

An advertisement for Welch's "Cocoanut" Bars explicitly called out mom for failing to satisfy a child's candy needs.[15] If kids were nostalgic for mom's chocolate baking, and she wasn't forthcoming with the goods, they should pick up a candy bar instead at the corner store with their own money. In addition to impulse purchases, toymakers and clothing brands began to promote heavily in advance of the holiday shopping season in catalogs, magazines, store displays, and via direct mail.

How would they get the information they needed to refine their strategies? They'd ask – not in a survey, as such. Advertisers were far more creative than that. In one of many examples, Daisy Air Rifles sponsored a nationwide essay contest asking "Why the Daisy is the Favorite Boys' Gun" and offered prizes to the best responses. For the advertiser, even the losing entries proved instructive. They told the company what was on

---

14 The Boy Scouts were founded in 1910. The Girl Scouts were founded two years later, in 1912.

15 Think cacao, as in the cacao nut, the base ingredient in chocolate (not the white, flaky tropical fruit). Not surprisingly, advertising for kids simplified its language to "chocolate" in short order.

their consumer's minds in a way no survey could replicate.

As Jacobson puts it in her book *Raising Consumers: Children and the American Mass Market in the Early Twentieth Century*, "the most striking development in the 1920s was a new willingness among advertisers to contemplate the short-term benefits of targeting children."

That said, much of the literature in the past 100 years focuses on the critique that these advertisements only reached more "privileged" children. Jacobson states:

> Reaching a predominantly white, middle-and upper-class juvenile audience, *St. Nicholas, American Boy, American Girl, Open Road for Boys, Youth's Companion,* and *Boy's Life* enjoyed circulations that ranged from 80,000 to 500,000—all easily surpassing the 50,000 minimum needed to attract the lucrative accounts for nationally advertised branded goods.

That might be true, but it's incomplete. According to one estimate, juvenile magazine advertisers were reaching about 12 million children *directly* by 1928, ranging in age from 10 to 20.2. When you compare that U.S. Census data from that same period (and adding in slightly younger kids not counted in the estimate above but who certainly were reached along with their older siblings and friends), advertisers reached more than *half* of the child population. Those can't all be "children of means." But even if we take Jacobson's assessment at face value, we must understand that radio was the new advertising player in the game in the 1920s, and it could reach *anyone*.

As we learned in Chapter 8, many of the first radio programs were aimed at children. (If you were wondering when children began using media as a babysitter, now you know.) Radio was a much more efficient way to reach children of all income brackets as radios became more popular – and they became popular outside of the home. You didn't need to be wealthy to own one, and *most* households did. Children loved the radio and accepted the new technology in a way their parents never would.

Over the decade, advertising became so sophisticated as to encourage children to view themselves as part of the "consumer economy" and "intelligent consumers" whose purchase of advertised goods was critical in lowering prices and improving quality. Jacobson noted that "such empowering rhetoric gave children nothing less than a stake in maintaining the national standard of living."

That's all pretty high-minded rhetoric. Is that what children really thought? It's safe to assume that neither Victorian nor Marxist moralists could peer into the youthful mind, but were advertisers any better? Yes, they had a direct monetary incentive, and yes, they did evolve their approach. That much is clear. What can all this tell us about what children were thinking and how they processed the world around them?

Quite a bit, actually.

The 1920s was a decade of monumental change on a level we can't quite fathom today. In a time when there was so much that was new, children were *better* equipped to handle the situation than their parents. Remember, their parents were born in a completely different world. For their children, it was the only world they knew. They accepted consumer culture at face value, like children in the 1960s accepted rock and roll, children in the 1980s accepted video games, and children in the 2000s accepted the internet. Only those changes were far less consequential.

Angelo Patri was onto something here. He understood that the parent's role should be a "tutor," not a controller. More families involved children in a "family firm" where the business of the family – its purchase decisions – were made as a collaborative group. No, not every family (yours might have been very different), but the numbers paint a clear picture. Moralists bemoaned the boundary between spiritual ethics and marketplace ethics, but children didn't have a problem with balancing both.

Just like their parents, children wanted to be involved, make decisions, and experience the joy of getting. In doing so, especially with newer mediums in advertising, they were savvier than their parents. It didn't take them long to realize that the gum they spent their hand-won nickel on "didn't last forever," the indestructible movie projector broke the first day they played with it, or the soup wasn't really hiding the vegetables. They became skeptical, discerning consumers very early, learning critical thinking skills they would take into the marketplace in the following decades.

. . .

It's surprising how *little* has changed between then and now.

A study by the National Retail Federation published in 2019 confirms what most parents already know: About half (48 percent) of parents say their children influence purchases specifically for the child, and about a third (36 percent) say their children have a broader influence in household purchases not specifically for the child. One suspects the other 52 and 64 percent, respectively, aren't yet ready to admit it…or their children are too young to ask.

Where does that influence show up? Some of this you could guess. The top categories are toys and games, clothes and shoes, food and drink, dining out, events, and music and books. Parents admit their children have some influence over electronic products, but when so many toys, games, and media are consumed electronically, one thinks the survey respondents didn't quite know how to categorize a child's influence over a new television, smartphone, or tablet.

But it's more than simply specific categories of products; children also influence a parent's choice in brands (52 percent), product features (48 percent), and even specific retailers (41 percent). Parents also involve their children quite early in the decision process – researching online and watching advertising. Children are less involved in the actual purchase process or leaving reviews after the fact, but those numbers aren't zero. Some kids swipe the family credit card or ask Amazon's Alexa to buy stuff.

Retailers (both online and physical) have caught on and go out of their way to ensure the shopping experience is child-friendly. Yes, that involves play areas, but it's also about product demonstrations and displays at child-applicable heights in the store.

But we're still talking about *influence*, aren't we? What happens when we flip the question and ask what decisions children make when given a choice?

A 2019 study by consulting firm Wunderman Thompson that surveyed 4,000 children between the ages of six and 16 again shows what children already know.[16] Who has the biggest influence on what children buy with their own money? Peers are the top source, with 28 percent of kids citing them. What's interesting is that parents and family are *not* in second place. *Influencers* are – social media personalities hold the number two spot at 25 percent, with families just behind *them* at 21 percent. Like

---

16 The title of the Wunderman Thompson report is aptly-titled "Generation Alpha: how and why today's children will shop differently." Based on what we now know about children of the 1920s, it doesn't seem like kids will prove as "different" as advertised.

their 1920s counterparts, children in the 2020s are tech-natives. In this era, "Generation Alpha" use social purchasing and subscription services like their great-great-grandparents used magazines and radio.

However, children aren't quite as savvy as we might believe. When asked, children claim immunity from sales and advertising approaches. Similar to responses from adults, children believe they can identify and resist promotional messaging when they see it. That may be true to an extent, but based on the paragraph you just read, it may be just as likely that they don't quite recognize the shift in advertising tactics – from direct marketing appeals to sales pitches delivered by people children know and trust.

Even the seemingly modern demand that children expect (and will support) brands that "do good in the world" (70 percent of respondents) isn't an invention of kids who grew up in the 2000s. Brands that advertised in *Boy's Life* to support scouting in the 1920s are some of the same ones supporting today's outdoor causes. With their dollars and influence, children in both eras rewarded brands aligned with their values. Children are often the least concerned with other matters and tend to focus on causes that speak to them without the added burdens and responsibilities of adulthood. Advertisers have learned that if they truly want loyalty in adults, they need to establish that when their customers are most paying attention: when they're children.

Parents didn't teach their children consumer culture. Children taught (and continue to teach) their parents.

26
FIVE-STAR WONDERLAND

> One who goes into the market to buy a motor car today is naturally confused. He has read the words best and greatest so often that they have ceased to be convincing. Where all are best, he reflects, there can be no best. Thousand-dollar cars have been described to him in ten-thousand-dollar language. And vice versa. He finds himself the target in a war of adjectives, the helpless victim in a gigantic competition of words. And so he is forced to rely on the advice of friends or his own limited experience.
> – *Stuart Chase and Frederick Schlink*

Does the American consumer *really need* 63 kinds of peanut butter?[1]

You'd be tempted to think most varieties simply represent different package sizes, and you'd be partly correct. You can buy 16-, 28-, and 40-ounce jars, along with individually-portioned "snack packs" of the same mushy legume goo.[2] That's only the "creamy" choices. You need to double your estimate when you consider the less-mushy version – commonly known as "chunky" – which seems like a way to charge you the same price for less work hammering peanuts into submission. Don't forget "extra" chunky, which is even less abusive. One wonders why they don't sell a jar of peanuts that have been only mildly scolded. Someone would buy them.

Add in options from a few competing major national brands, a handful of regional favorites, commercial kitchen sizes, refrigerated options (which makes you wonder why the others *aren't* refrigerated), a generic store brand, "natural" varieties (whatever that means), one with jam mixed in (for those too lazy to buy *two* bottles), a candy bar brand collaboration, a no-sugar-added version (as if that would make it more healthy), a squeeze pack, balled peanut butter (you don't want to know), and even powdered stuff to make your peanut butter smoothies less gloppy.

At this point, 63 kinds seem positively draconian, right? *Only 63?* What else are we missing?!

What is the average person supposed to do when confronted with

---

[1] This is no exaggeration. This number represents a live count of peanut butter options in a Minnesota grocer in July, 2022. Other stores had *more* choices, but who would believe it?

[2] Peanuts are legumes, not nuts. In other words, eating peanut butter is sort of like eating crunchy beans. If that's true, why don't we have kidney bean butter? Do we?

an orgy of peanut butter? It's as if choices mated in the minds of marketing executives and gave birth to bastard children like reduced-fat, super-chunk, peanut butter balls. What's next, peanut butter bath balls? (Don't laugh. There's avocado shampoo.)

Before the 1920s, this sort of situation would have been unthinkable. You were lucky to find peanut butter *at all*, much less in dozens of varieties. To solve that "problem," manufacturers and advertisers – responding to a virtuous cycle of consumer expectations – worked together to create an unparalleled wonderland of choice.

But where advertisers saw a "wonderland," Stuart Chase saw an abomination. Chase didn't only see marketing mischief in ads for food, medicines, automobiles, and household items. Flouncy language was everywhere – on the radio, in newspapers, in the mailbox, and from the mouths of door-to-door hucksters. Mass production and mass merchandising were getting too far ahead of mass skepticism. Consumers were fooled into buying lesser quality items for higher prices by salespeople who had learned to manipulate them and play to their emotions. Advertisers drew from a sophisticated toolbox of devilish implements and had no compunction about using them: Lies, damned lies, and statistics. Not enough information. Too much information. The wrong kind of information. Or when all else failed: Show cleavage.

The American consumer was under constant attack and had nothing but their wits to protect them. That might have been okay 20 years earlier and 1/20th of the choices, but in the 1920s, consumers were overwhelmed.

Chase went on a mission to fix it. Think of him as the Torquemada for his own personal marketing inquisition. He wanted to replace emotional appeals with rational science. He wanted to objectively measure if a product did what it said it would do. He wanted to publish those results so people could make up their own minds. He'd write books. He'd give speeches. He'd give interviews. *Chase was relentless.*

They're all great fun to read, but you might know him better for his most lasting creation: *Consumer Reports.*

. . .

Stuart Chase was a nerd's nerd.

He attended college at Harvard and the Massachusetts Institute of

Technology, graduating as a public accountant. As you might guess, Chase was the no-nonsense type. MIT will do that for you. *In God we trust; all others must bring data.*[3] However, his time at Harvard gave him a flair for literary drama, a sharp pen, and a rasping wit. It meant that this accountant could speak with the rest of us humans in a language we could not only understand, but also deeply enjoy. The detail of a CPA and the verve of the most pugnacious muckraker. The perfect balance of substance and style.

After graduation, Chase went to work for the newly created Food Administration Department of the also newly created Federal Trade Commission. His formative experience would be researching the meat packing industry – an industry that had struggled to reform under pressure brought to bear the decade before from its portrayal in Upton Sinclair's *The Jungle* and President Theodore Roosevelt's famous bully pulpit.[4]

Sinclair described it as a "disassembly line" – whole animals came in one end; parts came out the other. What happened between points A and B was…let's just say…*unsanitary*. We'll leave it at that. Beyond filthy (de)production facilities, much of what did come out of the plants was mislabeled. If you're thinking brisket passed off as a filet, that's the *best-case* scenario. Let's just say not everything you bought was the animal you thought it was. In short, consumers were getting more than they bargained for (intestinal parasites and nasty bacteria) and less than they paid for (mixed species "parts").

That experience would shape Chase's worldview.

It was a worldview that fit the times. This was the so-called Progressive Era when many people on both sides of the political spectrum saw

---

3 That wasn't Chase, although he would have shared the sentiment with his contemporary, the Yale-educated mathematician and physicist William (W.) Edwards Deming.

4 There's a misperception that TR read *The Jungle*, unfeelingly skipped over all the human suffering, and only concentrated on the meat-packing industry and its mislabeling and unsanitary practices. That's inaccurate. Roosevelt routinely visited tenement homes. He believed in seeing problems for himself, rarely relying solely on the opinions of others. He understood what was going on, often more than the people who criticized him.

a larger, positive role for government in American daily life.[5] Further to the left of the aisle were the socialists and communists – buoyed by the apparent success of the Russian Revolution in 1917 in overthrowing its oligarchs.[6] They saw a similar path to unseating the capitalists and industrialists of their day. Where they might not be keen to start a violent revolution (some anarchists were, but they were a small bunch), they would find common cause with leaders like Republican Herbert Hoover. The Commerce Secretary and future president was extremely popular during the mid-1920s, bringing government and business together to set standards for food and medicines, establishing the first traffic rules, promoting Hollywood film-making, and encouraging the first commercial air travel (among many other things). He was not only Chase's first boss, but Hoover's approach would be the intellectual center of gravity for the young accountant.

Chase saw that he could apply that Progressive philosophy to consumer information. He observed that the government could purchase commodities (like food, construction supplies, and other raw materials) efficiently because it bought in enough volume. That purchasing volume not only meant that the government needed to create standards and specifications, but it could also insist that its suppliers met those standards. And government vendors weren't on the honor system; regulators (like Chase) would establish labs to test random samples of incoming shipments to ensure compliance. In other words, when the War Department purchased 10 million cans of beans for the Army, it needed to know where the beans came from, that they were (in fact) beans, that each standard-sized can weighed the same amount, that it didn't contain too much sauce, that it arrived on time, and that the invoice matched the original purchase order. Suppliers might grumble, but they largely played by the rules. The volume was worth it.

The average consumer, however, had no such guarantee. Yes, some

---

5   Most people think that changed with the New Deal programs of the 1930s. Not so. The Progressive Era traces its roots to the late 1800s and only climaxed with FDR's programs. His older cousin, Theodore, would use his presidential authority to create the bulk of the National Park system out of thin air and the phrase, "I so declare it."

6   It hadn't yet turned horrifying. The truth of the genocide of this era in the Soviet Union would be hidden for decades.

large retailers and wholesalers were large enough to buy in bulk, but even the largest couldn't insist on the same quality controls the government enjoyed. Corner-cutting was a real problem. As the 1920s rolled on and the number of consumer goods exploded, the problem turned from *caveat emptor* to *timeo emptor*.[7]

Here's where Chase's accounting training paid off: He saw the problem at the consumer level as an issue of waste. That was the driving force. If people knew what they were getting, they could make better decisions. And if products were better made, consumers would need fewer of them. Less waste led to better quality, more value for the dollar, and a happier consumer. Chase wasn't against people making their own choices per se; he felt they needed the information to make *good* choices. People with better information would make better choices and desire fewer (better) goods. Better information. Less waste. That was the logic. It sure sounded good.

The group standing in the way of this utopian ideal? *Advertising.*

. . .

Okay, not so fast.

Before we get to Chase's epic rant against the advertising industry of his day, we need to dive a bit deeper into what he meant by "waste." That word might not mean what you think it means.

Let's take the peanut butter example we discussed earlier. For most of us, "waste" means throwing away half the jar because it's too much to use before it begins to taste funny. But that's not what Chase was thinking. Using his logic, you only needed one kind of peanut butter. Presumably, that would be the "chunky" variety because, with some elbow grease, you could convert chunky to creamy on demand. All those other options lead to higher costs, confusion, and…waste.

Chase saw wastefulness throughout the entire *production* chain, not just at the grocery counter. Farmers could much more efficiently grow, harvest, and process just one type of legume instead of several varieties to produce multiple flavors. Processing facilities would need only two

---

7 *Buyer beware* became *Buyer be afraid.*

types of containers – a larger version for restaurants and a smaller one for homes. With fewer container sizes, packaging and transportation are cheaper and easier. Maintaining appropriate stocking levels at the grocery store gets easier, not to mention how easy it is to buy when you only have one choice.

If peanut butter is too trivial of an example, what about home construction materials? Plumbing fixtures should be standardized, right? What about medicines? How many have real benefits, and how many are just in the mind of the beholder? Many of these would indeed fall under industry standards in future decades, but this was still the 1920s. It was a consumer wild west.

But the true thumbtack on the chair was *advertising*. Ultimately, it was *their fault* that people "wanted" these choices. They were purposefully deceiving the public, and not only that, raising the cost of everything they touched. Remember, Chase was a trained public accountant. When he examined public companies' books, he noted (with horror) that nearly 80 percent of the cost of some commodities were so-called "selling expenses." In other words, marketing, advertising, and sales. How much cheaper would everything be if manufacturers didn't need to cover those costs?

It has an appeal, doesn't it? Now we can dig in.

. . .

Chase was a prolific writer, but his most famous work is a collaboration with Frederick Schlink titled, "Your Money's Worth: A Study in the Waste of the Consumer's Dollar," published in 1927.[8]

It's an extraordinary book. It's short, engaging, and was (no surprise) a huge hit with the middle-class audience of the Book of the Month Club. In other words, lots of people read it. The book, almost singlehandedly, created the modern debate between "wants" and "needs" in the consumer economy. We've been dancing around that issue since the beginning of this chapter. It's about time we hear how Chase framed his argument.

In chapter after chapter, Chase and Schlink use the "Alice in

---

8   Like many books of this era, this one is out of print. However, the good folks at Google have digitized it, meaning you can find a free scan of this book in several online databases. As of January 1, 2023, it entered the public domain.

Wonderland" metaphor to cast the average consumer as "Alice" walking through a bizarre, trippy "Wonderland" created by advertising. The symbolism wasn't lost on anyone. Alice was innocent, a bit naive, bumbling, and confused. The Wonderland wasn't *wonderful* at all – it had wonders, to be sure, but just like Lewis Carroll's story, it could be creepy, violent, nonsensical, and dangerous. The Cheshire Cat, the Mad Hatter, and the Flying Monkeys all made a (figurative) appearance.

Just get a load of a few of the chapter titles: Alice in Wonderland; The Acrobatics of Quality, Price, and Cost; Quack, Quack; and One Hundred Billion Dollars. If you wondered what you were in for as you cracked the spine, you wouldn't have to wait long. Nothing about the 1920s consumer experience is left to the imagination.

Because we used the "thousand dollar car in ten-thousand-dollar language" admonishment to start this chapter, it's worth going deeper. For Chase and Schlink, the alternative is clear:

> For the expenditure of about a million dollars, it would be possible to take every current type of motor car made, over a standardized 10,000-mile road test under controlled conditions. (One million dollars is roughly the equivalent of Mr. Ford's output every two hours.) At the close of the experiment, the figures for each make could be published in parallel columns, without comment. Just the cold figures - so many miles per gallon of gas and oil, so many failures of one kind or another per 1,000 miles, so much braking ability from a given speed, so much accelerating capacity, so much tire wear, and so on. Would this help you in choosing your next car? Not if you were buying primarily to make an impression on the neighbors. But if you really wanted to get back to the advertising, the high-powered salesman, and the dandy little jiggers on the dashboard, and find out what was the best car for your needs and for your money - it would help tremendously. As the motor car becomes increasingly a utility and decreasingly an emblem of swank, the help to the main body of purchasers would be untold. In the end, such a list would set up standards of performing excellence, and force persistently inferior types off the market altogether. For the million-dollar outlay - in a three billion-dollar-a-year industry - who shall say what savings in hundreds of millions would be repaid to the American people?

Pretty reasonable request, isn't it? (If it sounds a bit like the magazine you might be familiar with, stay tuned.) You can start to understand why the book was such a bit hit. Listen to the language. Inside the tightly-reasoned argument are pointed comparisons to Henry Ford's wealth, gentle ribbing of people buying a car to keep up appearances, cars as "emblems of swank," and whatever "dandy little jiggers" might be. It's excellent stuff.

Few consumer products escaped their gaze. Chase and Schlink questioned the logic of "bottled" water (they wouldn't be the last), railed against Listerine (the "best" mouthwash is a simple saltwater gargle), and even argued against using toothbrushes (okay, there's some not-so-good advice in there too). Of special concern are celebrity endorsers – Babe Ruth is a favorite target – or the common advertising practice of "repetition over reputation." In those cases, consumers will rely on familiarity without factual knowledge. Celebrities are good at making products seem familiar, but if that fails, repeat the jingle until people whistle it on the street. Either way works.

You can hardly blame consumers in the 1920s. The decade saw an explosion of never-before-seen products and more variety than at any other time in human history. Government standards, if they existed, lacked enforcement teeth. Objective product information was largely *non*-existent. What information you could find was a caustic mix of truth and fiction. Nowhere was that state of affairs more dangerous than health and medical products.

Patent medicines were the perfect example. The term "patent medicine" represents what you think it does – a proprietary formulation. However, to get patent protection, you needed to publish that formula. As in, file for a patent. If you did that, your ingredient list was public knowledge. Can you guess what happened next? Of course, you can. Unscrupulous types simply copied the formula and sold their own versions. In that era, it was much harder to find them, sue them, or otherwise stop them.

Because of the risk of copycats, many manufacturers would not publish their ingredient lists. That meant consumers couldn't (truly) know what they were getting other than an assurance from the manufacturer that what was in the bottle was what was supposed to be in it. Can you guess what happened next? Of course, you can. You may have heard urban legends that cocaine was a popular drug used in cough drops and "pick-me-ups" in the era before federal drug laws. Those weren't urban legends. However, cocaine was more expensive than sugar, and you can't tell the difference by looking once they're dissolved in water. Plenty of magic elixirs were nothing more than sugar water with a few herbs. Lucky, huh?[9]

Sure, we know that *now*, but in the 1920s, without government standards, it was nearly impossible for the consumer to know what they were getting. Chase and Schlink were among the first to expose this pharmaceutical mess for what it was.

Of course, not every consumer product conveyed the same risk as unsafe automobiles, faulty construction materials, and amphetamine-laced cough drops. Chase and Schlink take pains to distinguish "wants" from "needs" in their writing. For example, they aren't writing to make a judgment call on "the prettiest feathers on the hat," but rather to decide if the hat is what it says it is. If the hat says it's size 6, is it really size 6? What, precisely, is size 6 in *standard* measurements people know (e.g., inches or centimeters in diameter)? Is the hat made with the "tropical bird feathers" it says it is? Or are goose feathers painted at a factory? The idea isn't to decide what's good or bad; that's for the consumer to say. But the consumer should have objective information to make that decision.

Or, at least, that's the idea.

However, the entire book is written in a way that you can't help but come away whipped up and angry. It's advocacy at its most pure. Chase and Schlink use the same emotional techniques in their attack on advertising that advertisers use when communicating with the public. That was not a mistake. They're fighting fire with fire.

The rest of the book continues this theme. It's a rant – probably the most epic anti-consumerism rant of all time – but a rant nonetheless. And that's where it can suffer. The authors are at pains to hedge the worst of their criticisms. Most manufacturers try to be honest…but can't compete effectively with the liars. They extol local craftspeople and products as the ideal…but are forced to admit that mass production leads to higher overall quality and lower costs. Most advertising is wasteful…except when it's for the "right" reasons (for example, social goods). Chase and

---

9   It wasn't so lucky with radium. Once scientists discovered radioactivity, adding "hot" elements to patent medicines became trendy. Many of them were sugar water…which was lucky. Some were not…which was less lucky. They were expensive, so it was only the wealthy who could afford to use them consistently. There are plenty of stories of trendy industrialists physically deteriorating (painfully) from the effects of aggressive radiation poisoning and nasty cancers.

Schlink make liberal use of the unanswered "reasonable question" rhetorical strategy to leave the reader with the impression of nefarious, hidden intent. For example, why would advertisers craft store displays designed to stop traffic? The question is left unanswered, as if your local department store wanted to cause an auto accident, when the answer is...well...quite pedestrian. They're simply displaying the most appealing seasonal products. And if you're tempted to think the authors don't have an opinion on what constitutes a "want" versus a "need," and that consumers should be left to make that decision for themselves, you shouldn't be. In their centrally-controlled system, manufacturers would only compete on price for the same product. Because of a much narrower set of choices, the consumer would benefit from the lowest price and the highest quality.[10]

In the book's final chapters, the authors step back a bit from the ledge of central economic control and lay out the role they envision for government – primarily in setting objective standards, auditable business practices, and consistent labeling. When the government couldn't act fast enough (or didn't have the requisite niche expertise), Chase and Schlink saw a strong role for private standards organizations. Those groups would be funded by taxes levied on industry rather than directly controlled by the industries. The manufacturers might have the best knowledge, but they couldn't be trusted to regulate themselves.

However, it's unlikely the average reader got this far in the book. Once the authors explore government regulations and industry standards, their writing style dries up. It's hard to get people fired up about measurement standards for plumbing fixtures.

---

10   Chase would pen the phrase "New Deal" for President Roosevelt in 1932. During the Great Depression and for decades to come, he would only sharpen his call for government intervention in economic life.

That's too bad. Because it's in the final chapters that we see Chase and Schlink plant the seeds for the true legacy of consumer advocacy.

. . .

Several themes appear throughout the book: Objective results should trump emotional appeals. Consumers should have access to the raw data to make up their minds. Ideally, product offerings should be standardized and simplified as much as possible.[11]

However, the book was largely silent on how that was supposed to happen in practice. "Your Money's Worth" might be a satisfying rant, but ultimately, it's a bit of a let-down unless something changes. Implementing its recommendations would be harder than complaining about their absence, and they wouldn't be content to simply complain.

> One of the authors, with the encouragement and assistance of technical experts of his acquaintance, has established an information service and rudimentary experiment station administered as a "Consumers' Club." It may be worth watching as a point of departure for other groups. Two lists of goods are being prepared, usually giving maker and brand. The first list carries products considered to be of good value in relation to their price; the second, products one might well avoid, whether on account of inferior quality, unreasonable price, or of false and misleading advertising. The basis for judgment lies in the work of the outpost agencies, already reviewed. The help of high school teachers of chemistry and physics is also to be enlisted for analysis and performance studies.

---

11 To some, that might sound quite appealing. Frustrated by the stunning variety of choices for everyday items (like peanut butter), many shoppers purposely choose grocery stores that offer a narrower set of options. Aldi and Trader Joe's are popular options today. Those shoppers might cheer Chase and Schlink's quest for efficiency… until you told those same shoppers that they only get one type of computer, one style of shirt, or one "multi-catch" fishing lure. As much as they might complain about it, consumers resist having their choices made for them.

The author in question was Schlink.[12] The idea was simple: Consumers would pay a small fee to belong to the "club." Their subscription would pay for a small army of scientists and engineers to conduct tests and publish their findings for the club members' benefit. The organization would, by necessity, need to focus on bigger ticket items like automobiles and home appliances, at least in the early days. Retailers and wholesalers also had the incentive to pay attention. They had a vested interest in selling the best possible goods – they were *consumers* as well. In fact, giving consumers the information they needed to make good decisions would have a positive ripple effect *backward* through the entire supply chain – from the end consumer, to the retailer, to the wholesaler, and finally, all the way to the manufacturer. Seeing a reduction in sales, manufacturers would improve their products to fend off competitors who *would* make those changes. And so on. And so on.

But it wasn't quite a "business" just yet. This "Consumers' Club" was just an idea. It wouldn't be for long.

. . .

A year after the commercial success of their book, Schlink went out in search of support – money, of course, but also writers and scientists. The new organization would offer consumers the unbiased services of "an economist, a scientist, an accountant, and goodness knows what more." Within a year, Schlink had the backing he needed. He founded Consumers' Research in 1927.

Because the fledgling organization needed to remain independent from outside influence, it could not accept advertising. No matter how carefully you shielded the two sides of the business, they had learned from journalists that newspapers could never quite figure out how to divorce editorials and news coverage from their advertisers. However, even the *appearance* of bias would doom a consumer advocacy organization. What eventually would become *Consumer Reports* in 1936 would not accept

---

12 Chase would forever be the evangelist and advocate. He didn't quite have the stomach for the business side of it that Schlink had. It's one thing to advocate and another thing to make the compromises necessary to affect that change.

advertising.[13] To maintain objectivity, it would go so far as to "blind purchase" products. Everyone knows that restaurant reviewers get the best table and the chef's attention. Schlink would not allow manufacturers and advertisers a seat at the table. Ever.

In 1927, the magazine began life with a paltry 565 subscribers, but by 1932, the number had ballooned to over 42,000. The idea had clearly struck a nerve. However, it's fair to ask the obvious question: Only 42,000? That's a tiny fraction of the American consumer public. Why didn't more people sign on? Yes, magazines get shared with others, so the "real" number of readers likely reached double or triple the paid subscriber number. However, 100,000 (or so) people is still a drop in the bucket. Did consumers simply not care?

What the number can't convey is the cultural shift.

After 1927, manufacturers and advertisers had to watch their backs. They knew there was an unbiased source of objective product information – ready to dispute their claims and publish raw data. A faulty, dangerous, or misleading consumer product was (and is) the kind of story newspapers *love* to cover, further amplifying the magazine's reach. Over its nearly 100-year history, *Consumer Reports* has shamed multiple products into substantive revisions – or even removal from the market – after unfavorable test results. Additionally, that doesn't account for the "chilling effect" on manufacturers and advertisers to produce better products and the "warming effect" on consumers.

In addition to testing, *Consumer Reports* remains a tireless consumer advocate and lobbyist. It was among the first to call for seat belts, laws requiring seat belt usage, the dangers of cigarettes, structural issues in the mortgage industry (they warned the public well ahead of the "Great Recession" in 2008), and health care billing transparency.

Despite all that, perhaps the magazine's most recognizable feature is its "dot score" – an intuitive way to understand product quality. Its first iteration featured a red dot representing "Excellent," half-red for "Very

---

13 The magazine emerged in 1936 in its final form after a messy corporate divorce. It was "refounded" in 1936 by Arthur Kallet, Colston Warne, and others who felt that the established Consumers' Research organization was not aggressive enough. Both organizations still exist today, but the original is a shadow of its former self and provides more opinion than data.

Good," an empty black ring for "Good," half-black for "Fair," and a full black dot representing "Poor." (The red dot also served as the magazine's logo.) In 2018, the magazine improved the system, using the more intuitive "stop light" colors: Green, light green, yellow, orange, and red to represent the excellent to poor scale. In either case, the symbolic language is easily understood. It's one of the reasons savvy bikers started picking Hondas over Harleys in the 1980s.

But the true impact of consumer advocacy reaches further than scientific tests and lobbying for product standards. Chase and Schlink's most enduring legacy might be *review* culture – by consumers, for consumers. According to the latest figures, nearly *all* consumers read reviews before purchasing a product – well over 90 percent in most surveys, with some surveys showing nearly universal use of available reviews. That number varies depending on the product or service category, but it's more than just consumer products like electronics, toys, food, books, movies, and clothing. Consumers use reviews to select the best services as well – restaurants, hotels, real estate agents, and childcare, of course, but also physicians, cremation services, and even their religious affiliation. Hey, who doesn't want a five-star pastor? If there's a platform that collects reviews on a specific product or service, you'll find a consumer ready to use them. And there are a *lot* of those platforms. Amazon and Yelp might be the most recognizable, but Healthgrades (for doctors) and Angie's List (for contractors) are just as useful for consumers hunting for the best information.

More than simply providing information, the most important innovation has been how the platforms have reduced the barriers not only to *reading* reviews but also to *writing* them. Yes, there is still a role for "professional" reviewers, like *Consumer Reports*, but over the past ten years, consumers have democratized the review business. Many sites, like the movie review aggregator Rotten Tomatoes, publishes reviews from movie *critics* and movie *goers* side by side. And if you're wondering which side is more important, there's a direct correlation between box office performance and the *moviegoer* rating that disappears when you compare commercial success to the *critical* response.[14]

Some professional observers of "review culture" point to fraud and

---

14 Unless the "objective" is to impress critics and win an industry award.

manipulation that can creep into the process. They claim consumers are fooled by "1-star movies written about in 5-star language" (to paraphrase Chase in 1926). However, data show that consumers are smarter than their critics. Historian and sales expert Todd Caponi discovered that sales performance did *not* correlate directly with the number of stars in a review. In fact, a 4-star rating often outperformed a 5-star rating when it came to actual sales data.[15] Why? Consumers are savvy. They know fluff when they see it. A 4-star review (which notes a product's faults) seems more honest to them than a glowing 5-star review (that seems too good to be true).

The system isn't perfect. In the past ten years, we've seen examples of "review bombs" – that's when a group of people with an "agenda" will give a performer, restaurant, book, or movie purposefully-negative reviews (usually a large number of 1-star reviews) to reduce the overall rating, trick software algorithms into down-ranking it, dissuade consumers, and reduce sales. However, on the whole, that's quite rare. Doing that takes organization, commitment, and timing. Additionally, platforms aren't dumb. They've learned those patterns and made continual updates to prevent fraudulent reviews from being posted. (The platform has the financial incentive to protect its reputation.) In many cases, businesses that complain about "unfair" reviews (and try to get them removed) are simply taking a narrower view of what constitutes "fair." For example, if you visit a restaurant and you can't find a place to park, you might leave a poor review. Is it "fair" to blame the restaurant for the city's failure to provide street parking? Perhaps not, but the review is still *useful* to the consumer. People want to know if they're going to need to leave an extra 15 minutes ahead of time to find a parking spot. That review usually stays.

Does review manipulation happen? Yes. Are reviews 100 percent fair and objective? No. Does either of those facts invalidate reviews as a useful tool? Not in the slightest. Reviews are here to stay.

---

15   The best-performing rating? 4.3 out of 5. You can find much more on his research – and his advice to sales professionals – in his book, *The Transparent Sale*.

Stuart Chase passed away in 1985 at age 97. A *New York Times* obituary eulogized him this way:[16]

> Conservatives who opposed his economic views still marveled at the way he could discuss complicated economic problems in racy, colloquial, readable language. One wrote: "Mr. Chase's logic wobbles, but his sentences march. His thought is incurably superficial, but his gusto and relish, his flair for effective phrases, his power to dramatize his subject, are unfailing."

On reflection, would Chase have appreciated the state of consumer reviews? Would he have liked government standards-makers and professional testers taking a backseat to consumers helping consumers make the best choices?

If the ultimate goal of advocacy is solving the problem, then yeah, probably so.

---

16 You can find a digitized copy of Stuart Chase's obituary in the November 17, 1985 edition of the *New York Times* on page 44 of Section 1.

Conclusion
"THE CUSTOMER IS ALWAYS RIGHT."

The smell was the first clue.

Fresh from the factory, toilets can smell like many things – porcelain dust, enamel paint, packing foam, or cardboard. This toilet smelled like *none* of those things.

As the customer wheeled his unrequited throne up to the Costco return counter, one can imagine the frustration of the unlucky associate charged with getting to the bottom of this problem.[1] On closer inspection, the source of the smell revealed itself. Like a sanitary forensics investigator, the spray pattern inside (and outside) the bowl indicated this toilet was…not pristine. Those were stains. *Usage* stains.

This splattered, forlorn 60 pounds of porcelain clearly had braved a family of carnivores, enduring stoically until the day it was unceremoniously dethroned from its mounts, loaded into the family truckster, and scraped along the floor to the Customer Service desk. Glancing at the model number and recognizing it immediately, the associate notes (with dismay) that his fears are confirmed. The store hasn't sold these particular toilets in the past *two years*. For a family of four, assuming average usage, this commode had endured more than 3,000 "deposits." When you add liquid-only trips, that estimate grows exponentially.

"What's the reason for the return?" our unlucky associate asks.

"I'm not satisfied with this toilet," the customer responds.

(*What's there to be unsatisfied with? It's a toilet.*)

"Okay, do you have a receipt?" our associate continues.

"No," the customer snaps, clearly unashamed of the olfactory assault in progress.

(*Sigh. No one has a receipt anymore, and credit card lookups don't always work.*)

"How can I make this right for you," the associate parrots the scripted question.

"I'd like a refund," the customer demands.

(*Of course, you do.*)

One wonders what bizarre, otherworldly expectations the customer might have had for this toilet, but no matter, *the customer is always right.*

---

1   Retail associates *hate* working the return counter, though it does make for good storytelling when they return home each night.

The refund is issued. The customer leaves happy, walking into the vast warehouse to spend his refund in the store that day. However, the toilet in question will not be restocked. It has discharged its duty honorably and deserves its final rest.

Urban legends like this one abound in the annals of retail lore. Costco's famously-generous return policy generates an unfair number of these stories, but it's hardly alone. How about the man who wanted a refund for his cold burrito? It had failed to remain hot after he had driven it 50 miles from the Chipotle restaurant in Colorado across the border to his home in Wyoming. Or the man who returned a half-empty tube of sexual lubricant to Walgreens because it failed to provide the "intense pleasure" promised on the label? Or the prom-goer returning her dress to Macy's, the day *after* the big dance, reeking of alcohol and body odor?

Anyone who's ever worked in retail has a story like this. The truth of the accounts or the specific details hardly matter. On internet message boards, associates often claim vindication – *we rejected that return!* – but retail statistics tell a different story.

In 2021, consumers returned 10.6 percent of *all* purchases, but that number hides wide disparities by category and channel. Food is lower. Clothing is higher. (Sadly, the specific return rate for toilets is not shown in the aggregate data from the National Retail Federation.) Intuitively, in-store purchases have a lower return rate than items bought online, with return rates for impulse clicks for clothing approaching a staggering 30 to 40 percent. And that's *legitimate* returns. Return fraud – people who return empty boxes of high-value electronics, for example – cost retailers $5.90 for every $100 they earn.[2]

Although specific return policies vary by merchant, even when confronted with the most ridiculous of reasons, most retailers are happy to accept returns. Why would they do that? Blame the "golden rule." No, not *that* golden rule. The other one: *The person with the gold makes the rules.* In other words, customer returns are a valuable lens for seeing the usually-hidden display of raw consumer power.

Customers may not be right. They're certainly not "always" right. But

---

[2] The National Retail Federation publishes this data annually. Surprisingly, aside for some blips in the data during the COVID-19 pandemic years, return and fraud data remain remarkably consistent.

businesses that survive have learned to act like they are. And increasingly, consumers have learned to exercise their power in all aspects of their lives, not just at the checkout counter. They expect prompt service at the doctor's office. They want college dorm rooms to offer granite countertops. They demand complete transparency from their elected officials, even in their personal lives.

That was the true subject of this book: *power* – who has it, how they wield it, and how that all came to be.

. . .

There's some debate on the first use of the iconic consumer anthem.[3] However, most people attribute the *popularization* of the phrase to retail department store legend Marshall Field around the turn of the century.

> ...no matter how very wrong a customer was, she must be considered right. There must *never* be an argument with a customer. And on this policy, Mr. Field built up one of the greatest mercantile houses the world has ever known.[4]

What had become the equivalent of oral history and an article of faith – passed down from salesperson to salesperson for (probably) hundreds of years – became formalized in 1917 with Ralph Starr Butler's groundbreaking textbook, *Marketing Methods*. A professor at the University of Wisconsin, his work would train the first generation of modern business

---

3   As far back as 1830, A Course in English for Engineers, Volume II says, "there are a good many firms whose policy [is] that 'the customer is always right' …". We find it even in Supreme Court transcripts, in a case about manufacturing prices in 1832. Both sources (and others) indicate the phrase must have been in use long before then. By the turn of the century, Tarbell's *Teacher's Guide to the International Sunday-school Lessons* in 1906 made the case that the phrase is biblical in origin. You won't find the phrase in the King James version of the Bible, but some versions of it can be inferred from Issac's willingness to accept the occasional imposition. That seems like a stretch, but what's important is that people found many reasons – their own reasons – to use this phrase in business. Thanks to sales historian Todd Caponi for the legwork on these obscure sources.

4   This quote comes from the advertising trade journal *Batten's Wedge*, published in February 1909. You'll find several similar examples. Marshall Field was like the Steve Jobs of his day and his aphorisms were endlessly quoted.

leaders.[5] Marshall Field may have had the right idea, but besides a snappy slogan, he didn't provide much instruction for how "customer rightness" would happen in practice. What products were on offer? At what prices? Where would you buy them? What messages would convince people? In other words, how do you mass-produce customer satisfaction?

Simply mass-producing products wasn't enough. That was the great challenge of the *Industrial Revolution*, which had been (largely) solved by 1920. Something more was needed. Making the customer "right" meant getting four other rights right: right product, right price, right place, and right message. That formula would not only form the foundation of the practice of *marketing* for the next 100 years, but it also would become the operations manual for the coming *Consumer Revolution*.

In that, Butler proved prophetic. After World War I, the number of consumer products exploded – automobiles, of course, but also hundreds of other gadgets, everything from clothes washers to electric razors. The iconic Sears catalog may have shown what was possible in 1894. Retail innovators like Marshall Field might have created magical shopping experiences in the first two decades of the new century. Still, neither one prepared American society for what was to come next.

To Butler and his contemporaries, *The Customer Is Always Right* wasn't just a slogan. It was the central creed of the new consumer religion.

And it all comes back to *power*.

. . .

The power to *vote with your wallet* was the most transformative cultural achievement of the 20th century. Most people don't think of it that way. We're

---

[5] Butler was a doer, not just a professor. He left academia to take over as the head of advertising for General Foods Corporation in the 1920s. Was he the first person to use the word "marketing?" Probably not, but he was certainly the first person to popularize it. He mentions in the textbook that he had been developing and teaching the course before he published the book as early as 1909. In other words, he had been working on this for nearly a decade. One more thing. If you search for your own copy (and I'd recommend you do), you can find publication dates for Butler's book of both 1917 and 1918. The correct answer is obvious when you look at the cover page. Don't worry; they're the same book. Aside from some archaic language here and there, you'll be shocked at how well Butler's advice holds up more than 100 years later.

more comfortable with other types of power we see in our everyday lives.

Governmental power is easy to see. As citizens, we follow laws we'd rather not follow and pay taxes we'd rather not pay. However, we also enjoy driving on public roads, walking through public parks, and drinking clean water. In some places (the United States is one), we get to vote for the people who decide those things on our behalf. The system isn't perfect, of course, but it works surprisingly well most of the time.[6]

In the 1920s, we saw different visions of governmental power on the world stage, most notably in the communist Soviet Union. However, that vision came with its own set of upsides and downsides. On the positive side of the ledger was "a chicken in every pot." On the negative side was a one-way ticket to Siberia for anyone Joseph Stalin didn't like. It was easy to become enamored with the benefits of Soviet central economic planning in the Roaring 20s when outsiders only saw the chickens.[7]

The power of big business is easy to see as well. In the 1920s, names like Ford, Standard Oil, RCA, and General Mills seemed like they were everywhere, all at once. They not only controlled many of the products you could buy, but they also had a strong influence on the wages you could earn. And the media's watchdog role – especially on the unfair monopolistic practices of companies like Standard Oil and the anti-union stance of General Motors? Remember, the media is a big business as well. Scandals sold papers. (They still do.) Their motivations weren't (and aren't) as noble as you might believe.

However, *consumer power* is different. This type of power involves individual consumers making the best choices they can, given the options available to them at the time. Because no *one* of those choices is as consequential as a groundbreaking piece of legislation or snappy new model

---

6   Think of "government" like you think of the power company. It works better than 99.9 percent of the time. We only notice when it doesn't. Additionally, we have an entire industry (the media) that makes its living finding and hyping the 0.1 percent. That's not to say we shouldn't fix what's not working, but it's important to tell the difference between the tail and the dog.

7   Lots of smart people were hoodwinked by Stalin. He only showed American and European visitors what he wanted them to see. American socialist icon Eugene Debs was a great example, but hardly the only one. To be fair, people like Debs very much wanted to see how the Soviet collective experiment played out, they believed in the vision, and saw what *they* wanted to see as well. It happens to all of us.

year Cadillac, it's easy to dismiss consumer power as somehow less than either of those showier versions. As we've seen in this book time and again, underestimating consumer power would be a mistake.

Do consumers exercise that power responsibly every time? Clearly not. In the 1920s, we learned how Alfred Sloan and Billy Durant helped people get just the car they wanted at a price they could afford. However, consumers often overextended their finances. Coco Chanel helped women (and later, men) create their identities through fashion choices. However, the proliferation of cheap clothing has proven hugely wasteful. Charles Fisher and his contemporaries built the Florida housing market, offering a getaway from brutal northern winters in a freer, funner atmosphere. It was also an environmental disaster and financial bubble of the first order, likely contributing more than its fair share to the Great Depression. Consumers can also be crude, unreasonable, silly, and dishonest, as we saw with the toilet, burrito, sexual lubricant, and prom dress. Each chapter was careful to show both sides of the coin. The mistake would be looking at only one side.

Like any other form of power, consumer power is not good *or* bad. It's simply a tool. It's how we use that power that counts.

The enduring legacy of exercising the power to choose is hard to understate. The 1920s may have been the cradle of consumer culture, but contrary to conventional wisdom, the baby survived the stock market crash. The Great Depression proved to be more like the "tough toddler" years. How can we say that? Let's look at the quantitative evidence and not just the stories of suffering that stick in our collective memories.

The unraveling that began with the stock market crash (actually a series of stumbles) on October 24, 1929, signaled the end of the "Roaring 20s" and a return to earth for the consumer economy. And yes, the economic data of that time bear out *some* of that sentiment.[8] Every consumer spending category dropped; how far was simply a matter of degree. In the worst year, 1933, consumer expenditures for food and beverages, household furnishings, and transportation dropped a staggering 40 percent from their 1929 peak. Clothing and recreation fell even further – more

---

[8] See for yourself. Search for the "Historical Statistics of the United States: Colonial Times to 1970" published by the U.S. Department of Commerce. Consumer expenditures are found in Chapter G (416-469, specifically), but there is *plenty* more.

than 50 percent. Housing spending (mostly mortgage and rent) sank 25 percent. Even spending on *medical care* dropped by a third.

However, by 1939 – ten years later and right before the outbreak of World War II – consumer spending had largely recovered.[9] In other words, the consumer economy proved remarkably resilient. This book provides part of an explanation for that: Consumers enjoyed their newfound power and were not willing to give it up, even in the darkest days of the Great Depression.

Setting the data aside, the legacy of consumer culture is more than simply what we buy and how we buy it, as we've seen repeatedly through this book. While people were watching products advertised on television for the first time, civil rights leaders saw a path to use consumer power for social change. In December 1955, they organized the Montgomery Bus Boycott. They voted by *not* using their wallets. It took over a year, but it worked. Consumer activism like this would become a key strategy in the non-violent resistance movements of the 1960s and many social movements that followed. Consumer power has shown itself more than a match for governmental power (or its lagging response, in this case).

To build on that, a 2021 survey by the McKinsey consulting group found that two out of three shoppers claim their social values shape their purchase decisions, including 45 percent who believe retailers should specifically support Black businesses and other marginalized groups.[10] In other words, consumers demand social change through where they spend their money. Though it should be noted, there's a big difference between what consumers say they want and what they're willing to buy. That's another key theme in this book. Consumer culture is comfortable with this contradiction, and anyone who serves consumers learns to manage it…or else.

However, perhaps the best way to understand consumer power is to examine company longevity. In other words, how long does the average

---

9   The stock market, however, wouldn't return to 1929 levels until the 1950s.

10 Search for "The rise of the inclusive consumer," published February 8, 2022, on the McKinsey & company website, authored by Pamela Brown, Tiffany Burns, Tyler Harris, Charlotte Lucas, and Israe Zizaoui. Be warned: Consultants often write studies to sell consulting work, so take this one with a grain of salt. It shares the results of opinion polling but is light on evidence that consumer opinion translates into consumer behavior.

company survive? If a company meets and exceeds consumer expectations, it gets to keep operating. When it fails to do that, its days are numbered. Small businesses are especially susceptible to this basic truth – most fail in their *first year*. But big business doesn't get a pass; it simply may take longer for them to circle the drain. Management consulting firm McKinsey crunched the numbers. In 1958, the average life expectancy of a firm on the Standard & Poor's 500 index was 61 years. By 2020, it was less than *18 years*. They estimate that by 2027, 75 percent of all companies on that list will have ceased to exist. The traditional explanation for this trend is that competition *between businesses* has sharpened, that the pace of change is accelerating, and that big companies struggle to balance profitability and innovation. However, after reading this book, you have another explanation: Consumers are getting *better* at exercising their power, and they're putting companies out of business faster than ever.

. . .

All of this talk about power begs the question, doesn't it? Is the power to choose a good thing or a bad thing? Are we happy to have that power? Does it improve our everyday lives?

The reflexive answer might be *yes, of course*, but researcher Barry Schwartz questions that premise. In his groundbreaking 2004 book, *The Paradox of Choice: Why More is Less*, he shatters the conventional wisdom that more choice automatically leads to a happier experience.

Let's step back to the example of my mom hunting for a new coffee maker. Imagine a scenario in which we arrived at Target to find only *three* choices for a new coffee maker: one drip model, one pour-over carafe, and one espresso maker. My mom would have had a "choice," to be sure, but it wouldn't have taken her long to make it. She doesn't mess with pour-overs and doesn't want to learn to make espresso. Her choice is simple. In that world, she leaves Target confident that she made the best choice.

Now, let's change the scenario and take the other extreme. In this case, my mom sees not only pour-over and espresso machines but also two dozen *drip coffee maker* choices. She can easily eliminate pour-overs and espresso makers, but she's still faced with choosing between *24* different drip models. The chance of making the optimal choice is 1-in-24, or a little better than four percent. Read another way; there is a *96 percent chance* that my mom will *not* choose the best model for her needs. As Schwartz explains, consumers don't do the math in their heads like this. However, they know intuitively that they're ill-equipped to make a decision with so many choices. They may try to rely on reviews, referrals, or a salesperson to assist them, but ultimately, they leave *less satisfied* because they worry about the choices they *could have made* – even if the one they chose was, indeed, the "best" choice.[11]

Schwartz argues, quite convincingly, that more choice makes us less happy because of the overwhelming number of choices we could *not* make.

But Target seems to have read Schwartz's book too. Have you noticed what's happened since his book was published? Target doesn't want my mom to leave unhappy; that's bad for business. So Target purposefully curates the number of coffee makers in each category to an optimal number of choices – in my mom's case, she had five models that met her needs, and three of *those* were different colors. In short, my mom could feel good about choosing without getting overwhelmed.

Ultimately, though, choice-making is not about happiness. It's about power. To paraphrase a cultural icon (actually, his uncle or aunt, depending on the version), *with great power comes great responsibility*. After this book, you should understand that power better. Now, it's up to you to accept the responsibility part.

Choose wisely.

---

11 Schwartz didn't use the term FOMO (Fear Of Missing Out) in his book, but he certainly coined the idea.

KEY PEOPLE

Listed Alphabetically by Family Name

Cyrus Stevens Avery (1871–1963), Chapter 20
Avery was an Oklahoma businessperson and investor. He is among the people most singularly responsible for the creation of Route 66. He is also (at least partly) responsible for the U.S. highway "badge" design still in use today. Although not the first transcontinental highway (the "Lincoln Highway" predates it), Route 66 remains a cultural icon and was central to automobile culture, human migration during the Great Depression, hippie culture in the 1960s, and the idea of the "road trip."

Bruce Fairchild Barton (1886–1967), Chapter 15
Barton was one of the most prominent advertising executives of the early 20th century. He founded the Batten, Barton, Durstine & Osborn (BBDO) advertising agency, which was credited with groundbreaking campaigns for General Motors and General Electric. Barton authored two books, The Man Nobody Knew (about Jesus) and The Book Nobody Knew (about the Bible). He crafted the promotional campaigns designed to get Calvin Coolidge the vice-presidential nomination alongside Warren Harding in the 1920 presidential campaign, and the campaign to win the presidency in 1924. He served as a Republican member of the U.S. House of Representatives from 1937 to 1941 (NY-17).

Roy F. Bergengren (1879-1955), Chapter 24
Bergengren was a central figure in the popularization of the credit union in the United States. A lawyer by training, specializing in poverty law, he accepted a job offer from department store magnate Edward Filene in 1921 to lobby state legislatures to pass laws allowing credit unions to form and then supporting their development. Bergengren founded the Credit Union National Extension Bureau, the precursor to the national organization.

Clarence Birdseye (1886-1956), Chapter 3
Birdseye is generally recognized as the first person to commercialize frozen food in the United States through a process of "flash freezing." This method rapidly uses a chemical reaction to rapidly freeze food, reducing the time ice crystals need to form and improving the taste of reheated food. His name appears on

more than 200 patents in a variety of areas beyond the freezing process.

Dr. John Romulus Brinkley (1885-1942), Chapter 8

"Doctor" Brinkley received a mail-order medical degree and is largely dismissed as a quack. He believed transplanting goat reproductive tissue into a human would increase virility (it does not). However, because of his efforts to promote his procedure to the general public, he became – somewhat unwittingly – a pioneer in radio broadcasting and advertising.

William Jennings Bryan (1860-1925), Chapter 11

Bryan is best known for his speaking skills, earning the nickname, "The Boy Orator" because of his youthful appearance – even as he aged. He was a force in Democratic party politics, serving in the U.S. House of Representatives and as President Woodrow Wilson's Secretary of State. He ran unsuccessful bids for president in 1896, 1900, and 1908. He sat at the prosecutor's table during The State of Tennessee v. John Thomas Scopes, more well-known as the "Scopes Monkey Trial." His exchanges defending the Bible with defense attorney Clarence Seward Darrow became part of the mythology of the trial.

Charles P. Buchanan (1898-1984), Chapter 12

Buchanan was a Black civic leader and businessperson most notable for operating the Savoy Ballroom in Harlem, New York, for 32 years. He was born in Barbados and arrived in the United States when he was six years old, becoming a key figure in the "Harlem Renaissance" of the 1920s. In addition to his time at the Savoy Ballroom, he was chairman of the United Mutual Life Insurance Company, the only Black-operated mutual insurance company chartered in New York State.
*He has no Wikipedia page, by the way, and he should.

Alphonse Gabriel Capone (1899-1947), Chapter 5

Al Capone, nicknamed "Scarface" after a knife fight, was one of the most notorious gangsters in the Prohibition era. Based in Chicago, Capone waged a ruthless campaign to eliminate his rivals. He's famous for his ostentatious style, elegant dress, and positive relationship with the media. Where other mob bosses preferred to remain quiet, and behind the scenes, Capone helped craft a romanticized image of gangsters who simply "gave the people what they wanted." He was finally convicted of income tax evasion and spent the last 11 years of his life in prison.

Gabrielle Bonheur "Coco" Chanel (1883-1971), Chapter 22
Chanel was a French fashion designer and businessperson. She is largely responsible for the "casual chic" style for women popularized after World War I. In contrast to the complex, multi-layered fashions until that point, Chanel's clothing styles were simpler, easier to manage, more comfortable, and less expensive. She is most famous for the iconic "little black dress" that still forms the foundation of women's dresses more than 100 years later.

Stuart Chase (1888-1985), Chapter 26
Author of several books, Chase was a staunch advocate for consumer protections and a frequent critic of advertising practices. His 1932 book, The New Deal, is often credited with prompting President Franklin Roosevelt to use that language to describe his economic programs, though that claim is disputed and impossible to verify. In the late 1920s, Chase traveled to the Soviet Union and praised its collective economic practices. However, he became critical of the Soviet government in the 1950s because it had not given workers and farmers the power communism had promised. Along with Frederick Schlink, he founded Consumers' Research, a precursor to the magazine, Consumer Reports.

Calvin Coolidge (born John Calvin Coolidge Jr.) (1872–1933), Chapter 15
Coolidge served as governor of Massachusetts, Vice-President of the United States, and President of the United States. He was principled, well-read, deeply religious, and famously quiet. Coolidge believed in a limited role for government intervention in American daily life, in contrast to the "Progressive" trend at the time. His wide use of modern consumer marketing techniques (designed by advertising executive Bruce Barton), marked a turning point in political campaigns.

Émile Coué de la Châtaigneraie (1857-1926), Chapter 23
Coué was a French psychologist and pharmacist most famous for advocating and popularizing conscious autosuggestion. That process refers

to repeating positive words or phrases to train the unconscious mind. (According to Coué, the process also works in reverse, and often without us knowing it – aka "negative self-talk.") He is largely credited with birthing the self-help movement (and industry) in the United States through the vigorous work of his followers.

Dr. Caroline Bartlett Crane (1858-1935), Chapter 7
Nicknamed "America's Housekeeper," Crane left her early career in public health and teaching to focus on journalism and activism. She is best known for her work to improve public sanitation in the United States and was an early proponent of the Euthenics movement. Euthenics is a collection of ideas that explore how the physical environment (e.g., the home) impacts physical and emotional health. Like Marie Mattingly Meloney, she participated in the Better Homes of America movement, but with it a decidedly "Midwest" approach.

Betty Crocker (1921-Present), Chapter 21
Betty Crocker is a fictional person, credited by the Washburn-Crosby Company, the forerunner of today's General Mill, to serve as a spokesperson for the company. Through various actors and writers, she appeared in cooking demonstrations, radio programs, cookbooks, product packaging, and contests. Over the past 100 years, her official "image" has been updated to reflect the prevailing style of the archetypal homemaker.

Clarence Seward Darrow (1857-1938), Chapter 11
Darrow was one of the most high-profile attorneys of his era. As a leading member of the American Civil Liberties Union (ACLU), he led the defense of John Thomas Scopes in The State of Tennessee v. John Thomas Scopes, more well-known as the "Scopes Monkey Trial." Ultimately unsuccessful in his defense (largely because of his own grandstanding), his public sparring match with prosecutor William Jennings Bryan stole the show when he asked Bryan to take the stand as a "Bible expert."

William Crapo "Billy" Durant (1861-1947), Chapter 4
Auto pioneer and founder of General Motors, Durant was the first to bring together multiple car brands under one holding company. Those brands included Buick, Chevrolet, Oldsmobile, Cadillac, Oakland (later replaced

with Pontiac), and others. He also founded the Frigidaire company to capitalize on the explosive growth in commercial and home refrigeration. Durant's most impactful innovation might have been the popularization of the installment loan for auto purchases through the General Motors Acceptance Corporation (GMAC).

Edward Albert Filene (1860-1937), Chapter 24
Along with his brother Abraham, Filene founded what would become Filene's department store in Boston, Massachusetts. By 1928, he left the company (or was removed by its board; it depends on who you ask) to focus on his civic and philanthropic ventures. He provided significant support and guidance to Roy Bergengren and together, they pushed for new state and federal credit union legislation.

Charles Thomas Fisher (1880-1963), Chapter 13
Fisher was an early automobile pioneer and real estate developer. He made his initial fortune developing the standard headlamp design for early automobiles. Fisher parlayed that investment into auto racing and was a principal investor in what would become the Indianapolis Motor Speedway. Later in life, he was a major figure in the south Florida real estate boom in the early to mid-1920s, developing hotels, attractions, and housing in the Miami and Miami Beach areas. The overheated market eventually took on the hallmarks of a Ponzi scheme and the real estate market (and his investments) significantly declined by 1928.

Briton Hadden (1898-1929), Chapter 18
Along with Henry Luce, Hadden founded Time Magazine in 1923. It was the first so-called "news magazine" – a publication that summarized and interpreted the week's news. Time was known for its unique writing style, highly-readable (and short) articles, and broad coverage. Hadden provided the creative energy for the new publication and is largely responsible for its fearless and (sometimes) acerbic coverage. He died at 31 from a likely bacterial infection that invaded his bloodstream.

Herbert Clark Hoover (1874–1964), Multiple Chapters
A trained mining engineer and progressive politician, Hoover served as the first Secretary of Commerce and President of the United States. He

was extremely popular before the stock market crash of 1929, mainly due to his humanitarian work in Europe during World War I, active efforts to support public/private partnerships to increase homeownership, working with the steel industry to set an eight-hour workweek, craft automobile traffic guidelines, promote Hollywood movies, and set the stage for commercial air travel. Many of his progressive policies to counteract the impacts of the Great Depression were expanded by his successor, Franklin Roosevelt.

Jack Arthur Johnson (1878-1946), Chapter 12
Johnson was an American boxer who became the first Black world heavyweight boxing champion, holding the title from 1908 to 1915. In addition to his boxing career, the "Galveston Giant" also became a club owner. His first effort was a desegregated nightclub called the "Black and Tan," which he ran with his wife (a White woman). Before he was hired on as manager of the revamped Cotton Club, Johnson served a jail sentence for violating the Mann Act – a racially-motivated law (and charge).

James Mercer Langston Hughes (1901-1967), Chapter 12
Known by most as Langston Hughes, he was a Black poet in the early 20th century and a key figure in the "Harlem Renaissance." One of his best-remembered observations was his writing about the 1920s when "the Negro was in vogue," later paraphrased to "when Harlem was in vogue." He wrote extensively about the full spectrum of Black working-class life in the United States – racism and struggle, of course, but also pride, joy, and music.

Rupert Hughes (1872–1956), Chapter 16
A novelist and film producer in the early years of Hollywood. His most notable work (a novel and film) was Souls for Sale, a satirical look at Hollywood scandals of the early 1920s. In it, he described the cultural conflict between organized religion and progressive Hollywood – the broad outlines of which continue more than 100 years later. He's also known for one of the first historically-accurate depictions of General and President George Washington. (For example, debunking the myth of the "cherry tree.") Hughes wrote over a dozen books and more than 50 films (mostly

in the silent era) over his career.

Charles Augustus Lindbergh (1902-1974), Chapter 9
Lindbergh was a pilot, inventor, and activist. On May 20–21, 1927, he flew solo from New York City to Paris nonstop. He was one of the first examples of a modern celebrity, meeting with presidents and leaders of multiple nations, including the Nazi German high command (from which some of his purported Nazi sympathies arise). He was an outspoken critic of American wartime involvement, though as a private citizen, he flew military missions in the Pacific theater in World War II. (His father, Charles August – not Augustus – Lindbergh, was a congressperson from Minnesota.)

Henry Robinson Luce (1898-1967), Chapter 18
Along with Briton Hadden, Luce founded Time Magazine in 1923. It was the first so-called "news magazine" – a publication that summarized and interpreted the week's news. Time was known for its unique writing style, highly-readable (and short) articles, and broad coverage. Luce also founded Life, Fortune, and Sports Illustrated during his decades-long career. Born in China to American missionary parents, Luce graduated from Yale University and was a member of its "Skull and Bones" society. He's been called the most influential private citizen of the 20th century.

Marie Mattingly Meloney (1878-1943), Chapter 7
Nicknamed "Missy," Meloney was one of the leading journalists in the 1920s. She worked as a journalist in several major east coast publications, and by 1920, was the editor of The Delineator, a publication that focused on women's issues. That magazine served as a platform for her efforts with the Better Homes of America (BHA) movement. The BHA helped set the expectations for "homemaking" in the United States and also sponsored neighborhood model home exhibitions around the country.

Caroline Amelia Nation (1846-1911), Chapter 14
Also known as the "Hatchet Granny," Nation was a staunch prohibitionist. She earned her nickname by entering saloons and physically destroying the bar. She sincerely believed drunkenness was the root cause of society's ills and that she was called by God to purge the United States of

this evil. In addition to her work with the ax, she established the model for what would later become shelters for battered and abused women and their children.

B.J. Palmer (1882-1961), Chapter 2
Joshua Bartlett Palmer (no, not Bartlett Joshua, according to his biographer) was the son of Daniel David (D.D. Palmer), the founder of chiropractic. B.J. popularized and further developed chiropractic, establishing a training school, publications, and one the first radio stations in the United States (W.O.C. in Davenport, Iowa). He's credited with developing one of the first leasing business models for his Neurocalometer therapeutic device.

Angelo Patri (1876-1965), Chapter 25
An Italian-American immigrant and prolific writer and author, Patri was the first Italian to become a principal in the New York Public School System in the early 1900s. He was one of the leading voices in child-rearing advice for parents, and one of the first to promote the idea of an "allowance" to train young people to manage their money.

Carlo Pietro Giovanni Guglielmo Tebaldo Ponzi (1882-1949), Chapter 13
More commonly known by his Americanized name, Charles Ponzi, he is most famous for the type of financial scam that bears his name. In a "Ponzi Scheme," early investors are promised out-sized returns. Those returns are paid off with new investor money, not with actual investment performance gains. The scheme continues so long as new investors participate and it collapses quickly when they do not. Ponzi was jailed multiple times in the United States and Canada, eventually fleeing to Italy to continue his schemes, and finally to Brazil, where he died broke.

Charles Cassius (C.C.) Pyle (1882–1939), Chapter 20
Pyle (also known by the nickname "Cash and Carry") was a sports promoter and showman in the mold of P.T. Barnum. He organized the so-called "Bunion Derby," a 3,400-mile footrace from Los Angeles to New York in 1928 to promote road-building in the United States. Despite a disappointing showing and poor organization, the race did

raise publicity for the newly-named Route 66.

Helen Bayless Lansdowne Resor (1886–1964), Chapter 17
Lansdowne (married name Resor) was an advertising executive with the J. Walter Thompson advertising agency in New York. She was the first female copywriter at the agency, making a name for herself with top accounts such as Procter & Gamble, Red Cross Shoes, and Woodbury's Facial Soap. Her work is still regarded as some of the best advertising work of all time, and in 1967, she was posthumously inducted into the Advertising Hall of Fame.

Julius Rosenwald (1862–1932), Chapter 6
Rosenwald took over leadership of Sears, Roebuck and Company in 1895 and served as its president until he recruited Robert Elkington Wood in 1924. He's credited with rescuing the company from a precarious financial position following the Panic of 1893 and dramatically scaling its catalog and mail-order business. He's also remembered for his philanthropy, especially his support of education for Black children. At the request of his friend and fellow activist, Booker T. Washington, Rosenwald served as chair of the Tuskegee Institute from 1912 until he died in 1932.

George Herman "Babe" Ruth Jr. (1895-1948), Chapter 14
Ruth was an American Major League Baseball (MLB) player for 22 seasons (1914 through 1935). He began his career with the Boston Red Sox, but he was most famous for his hitting and home runs with the New York Yankees. (Many of his batting records stood for decades.) Ruth helped inaugurate a new type of "sports celebrity" during the 1920s and 1930s. In addition to re-energizing baseball after the so-called "Dead Ball Era," his personal exploits (namely drinking and womanizing) were widely followed by the media.

Margaret Higgins Sanger, aka Margaret Sanger Slee (1879-1966), Chapter 19
Sanger was a nurse, feminist, and social activist. She is best known for her advocacy of birth control and abortion rights in the United States. Her most well-known works on the subject are "Family Limitation" (1914) and "What Every Girl Should Know" (1916). Both are remarkable for

their explicit and direct language regarding anatomy and sexual behaviors. In 1921, she founded the American Birth Control League, the precursor to Planned Parenthood.

Harry Scherman (1887–1969), Chapter 10
Scherman was a copywriter at the J. Walter Thompson advertising agency in New York. He left JWT to found his own agency exclusively devoted to book marketing after his success with the "Little Leather Library," a company that repackaged classic literature and sold it through the mail. He went on to co-found the Book of the Month Club and write four books on economics.

John Thomas Scopes (1900-1970), Chapter 11
A science teacher in Tennessee, Scopes was the defendant in The State of Tennessee v. John Thomas Scopes, more well-known as the "Scopes Monkey Trial." It was a test case, brought by the American Civil Liberties Union (ACLU) to challenge the Tennessee state law preventing the mention of Darwin's theory of evolution by natural selection in any public classroom. Scopes was found guilty at the end of the trial and fined $100. He was offered his teaching job back, so long as he apologized and refused to mention evolution again. Scopes refused.

Alfred Pritchard Sloan Jr. (1875–1966), Chapter 1
Sloan became president of General Motors in 1923 and chairman of the board in 1937, guiding the company's growth from a struggle gaggle of car makes to the largest auto manufacturer – and largest company – in the world for decades. He introduced the "product ladder" of low-to-high-priced car options, the annual model year change, and the General Motors Acceptance Corporation (GMAC) – the company's financing arm.

Judith Cary Waller (1889-1973), Chapter 14
Known as the "First Lady of Radio," Waller got her broadcasting start at Chicago's brand new WMAQ radio station. Despite knowing "nothing" about radio (her boss admitted that he didn't either), Waller created the radio business model from scratch. Her success in Chicago created the prototype for other stations across the country, as well as other female radio station managers in Minneapolis and New York. Waller was

instrumental in Wrigley's strategy to transform baseball into a "radio" sport; she acquired the rights to broadcast all Chicago Cub home games, building both the radio station's business as well as bolstering the baseball club's finances.

Wayne Bidwell Wheeler (1869-1927), Chapter 5
Wheeler was the driving force behind the 18th Amendment to the U.S. Constitution prohibiting the sale, manufacture, and transportation of "intoxicating beverages" – aka Prohibition. As the leader of the Anti-Saloon League (ASL), Wheeler pioneered the single-issue political strategy. The ASL would support any candidate for office from any political party so long as they were prepared to vote "dry." (The ASL cared less about those politicians' private views or even their actions. All that mattered was their vote.) Wheeler died just as Prohibition enforcement had become largely unworkable due to underfunding, inconsistent enforcement, and increasing draconian penalties.

Robert Elkington Wood (1879–1969), Chapter 6
A military officer and extraordinary logistics expert, Wood became a retail business executive after his Army service. He first joined Montgomery Ward, but Julius Rosenwald recruited him to join Sears in 1924. Wood successfully launched the first suburban "big box" retail store concept. Wood took over as president of Sears, Roebuck and Company from 1928 until 1939 and continued as chairman from 1939 until 1954.

William Mills Wrigley Jr. (1861-1932), Chapter 14
Wrigley is most famous for founding the chewing gum manufacturer, Wm. Wrigley Jr. Company, in 1891. In addition to spearheading housing developments in California, Wrigley assumed majority control of the Chicago Cubs baseball team in 1921. Ever the innovator, he saw the potential of radio broadcasts to widen the appeal of the sport to far-flung rural communities outside of the Chicago metropolitan area. Instead of decreasing admissions to live games (as many predicted), radio broadcasts encouraged in-person visits to the park.

FURTHER READING

Introduction: "Coffee for Every Purse and Purpose."

Allen, F. L. (1931). *Only Yesterday: An Informal History of the 1920s.* Harper Perennial Modern Classics.

Miller, N. (2010). *New World Coming: The 1920s and the Making of Modern America.* Scribner.

Russell, T. (2010). *A Renegade History of the United States.* Free Press.

Chapter 1: Manufacturing Desire

Dorner, D. (1997) *The Logic Of Failure: Recognizing And Avoiding Error In Complex Situations.* Basic Books.

Sloan, A., et al (1963). *My Years with General Motors.* Alfred P. Sloan, Jr. (Available in multiple reprints.)

Tenner, E. (1997) *Why Things Bite Back: Technology and the Revenge of Unintended Consequences.* Vintage (Reprint Edition)

Chapter 2: The Manipulation Messiah

Keating, J. C. (1997). *B.J. of Davenport: The Early Years of Chiropractic.* The Association for the History of Chiropractic.

Keating, J. C. (1997). *Chronology of the Neurocalometer.* National Institute of Chiropractic Research. Retrieved from https://www.chiro.org/Plus/History/Persons/Neurocalometer/ncm_chronology.pdf.

Chapter 3: Flash Food

Kurlansky, M. (2012). *Birdseye: The Adventures of a Curious Man.* Doubleday.

Chapter 4: Cars on Time

Calder, L. (1999). *Financing the American Dream – A Cultural History of Consumer Credit.* Princeton University Press.

Pelfrey, W. (2006). *Billy, Alfred, and General Motors: The Story of Two Unique Men, a Legendary Company, and a Remarkable Time in American History.* AMACOM.

Chapter 5: Consumer Rebellion

Okrent, D. (2010). *Last Call: The Rise and Fall of Prohibition.* Scribner.

Bair, D. (2016). *Al Capone: His Life, Legacy, and Legend.* Doubleday.

Chapter 6: Opening the Big Box

Acosti, P. (2006). *Julius Rosenwald: The Man Who Built Sears, Roebuck and Advanced the Cause of Black Education in the American South.* Indiana University Press.

Worthy, J. (1984). *Shaping an American Institution: Robert E. Wood and Sears, Roebuck.* University of Illinois Press.

Chapter 7: Housing Feminism

Des Jardins, J. (2020). *American Queenmaker: How Missy Meloney Brought Women Into Politics.* Basic Books.

Richards, E. H. S. (1842). *Euthenics, the Science of Controllable Environment.* (Public Domain. Available in multiple digital and paperback reprints.)

Chapter 8: When Advertising Grew a Pair

Garratt, G. (1994). *The Early History of Radio: From Faraday to Marconi.* The Institution of Engineering and Technology.

Rudel, A. (2008). *Hello, Everybody!: The Dawn of American Radio.* Houghton Mifflin Harcourt.

Chapter 9: America's First Equal Opportunity Employer

Inglis, F. (2010). *A Short History of Celebrity.* Princeton University Press.

Marcus, S. (2021). *The Drama of Celebrity.* Princeton University Press.

Chapter 10: Subscribing to Culture

Radway, J. (1997). *A Feeling for Books: The Book-of-the-Month Club, Literary Taste, and Middle-Class Desire.* University of North Carolina Press.

Chapter 11: The First District Court of Public Opinion

Hunter, G. W. (1914). *A Civic Biology: Presented in Problems.* American Book Company. Original from the University of California, Digitized Oct 11, 2007

Larson, E. J. (2020). *Summer for the Gods: The Scopes Trial and America's Continuing Debate Over Science and Religion.* Basic Books.

Chapter 12: Happy Feet

Brothers, T. (2014). *Louis Armstrong: Master of Modernism.* W.W. Norton & Company.

Gioia, T. (2019). *Music: A Subversive History.* Basic Books.

Haskins, J. (1977). *The Cotton Club.* Random House.

Huggins, N. I. (1971). *Harlem Renaissance.* Oxford University Press

Chapter 13: Swampland

Knowlton, C. (2020). *Bubble in the Sun: The Florida Boom of the 1920s and How It Brought on the Great Depression.* Simon & Schuster.

Chapter 14: Changing the Game

Halfon, M. (2014). *Tales from the Deadball Era: Ty Cobb, Home Run Baker, Shoeless Joe Jackson, and the Wildest Times in Baseball History.* Potomac Books.

Leavy, J. (2018). *The Big Fella: Babe Ruth and the World He Created.* Harper.

Walker, J. (2015). *Crack of the Bat: A History of Baseball on the Radio.* University of Nebraska Press

Chapter 15: Marketer in Chief

Fried, R. M. (2005). *The Man Everybody Knew: Bruce Barton and the Making of Modern America.* Dee.

Johnson, C. C. (2013). *Why Coolidge Matters: Leadership Lessons from America's Most Underrated President.* Encounter Books.

O'Toole, G. (2017). *Hemingway Didn't Say That: The Truth Behind Familiar Quotations.* Little A.

Shlaes, A. (2014). *Coolidge.* Harper Perennial.

Voiovich, J. (2021). *Marketer in Chief: How Each President Sold the American Idea.* Jaywalker Publishing.

Chapter 16: Five-Cent Trip to Hell

Hughes, R. (1922). *Souls for Sale.* (Public Domain. Available in multiple digital and paperback reprints.)

Kemm, J. (1997). *Rupert Hughes: A Hollywood Legend.* Pomegranate Press.

Lindvall, T. (2021). *Souls for Sale: Rupert Hughes and the Novel Hollywood Religion.* Cascade Books.

Stewart, J. (2021). *Mystery at the Blue Sea Cottage.* Wildblue Press.

Chapter 17: Mad Women

Marchand, R. (1985). *Advertising the American Dream: Making Way for Modernity, 1920-1940.* University of California Press.

Fox, S. (1984). *The Mirror Makers: A History of American Advertising and Its Creators.* Morrow.

Butler, R.S. (1917). *Marketing Methods.* (Public Domain. Available in multiple digital and paperback reprints.)

Chapter 18: The Sensemakers

Brinkley, A. (2010). *The Publisher: Henry Luce and His American Century.* Alfred A. Knopf.

Wilner, I. (2009). *The Man Time Forgot: A Tale of Genius, Betrayal, and the Creation of Time Magazine.* HarperCollins.

Chapter 19: Family for Sale

MacNamara, T. (2018). *Birth Control and American Modernity: A History of Popular Ideas.* Cambridge University Press.

Sanger, M. (1914). *Family Limitation.* (Public Domain. Available in multiple digital and paperback reprints.)

Sanger, M. (1916). *What Every Girl Should Know.* (Public Domain. Available in multiple digital and paperback reprints.)

Chapter 20: How You Got Your Kicks

Kelly, S. C. (2019). *Father of Route 66: The Story of Cy Avery.* University of Oklahoma Press.

Chapter 21: All-Natural Ingredients. Artificial People.

Marks, S. (2005). *Finding Betty Crocker: The Secret Life of America's First Lady of Food.* Simon & Schuster.

Chapter 22: Democratizing Fashion

Garelick, R. (2014). *Mademoiselle: Coco Chanel and the Pulse of History.* Random House.

Zeitz, J. (2006). *Flapper: A Madcap Story of Sex, Style, Celebrity, and the Women Who Made America Modern.* Crown.

Chapter 23: Buying a Better You

Coué, E. (1922). *Self-Mastery Through Conscious Autosuggestion (1922).* (Public Domain. Available in multiple digital and paperback reprints.)

Chapter 24: "Please, can I…"

Patri, A. (1922). *Child Training.* D. Appleton and Company. (Also available digitally from the Internet Archive.)

Jacobson, L. (2004). *Raising Consumers: Children and the American Mass Market in the Early Twentieth Century.* Columbia University Press.

Chapter 25: Capitalism without the Capitalists

Bergengren, R. (1952). *Crusade: The Fight for Economic Democracy in North America, 1921-1945*. Exposition Press.

Chapter 26: Five-Star Wonderland

Chase, S. & Schlink, F. (1927). *Your Money's Worth: A Study in the Waste of the Consumer's Dollar.* (Public Domain. Available in multiple digital and paperback reprints.)

Caponi, T. (2018). *The Transparency Sale: How Unexpected Honesty and Understanding the Buying Brain Can Transform Your Results*. Ideapress Publishing.

Conclusion: "The Customer Is Always Right."

Butler, R. S. (1917). *Marketing Methods.* (Public Domain. Available in multiple digital and paperback reprints.)

Schwartz, B. (2004). *The Paradox of Choice: Why More Is Less*. Ecco.

ACKNOWLEDGMENTS

> "I think you should make a smoother transition to your non-testicular content."

I'm pretty lucky to be in a position to write a book that gets serious feedback like this. (Thanks, Victoria.) I'm lucky to traipse through reference libraries to find out-of-print books. (Thanks, Gale Family Library.) I'm lucky to read about amazing people history seems to have forgotten about. (Thanks, Helen Lansdowne.) I'm lucky to find the historians who hadn't forgotten about them, and who languish with three or four reviews for their labor of love on Amazon. (Thanks, Trent MacNamara.) I'm lucky to make innumerable corrections to Wikipedia…and even add a starter page or two for people who deserve it. (Thanks, Charles Buchanan.) I'm lucky to have people who will really read a manuscript and weren't afraid to say parts of it were terrible. (Thanks, Terry.) And I'm mostly lucky to be married to someone who will read every word and watch my buts. (Thanks, dear.)

It's been an honor. I hope you enjoy reading (or listening) to this book as much as I enjoyed writing it.

ABOUT THE AUTHOR

My arrival in marketing started early. I was born into a family of artists, immigrants, and entrepreneurs. Frankly, it's lucky I didn't end up as a circus performer. I'm sure I would have fallen off the tightrope by now. My father was an advertising creative director. One grandfather manufactured the first disposable coffee filters in pre-Castro Cuba. Another grandfather invented the bazooka. A great-grandfather invented Neapolitan ice cream. I was destined to invent the first disposable soft-serve grenade launcher, but the ice cream just kept melting!

I took bizarre ideas like those to the University of Wisconsin, the University of Minnesota, and the MIT Sloan School of Management. It should surprise no one that they are all embarrassed to have let me in.

I've launched hundreds of new products over a career that's spanned more than 25 years – as an entrepreneur, product designer, advertising strategist, and executive – everything from medical devices, to virtual healthcare, to non-dairy consumer cheese, to next-generation alternatives to the dreaded "cone of shame" for pets, to sex aides for cows (really!).

The Roaring 20s was a natural subject of curiosity for someone like me. That decade not only saw the emergence of so many new products, but also an entirely new way to think about ourselves, our world, and our place in it.

ALSO BY THE AUTHOR

Marketer in Chief: How Each President Sold the American Idea
Available in paperback, ebook, and audiobook.

Connect with Jason:
Website: jasontvoiovich.com
LinkedIn: https://www.linkedin.com/in/jasonvoiovich/
Twitter: https://twitter.com/JasonTVoiovich

Made in the USA
Monee, IL
18 March 2024